FEMINIST ETHNOGRAPHY

THINKING THROUGH METHODOLOGIES, CHALLENGES, AND POSSIBILITIES

Second Edition

DÁNA-AIN DAVIS AND CHRISTA CRAVEN

ROWMAN & LITTLEFIELD

Lanham • Boulder • New York • London

Acquisitions Editor: Jon Sisk
Acquisitions Assistant: Sarah Sichina
Sales and Marketing Inquiries: textbooks@rowman.com

Cover Designer: Kathi Ha
Cover Art: Thinkstock
Credits and acknowledgments of sources for material or information used with permission appear on the
appropriate page within the text.

Published by Rowman & Littlefield
A wholly owned subsidiary of The Rowman & Littlefield Publishing Group, Inc.
4501 Forbes Boulevard, Suite 200, Lanham, Maryland 20706
www.rowman.com

86-90 Paul Street, London EC2A 4NE, United Kingdom

British Library Cataloguing in Publication Information Available

Library of Congress Cataloging-in-Publication Data

Names: Davis, Dána-Ain, 1958– author. | Craven, Christa, author.
Title: Feminist ethnography : thinking through methodologies, challenges, and possibilities /
    Dána-Ain Davis and Christa Craven.
Description: Second edition. | Lanham : Rowman & Littlefield, [2023] | Includes bibliographical
    references and index. | Summary: "This book is a cross-cultural and interdisciplinary text that employs a
    problem-based approach to guide readers through the methods, challenges, and possibilities of feminist
    ethnography. The authors tease out the influences of feminist ethnography across a variety of disciplines
    including women's and gender studies, critical race studies, ethnic studies, and others"— Provided by
    publisher.
Identifiers: LCCN 2021054685 (print) | LCCN 2021054686 (ebook) |
    ISBN 9781538129791 (cloth) | ISBN 9781538129807 (paperback) |
    ISBN 9781538129814 (epub)
Subjects: LCSH: Feminist theory. | Feminism—Research. | Women's studies—Methodology. |
    Social sciences—Research—Methodology. | Feminists—Biography.
Classification: LCC HQ1190 .D385 2023 (print) | LCC HQ1190 (ebook) | DDC 305.4201—dc23/
    eng/20211228
LC record available at https://lccn.loc.gov/2021054685
LC ebook record available at https://lccn.loc.gov/2021054686

*Dedicated to the memory of Leith Mullings,
the community of feminist ethnographers she drew together,
and the space she made for generations of students*

Brief Contents

Acknowledgments   xiii

Preface to the Second Edition   xv

About the Authors   xix

Timeline   xxi

Introduction   1

1   What Is the "Feminist" in Feminist Ethnography?   7

2   Historicizing Feminist Ethnography   35

3   Debates and Interventions in Feminist Ethnography   61

4   How Does One *Do* Feminist Ethnography?   91

5   Challenges for Feminist Ethnographers   123

6   Producing Feminist Ethnography   151

7   Feminist Activist Ethnography   181

8   Thinking Through the Futures of Feminist Ethnography   205

Glossary   209

Bibliography   213

Index   231

Contents

Acknowledgments   xiii

Preface to the Second Edition   xv

About the Authors   xix

Timeline   xxi

Introduction   1

Thinking Through This Text   3

Unique Features of This Book   4

1 What Is the "Feminist" in Feminist Ethnography?   7

Spotlight: Zenzele Isoke on Feminist Concepts   8

What Is Feminist Ethnography?   9

Spotlight: Dyese Osaze on Meaningful Ethnography   12

Essential: Commentary on Doing Feminist Ethnography by
Rosemarie A. Roberts   13

Spotlight: Scott L. Morgensen on the Influence of Feminist Ethnography   15

What Contributed to the History of Feminisms?   15

Reconsidering "The Waves"   15

The Time of Suffrage   17

Essential: A Portion of the Seneca Falls Declaration of Sentiments, July 19, 1848   17

Radical Movement Building   19

Expanding a Feminist Legacy   22

Thinking Through . . . Foremothers of Feminism   23

How Are Feminist Perspectives Categorized?   24

Spotlight: Gayle Rubin's Influence   26

Essential: Excerpt from the Combahee River Collective Statement   28

Essential: Excerpt from "Under Western Eyes Revisited" by Chandra Talpade
Mohanty   30

Thinking Through . . . Feminisms   31

Conclusion   31

Thinking Through . . . Feminist Perspectives and Key Texts   32

2 Historicizing Feminist Ethnography   35

Who Were Some of the Early Contributors to Feminist Ethnography?   36

Essential: Excerpt from *The Omaha Tribe* by Alice Fletcher and Francis LaFlesche   37

How Did Feminist Ethnography Mature between the 1920s and 1960s?   40

Essential: Excerpt from *Mules and Men* by Zora Neale Hurston   41

What Impact Did the Women's Movement of the 1960s Have on the Next Phase of Feminist Ethnographic Production? (1960s–1980s)   42

Thinking Through . . . Restudying Culture   43

Spotlight: Florence Babb on the Impact of *Woman, Culture, and Society* and *Toward an Anthropology of Women*   44

Essential: Excerpt from "Too Queer for College" by Esther Newton   46

Spotlight: Louise Lamphere on the Legacy of *Lamphere v. Brown*   48

Thinking Through . . . Faculty Composition at Your Institution   50

What Interventions Came Out of Feminist Ethnography from the 1990s Through the Present?   50

Essential: Excerpt from "Methodological Gifts in Latina/o Studies and Feminist Anthropology" by Gina Pérez   52

Spotlight: C. Riley Snorton on Feminist Anthropology and Trans Studies   55

Spotlight: Lee Baker on Feminist Histories   57

Conclusion   58

Thinking Through . . . Critiques and Reviews of an Ethnography   58

3   Debates and Interventions in Feminist Ethnography   61

Who Should Be Claimed as a Feminist Ethnographer?   62

Essential: Excerpt from *Decolonizing Methodologies: Research and Indigenous Peoples* by Linda Tuhiwai Smith   63

Can There Be a Feminist Ethnography?   64

Essential: Excerpt from "Can There Be a Feminist Ethnography?" by Judith Stacey   65

Essential: Excerpt from *Feminism and Method* by Nancy A. Naples   68

How Have Feminist Ethnographers Approached the Insider/Outsider Dilemma?   69

Essential: Excerpt from "Feminist Insider Dilemmas" by Patricia Zavella   70

Spotlight: Shannon Speed on Fieldwork and Identity   72

What Is the Role of Citational Politics in Feminist Ethnography?   75

Spotlight / Essential: Christen A. Smith on Citing Black Women   76

Essential: Excerpt from "Making Feminist Points," on the *feministkilljoys* Blog by Sara Ahmed   80

Thinking Through . . . An Intellectual Genealogy   81

Can an Ethnographer's Personal Experience Be a Part of a Study?   81

Spotlight: Laura Mauldin on the Impact of Life Experiences   82

How Involved or Engaged Should a Feminist Ethnographer Be?   84

Spotlight: Brenna McCaffrey on the Political Stakes of Feminist Ethnography   85

Spotlight: Mary L. Gray on the Labor of Feminist Ethnography   86

Conclusion   88

Thinking Through . . . What Would a Feminist Ethnographer Do?   88

4   How Does One *Do* Feminist Ethnography?   91

Essential: Excerpt from "Feminist Methodology . . ." by Faye V. Harrison   92

How Should a Feminist Ethnographer Choose a Topic?   94

Spotlight: Elisabeth Engebretsen on Choosing Methods and Shifting Knowledge   95

What Methods Have Been Useful to Feminist Ethnographers?   97

Participant-Observation   98

Essential: Excerpt from *Queer Activism in India* by Naisargi Dave   99

Ethnographic Interviewing   100

Spotlight: Class of 2021 Undergraduates on Fieldwork during a Pandemic   102

Oral History/Life History   106

Spotlight: Tracy Fisher on Using Oral/Life History to Address Feminist Ethnographic Questions   106

Survey   108

Analysis of Cultural Material   109

Social Media Research   110

Ethnohistory   113

Spotlight: Whitney Battle-Baptiste on Historical Archaeology and Literary Fiction   114

Participatory Research   115

Essential: Excerpt from "Photovoice" by Caroline C. Wang and Mary Ann Burris   116

Interpretive Communities   118

Conclusion   119

Thinking Through . . . Three Options to Explore Methodological Possibilities   120

Thinking Through . . . Word Cloud Magic!   120

5   Challenges for Feminist Ethnographers   123

Spotlight: Elizabeth Chin on Envisioning a Feminist IRB Process   125

What Logistical Constraints Arise in Feminist Ethnographic Research?   126

Essential: Excerpt from "Following as Method" in *Mobile Subjects: Transnational Imaginaries of Gender Reassignment* by Aren Z. Aizura   128

Essential: Excerpt from "Cast among Outcastes" by Delores Walters   131

Essential: Excerpt from "Toward a Fugitive Anthropology: Gender, Race, and Violence in the Field," by Maya J. Berry, Claudia Chávez Argüelles, Shanya Cordis, Sarah Ihmoud, Elizabeth Velásquez Estrada   134

How Do Ethical Concerns Shape the Research Encounter? 136

Thinking Through . . . Difficult Ethnographic Experiences 137

Spotlight: Loretta J. Ross on Working with Former Skinhead White Supremacists 138

Spotlight: Tanya Erzen on the Politics of Reciprocity and Mediation 141

How Can We Assess the (Potential) Impacts of Feminist Ethnography? 144

Spotlight: Kiersten Downs on "Feminist Curiosity" and Stamina 144

Spotlight: Sandra Morgen on Movement Building 146

Thinking Through . . . Ethical Dilemmas 148

Conclusion 148

6 Producing Feminist Ethnography 151

How Does One Write Feminist Ethnography? 152

Essential: Excerpt from *Alive in the Writing* by Kirin Narayan 156

Essential: Excerpt from *Progressive Dystopia: Abolition, Antiblackness and Schooling in San Francisco* by Savannah Shange 157

Essential: Excerpt from *Playing with Fire* by the Sangtin Writers Collective and Richa Nagar 160

What Creative Possibilities Exist for Writing and Circulating Feminist Ethnography? 161

Spotlight: Asale Angel-Ajani on Writing (Without Swagger) 162

Fiction 163

Essential: Excerpt from *A World of Babies* by Judy DeLoache and Alma Gottlieb 164

Parallel Writing 165

Autoethnography and Ethnographic Memoir 166

Essential: Excerpt from *Downtown Ladies*, "My Jelly Platform Shoes" by Gina Athena Ulysse 167

Thinking Through . . . Citational Politics, Revisited in the Age of #MeToo 170

How Can We Make Feminist Ethnography Publicly Accessible? 170

Spotlight: Harjant Gill on Film as a Powerful Feminist Medium 172

How Do Feminist Ethnographers Engage in Creative and Artistic Projects? 175

Thinking Through . . . Experimental Design 176

Conclusion 177

Thinking Through . . . Developing Creative Ethnography 178

7 Feminist Activist Ethnography 181

What Does It Mean to Be a Feminist Activist Ethnographer? 183

Thinking Through . . . Engaging in Public Scholarship 185

What Should Feminist Activist Ethnography Seek to Accomplish? 185

Essential: Excerpt from "Water Is Life—Meters Out!" by Susan Brin Hyatt 186

Is Feminist Ethnography Inherently Activist? 187

What Forms Can Feminist Activist Ethnography Take? 189

Essential: Excerpt from *Black Autonomy: Race, Gender, and Afro-Nicaraguan Activism* by Jennifer Goett 190

Collaboration and Participatory Action Research 190

Essential: Excerpt from "Makes Me Mad! Stereotypes of Young Urban Womyn of Color" by the Fed Up Honeys 191

Social Media and Film 194

Spotlight: Tom Boellstorff on New Technologies and Activism 194

Thinking Through . . . Working with Activists 196

Spotlight: Michelle Téllez on Activism Through Storytelling in Visual Media 196

Serving as an Interlocutor 197

Essential: Excerpt from "Introduction: Comparative Perspectives on the Indigenous Rights Movement in Africa and the Americas" by Dorothy Hodgson 198

How Can Feminist Activist Ethnographers Reflect upon Our Practice? 199

Spotlight: Leith Mullings on Keeping Feminist Ethnography Meaningful 201

Conclusion 201

8 Thinking Through the Futures of Feminist Ethnography 205

Glossary 209

Bibliography 213

Index 231

Acknowledgments

Many people have contributed to this book, and our gratitude now spans far beyond those we named in the first edition. Shortly after the book was published, we lost the friend who had inspired our original acknowledgments for this textbook, feminist anthropologist and activist Sandi Morgen. Yet her insights are more prescient now than ever. Over the years, we had several conversations with her that got us thinking deeply about the debts we owe to academic friendships. During her battle with ovarian cancer—through which she also became a fierce advocate for cancer patients—she recalled having to explain to baffled family and friends how academic friendships were essential to her well-being as a scholar, but also as a person. Connecting for twenty minutes at conferences year after year, collaborating on panels, building on each other's scholarship, and engaging in activism together were meaningful in ways that moved beyond what most of us think of as "professional connections." Likewise, the scholarly connections that have inspired and nurtured our scholarly, activist, and personal journeys are many and deeply valued.

Throughout our work on this book, collectively (as coauthors, coeditors, and friends) and individually (as feminist ethnographers and activist-scholars), we have been the recipients of tremendous support. During revisions for the second edition, we received ideas, critiques, and feedback from reviewers formal and informal. We are grateful for the continued enthusiasm we have received from so many supportive colleagues who have invited us to engage with them and their students about this work, including Rajani Bhatia, Laurian Bowles, Sue Hyatt, Zenzele Isoke, Scott L. Morgensen, Richa Nagar, Juno Salazar-Parreñas, and Margot Weiss. We thank Rowman & Littlefield's reviewers—for both the first and the second editions—for their insightful comments and helpful references. The College of Wooster and Queens College, CUNY, our home institutions, have supported our work, and we particularly thank the students we were able to work with as a result. College of Wooster students (many now alums!) Jacob Danko, Angela Danso Gyane, Tina Lam, Hannah Lane-Davies, Ella Lang, Regina McCullough, Evangeline Smith, Emery Stewart, and Sara Tebeau assisted with translation, found sources, and conducted some of the interviews with feminist ethnographers featured here and in the first edition. At the CUNY Graduate Center, Brenna McCaffrey, now Dr. McCaffrey, assisted us with revisions, the timeline, and the glossary (and a *Spotlight* on her doctoral research appears in chapter 3). Eileen Liang served as an editorial assistant for the second edition assisting us with compiling all of the photos, edits, and consents. Finally, we are grateful to Jackson Siegel, a graduate of College of Wooster, for designing the shell-themed artwork that demarcates elements, such as *Essentials* and *Spotlights*, in the text, mirroring the Haitian cone shells offered on the cover.

We have also received tremendous support from our families, who have sustained us—emotionally, physically, and intellectually—during this project. Dána-Ain is blessed to have an amazing family of choice and birth: Ricci, Sadan, Emmy, LaFredia (aka Fefa), India-Rose, Deirdre, Uncle Max/Myron Kalin, Liz, Alex, and Ethan. And Christa is grateful for the enduring support of Donna, Stephen, and David Craven, B Murphy for understanding the bizarre madness that is writing, and her twins Rosalie and Braxton Murphy-Craven for especially fun writing breaks.

It has been a journey and we thank each other. It is an amazing experience to collaborate with someone who knows how to motivate you. When one of us was distracted, bound by other obligations, or facing family crises, the other held things together and moved this project forward. All academics should be so fortunate to have someone to collaborate with who makes the work such a joy. It is a pleasure to be in each other's company again as we revised this textbook for its second edition. Cheers to an enduring friendship, critical conversations, and more collaborative scholarship long into our futures.

Preface to the Second Edition

Writing now in 2022—in the midst of the global COVID-19 pandemic and having witnessed the intensification of anti-Black violence, anti-immigrant sentiment, and white supremacist mobilization in 2020 and 2021—the need for feminist ethnography as a tool and a guiding framework has become even more urgent. As we continue to encounter a world marked by stark inequities and structures of power that incite violence—physical, political, and social—against those less powerful, we reaffirm our commitment to you as students. Being exposed to the work of a broad range of feminist ethnographers and training to be critical observers, active participants, and effective writers and creators who can convey that knowledge is, in itself, a political act.

We initially wrote *Feminist Ethnography: Thinking Through Methodologies, Challenges, and Possibilities* to share perspectives from a diverse array of feminist ethnographers on how to integrate activism, theory, and fieldwork into crafting ethnography with liberatory potential. We sought to help students untangle various threads of feminist ethnography—its multiple histories, meanings, hopes, dilemmas, praxis, and necessity—by foregrounding the importance of feminist ethnography to the development of ethnographic methods. Some have claimed feminist ethnography is an impossibility, others have attempted to neutralize its intent, and even those who count themselves a part of this field sometimes find feminist ethnography difficult to fully and unequivocally define. This textbook remains devoted to the task of drawing out its important interdisciplinary lineages and charting a path for feminist ethnography into the future.

How We Got Here: Serendipity and the Origin of Our Collaboration

Students often ask how we came to write this book, which is really embedded in the story of how we met and have embarked upon several scholarly projects together. We met, quite by accident, at an American Anthropological Association (AAA) conference in the early 2000s. We were both sitting in the back of the room during a panel discussion interrogating globalization and transnational labor politics. Dána-Ain had recently been hired in a tenure-track position following a career in public health and activist work; Christa was a graduate student in anthropology. Sitting a few seats away from each other, we were both taken aback as we watched the panel unfold. After a noted feminist anthropologist articulated how insights from Black feminism could contribute to rethinking transnational labor politics, she was summarily dismissed by the white male anthropologists and activists on the panel, as well as the predominantly white male audience. We both intermittently sighed, exasperated by the male panelists' disregard. We were each keenly aware of the vibrant history of feminist ethnography and the ways in which that research had contributed to feminist, antiracist, and anti-colonial efforts far beyond the academy. Frustrated, and looking around the room to see how others were bearing witness to the devaluation of Black feminist research, we caught each other's glance, exchanged a few muffled comments, and quickly agreed that grabbing coffee together would be a far better use of our time. Over coffee, we found that we had much in common as both activists and scholars, which led to conference panel proposals and eventually larger collaborations, more often than not centered around issues and ideas related to feminist ethnography.

Those conversations between us and with other feminist anthropologists led us to compile an edited volume in 2013, *Feminist Activist Ethnography: Counterpoints to Neoliberalism in North America*. It was the unexpected, but affirming, response from colleagues beyond anthropology that inspired us to write this textbook, a more historical, cross-cultural, and interdisciplinary discussion of feminist ethnography. Our disciplinary background in anthropology led us to approach this textbook with keen attention to the colonial and racist legacies of our discipline. But we also situate ourselves as interdisciplinary feminist scholars and have been influenced by feminist scholarship, ethnography, and practice that span many academic and activist spaces. This sense of ourselves infuses our approach to exploring the scope and applications of feminist ethnography.

We have now worked collaboratively on this textbook for over a decade, exchanging innumerable phone calls, texts, emails, and back-and-forth chapter drafts. We also had an opportunity to work together in person on several occasions. The bulk of the textbook was written during the Spring of 2015, when we were able to work for a week in Wooster, Ohio, and a week in New York, our respective homes. Even our "downtime" during these visits reinforced the importance of writing this text. During Dána-Ain's visit to Wooster, we had the pleasure of meeting philosopher and activist Angela Y. Davis during the College of Wooster's Colloquium on Global and Postcolonial Ethics, when she spoke with faculty about teaching in the context of liberation and transnational solidarity. Davis is well known for her political activism around prison reform, her leadership in the Communist party, and her scholarship. On the day we saw Davis, what was profound about her talk on teaching was her reminder about the impact one can make in classrooms—not only by professors but also by students engaging deeply with texts and materials that promote social change. Indeed, we aim for this text to prompt such discussions, including how feminist ethnography can contribute to a more transformative politics.

During a subsequent meet-up to write together in New York City, we took a break from writing to attend an art exhibit at the Brooklyn Museum: "Kehinde Wiley: A New Republic." The exhibit featured Wiley's impressive portraits, which foreground people of color, particularly Black men. His artwork fuses classical representations of European heroes and elite men—in styles ranging from French Rococo to Baroque of the European Renaissance to Islamic architecture to West African textile design—with contemporary images of young men he has seen on the street. Dressed in their everyday common attire—jeans, T-shirts, sneakers, et cetera—the men assume the heroic poses of classical paintings. Wiley describes his work as "interrogating the notion of the master painter, at once critical and complicit." The exhibit also displays Wiley's reflection on the importance of representation in his work:

> Painting is about the world that we live in. Black men live in the world. My choice is to include them. This is my way of saying yes to us.
>
> —Kehinde Wiley, American, born 1977

As we moved through—and were moved by—the exhibit, we also noted the number of people of color in attendance, especially young Black men, Black families, and multiracial groups of patrons. The attendance at the exhibit is a stark contrast to First Lady Michelle Obama's important observation in a speech at the dedication of the Whitney Museum of American Art in New York, when she underscored how museums are often seen as "white spaces." Yet the Brooklyn Museum, which has become well known for featuring work by artists of color over the past few decades, reports that 40 percent of its visitors are minorities.[1] Visiting this exhibit reinforced what can happen when you bring people's lives to the center as subjects, artists, and authors—whether in museums, ethnographic texts, or other creative spaces. Being critically attuned to issues of representation—who and what is represented and who decides—has been central to our ongoing discussions. We have consciously modeled this commitment throughout the text.

In the spirit of collaborative feminist practice, we welcome comments, critiques, and suggestions from teachers, students, and activists who engage with the book. Please feel free to contact us.

Note

[1] Arun Venugopal, "Museums as White Spaces," accessed May 21, 2021, https://www.wnyc.org/story/museums-white-spaces/.

Dána-Ain Davis is professor of Urban Studies and Anthropology at Queens College and Graduate Center, City University of New York. She directs the Center for the Study of Women and Society at the Graduate Center, City University of New York (CUNY). Her work centers on examining the manifestations and articulations of neoliberalism in a range of contexts: race, reproduction, violence against women, and welfare reform policy. She is the author of *Reproductive Injustice: Pregnancy, Racism, and Premature Birth* (2019) and *Battered Black Women and Welfare Reform: Between a Rock and a Hard Place* (2006). Davis is coeditor, with Sameena Mulla, of *Feminist Anthropology*, the inaugural journal of the Association of Feminist Anthropologists. She also coedited *Black Genders and Sexualities* with Shaka McGlotten (2012), coedited *Feminist Activist Ethnography: Counterpoints to Neoliberalism in North America* with Christa Craven (2013), served as coeditor with Aimee Meredith Cox of *Transforming Anthropology*, the journal of the Association of Black Anthropologists (ABA), and served as president of ABA.

Christa Craven is a professor of Anthropology and Women's, Gender, and Sexuality studies (WGSS) at the College of Wooster, a small liberal arts college in Ohio. She is currently Dean for Faculty Development. Her research interests include women's health and reproductive justice, lesbian/gay/bi/trans/queer reproduction, midwifery activism, feminist ethnography & activist scholarship, and feminist pedagogy. She is the author of *Reproductive Losses: Challenges to LGBTQ Family-Making* (2019) and *Pushing for Midwives: Homebirth Mothers and the Reproductive Rights Movement* (2010) and coeditor of *Feminist Activist Ethnography: Counterpoints to Neoliberalism in North America* with Dána-Ain Davis (2013). She has served as cochair of the Society of Lesbian and Gay Anthropologists (now the Association for Queer Anthropology) and the Program Administration and Development for the National Women's Studies Association.

Timeline

Some people set the origins of feminism to coincide with specific revolutionary women in early history—for example, Sappho in Greece (600 BCE)—while others point to waves of activism around particular issues, such as women's suffrage. For the sake of highlighting the long, rich, and geographically diverse history of feminism(s) in a manageable overview, the following timeline presents key dates in feminist ethnography against the backdrop of representative issues raised in this text, including events and dates from varied strands of feminism and intersecting social movements. When we mention specific individuals featured in the *Spotlights* or *Essentials* boxes, we also include chapter numbers where you can find more information.

The number of timelines exploring the history of feminism and related movements has increased substantially since we published the first edition of *Feminist Ethnography*. Here we include a few recommendations for viewing this history through alternative lenses, roughly by the date they were created from newest to oldest. But we also encourage students to search online, particularly for histories on the geographical area you are learning in and your places of origin. History is often told by those in power and reflects the legacies of colonialism, racism, and other injustices documented in this book. For that reason, we encourage you to approach these timelines through a critical lens and to seek out those compiled by feminists of color and others who have been marginalized. And if those timelines aren't available? It would make a fantastic class project to collaborate on launching one!

- *Women of the World, Unite!* Interactive Timeline by the United Nations Women (n.d.), available in English, Español, and Français at https://interactive.unwomen .org/multimedia/timeline/womenunite/en/index.html#/1840.
- *Women's Footprint in History* Interactive Timeline by the United Nations Women (n.d.), available at https://interactive.unwomen.org/multimedia/timeline/womensf ootprintinhistory/en/index.html#intro1.
- *Women's Suffrage Timeline* (before 1920, multimedia) from the U.S. National Women's History Museum (n.d.), https://www.womenshistory.org/resources/time-line/womans-suffrage-timeline.
- *OutHistory Timelines*, including the Transgender History Timeline (first published July 28, 2016), available at https://outhistory.org/exhibits/show/trans-timeline/timeline.
- Suppressed Histories Archives (n.d.), http://www.suppressedhistories.net/.
- *Women's History: Native Americans* by Denize Oliver Velez (March 2, 2014) in the *Daily Kos*, available at http://www.dailykos.com/story/2014/3/2/1280488/ -Women-s-History-Native-Americans.
- *A Brief History of African Feminism* in *Ms. Afropolitan* (July 2, 2013), available at http://www.msafropolitan.com/2013/07/a-brief-history-of-african-feminism.html.
- *Timeline of Legal History of Women in the United States*, National Women's History Project (2013), available at http://www.nwhp.org/resources/womens-rights -movement/detailed-timeline/.
- Cross-national timeline of the women's movement in Asia in *Women's Movements in Asia: Feminisms and Transnational Activism* (2010), edited by Mina Roces and Louise Edwards, 224–42. London: Routledge.

- *The Struggle for Women's Equality in Latin America* by Donna Goodman (March 13, 2009) in *Dissident Voice*, available at: http://dissidentvoice.org /2009/03/the-struggle-for-womens-equality-in-latin-america/.
- *British Women's Emancipation since the Renaissance* (2009), available at: http://www.historyofwomen.org/timeline.html.
- *The Women's Struggle Timeline*, 1905–2006 (South Africa), available at: http://www.sahistory.org.za/topic/womens-struggle-timeline-1905-2006.
- *Contextualizing the Sexuality Debates*, in Nan D. Hunter's (2006) *Sex Wars: Sexual Dissent and Political Culture*, by Lisa Duggan and Nan D. Hunter, 15–28. New York: Routledge.
- *Timeline*, Australian Women's History Forum (2002), available at: https://awhf .wordpress.com/timeline/.
- *Selected Chronology of the Transexual Menace and Gender PAC*, in Riki Anne Wilchins's (orig. 1997) *Read My Lips: Sexual Subversion and the End of Gender*, 209–35. Riverdale, NY: Mangus Books, 2013.
- *Timeline of Canadian Women's History: From Moira Armour and Pat Stanton* (1992) in *Canadian Women in History: A Chronology*, 2nd ed. Toronto: Green Dragon Press. Available at: https://people.stfx.ca/nforeste/308website/ women'shistorytimeline.html.

TIMELINE

1837 British writer Harriet Martineau, often cited as the first female sociologist, published *Society in America* based on her long trip to the United States in the mid-1830s, which criticized the state of women's education

1885 Matilda Coxe Stevenson became the first president of the Women's Anthropological Society of America

1911 Alice Fletcher and Omaha collaborator Francis LaFlesche (see Ch. 2) published *The Omaha Tribe*

Margaret Mead published *Coming of Age in Samoa* on adolescence **1928**

Ruth Benedict published *Patterns of Culture,* a **1934** cross-cultural analysis of culture and personality

Zora Neale Hurston (see Ch. 2) published *Mules and Men,* **1935** a novel on Black American folk tales

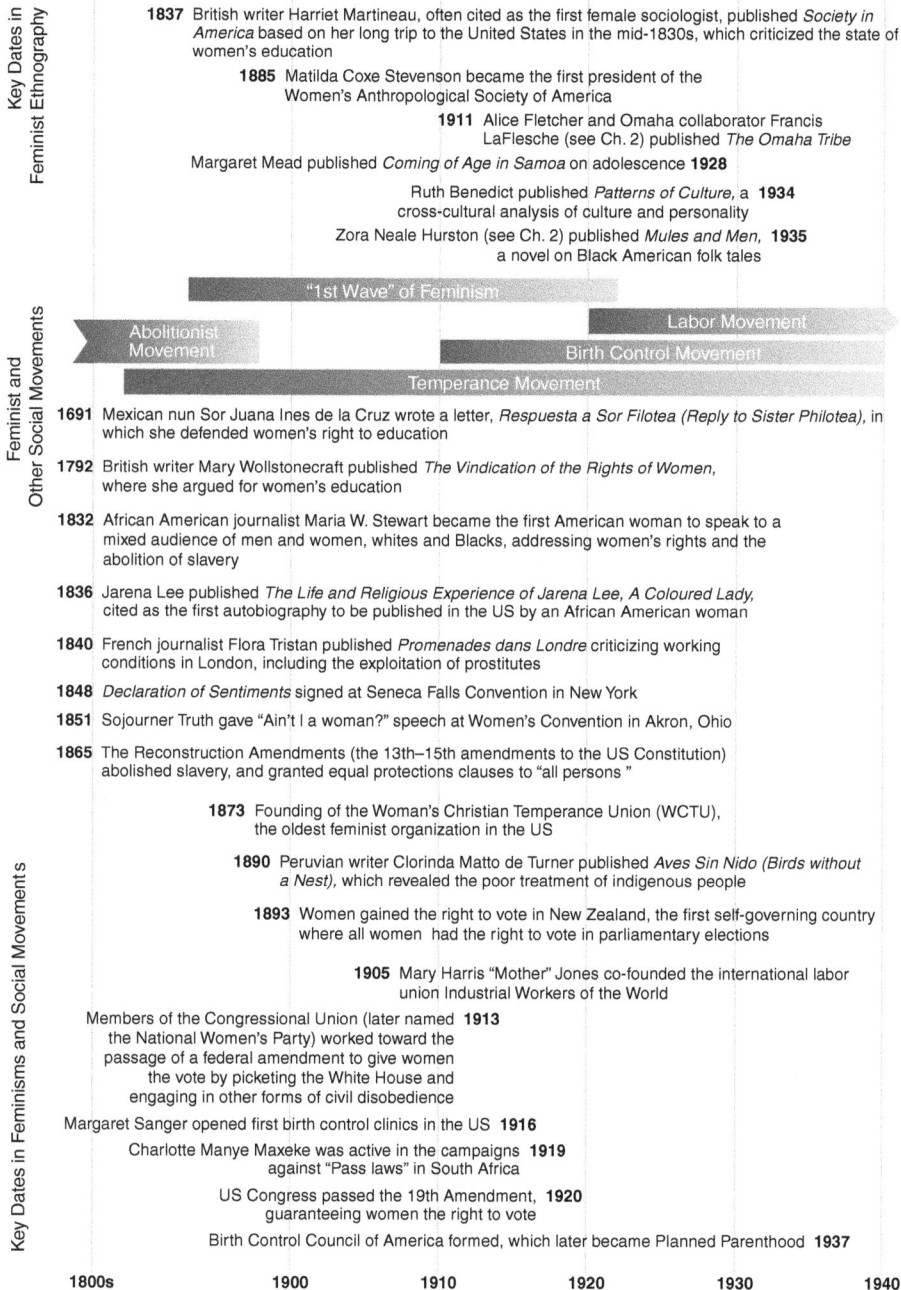

"1st Wave" of Feminism

Abolitionist Movement

Labor Movement

Birth Control Movement

Temperance Movement

1691 Mexican nun Sor Juana Ines de la Cruz wrote a letter, *Respuesta a Sor Filotea (Reply to Sister Philotea),* in which she defended women's right to education

1792 British writer Mary Wollstonecraft published *The Vindication of the Rights of Women,* where she argued for women's education

1832 African American journalist Maria W. Stewart became the first American woman to speak to a mixed audience of men and women, whites and Blacks, addressing women's rights and the abolition of slavery

1836 Jarena Lee published *The Life and Religious Experience of Jarena Lee, A Coloured Lady,* cited as the first autobiography to be published in the US by an African American woman

1840 French journalist Flora Tristan published *Promenades dans Londre* criticizing working conditions in London, including the exploitation of prostitutes

1848 *Declaration of Sentiments* signed at Seneca Falls Convention in New York

1851 Sojourner Truth gave "Ain't I a woman?" speech at Women's Convention in Akron, Ohio

1865 The Reconstruction Amendments (the 13th–15th amendments to the US Constitution) abolished slavery, and granted equal protections clauses to "all persons"

1873 Founding of the Woman's Christian Temperance Union (WCTU), the oldest feminist organization in the US

1890 Peruvian writer Clorinda Matto de Turner published *Aves Sin Nido (Birds without a Nest),* which revealed the poor treatment of indigenous people

1893 Women gained the right to vote in New Zealand, the first self-governing country where all women had the right to vote in parliamentary elections

1905 Mary Harris "Mother" Jones co-founded the international labor union Industrial Workers of the World

Members of the Congressional Union (later named **1913** the National Women's Party) worked toward the passage of a federal amendment to give women the vote by picketing the White House and engaging in other forms of civil disobedience

Margaret Sanger opened first birth control clinics in the US **1916**

Charlotte Manye Maxeke was active in the campaigns **1919** against "Pass laws" in South Africa

US Congress passed the 19th Amendment, **1920** guaranteeing women the right to vote

Birth Control Council of America formed, which later became Planned Parenthood **1937**

| 1800s | 1900 | 1910 | 1920 | 1930 | 1940 |

1940s Anthropologists recruited by the US government to assist with war efforts

1941 Elsie Clews Parsons became the first female president of the American Anthropological Association (AAA)

1947 Ruth Benedict served as president of the AAA for 6 months

1949 The Society of Applied Anthropology adopted the first Code of Ethics in a social science organization under the direction of Margaret Mead

Margaret Mead became president of the AAA **1960**

Anthropologists recruited by the US Army to participate in Project Camelot, **1964** a counterinsurgency study in Latin America

"2nd Wave" of Feminism

Labor Movement

Civil Rights Movement

Anti-Vietnam War Movement

American Indian Movement (AIM)

Abortion Right's Movement

1942 "We Can Do It!" posters featuring a woman who later became known as "Rosie the Riveter" encouraged American women to work in factories and shipyards during World War II producing munitions and war supplies; during this time, nearly 19 million women held jobs, but many were fired when men returned from the war

1949 Feminist journalist, Black Nationalist, and member of the Communist Party USA Claudia Jones published "An End to the Neglect of the Problems of the Negro Woman" in *Political Affairs*

1954 US Supreme Court case *Brown v. Board of Education* ruled that establishing separate public schools for Black and white students was unconstitutional, a major victory for the Civil Rights Movement

Activist Yuri Kochiyama met Malcolm X and joined the Organization of **1963** Afro-American Unity

Betty Friedan published *The Feminine Mystique*, which some credit as sparking **1963** "Second Wave" Feminism in the US

The US Civil Rights Act outlawed discrimination based on race, color, religion, **1964** sex, or national origin

US Voting Rights Act extended the right to vote to all adult citizens **1965**

Griswold v. Connecticut made it unconstitutoional to prohibit **1965** married couples from using birth control

National Organization for Women (NOW) founded with 300 charter members **1966**

US Civil Rights Act signed, including the Fair Housing Act **1968**

The Redstockings and New York Radical Feminists protested the Miss America Pageant **1968**

Shirley Chisholm became the first Black woman elected to the US Congress **1968**

The Stonewall Riots, following a police raid on a gay tavern in New York City, are often cited as the **1969** beginning of the Gay Liberation or LGBTQ Movement

1940   1950   1960   1970

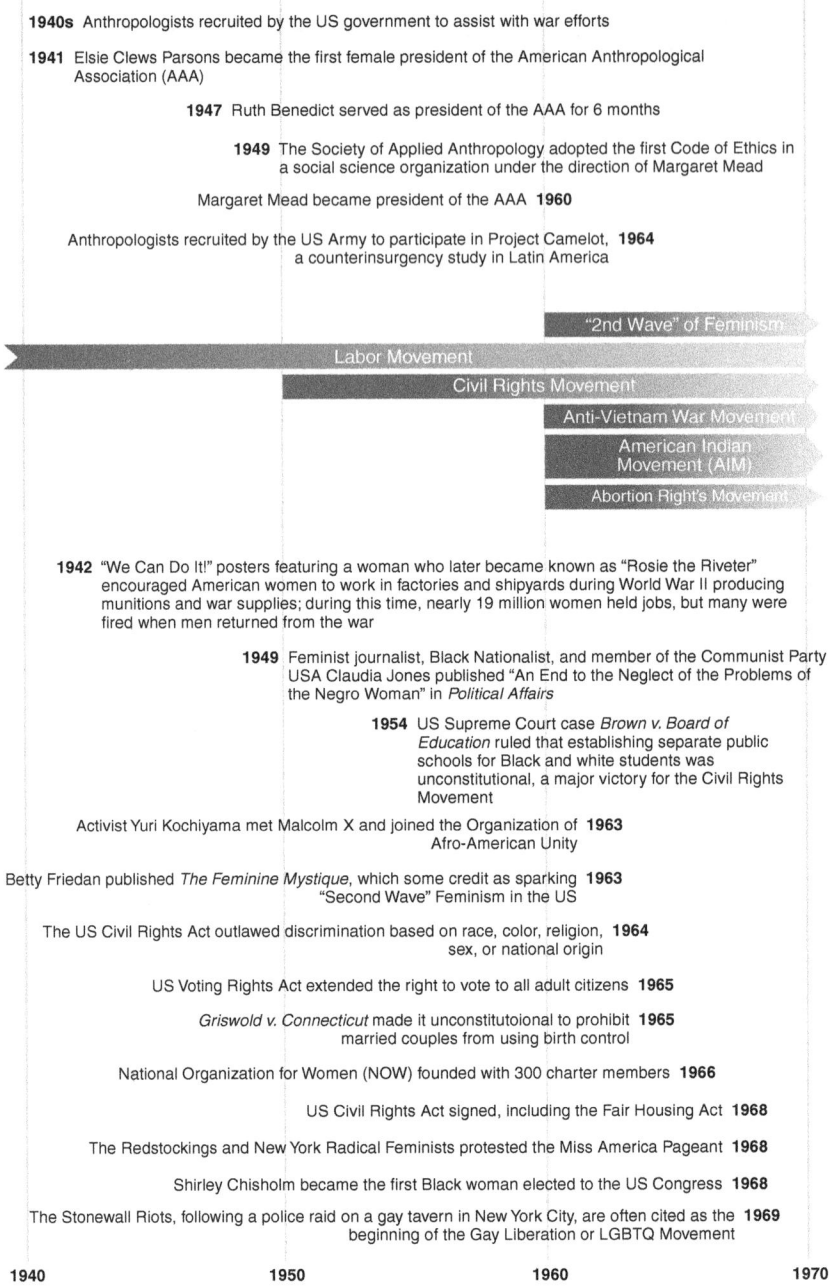

Key Dates in Feminist Ethnography

Feminist and Other Social Movements

Key Dates in Feminisms and Social Movements

Key Dates in Feminist Ethnography

1970 Association of Black Anthropologists (ABA) established; ABA leadership has included Lee Baker (see Ch. 2), Whitney Battle-Baptiste (see Ch. 4), Lynn Bolles (see Ch 3), Elizabeth Chin (see Ch. 5), Dána-Ain Davis, Faye Harrison (see Ch. 7), Leith Mullings (see Ch. 7), Cheryl Rodriguez, Bianca Williams, and Riché Barnes, among others

1972 Eleanor "Happy" Leacock was named chair of Anthropology at City College of New York, after teaching as an adjunct instructor for decades; she credited her appointment to pressure from feminist activists for institutions of higher education to diversify their faculty

1972 *Feminist Studies* established, the first journal in women's studies

1974 *Women, Culture, and Society* published

1974 Louise Lamphere (see Ch. 2) denied tenure at Brown University; she filed a successful Title VII Sex Discrimination Case the following year

Toward an Anthropology of Women published **1975**

Signs: The Journal of Women in Culture and Society established **1975**

National Women's Studies Association established to promote and **1977** support the production and distribution of knowledge about women and gender through teaching, learning, research, and service in academic and other settings

Feminist and Other Social Movements

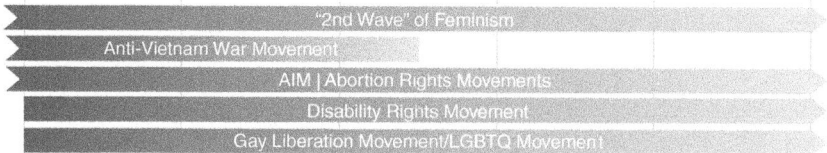

"2nd Wave" of Feminism

Anti-Vietnam War Movement

AIM | Abortion Rights Movements

Disability Rights Movement

Gay Liberation Movement/LGBTQ Movement

Key Dates in Feminisms and Social Movements

1970s The first Rape Crisis Centers were established

1970 Comisión Femenil Mexicana Nacional founded to address issues of concern to Chicana women

1971 Anna Nieto-Gómez founded a women's group and feminist Chicana newspaper, both named *Hijas de Cuauhtémoc* after a Mexican women's underground newspaper published during the 1910 Mexican revolution

1971 The Boston Women's Health Book Collective published the first edition of *Our Bodies, Ourselves*, encouraging women's active engagement with their health and sexuality

1972 Shirley Chisolm became the first major-party Black candidate for President of the US and the first woman to run for President of the US

1973 *Roe v. Wade* legalized abortion during the first trimester of pregnancy

1973 Lesbian feminists attempted to exclude Sylvia Riviera, a Latina drag queen and transgender activist who had been part of the Stonewall riots, from speaking at a gay pride event commemorating Stonewall

1973 COYOTE (Call Off Your Tired Old Ethics), a prostitutes' rights organization, formed to repeal prostitution laws and end the stigma associated with sex work

1974 Equal Rights Advocates (ERA) was founded as a nonprofit women's rights organization dedicated to protecting and expanding economic and educational access and opportunities for women and girls

1974 Native American civil rights activists, including Lorelei DeCora Means and Madonna Thunderhawk, established Women of All Red Nations (WARN)

The first United Nations (UN) World Conference on **1975** Women held in Mexico City to inaugurate the Decade of Women (1976-1985)

Women Against Violence Against Women (WAVAW) formed **1976** to end all forms of violence against women

Combahee River Collective Statement published (see Ch. 1) **1977**

National Center for Lesbian Rights (NCLR) was founded by lesbian **1977** feminist activists who were members of ERA

| 1970 | 1972 | 1974 | 1976 | 1978 | 1980 |

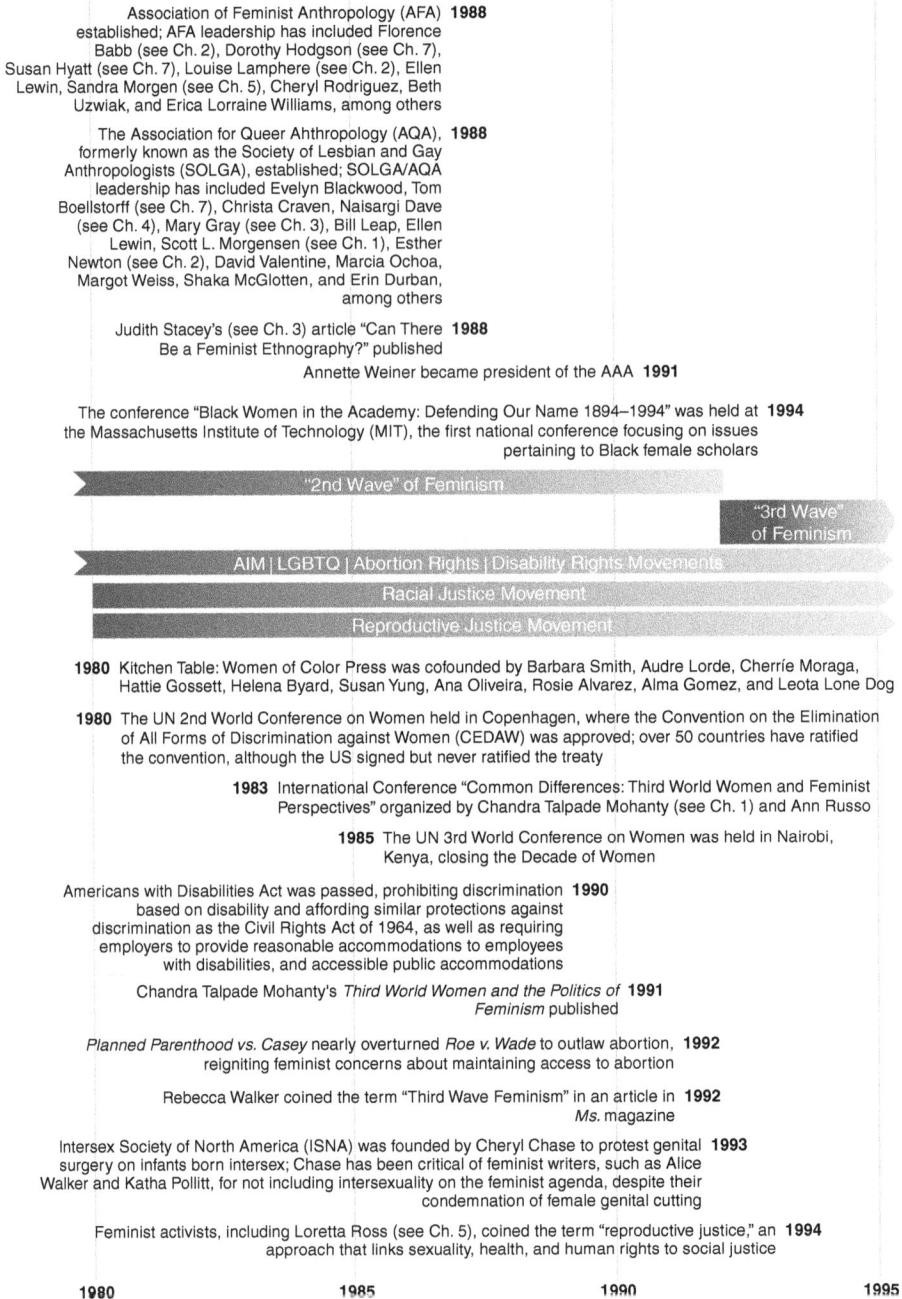

Association of Feminist Anthropology (AFA) **1988** established; AFA leadership has included Florence Babb (see Ch. 2), Dorothy Hodgson (see Ch. 7), Susan Hyatt (see Ch. 7), Louise Lamphere (see Ch. 2), Ellen Lewin, Sandra Morgen (see Ch. 5), Cheryl Rodriguez, Beth Uzwiak, and Erica Lorraine Williams, among others

The Association for Queer Ahthropology (AQA) **1988** formerly known as the Society of Lesbian and Gay Anthropologists (SOLGA), established; SOLGA/AQA leadership has included Evelyn Blackwood, Tom Boellstorff (see Ch. 7), Christa Craven, Naisargi Dave (see Ch. 4), Mary Gray (see Ch. 3), Bill Leap, Ellen Lewin, Scott L. Morgensen (see Ch. 1), Esther Newton (see Ch. 2), David Valentine, Marcia Ochoa, Margot Weiss, Shaka McGlotten, and Erin Durban, among others

Judith Stacey's (see Ch. 3) article "Can There **1988** Be a Feminist Ethnography?" published

Annette Weiner became president of the AAA **1991**

The conference "Black Women in the Academy: Defending Our Name 1894–1994" was held at **1994** the Massachusetts Institute of Technology (MIT), the first national conference focusing on issues pertaining to Black female scholars

"2nd Wave" of Feminism

"3rd Wave" of Feminism

AIM | LGBTQ | Abortion Rights | Disability Rights Movements

Racial Justice Movement

Reproductive Justice Movement

1980 Kitchen Table: Women of Color Press was cofounded by Barbara Smith, Audre Lorde, Cherríe Moraga, Hattie Gossett, Helena Byard, Susan Yung, Ana Oliveira, Rosie Alvarez, Alma Gomez, and Leota Lone Dog

1980 The UN 2nd World Conference on Women held in Copenhagen, where the Convention on the Elimination of All Forms of Discrimination against Women (CEDAW) was approved; over 50 countries have ratified the convention, although the US signed but never ratified the treaty

1983 International Conference "Common Differences: Third World Women and Feminist Perspectives" organized by Chandra Talpade Mohanty (see Ch. 1) and Ann Russo

1985 The UN 3rd World Conference on Women was held in Nairobi, Kenya, closing the Decade of Women

Americans with Disabilities Act was passed, prohibiting discrimination **1990** based on disability and affording similar protections against discrimination as the Civil Rights Act of 1964, as well as requiring employers to provide reasonable accommodations to employees with disabilities, and accessible public accommodations

Chandra Talpade Mohanty's *Third World Women and the Politics of* **1991** *Feminism* published

Planned Parenthood vs. Casey nearly overturned *Roe v. Wade* to outlaw abortion, **1992** reigniting feminist concerns about maintaining access to abortion

Rebecca Walker coined the term "Third Wave Feminism" in an article in **1992** *Ms.* magazine

Intersex Society of North America (ISNA) was founded by Cheryl Chase to protest genital **1993** surgery on infants born intersex; Chase has been critical of feminist writers, such as Alice Walker and Katha Pollitt, for not including intersexuality on the feminist agenda, despite their condemnation of female genital cutting

Feminist activists, including Loretta Ross (see Ch. 5), coined the term "reproductive justice," an **1994** approach that links sexuality, health, and human rights to social justice

1980   **1985**   **1990**   **1995**

Key Dates in Feminist Ethnography

Feminist and Other Social Movements

Key Dates in Feminisms and Social Movements

1995 The Committee on the Status of Women in Anthropology (COSWA), which later became the Committee on Gender Equity in Anthropology (CoGEA), was established to monitor the status of gender equity in the discipline and the AAA, and annually awards the CoGEA Award (formerly known as the Squeaky Wheel Award), which has gone to Louise Lamphere (see Ch. 2) and Sandra Morgen (see Ch. 5), among others

1996 Race, Gender and Class Section of the American Sociological Association (ASA) established; Mignon Moore and Nancy Naples (see Ch. 3) have served as president in 2011 and 2015, respectively

1999 Louise Lamphere became president of the AAA

AAA issued a statement opposing President George W. Bush's call for a **2004** constitutional amendment banning gay marriage as a threat to civilization

Anthropologists began to be recruited to serve on Human Terrain Systems, **2007** embedded with US military personnel in Iraq and Afghanistan

"3rd Wave" of Feminism

AIM| LGBTQ | Abortion Rights | Disability Rights | Racial Justice| Reproductive Justice Movements

Anti-Globalization Movement

1995 The UN 4th World Conference on Women in Beijing, China endorsed "women's right to control [their] sexuality"

1995 Riki Anne Wilchins founded transgender advocacy group GenderPAC on explicitly feminist principles to lobby against hate crimes and employment discrimination

1996 President Bill Clinton signed the Defense of Marriage Act (DoMA), which established marriage as an institution between one man and one woman

1997 Loretta Ross cofounded the SisterSong Women of Color Reproductive Justice Collective

1997 The Audre Lorde Project opened in New York, a community center for lesbian, gay, bisexual, two spirit, and transgender (LGBTT) people of color

1997 NOW passed a trans-inclusion resolution in consultation with GenderPAC

The Netherlands became the first country to legalize **2001** same-sex marriage

AVEN, the Asexuality Visibility and Education Network, **2001** was established

The Consensus Statement on Treatment of Intersex Individuals was revised to prioritize **2006** psychosocial support for children and families due to activism by the ISNA and the Accord Alliance

| 1995 | 1998 | 2001 | 2004 | 2007 |

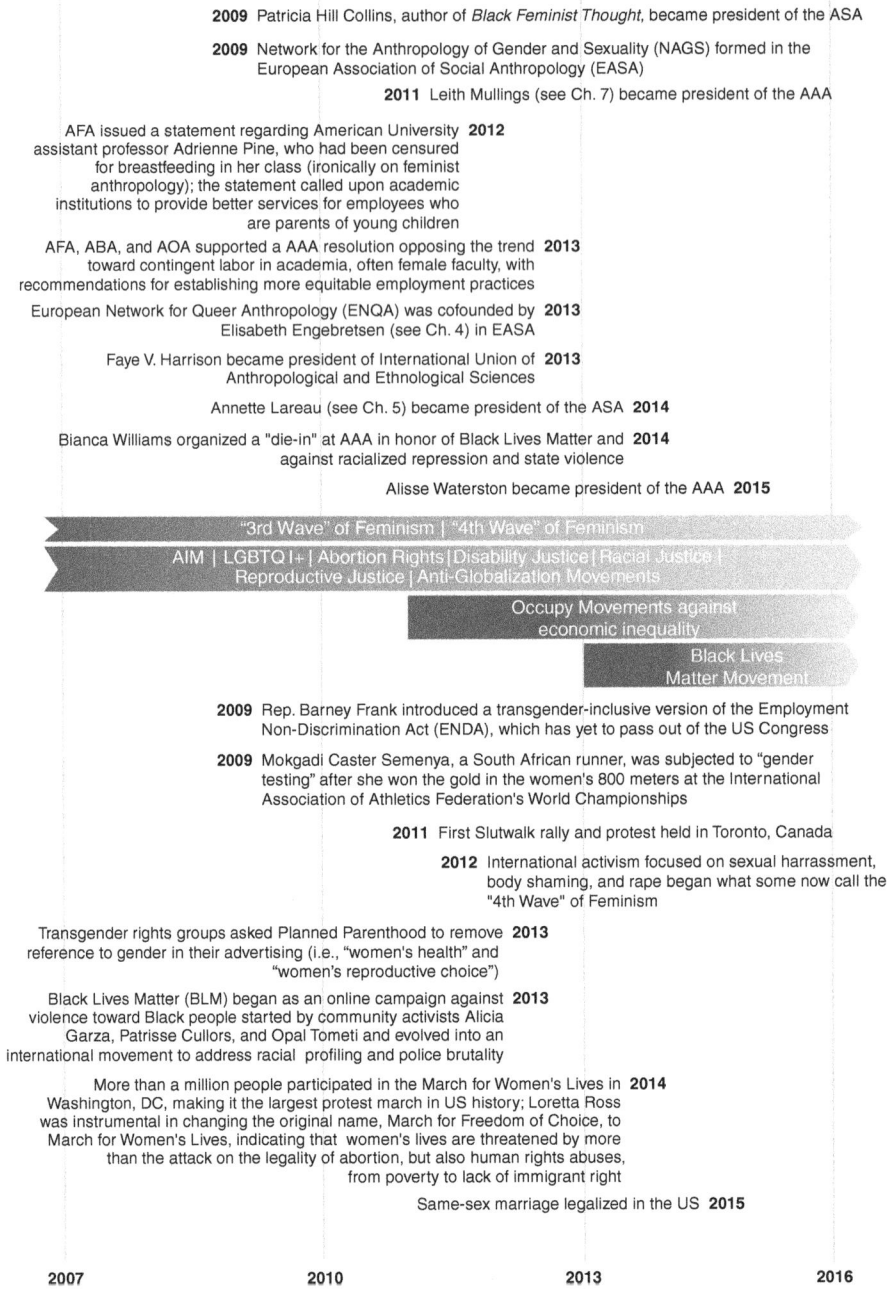

Key Dates in Feminist Ethnography

2009 Patricia Hill Collins, author of *Black Feminist Thought*, became president of the ASA

2009 Network for the Anthropology of Gender and Sexuality (NAGS) formed in the European Association of Social Anthropology (EASA)

2011 Leith Mullings (see Ch. 7) became president of the AAA

AFA issued a statement regarding American University **2012** assistant professor Adrienne Pine, who had been censured for breastfeeding in her class (ironically on feminist anthropology); the statement called upon academic institutions to provide better services for employees who are parents of young children

AFA, ABA, and AOA supported a AAA resolution opposing the trend **2013** toward contingent labor in academia, often female faculty, with recommendations for establishing more equitable employment practices

European Network for Queer Anthropology (ENQA) was cofounded by **2013** Elisabeth Engebretsen (see Ch. 4) in EASA

Faye V. Harrison became president of International Union of **2013** Anthropological and Ethnological Sciences

Annette Lareau (see Ch. 5) became president of the ASA **2014**

Bianca Williams organized a "die-in" at AAA in honor of Black Lives Matter and **2014** against racialized repression and state violence

Alisse Waterston became president of the AAA **2015**

Feminist and Other Social Movements

"3rd Wave" of Feminism | "4th Wave" of Feminism

AIM | LGBTQI+ | Abortion Rights | Disability Justice | Racial Justice | Reproductive Justice | Anti-Globalization Movements

Occupy Movements against economic inequality

Black Lives Matter Movement

2009 Rep. Barney Frank introduced a transgender-inclusive version of the Employment Non-Discrimination Act (ENDA), which has yet to pass out of the US Congress

2009 Mokgadi Caster Semenya, a South African runner, was subjected to "gender testing" after she won the gold in the women's 800 meters at the International Association of Athletics Federation's World Championships

2011 First Slutwalk rally and protest held in Toronto, Canada

2012 International activism focused on sexual harrassment, body shaming, and rape began what some now call the "4th Wave" of Feminism

Transgender rights groups asked Planned Parenthood to remove **2013** reference to gender in their advertising (i.e., "women's health" and "women's reproductive choice")

Black Lives Matter (BLM) began as an online campaign against **2013** violence toward Black people started by community activists Alicia Garza, Patrisse Cullors, and Opal Tometi and evolved into an international movement to address racial profiling and police brutality

More than a million people participated in the March for Women's Lives in **2014** Washington, DC, making it the largest protest march in US history; Loretta Ross was instrumental in changing the original name, March for Freedom of Choice, to March for Women's Lives, indicating that women's lives are threatened by more than the attack on the legality of abortion, but also human rights abuses, from poverty to lack of immigrant right

Same-sex marriage legalized in the US **2015**

Key Dates in Feminisms and Social Movements

2007   2010   2013   2016

2016 Laws banning anti-discrimination protections based on sexual orientation and requiring transgender people to use bathrooms that match the sex on their birth certificates passed in several US states

2016 Native Americans at Standing Rock, North Dakota, and allies across the world protested to protect access to clean water for Indigenous communities and sacred burial grounds during the government-funded construction of the oil transport system, the Dakota Access Pipeline (DAPL)

2017 The #MeToo movement spread virally throughout the world as a hashtag on social media in the wake of widespread sexual abuse allegations against film producer Harvey Weinstein. Civil Rights actvist Tarana Burke, who first used the hashtag in 2006, is credited as the founder of this movement to raise awareness about sexual abuse and assault.

2017 Christen A. Smith (see Ch. 3) created Cite Black Women as a campaign to push people to engage in a radical praxis of citation that acknowledges and honors Black women's transnational intellectual production

2017-2020 Executive orders and legal changes during Donald Trump's presidency rolled back numerous civil rights, instituting a Muslim travel ban, the deportation of refugees and separation of Central American families, the reversal of many protections for transgender people, and restrictions on reproductive rights, among others

2019 The American Anthropological Association hired an Accessibility & Meetings Coordinator and commited to more robustly addressing accessibility needs

The first issue of the journal *Feminist Ethnography* was released, **2020** with a commitment to magnify and center scholarship that incorporates multi-disciplinary research, interviews, poetry, creative fiction and non-fiction, visual art, and the praxis of teaching and mentoring.

Black Lives Matter

AIM | LGBTQI+ | Abortion Rights | Disability Justice | Racial Justice | Reproductive Justice
Anti-Globalization Movements

The global COVID-19 pandemic began, disproportionally **2020** impacting women and minority populations worldwide

Protests for racial justice reverberated **2020** across the US and internationally after the murders of George Floyd, Breonna Taylor, and other Black victims of police brutality. Calls for educators, political officials, and others to reckon with racist histories led to the removal of many Confederate statues and renaming of academic buildings and public spaces across the country.

White supremacists led an insurrection on the US Capitol in protest of **2021** the presidential election results in favor of Democrat Joe Biden and Kamala Harris, the first woman, the first Black American, and the first South Asian American to be elected Vice President

The US issued the first American passport displaying **2021** "X" rather than an "F" or "M" gender marker

Hundreds of local rallys were held in opposition to restrictive abortion legislation **2021**

2016   2018   2020   2022

Introduction

Feminist Ethnography: *Thinking Through Methodologies, Challenges, and Possibilities* (FE) was designed with the hope that feminist ethnography can play an integral role in your thinking about how to productively respond to the injustices we encounter in our everyday lives. In this case, the subtitle "Thinking Through . . ." has two meanings. First, we hope you will use the discussions in the book to arrive at some understanding of how feminist frameworks and writing can be useful as a critical approach to everyday experiences. The other meaning is to consider carefully, or think through, aspects of planning and the implementation of a project. To facilitate your ability to learn about feminist ethnography, we use a problem-based approach, which is based on inquiry and investigation. Problem-based learning is an opportunity to ask and respond to critical questions, as well as complete assignments or tasks to enhance the integration of the ideas presented.

FE was written expressly with students in mind, in part, because feminism and feminists—and consequently academic inquiry associated with feminism—have gotten a very bad rap over the past few decades, particularly in popular media. What many have described as "Third Wave" and now "Fourth Wave" feminism—a diverse resurgence of young feminists in the 1990s demanding attention to a range of issues addressing not only gender equity but also antiracism, anticolonialism, queer rights, reproductive justice, and antiviolence initiatives—came on the heels of the conservative political environment of the 1980s and 1990s, which led to public resistance to the term feminism. In 2014, *Time* magazine included the word "feminist" in a readers' poll inquiring which words should be banned from public use. Although *Time* later recanted and apologized, its contrition was the result of public outcry.[1] Despite the magazine's apology, the fact remains that feminism has often been viewed as a "dirty word," as evidenced by the sheer number of blog posts that make and/or refute the claim. As a nonscientific test, we googled "Feminist a Dirty Word" in December 2021 and received nearly seven million results (which had more than quadrupled since we initially published this book in January 2016)!

Given the negative public perception and the ways in which the lives of women, lesbian, gay, bisexual, trans, queer, and intersex people (LGBTQI+),[2] and Black, Indigenous, Asian and Pacific Islander, and Latinx people are under attack,[3] we want to impress upon you the possibilities that exist when doing feminist ethnographic research, which can serve as a potent response to these inequities. As journalist and blogger Samantha Blake, who publishes regularly in popular millennial and Gen Z media outlets such as *Bustle*, *Her Campus*, and *Medium*, states:

> In order to incite real change, we need more people to understand and begin to see value in the roots of the [feminist] movement, even if they don't agree with the terminology. . . . In short, we want to have the same opportunities and be able to make our own decisions, and a lot of men (though not exclusively) seem to keep standing in the way of that.[4]

A poll with the hashtag poll with the hashtag #FeminismInMyCountry—"What does it mean to be a 'feminist' in your country? How do your belief systems and cultural traditions shape your view of how a woman should exercise her rights?"— generated heated discussion on social media in areas throughout the world, including South Korea, Rwanda, Poland, Portugal, Tanzania, and the United States.[5]

On some level, we are inclined to just own it! Feminism has been, is, and will likely continue to be a contested term. Rather than suggest one monolithic set of tenets, we draw on the concept of *un choque*, or "cultural collisions," discussed by Chicana feminist Gloria Anzaldúa. For those who inhabit more than one culture— as so many of us do—we frequently receive multiple, often conflicting messages, as Anzaldúa describes them "self-consistent but habitually incomparable frames of reference."[6] In her work, the collision of cultures forces *la mestiza* to engage in self-making—that is, the creation of her own identity. We apply the concept of *un choque* in the text when we present ideas that are sometimes contradictory or challenging within feminist thinking. The ability to work through tensions and contradictions, as we see it, is itself a source of knowledge and part of the production of feminist ethnography and ideology. For example, across race and ethnicity, there are no uniform perspectives about the role, or even the meaning, of feminism. Nor will you find singular feminist analyses of issues within transnational politics or across political perspectives. This text then not only reveals the challenges within feminism but also positions those challenges as the *work* of feminism; in other words, parts of this text and the discussions and contradictions herein represent the concept of *un choque*.

Our point is to expose you to the breadth and history of feminist ethnography and the broad interdisciplinary application of feminist ethnographic methods. Feminists have examined many issues that expand our thinking on contemporary political and social concerns. Political scientist Cathy Cohen, for example, is the principal researcher on the Black Youth Project,[7] which produces research about the ideas, attitudes, decision-making, and lived experiences of Black youth, aimed at encouraging civil engagement and mobilizing communities of color beyond electoral politics. Anthropologist Daisy Deomampo's research conducted on the global surrogacy industry in Mumbai, India, looks at the complex transnational issues surrounding gestational surrogacy, egg donation, and in vitro fertilization.[8] Sociologist Katherine Cross studies online harassment and gender in virtual worlds and writes regularly for the blogs like Feministing.org and Rewire News on topics such as the Black Lives Matter movement, online harassment through #GamerGate, Europe's "refugee crisis," transgender politics, sexual shaming, and the #SayHerName and #MeToo campaigns.[9]

An important thing that we noticed in our research for this book is that although feminists across a range of disciplines have embraced feminist ethnography, some have admitted to being unfamiliar with ethnographic work outside of their own disciplines.[10] It is our goal to highlight the strong tradition of feminist ethnography that began (largely) in anthropology, but to also consider the contemporary application of feminist ethnography across a variety of disciplines—including archaeology, biocultural anthropology, communication, education, human geography, linguistics, performance, political science, psychology, sociology, and in a range of **interdisciplinary** fields such as American studies, critical race studies, ethnic studies, Africana studies, **Chican@/Xicanx/Latin@/Latinx** studies,[11] and women's, gender, and sexuality studies, among others.[12] We also want to speak to broader audiences that interface with academia, such as activists and transformative education efforts like the medical humanities and the Inside-Out Program that offers pedagogical approaches for teaching and learning among college students and people who are incarcerated.

This book is your guide to feminist ethnographic approaches. You will come to understand its history and its varied methodologies. You will see how it has been produced and circulated, and you will explore the challenges and possibilities that open up when you engage feminist ethnography as a theoretical, empirical, political, and potentially activist project. We also hope that the people who teach and read this material will bring their own topical and disciplinary expertise to bear in thinking through feminist ethnography.

Thinking Through This Text

Before we tell you about the structure of the book, we want to offer a brief note on terminology. We follow scholars such as anthropologist Leith Mullings, sociologists Maxine Baca Zinn and Bonnie Thornton Dill, and Native American activist and environmentalist Winona LaDuke who capitalize terms that represent historically marginalized groups, such as Indigenous, Aboriginal, Native, Black, Chicanx, Latinx, et cetera. However, we strategically utilize lowercase for the term "white" in an aim to decenter whiteness, the racialized identifier that has long served as the norm in disciplines that employ ethnography.

FE is organized into eight chapters. Chapter 1 provides an introduction to feminist perspectives and their meanings over time. It establishes the importance of feminist ethnography and offers our working definition of the term. Chapter 2 is an historical overview of feminist ethnography, noting that the feminist ethnographic approach is not always identified as such by authors. Chapter 3 enumerates recent debates among feminist ethnographers as the field expanded from the 1980s through the present. Chapter 4 examines feminist methodologies. It answers the question, how does one *do* feminist ethnography? While we do not cover every possible method for feminist ethnography, we explore participant-observation, oral history, narrative analysis, and participatory action research, among others. Chapter 5 investigates the challenges of doing and producing feminist ethnography, including the ethical dilemmas and logistical constraints faced during fieldwork and writing. In chapter 6, we further explore the production and distribution of feminist ethnography with attention to both traditional and creative ways that ethnography can be circulated, including ethnographic texts, blog posts, novels, film, and performance. Chapter 7 discusses what it means to be a feminist activist ethnographer and highlights strategies for integrating scholarly and activist work through contributions to advocacy efforts and public policy. In chapter 8, we ask: What is your vision? What impacts do you want to make on the future of feminist ethnography?

We incorporate a range of people whose contributions to feminist ethnography are often overlooked, particularly those from groups that have not always been featured prominently in collections on feminist ethnography. Some of these are scholars and activists we have met during our professional careers, some were our students, and others were "cold calls," so to speak, to those whose work we deeply admire. After the first edition, we continued to encounter—and had generous colleagues continue to introduce us to—the work of other scholars that expanded our vision of the field.

As with the first edition, over half of the textboxes include work by scholars of color, several are international scholars trained outside the United States, others identify as queer and trans, some are activists, or activist-scholars. In addition, in contrast to many earlier texts on feminist ethnography, feminist anthropology, and feminist methods, we interviewed **cisgender** men who identify as feminist ethnographers or have a feminist sensibility and view their scholarship to be heavily influenced by feminists. By feminist sensibility, we mean the ability to appreciate and respond to the complex intellectual and theoretical influences of feminist theory, thought, practice, and politics. Frankly, this is a project that we believe necessitates participation by *all* people—cisgender women (and men), trans women and trans men, as well as intersex and nonbinary people. We recognize that this may appear controversial to some who wish to emphasize the ways that sexism has marked women's scholarship historically and in the present—a fact that we are not inured to and also highlight in the text. Yet, as we look toward the future of feminist ethnography, we find many students and colleagues across the gender spectrum (or gender polyhedron, a three-dimensional shape, as one of Christa's former students, Maram Ghanimeh, aptly described "the mess that is gender identity and expression") are deeply inspired and influenced by feminist ethnographic work. Indeed, as we conducted our interviews and historical research for this book, we focused our inquiry on ethnographers who articulate a feminist sensibility in their research and writing, not because of the sex they were assigned at birth or their present gender identity.

Unique Features of This Book

As we prepared (and then revised) this textbook, the process was much like a feminist ethnographic project. Between the two of us, we conducted informal fieldwork—participant-observation and informal conversations about the field—at nearly fifty conferences for more than a decade (such as the annual meetings of the American Anthropological Association, American Studies Association, Association for the Study of the Worldwide African Diaspora, European Association of Social Anthropologists, National Women's Studies Association, American Psychological Association, and several smaller interdisciplinary conferences). We also interviewed over forty feminist ethnographers about the intricacies of their work.[13] These interviews introduce into the text the perspectives and reflections of seasoned feminist ethnographers who have participated in the field's growth since the 1970s, those who witnessed the debates that emerged during the 1980s and 1990s, and newer scholars inspired to incorporate feminist ethnography in their work, including several students.

Each chapter takes a "problem-based" approach guided by several critical questions. The beginning of each chapter offers an abbreviated snapshot of the contents, designed to make it easier to distinguish important elements of the text. The problem-based questions will also be useful to return to after reading the chapter, particularly in the context of the *Spotlights* and *Essentials* highlighting a broad range of ethnographers and issues. Each chapter features several *Spotlights*, excerpts from interviews conducted to explore the meaning and practice of feminist ethnography. *Spotlights* include a photograph and a brief introduction of the speaker (including their interests, academic and/or activist training and affiliations, and major or newest publications). Chapters also include several *Essentials*, excerpts of texts that we consider "classics" or influential texts to give you a deeper sense of the history and practice of feminist ethnography. *Essentials* also include a photograph and brief background on the author(s). In addition, you will find activities labeled *Thinking Through . . .* that encourage you to further engage the concepts that we have presented. It is the "doing" of feminist ethnography that offers the best opportunity to learn and encourages you to reflect on the challenges and possibilities of feminist ethnographic approaches. At the close of each chapter, we provide a list of additional *Suggested Resources* for those of you who wish to pursue the topics we present in more depth. These are largely new materials, ones that we do not explore elsewhere in the textbook. We also recommend reading the materials highlighted in the *Essentials* and *Spotlights* and other ethnographies that we profile in each chapter. Throughout the text, you will find words and phrases in **bold** that are defined on the first mention in the text and included in the Glossary of definitions. Finally, directly preceding this chapter we have included a timeline of events, related to feminism and feminist ethnography. It reflects the issues we cover in the textbook and highlights important people and events in movements for social justice.

We believe that feminist ethnography offers valuable contributions to both scholarship and activism. This textbook will engage you in critical thinking about its production and circulation. Ultimately, it is your reactions, responses, and projects that will shape what lies in its future.

Notes

1 Katy Steinmetz, "Which Word Should Be Banned in 2015?" *Time*, November 12, 2014, http://time .com/3576870/worst-words-poll-2014/.

2 We use + to include non-Western and non-EuroAmerican understandings of gender and sexuality, as well as identities, such as pansexual, omnisexual, asexual, and so on. We use different acronyms throughout the text to indicate particular historical moments—for instance, when LGBT politics and identities have been foregrounded.

3 Use of the term BIPOC (pronounced bye-pock)—Black, Indigenous, (and) people of color—came into common usage in the United States in 2020 when racial justice organizers used it to emphasize solidarities among all people of color in opposition to white supremacy; see, for instance, the BIPOC Project, https://www.thebipocproject.org/. Although ubiquitous on left-leaning social media platforms, we use this term sparingly. While BIPOC is a term that has gained popularity in the United States, it does not have the same resonance everywhere (see, for instance, philosopher Joseph Heath's 2021 discussion of BIPOC in a Canadian context), nor is it universally embraced within the United States (see Sandra E. Garcia's "Where Did BIPOC Come From?" *New York Times (Online)*, June 15, 2020). Other terminology, like women of color, has a deep history and continues to have important resonance for many feminists. We believe that these legacies are also important to preserve. The power of self-naming is at the heart of reproductive justice activist Loretta J. Ross's viral 2011 YouTube clip that begins "Y'all know where the term 'women of color' came from?" Ross narrates the story of how the "Women of Color Agenda" was created at the 1977 National Women's Conference in Houston, Texas. The document that was initially brought by Black women from Washington, DC, began as the "Black Women's Agenda," but when other "minority" women wanted to sign on, the group worked collaboratively and agreed to the "Women of Color Agenda" as a commitment to working in solidarity with others who had been minoritized by oppression. Throughout this textbook, we favor (1) specificity when describing particular contexts of oppression, such as anti-Black violence and the erasure of Indigenous peoples, and (2) self-naming, in that we prioritize using the terminology adopted by a particular writer or speaker in a particular historical and political moment.

4 Samantha Blake, "Why Some People Still Think 'Feminist' Is a Dirty Word," *Medium*, 2020.

5 Malaka Gharib, "A Rallying Cry, a Dirty Word: People Around the World Talk About 'Feminism,'" *NPR.Org*, August 4, 2016.

6 Gloria Anzaldúa, *Borderlands/La Frontera: The New Mestiza*, 1987, 78.

7 Cathy J. Cohen, "Black Youth Project." *Black Youth Project*. Accessed October 4, 2015. http:// www.blackyouthproject.com/. Cohen is also the author of *Democracy Remixed: Black Youth and The Future of American Politics*, 2010.

8 Deomampo, Daisy. *Transnational Reproduction: Race, Kinship, and Commercial Surrogacy in India*. New York: New York University Press, 2016.

9 Feministing, "Katherine Cross Archive," http://feministing.com/author/katherinecross/ and Rewire News, "Katherine Cross: All Work," https://rewire.news/author/katherine-cross/, both accessed January 8, 2020.

10 For example, see Annette Lareau, "Common Problems in Fieldwork," in *Journeys Through Ethnography*, eds. Annette Lareau and Jeffry Shultz, 1996, 225.

11 There have been a variety of linguistic resistances to the binary gendering and colonial inheritance of the Spanish language. The terms *Chicano* and *Chicana* (also combined as Chicano/a) became widely used during the 1960s to express political and cultural solidarity with the "Chicano" movement against Eurocentrism and the oppression of Mexican-descended people. Feminists popularized the use of the *arroba* symbol (the Spanish and Portuguese word for the "at symbol" @) in Chican@ and Latin@—conjoining the "o" and the "a" as a gender-neutral, though still binary, descriptor. In her 1994 book *Massacre of the Dreamers: Essays on Xicanisma*, novelist Ana Castillo replaced the "Ch" at the beginning of Chicano/a with "X" as a means to more directly identify with the Indigenous Mayan and Aztec etymology of the term. As the key command "@" became popular in online spaces, feminist and queer activists and artists adopted the ending "x" as an intervention which invoked both a politics of decolonization and the deliberate inclusion of nonbinary people (Shange 2019: 167, n3). Similar linguistic shifts are seen with mestizx and Filipinx, among others. For a more in-depth discussion of the implications of "x," particularly for Afrxlatinx communities, see Johnson (2015).

12 In our discussion, we frequently mention the disciplinary background of authors we cite, not to instantiate them in a single field (indeed, many are decidedly interdisciplinary in their approaches) but to highlight the multiple disciplines that constitute and contribute to the field of feminist ethnography.

13 Interviews were recorded when possible (in person, over the phone, or by Skype) or collected as email exchanges.

CHAPTER 1

What Is the "Feminist" in Feminist Ethnography?

This chapter provides an overview of feminism and feminist ethnography. You will learn definitions, histories, and categorizations using the following questions as your guide:

- What is feminist ethnography?
- What contributed to the history of feminisms?
- How are feminist perspectives categorized?

Spotlights *in this chapter:*

- Zenzele Isoke on Feminist Concepts
- Dyese Osaze on Meaningful Ethnography
- Scott L. Morgensen on the Influence of Feminist Ethnography
- Gayle Rubin's Influence

Essentials *in this chapter:*

- Rosemarie A. Roberts, "Doing Feminist Ethnography"
- Seneca Falls, "Declaration of Sentiments"
- Combahee River Collective Statement
- Chandra Talpade Mohanty, "'Under Western Eyes' Revisited"

*You will also be **Thinking Through** . . .*

- Foremothers of Feminism
- Feminisms
- Feminist Perspectives and Key Texts

This chapter is designed to orient you to feminism and the shifts it has undergone, as well as how feminists have engaged in an internal critique of their own work over time. Feminist ethnographic research is generally understood to have emerged during the women's movement of the 1960s and 1970s. It is important to understand what led up to the development of feminist ethnography, frequently referred to as the "waves" of feminism—a concept we problematize in this chapter. The notion of waves focuses upon a Euro-American history of feminism. Yet feminist activism has occurred at various times in many locations. We rely on this metaphor sparingly and include it in our timeline to provide reference points that can help to make feminist influences on ethnography legible.

We use an interdisciplinary approach to explore the influence of many different strands of feminism. Therefore, following a broad introduction of feminist ethnography, we consider the emergence of feminist thinking as it intersects with critical race, disability, gender, sexuality, and class analyses. The phases of feminism we identify represent time periods in which particular issues were raised. This is followed by a discussion of the political inclinations of several different feminist perspectives. We distinguish between the waves and perspectives because perspectives do not always overlap with a single time period. For example, although liberal feminism emerged during the 1800s (aka the First Wave), one can see liberal feminism in many contemporary feminist struggles throughout the twentieth century. Further, one could have been a socialist feminist in the early 1900s, although this perspective became more common among what people often describe as the Second Wave in the 1960s and 1970s. So, it is important to keep in mind that waves and perspectives are not necessarily congruent.

Despite the different impulses that have been important to the development of feminism, many would argue that the simplest definition of being a feminist is someone who is committed to the idea that there should be equality between women and men. For feminist ethnographers, this would entail scoping out specific projects to make women's experiences visible as the political imperative. Yet the feminist project has come to mean more than solely focusing on women's experiences—it also encompasses prioritizing projects that impact those who are marginalized, including people of color, disabled people, LGBTQI+ people, and poor or low-income people. Thus, feminist thinking is organized around supporting the struggles of people whose lives are marked and marred by structural inequalities.

✈ SPOTLIGHT ✈

Zenzele Isoke on Feminist Concepts

Photo Credit: University of Minnesota, Twin Cities.

Zenzele Isoke *is a Black feminist theorist, urban ethnographer, and political storyteller in the Department of Gender, Women & Sexuality Studies at the University of Minnesota. She writes across the fields of geography, political science, and urban ethnography and her scholarship spans several cities in the United States, the Middle East, and the Caribbean. Her new writing projects develop a set of "counterpoetic" writing practices to theorize and explore Black female life through the mediums of collaborative art-making, breath and meditation, memoir, and integrating ethnography with the lyric essay form. The following interview excerpt is her response to the question: How do you define feminist ethnography?*

I think of feminist ethnography as a form of community engagement and community-immersive participatory research that provides opportunity for prolonged mutual reflection on some sort of knowledge that has an ultimately emancipatory aim. Ethnography, of course, in its most simple and broadest formulation simply meaning the writing of human life. Human life happens in place and space. Traditionally speaking a place can be a town, a city, a campus, a prison, a region, a street corner, a hair salon, or really any kind of place where human come together to live and make meaning together. A space, on the other hand, is something that is created by the intention of humans working together to create new meanings and practices around some coalescing vision. This includes creating physical, social, or intimate space where people who are similarly minded can come together to simply be. I have studied all kinds of places and spaces that Black women have made to do different kinds of emancipatory and sometimes even insurrectionist work.

What makes an ethnography feminist does not have as much to do with the self-definition of the researcher, as much as it has the potential to transform the lives of those who participate in the making of the research. This includes the ethnographer, the respondents, and also future generations of scholars and communities who will pick up the work. Importantly, I believe that feminist research must in some way respond to and possibly intervene in some significant genealogy of feminist knowledge formation.

My work rests in the legacy of radical Black feminists including folks like Barbara Smith, bell hooks, and other transformative Black feminist social theorists like Patricia Hill Collins, Cathy Cohen, and Audre Lorde. In fact, it was by reading and studying and rereading and restudying, the Combahee River Collective, that my conviction that my work may be best understood as both transdisciplinary and antidisciplinary knowledge formations seeded in a love of Blackness and Black femaleness. One of the most compelling aspects of feminist ethnography is that it allows us to connect the microstructure of individual lives with the macrostructures of community, states, nations, and all of the messiness of social networks and social formations that are nested between them.

I think there are a few key concepts that I used above that need to be fleshed out. First, what makes a feminist work emancipatory? By emancipatory, I mean that this work seeks to clearly explain the conditions of the most vulnerable and oppressed groups in the researcher's communities, while refusing uncritically reproduce white and Eurocentric ways of thinking and being that continue to stifle the production of knowledge within Black, Indigenous, Asian and other people of communities in the United States and all around the planet. By insurrectionist, I mean that the work, or the ethnography, ignites newer and more imaginative modes of knowledge making that inspire others to craft projects that make fuller use of the ranges of the unique perspectives and worldviews that the ethnographer possesses and that the communities themselves nurture to make their lives more liveable. The goal of feminist ethnography is transgression toward the heightened aim of freedom.

What Is Feminist Ethnography?

A common question about feminist ethnography is: what is it that makes feminist ethnography different from just good ethnography? Our answer is laid out more comprehensively below and woven throughout the text, but in essence, feminist ethnography attends to the dynamics of power in social interaction that *starts* from a gender analysis. By gender analysis, we mean that a feminist ethnographic project takes into account all people in a field site/community/organization, and pays particular attention to gender by honing in on people's statuses, the different ways in which (multiple) forms of privilege allow them to wield power or benefit from it, and the forces and processes that emerge from all of the above. For instance, in Christa's book *Pushing for Midwives: Homebirth Mothers and the Reproductive Rights Movement* (2010), she chose to foreground the voices of homebirth mothers and midwives over the opposition to midwifery, which consisted mostly of physicians and public health officials (largely, though not entirely men) who were well positioned to be heard by legislators and the public through lobbyists, newspaper op-eds, as experts in court cases, et cetera. Within the midwifery movement, made up primarily of women, Christa was attentive to power dynamics, highlighting the socioeconomic class tensions that emerged between wealthy and middle-class organizers who promoted advocacy for access to midwives as a "consumer's right," and low-income homebirthers who did not identify as "typical midwifery consumers" who had a choice of options for childbirth providers. Her feminist commitment as an ethnographer led her to look at inequities and power dynamics—first through gender and then within it. Really, *any* good ethnographer should be examining power dynamics and inequities in their research; what sets feminist ethnographers apart, however, is their focus on a feminist framework for gendered analysis at the outset and throughout their projects, analyses, and choices concerning the production and circulation of their work.

This leads to the question: What are the ways that activists and scholars define "feminist" and how do those definitions fit into a discussion of feminist ethnography? There is an old joke that if you ask ten feminists to define feminism, you'll get at least eleven answers. Scholars across academic disciplines, activists engaged in social justice work, and public policy makers who sometimes utilize our work to justify political change use the term feminist and often feminist ethnography. Some say that feminist ethnography is a framework that influences the kind of research that one undertakes or that it reflects a feminist **epistemology**, an examination of how knowledge is produced from a feminist standpoint. Others present feminist ethnography as a range of methods—including, though hardly limited to, participant-observation, in-depth or life history interviewing, and participatory research. Still others would say that feminist ethnography is a research practice informed by a politics of social justice and that it must be accompanied by a social justice project. So, is it a research project? Is it a way of doing research? Is it an ideology or theory? Is feminist ethnography a way of writing or performing scholarship? Is it an activist engagement? Ultimately, it can be all of these! Feminist ethnography produces knowledge about people and situations in specific contexts with attention to power differentials and inequities that emerge from the various strands of feminism we introduce later in this chapter.

Like feminism, ethnography also has a long history, as well as disputed definitions—though we would argue less so than the term feminism. Ethnography has long been considered the primary research method in anthropology, employed across other social sciences such as sociology, and more recently by journalists. The difficulty in defining ethnography is that the term has been used in an unsystematic way, including by some who claim to be ethnographers after only brief stints interviewing and/or living for a few days among a particular group of people. Most social scientists would agree that ethnography is a form of qualitative research that centers on studying people and what they do and the contexts in which they live *over time.*

Ethnography typically involves long-term interactions through **participant-observation**. While its history dates back to Herodotus in the fourth century BCE,[1] ethnography assumed prominence across a range of disciplines in the twentieth century and involves becoming immersed in a situation and/or among a group of people to understand society from the point of view of those being studied—what contemporary ethnographers have come to call the **emic** perspective. Ethnographic description, including the **etic** or analytical point of view of the ethnographer, is thus a researcher's primary tool to convey knowledge about a particular cultural group. Ethnography was recognized more formally as a field of study in the mid- to late 1800s.[2]

One of the first social documentarians, or observers, of the conditions of the working class was Peruvian-born French feminist and socialist Flora Tristan (1803–1844), who recorded workers' exploitation in London. Although less well known than Friedrich Engels's often-cited *The Condition of the Working Class in England* published in 1845, Tristan's research on workers was published in 1840 under the title *Promenades dans Londres*.[3] Tristan was not an academic, but a socialist feminist who sought to bring attention to the impact of capitalism, the treatment of workers, and the links between the working class and women's rights. One of her primary arguments was that it was absolutely necessary to highlight the needs and experiences of women workers in order to address the needs of all workers. Tristan's work is a thread in the **intellectual genealogy** of contributions to (feminist) ethnography that emphasizes solution-based goals of documentary research.

Many academic disciplines and professions use participant-observation as a data collection method, but in anthropology, the origins of participant-observation are traced to Polish-British anthropologist Bronislaw Malinowski. Malinowski used participant-observation to generate anthropological knowledge among the Trobriand Islanders in 1914 and was among the first anthropologists to advocate using detailed descriptions of everyday life to understand societies. Across disciplines, practitioners now use ethnography to examine and understand how groups and people live their lives. The ethnographic account that results is a detailed description of that interaction and the product is also referred to as an ethnography. Far from being notable solely as a methodological choice, ethnography is as much about bridging theory and practice—**praxis**—grounded in an effort to explore situations from the perspective of those living the experiences being researched. In fact, one of the insights offered by early feminist ethnographers, that continues to be reiterated today, is that it challenges theories and ideas that privilege dominant groups but are made to seem like the only possibility for understanding culture.

Feminist ethnography originally emerged in the 1970s in an effort to correct women's absence from previous scholarship. Much of the previous male-centered research focused primarily on understanding culture, history, and everyday life from men's point of view. Women ethnographers in the field (and some men) made a concerted effort to correct this disparity by focusing on how life, politics, and sociocultural institutions were gendered and they sought to understand those issues by seeking out women's perspectives through the use of ethnographic methods. Sociologist Beverly Skeggs notes:

> The first location for feminist ethnography is in anthropology where ethnography is the central methodology. Here it has been strongly framed by colonialism and heterosexuality. The tradition of the heterosexual couple—him the distinguished anthropologist, her the interested and helpful wife, traveling to distant continents to spend years living in a "culture" in order to understand it—has led to the production of some exceedingly reflexive accounts.[4]

🐦 **SPOTLIGHT** 🐦

Dyese Osaze on Meaningful Ethnography

Dyese Osaze *is an anthropology graduate of the College of Wooster. Born and raised in Cleveland, Ohio, Osaze originally set out to become an OB/GYN, but, in light of the COVID-19 pandemic, she had the ability to tap into her creativity and spirituality, and she found her true calling as a doula. As part of her journey, Osaze is currently serving as an antenatal, perinatal, and postpartum doula in the Greater Cleveland area. Here, she discusses how anthropologist Leith Mullings has influenced her career path outside of academia.*

Photo Credit: Hashani Hettiarachchi.

One of the major public health issues facing the United States is the high mortality rates among African American women and infants. According to the Center for Disease Control (CDC), "the risk of pregnancy-related deaths for black women is 3 to 4 times higher than those of white women." The CDC has even called for a state of emergency regarding the pandemic. I came across Dr. Mullings's *Stress and Resilience: The Social Context of Reproduction in Central Harlem* while reading for a research project with Dr. Sarah Rubin, a medical anthropologist at Ohio University Heritage College of Osteopathic Medicine–Cleveland Campus.

Dr. Mullings's encouragement about making feminist ethnography "meaningful" resonated with me for two reasons. For one, I feel that her work has opened doors for me to use the lessons of medical anthropology as I continue my healthcare education. I can apply her insights to my practice as a midwife and will be able to address the many health disparities that Mullings highlights. Dr. Mullings has addressed many socioeconomic and environmental factors embedded in African American communities across the nation and I feel called to action.

Like Dr. Mullings, I too wish to create "meaningful" ethnography in my clinical practice. *Stress and Resilience* has inspired me to find ways I could immediately get involved in creating change. While Dr. Mullings focused on Central Harlem, I feel motivated to create change within my hometown of Cleveland because, as she reminds us, there is work to be done within our communities.

Ultimately, feminist ethnography does not have one single definition, nor can "doing" feminist ethnography be confined to a single scholarly trajectory. Just as important is the fact that feminist ideologies have shaped and been shaped *by* ethnographic processes. We offer you this working definition of feminist ethnography, which

1. involves a feminist sensibility and commitment to paying attention to marginality and power differentials; these include not only gender but also race, class, nation, sexuality, ability, and other areas of difference;

2. draws inspiration from feminist scholarship—in other words, our feminist intellectual genealogy is important;
3. challenges marginalization and injustice;
4. acknowledges and reflects upon power relations within the research context;
5. aims to produce scholarship—in both traditional and experimental forms—that may contribute to movement building and/or be in the service of organizations, people, communities, and issues we study.

Our goal is not to dispute multiple meanings and definitions, but rather to examine the ways that feminist ethnography is practiced, and how feminist research is produced and circulated. We also draw inspiration from dance scholar Rosemarie A. Roberts, who shared the following set of injunctions, or rules, that she attempts to follow in her own work to follow in her work.[5]

🐚 ESSENTIAL

Commentary on Doing Feminist Ethnography by Rosemarie A. Roberts

Photo Credit: Liam C. Muldro.

Rosemarie A. Roberts, *Dayton Professor of Dance at Connecticut College, holds an endowed professorship in the interdisciplinary study of the arts. Her artistic and scholarly work blends history, dance, and theater to conduct investigations of Afro-diasporic dance as embodiments of difference, knowledge, and resistive power. In addition to her dance practice and dance making, Roberts has published in the areas of intergroup and intragroup relations, qualitative research methods, participatory action research, curriculum, dance, gender, race, ethnic, and cultural identities. Roberts has also published in peer-reviewed journals, edited volumes, and coauthored a book/video project on conceptions of social justice in education and dance. Roberts's book titled* Baring Unbearable Sensualities: Hip Hop Dance, Bodies, Race and Power *examines the relationship among racialized bodies, knowledge, and power discontents. Here she discusses how she approaches feminist ethnographic research.*

Number 1: Build on knowledge that has come before your work. Don't knock down others in the interest of promoting one's own work as new or original. I know this goes against what I think so many of us have been trained to do—we have to show our projects as new and original, and we have to put somebody else down, or we have missed the main point. Building on and collaborating WITH is about changing the academy.

Number 2: Don't pay lip service to writing in accessible language. Actually write in accessible language that illuminates rather than obscures what you have come to say.

Number 3: Make sure your argumentation is carefully constructed and supported by evidence. For me, that means invoking qualitative data for the insights they offer, and using quantitative data for the trends and patterns they might suggest. The difference between qualitative and quantitative data is not a contest between subjective and objective, but it's about determining the methodologies that work best to get me to the understandings and nuances that I'm seeking.

Number 4: Practice Holism. That includes appreciating that intellectual reason is a part of, but is not the whole story. Practicing holism includes appreciating that the kinesthetic, affective, and emotional is also part of the whole. I tell myself, "Don't privilege reason over emotion, and don't privilege emotion over reason."

Number 5: Look for and cite those who continue to be marginalized, acknowledging their important contributions to our collective knowledge base.

Number 6: Remind yourself that self-promotion is problematic if you put yourself forth as the one who has developed a new philosophy or theory when actually, you haven't. Especially when the theory or approach comes from the communities you are studying. But, if you have created a work or developed new something, embrace it! Recognize and remind yourself that . . . it is not self-promotion in a negative way to let others know about your work and activities. That's good to do. After all, if you don't do it, who will?

Source: Roberts, Rosemarie. Roundtable Discussant Commentary, "Interdisciplinary Perspectives on Feminist Ethnography & Activism." National Women's Studies Association Annual Meetings, San Juan, Puerto Rico. 2014.

We explore the production of knowledge through the lens of feminist ethnography. When we talk about how knowledge is produced, that means we consider the sources of explanation. Historians can produce knowledge by searching through archival material. In the natural sciences, knowledge may be acquired through a series of experimental steps known as the scientific "method" that relies on **empirical**, or verifiable, knowledge. Feminists often produce knowledge by reconsidering how power operates differentially, prioritizing women's experiences and those of others who have been historically sidelined. Feminist knowledge is also important in identifying not only oppression but resistance as well.

Of course, it is important to recognize that the history of any research practice—and, as Morgensen highlights in the next *Spotlight*, our political perspectives—will often be told through the lens of dominant members of society. The history of feminist ethnography is no different. Some scholars have noted that feminist ethnography emerged in the United States at the same time as Second Wave feminism, in response to the eye-opening writings of liberal feminist Betty Freidan. Freidan's 1963 book *The Feminine Mystique* lamented the seeming destiny of suburban housewives—women whose lives, according to those Friedan interviewed, were almost devoid of meaning beyond shopping, decorating, and chauffeuring children to a host of activities.[6] Their displacement and sense of exclusion became a battle cry for what became known as the Second Wave of feminism in the 1960s and 1970s. But there were other influences as well.

✧ SPOTLIGHT ✧

Scott L. Morgensen on the Influence of Feminist Ethnography

Scott L. Morgensen *received his PhD in anthropology and women's studies from the University of California, Santa Cruz, and teaches in the Department of Gender Studies at Queen's University. His book,* Spaces between Us: Queer Settler Colonialism and Indigenous Decolonization *(2011), examined the shaping effects of white settler colonialism within North American LGBTQ politics, in conversation with anticolonial and antiracist work by Two-Spirit and QTBIPOC activists. His current writing examines queer anthropology, activist research, and the methodological contributions of queer and feminist ethnography to interdisciplinary gender studies. In this interview, Morgensen describes how feminist ethnography helps him address power and ethics in research.*

Paying attention to what people are telling me about themselves forces me to hold my own political investments in a critical light: not to let go of my politics, but to expose that they carry a culture and a history too. Feminist ethnography shows me how to have political stakes and also expose their situatedness. I think doing this makes research and writing better. I don't hesitate to get involved in politicized research because feminist ethnography checks my desires to control what I will learn or know. Feminist ethnographers aren't afraid of confronting the ways we are situated in relation to our subjects or topics of study. And when complex issues arise, feminist ethnography models ethical ways to address them. By this, I don't mean a bullet point list of "do this" and "don't do that," but the sensitivity to address how power is shaping everyone in every research relationship.

If we keep doing research in the future and all forms of oppression aren't gone yet, then we're going to keep confronting ethical problems. So, let's just be more clear about them—and thank you, feminist ethnography, for setting the bar!

What Contributed to the History of Feminisms?

Reconsidering "The Waves"

Histories can be told from many points of view, and that is the case with both the history of feminism and feminist ethnography. Typically, when people discuss Euro-American feminism, they do so in terms of waves, a metaphor that was coined in the 1960s. At that time, women's organizing around a broad range of issues—including sexuality, reproductive rights—was labeled the "Second Wave," in contrast to the movement for women's suffrage in the United States (achieved in 1920). Other scholars have used terms such as "phases" and "eras" in place of waves, but we find it more productive to broaden what constitutes the history of feminism both temporally and conceptually.

From a chronological perspective, historians cite feminist figures well before the late nineteenth century, such as lyric poet Sappho of ancient Greece, who wrote about passion and love for both women and men in ~600 BCE. Others born in or before the eighteenth century include writer and philosopher Mary Wollstonecraft (1759–1797) of Britain, who is considered one of the foremothers of the modern women's movement.

Women outside of a Euro-American framework who made contributions to what might now be considered feminism are also crucial to extending our understanding of feminist histories. This would include figures such as poet and nun Sor Juana Inés de la Cruz (1651–1695) of Mexico who promoted the right for women to have an education. In the United States, African American preacher Jarena Lee (1783–?) was an ardent supporter of equality for women and was the first woman authorized to preach by the African Methodist Episcopal (AME) church. Peruvian writer Clorinda Matto de Turner (1852–1909) caused controversy within Latin America as a woman of European ancestry who advocated for Incan Indigenous rights and authored *Aves Sin Nido* (*Birds Without a Nest*) about a love affair between a white man and an Indigenous woman—a book that ultimately led to her be excommunicated from the Catholic Church because it revealed the atrocious treatment of Peruvian natives. She was also a formidable supporter of women's education and her work has been compared to Wollstonecraft's (1792) *A Vindication of the Rights of Woman* because, like Wollstonecraft, she argued that marital egalitarianism could be achieved through educating women.

The notion of waves linked to suffrage, though, obscures activists who made women's concerns central to other movements. For instance, South African religious leader Charlotte Manye Maxeke (1871–1918) was active in the campaigns against pass laws that restricted Black South African's movement. She founded the Bantu Women's League of the South African Native National Congress (SANNC). As a leader of SANNC, Maxeke led the first demonstration against passes and was active in protests against low wages. Maxeke is likely to have been the first African woman to graduate university in the United States, Wilberforce University in Ohio, where she took courses under Pan-Africanist, W. E. B. Du Bois.[7] In the United States, Mary Harris Jones, better known today as Mother Jones, was an Irish American trade union activist who cofounded the international labor union Industrial Workers of the World in 1905. Mother Jones spent much of her life challenging the lax implementation of child labor laws that left many children permanently disabled, an essential issue for poor and working-class women at the turn of the twentieth century.

Conceptually, we take inspiration from the feminist activist organization INCITE: Women of Color Against Violence's slogan "Feminist since 1492," arguing that a single "History of Feminism" that privileges Euro-American Global North contributions loses sight of the important knowledge production of Indigenous feminist thinkers and women of color (WoC). The notion that feminist struggles ended when women gained the right to vote in the United States also conceals the extent to which activists and organizers between the 1920s and the 1960s brought women's issues to the center of civil rights struggles, labor organizing, international politics, and the Communist movement. For instance, Black nationalist and communist organizer Claudia Jones, who immigrated to New York from Trinidad and was later deported to Britain, made women's concerns central in political organizing within poor and working-class communities. She, like other women who don't fit in the context of organizing for suffrage, is too often omitted from this history.

What we find compelling across these biographies is that cumulatively the women represent a varied history that in some cases predates and in other cases disrupts the more widely accepted history of the "First Wave of feminism." The following sections trace the developments of feminism primarily in the United States, but we situate the foundation of these developments, acknowledging that other histories can also contextualize the emergence of feminism.

The Time of Suffrage

In the United States, what has been called the First Wave of feminism was connected to two other movements: the **abolitionist** and **temperance movements**, in that many of the members of the women's movement were also working toward the abolition of slavery and encouraging moderation in the consumption of alcohol. The "Women's Liberation" movement is generally understood to have been a nineteenth-century project that coalesced in 1848 at the Seneca Falls Convention in New York where 300 men and women came together to call for women's equality. It was there that Elizabeth Cady Stanton drafted the Seneca Falls *Declaration of Sentiments*, which laid out the movement's ideas and political strategies. Due to fear of retribution, the declaration was signed by only 100 of the 300 participants. This declaration ultimately gave rise to the US women's suffrage movement, advocating for women's right to vote and women's political participation. These two issues initiated important conversations about the differences between men and women, and the resulting rhetoric of equity was based on an assumption of women's moral superiority.

ESSENTIAL

A Portion of the Seneca Falls Declaration of Sentiments, July 19, 1848

A group of life-size bronze statues is the signature piece of art at the Women's Rights National Historical Park in Seneca Falls, New York. The statues depict Elizabeth Cady Stanton, Frederick Douglass and Lucretia Mott and other attendees to an 1848 Women's Rights Convention held in Seneca Falls, at which 100 women and men signed a Declaration of Sentiments modeled after the 1776 Declaration of Independence. Photo Credit: AP Photo/Michael Okoniewski.

When, in the course of human events, it becomes necessary for one portion of the family of man to assume among the people of the earth a position different from that which they have hitherto occupied, but one to which the laws of nature and of nature's God entitle them, a decent respect to the opinions of mankind requires that they should declare the causes that impel them to such a course.

We hold these truths to be self-evident: that all men and women are created equal; that they are endowed by their Creator with certain inalienable rights; that among these are life, liberty, and the pursuit of happiness; that to secure these rights governments are instituted, deriving their just powers from the consent of the governed. Whenever any form of government becomes destructive of these ends, it is the right of those who suffer from it to refuse allegiance to it, and to insist upon the institution of a new government, laying its foundation on such principles, and organizing its powers in such form as to them shall seem most likely to effect their safety and happiness. Prudence, indeed, will dictate that governments long established should not be changed for light and transient causes; and accordingly, all experience hath shown that mankind are more disposed to suffer, while evils are sufferable, than to right themselves by abolishing the forms to which they are accustomed. But when a long train of abuses and usurpations, pursuing invariably the same object, evinces a design to reduce them under absolute despotism, it is their duty to throw off such government, and to provide new guards for their future security. Such has been the patient sufferance of the women under this government, and such is now the necessity which constrains them to demand the equal station to which they are entitled.

Source: https://www.womenshistory.org/resources/primary-source/declaration-sentiments-and-resolution.

Of course, others contributed to the development of feminism during this time. Frederick Douglass, who escaped enslavement in 1838, was one of the most outspoken proponents of women's rights in the nineteenth century, supporting Elizabeth Cady Stanton and Susan B. Anthony in their quest for women's suffrage. Another formative moment was when Sojourner Truth, a Black abolitionist and Methodist preacher, walked into the predominately white Women's Convention in Akron, Ohio, in 1851, three years after the first Women's Rights Convention in Seneca Falls, New York. The white women at the conference did not want their struggle for suffrage to be mixed in with the issue of race, despite the fact that a Black man, Douglass, had kept the controversial issue of women's suffrage central at the first convention in Seneca Falls. Yet, when Truth rose to enter into the conversation, her speech—known as "Ain't I a Woman?"—in which she recounted the pain of having her thirteen children sold into slavery and enduring slavery herself, drew strong admiration. Truth subsequently spoke with many audiences about the importance of linking abolition and women's rights.

Suffrage is a widely accepted context for understanding early feminism in the United States. It took from 1848, the Seneca Falls Convention, to 1920 to ratify women's right to vote with the passage of the Nineteenth Amendment. Globally, there has been uneven realization of women's suffrage. Women had been voting in New Zealand since 1893 and in Australia since 1894. Women could not vote until 1944 in Jamaica, 1954 in Belize, 1945 in Italy, 1963 in Iran, and 1978 in Zimbabwe. Thus, women's access to the political arena has been uneven.

One issue that divided feminists at the time was expectations for women regarding childbearing. Many nineteenth-century feminists were involved in the temperance movement and strong supporters of the "womanly duty" to bear children. Indeed, Stanton described abortion as "the degradation of women," though she argued that voluntary motherhood—through access to birth control and the legal ability to say no to her husband's sexual demands—was key to women's salvation. Some US feminists, however, became ardent proponents of birth control during the early 1900s, and Margaret Sanger opened the first birth control clinics in the United States in 1916. Sanger, who founded the American Birth Control League (which later became known as Planned Parenthood), advocated for women's control over their fertility as a means of social mobility, albeit not without problems, as you will see shortly.

Feminist ideas, such as voting and birth control, were initiated as broad and bold political agendas ostensibly capable of encompassing the intersection of sexuality, gender, race, and class. But the "victories" of change brought about by these political struggles and agendas often ended up supporting white, elite, and heterosexual women. A case in point were the clinics founded by the American Birth Control League (ABCL). Initially, some US clinics reserved services for white women. It was only after pressure from African American women for birth control that the ABCL expanded access. Then **eugenics** proponents became primary funders for fertility control clinics in the United States, leading to controversial alliances between feminists and eugenicists who hoped that these technologies would limit births among poor and nonwhite women. Sanger herself promoted certain eugenicist ideas, particularly that "the unfit" should be eliminated. As a result, many African American women began to organize through their own community networks, both for access to fertility control and against the compulsory sterilization of many African American women.[8] Support for fertility control was not unanimous, however, and some African American and Native American women continued to resist birth control into the 1900s, arguing that it was an attempt at **genocide**, a policy designed to reduce the size of their populations. Thus, although there is some evidence of multiracial feminist activism during the early to mid-twentieth century, white women and WoC often worked in separate organizations toward suffrage, community reform, antisterilization efforts, and access to birth control and abortion.

As scholars and activists Jael Silliman, Marlene Gerber Fried, Loretta Ross, and Elena Gutiérrez emphasize in *Undivided Rights: Women of Color Organize for Reproductive Justice*, in 1920, following the achievement of women's suffrage, feminist activist campaigns quieted during the mid-1900s, though local struggles continued to demand access to education and reproductive services on a community level.[9] It became increasingly evident, however, that universal equality for women had not been achieved through suffrage alone. Women's rights—to equal pay, educational equity, and reproductive rights—had not been fully achieved, and remained significantly stratified by race and class.

Radical Movement Building

From the 1960s to the 1990s, feminism in the United States was often described as a "radical" movement, in part because of one event that precipitated its expansion: the Miss America Pageant in 1968. Radical groups, such as the Redstockings and New York Radical Feminists, staged a joint protest to expose the ways that women in these pageants were paraded like cattle. Walking down the Atlantic City boardwalk they staged a number of theatrical events to make their points, such as ceremoniously crowning a sheep as a pageant queen, and throwing bras, high heels, and other oppressive items in garbage cans. The "Second Wave" refracted multiple national tensions that were emerging during this time.

Inspired by the civil rights, lesbian and gay, and antiwar movements of the 1960s and 1970s—each of which critiqued capitalism and imperialism—feminists in this wave also critiqued **patriarchy**, systems in which men hold the power from which women are generally excluded. Differences between and among women caused various constituencies—including WoC, poor women, and lesbians—to challenge the organizing of what some call "mainstream feminists" for their tendency to **essentialize** womanhood—the reduction of womanhood to a set of basic characteristics. The critique was based on the fact that mainstream feminists modeled their understanding of feminism on issues affecting middle-class, white women. WoC, poor women, lesbians, and "Third World"[10] women viewed mainstream feminists as presumptuous regarding the idea that being a woman was enough to unite women in struggle. In fact, many argued that in order to understand women's experiences of oppression, feminists needed to acknowledge the different ways women—because of their particular histories and circumstances—had been subjugated. For example, whereas some white feminists argued that being in the home was repressive, there were many women who had traditionally worked—or been forced to work under slavery, or because of financial insecurity—outside the home. Their oppression did not come from having to stay home; rather, it came from having to engage in forced or wage labor *and* **reproductive labor**, which includes the social and household work that sustains society. A second example is the alienation African American women experienced both within male-led civil rights organizations and in primarily white feminist groups, leading many to participate in local organizations to make demands that emerged from their unique experiences of gender, race, and class oppression.

Multiracial coalition building was also important during this time. Civil rights activist Yuri Kochiyama (1921–2014), for instance, was influenced by her experience in a Japanese American internment camp during World War II and became a strong supporter of the Black Power movement during the 1960s. She later joined a group of Puerto Ricans who took over the Statue of Liberty to draw attention to the movement for Puerto Rican independence in 1977 and was active later in her life in opposition to police profiling of Muslims, Middle Easterners, and South Asians in the United States, which she saw as similar to the persecution of Japanese Americans during World War II.

Another coalition builder—through both her writing and her activist work—was Black lesbian poet Audre Lorde (1934–1992), who penned the essay that generated the familiar feminist adage: "The Master's Tools Will Never Dismantle the Master's House." Lorde's words captured the coalitional impulse to unite feminists across differences of race, nation, class, age, sexual orientation, and ability:

> Those of us who stand outside the circle of this society's definition of acceptable women; those of us who have been forged in the crucibles of difference—those of us who are poor, who are lesbians, who are Black, who are older—know that survival is not an academic skill. It is learning how to take our differences and make them strengths. For the master's tools will never dismantle the master's house. They may allow us temporarily to beat him at his own game, but they will never enable us to bring about genuine change. And this fact is only threatening to those women who still define the master's house as their only source of support.[11]

Lorde's vocal disagreement with prominent white feminists, such as radical lesbian feminist Mary Daly, about racism within the feminist movement marked her as an outsider in certain circles, as did her outspoken appeals for the inclusion of lesbians in feminist organizing.

Lesbian feminism emerged as a challenge to **heteronormativity**, the assumption that society should be structured around heterosexual relationships. Although many lesbians were active in feminist organizing in the United States, they were excluded from prominent organizations like the National Organization for Women (NOW), founded in 1966. Then-president of NOW Betty Friedan courted the ire of prominent lesbian feminists—such as Charlotte Bunch, Adrienne Rich, Audre Lorde, and Marilyn Frye—after firing several lesbian staff members, including Rita Mae Brown, and allegedly referring to the growing lesbian visibility within feminist organizing as the "lavender menace." Lesbian feminism intensified during the 1970s as a part of mainstream feminist organizing, as well as within the Gay Liberation movement, which encouraged "coming out" as a form of public activism, as well as community events such as pride marches, which remain popular internationally.

Like other social and political movements of the time, transgender activists were also mobilizing by creating issue-specific organizations and developing support network strategies that promoted autonomy and empowerment. Historian Susan Stryker's *Transgender History* documents how experiences with medicalization and police harassment from 1850 to 1950 foreshadowed the transgender liberation movement that took form in the 1960s.[12] As anthropologist David Valentine has written in his ethnography of the category "transgender," feminism intersected with transgender activism in pivotal ways.[13] For instance, historians have engaged in debates over who started the Stonewall riots during a 1969 police raid of the Stonewall Inn, a gay tavern in Greenwich Village, New York: a multiracial coalition of drag queens or an implicitly white group of "fluffy sweater boys, dykes, sissies, college students, boys in chinos and penny loafers."[14]

Tensions also surfaced when lesbian feminists attempted to exclude Sylvia Rivera, a Latina drag queen and transgender activist, from speaking at a gay pride event in 1973 commemorating the Stonewall riots. Following the publication of radical lesbian feminist Janice Raymond's *The Transsexual Empire: The Making of the She-Male* in 1979,[15] which controversially described transsexualism as a "patriarchal myth" that reinforced traditional gender stereotypes, transgender rights groups intensified throughout North America. By the 1990s, the Transexual Menace became the first national direct action group for transgender rights cofounded by transgender feminists Riki Anne Wilchins and Denise Norris. Hermaphrodites With Attitude became the first direct action group for the rights of intersex people, founded by Executive Director of the Intersex Society of North America (ISNA) Cheryl Chase. GenderPAC emerged as the first national transgender advocacy group, founded on explicitly feminist principles by Wilchins. Wilchins is also the author of *Read My Lips: Sexual Subversion and the End of Gender*, which is notable for linking trans* liberation to feminist ideology and politics.[16]

Another concern centered on issues of inclusion of Indigenous women. Beatrice Medicine (Lakota), a bilingual education proponent in Native communities and feminist anthropologist, conducted path-breaking work on Indigenous women and inspired a generation of Indigenous feminist scholars.[17] Medicine, in her 1988 article "Native American (Indian) Women: A Call for Research,"[18] emphasizes that there was no research agenda addressing Native American women. Medicine's argument existed within a Second Wave framework in terms of inclusion. Without the perspective Medicine calls for, Native women are frequently represented in stereotypical ways and the dominant context of their existence is often considered pathological. For instance, when male anthropologists conducted much of the initial research on Native Americans and Aboriginal people, research focused primarily on dropout rates, alcoholism, suicide, and homicide rates. Medicine advocated ethnographic research by Indigenous women on Indigenous women to highlight the importance of gender variation in Native communities and different roles among Native women that could influence feminist theory.

This era is also associated with struggles for sexual freedom, reproductive rights, and the development of disability rights and studies. As a result, some parochial ideas and norms about sex and sexuality shifted and the institution of marriage was no longer a requirement for sexual interactions. Medical advances, particularly the birth control pill, made it possible for people to pursue the pleasure of intimacy without linking it to pregnancy. Thus, controlling one's reproduction, particularly access to birth control and abortion, became an important feature of women's organizing. In the United States, the right to obtain legal access to birth control and abortion was achieved through a series of legal decisions that culminated in the 1973 US Supreme Court decision in *Roe v. Wade* to legalize abortion. Legal challenges since that time have added substantial waiting periods, parental consent, and other restrictions that have curtailed women's access to reproductive services. Similarly, as the legalization of abortion has become more common globally, access varies widely and is frequently limited by restrictive and complicated laws. This exemplifies once again the concept of *un choque* discussed in the introduction—a contradiction whereby abortion is legal in many areas but inaccessible.

We also see tensions surrounding abortion and disability rights. For example, bioethicist Adrienne Asch supported abortion in general as a woman's right but opposed it as a means of preempting the birth of disabled infants. Asch and Michelle Fine's article, "Shared Dreams: A Left Perspective on Disability Rights and Reproductive Rights,"[19] makes the argument that women have a right to an abortion and newborns have the right to medical treatment and that those rights, although unequivocal, are contested by politics. The rights are viewed separately, whereby some conservatives take a pro-family position arguing against abortion and a woman's right to control her own body. Some progressives have taken the position that abortion should be accessible if a woman determines that the fetus has a disability. The legitimacy of abortion, they argue, should not be in competition with the provision of treatment or the right for a disabled newborn to survive. However, the authors point out that the right of a disabled newborn should not be used as the "strawman" in arguing against women's rights to have an abortion. Emerging within these contradictions and internal disputes, in the 1990s, a new generation of feminists inaugurated what they called "Third Wave" feminism.

Expanding a Feminist Legacy

Manifesta: Young Women, Feminism, and the Future, written by feminist activists Jennifer Baumgardner and Amy Richards,[20] was a response to the "Second Wave" that grew out of a need for the feminist movement to speak to a new generation of young women. Many attribute the organizational structure of "Third Wave" feminism to Rebecca Walker, the daughter of prominent feminist novelist Alice Walker, who won the Pulitzer Prize for her 1982 novel *The Color Purple*. Rebecca Walker wrote an article for *Ms.* magazine in 1992, "Becoming the Third Wave," articulating the anger and desire for action in response to, among other things, the confirmation of Clarence Thomas as Supreme Court Justice amid controversy over allegations of sexual harassment by Anita Hill, an attorney who had previously worked for Thomas.

Third Wave feminists collaborated with many feminists of color who had been active in earlier organizing and worked together to articulate global alliances among women. They have placed greater emphasis on multiracial links among women and positioned inclusivity—with regard to economic disparities, transnational coalitions, and work for LGBTQI+ rights—at the center of organizing efforts. "Sex-positive" feminism promoting sexual freedom emerged as a response to the "sex wars" of the 1980s—heated debates over pornography, prostitution, BDSM,[21] and transgender rights/identities. The emergence of queer theory in the 1990s reignited controversies over the prominence of sexuality within feminist organizing efforts. With an emphasis on embracing gender fluidity, queer activists criticized essentialist understandings of gender, while a small group of radical feminists have maintained a vocal opposition to transgender liberation politics and denied intersections between feminist and queer activism. Mainstream LGBT efforts, such as the promotion of same-sex marriage and the expansion of adoption laws, have become widely supported by many women's rights organizations. This was despite earlier feminist critiques of marriage as a patriarchal institution that served primarily to limit women's autonomy.

Emi Koyama's "The Transfeminist Manifesto" evoked the polarization and fragmentation of feminist groups in the late twentieth century to call for more inclusive coalitional politics that includes and values the contributions of trans women:

> Every time a group of women previously silenced speaks out, other feminists are challenged to rethink their idea of whom they represent and what they stand for. While this process sometimes leads to a painful realization of our own biases and internalized oppressions as feminists, it eventually benefits the movement by widening our perspectives and constituency. It is under this understanding that we declare that the time has come for trans women to openly take part in the feminist revolution, further expanding the scope of the movement.[22]

Over the past few decades, well-known feminist organizations, such as the NOW, the Feminist Majority Campaign, and Planned Parenthood, have supported trans rights. Yet specific efforts to promote transgender inclusion, such as appeals to Planned Parenthood and the National Abortion and Reproductive Rights Action League (NARAL) in 2013 to remove reference to gender (i.e., "women's health" and "women's reproductive choice") in the names of their health clinics and reproductive justice campaigns, have continued to meet resistance among some cisgender feminist organizers.

Efforts to combat violence against women—including domestic violence, rape, and sexual harassment—that were central to feminist organizing in the 1970s when rape crisis centers were first established have taken new forms in the twenty-first century. The highly publicized Slutwalk protest marches, for instance, emerged in response to a Toronto police officer's admonishment that women should not dress like "sluts" so they do not become victims of (presumably) male sexual violence. In 2011, the first rally and protest occurred in Toronto and subsequent marches have been organized throughout Asia, Europe, Latin America, and North America. Prominent feminist pundits and bloggers have accused the movement of trivializing women's experiences and excluding WoC, reigniting concerns about racialized divisions in contemporary mainstream feminist organizing.

THINKING THROUGH . . .

Foremothers of Feminism

Choose a person who was influential to the development of feminism. Building on what you have read so far, pretend that you will conduct an interview with that person about their contribution to feminism. Develop a set of questions and fashion what you think would be likely "responses" based on additional research.

How Are Feminist Perspectives Categorized?

In the previous section, you see that feminists generally hold the view that when people are treated differently they have uneven access to resources and power. Feminists also believe that this inequity can be changed through social movements and by challenging cultural practices and norms. Holding a feminist perspective can encourage one to examine the roles that marginalized people in general, but women in particular, have in society and explore the ways in which inequalities are expressed in people's everyday lives. Generally, then, contemporary feminists pay attention to how people are stratified or **hierarchized** in terms of gender, race, class, ability, and other markers or categories of difference. Hierarchizing occurs when people are treated differentially in society allowing some people access to more power, control, and privilege than others.

There are many ways to explore these inequities and people often view the **etiology**, or cause, of stratification as having different sources. Thus, there are different variations of feminisms. If one were to ask, "How and why are women (or racial minorities, or poor lesbians, among other groups) less privileged and have less power?" there would be different starting points to answer the questions. There might even be different ways of asking the question because of how various feminists even *understand* a problem. For instance, would they highlight social, economic, political, or other factors in their answer? Some of the ways that feminisms are often categorized are Liberal, Radical, Cultural, Marxist, Socialist, Black, "Third World," Postcolonial and Transnational, and Postmodern. In this section, we include brief explanations of these perspectives. Although they are presented as unique forms of feminism, the lines between them are often blurred and the distinctions are not mutually exclusive. Additionally, the emergence of queer and trans feminisms (see previous section), as well as other forms of feminism inflected by Chicanx, Asian, Jewish, and Crip politics,[23] among many others, deepened and expanded this feminist lineage in important ways. While an exhaustive list is beyond the scope of this book, we encourage you to think through how different strands of feminism have contributed to feminist ethnography.

Liberal Feminism centers on the argument that while women may be universally subordinate, they are not inferior to men and can assert power within particular spheres. Mary Wollstonecraft, the eighteenth-century author of the book *A Vindication of the Rights of Women*, argued that women are not inherently inferior to men. Writing in the liberal tradition in 1792, she promoted individual rights. Liberal feminists believe that all people are equal and oppression exists because of the way that people are conditioned or socialized. Since it is societal norms that orchestrate how women and men are expected to act, the society must be changed. That change comes by making institutions accountable, not by eliminating the institutions themselves (as some other feminists suggest). Thus, liberal feminists argue that gender equality can be attained by working *within* institutions. The kinds of rights liberal feminists seek to secure have included voting rights, protection of women under the law, and equal funding for girls' education and sports. Since liberal feminists identify equal opportunity at the center of their analysis, they tend to hold the view that discrimination and barriers can be resolved through government reforms. They work within existing structures to create opportunities and use legislative and electoral politics to ensure equity. International efforts toward women's suffrage are associated with the liberal feminist efforts of the nineteenth and early twentieth centuries. A more contemporary example of liberal feminism would be the promotion of same-sex marriage legislation, aimed at alleviating legal inequities between heterosexual couples and lesbian and gay couples.

Radical Feminism is a perspective that emerged during the Civil Rights Movement in the 1960s. Radical feminists argue that women's oppressed status cuts across race, culture, and class and uses an analysis of the structure of sex/gender to understand women's oppression. Thus, all women are oppressed and oppression stems from male dominance. If the root of oppression lies in male dominance, it is that structure that needs to be dismantled. Radical feminists support movements that are about direct social change and even cultural revolution. Many radical feminists view violence against women and sexual violence as the primary reasons for women's subjugation. Therefore, understanding women's oppression would come from examining and analyzing violence in all of its forms as one of the most important strategies that facilitate the perpetuation of patriarchal society in which women are oppressed. Radical feminism has focused on how deeply entrenched the male/female division is across cultures, arguing that women have been oppressed and discriminated against in all areas and their oppression is primary. Radical feminists are generally skeptical of a reformist (liberal feminist) approach to address women's oppression. For example, they do not believe that antiviolence laws will end male supremacy. Yet they use the law as a protective strategy while seeking other avenues to eliminate patriarchal dominance.

Cultural Feminism is a perspective that some say followed a decline in radical feminism, representing a historical progression, but a particular formulation of feminism based on biological distinctions. It is rooted in the perspective that differences between men and women are primarily biological. These biological variations result in different behaviors. For example, cultural feminists might argue that women are inherently more nurturing than men because of their capacity to give birth. From the point of view of psychoanalytical sociologist Nancy Chodorow, women's domestic and nurturing work should be compensated and recognized as productively important. Cultural feminists are less interested in equality per se and instead argue for there to be a greater societal value placed on women's roles and work. Following radical feminists, cultural feminists reify the characteristics that they argue make men and women different. They advocate for a system of governing based on women's virtues and ways of being, which they consider more peaceful, nurturing, and collaborative, in contrast to male tendencies toward violence and competition. Chodorow's work, as well as that of other cultural feminists, was featured in some of the earliest publications in feminist anthropology, such as *Woman, Culture, and Society* in 1974. Although this perspective has since been heavily critiqued—by later feminist anthropologists, as well as many of those who published initially in the volume as graduate students—the influence of cultural feminism remains important to the genesis of feminist ethnography.

Marxist Feminism attributes women's oppression to the capitalist and private property system. Under the capitalist system, the **means of production** are controlled by those who have power, and in the process, women's labor is exploited. In other words, the rewards for production—be it the social reproduction of inequalities or manufacturing production of commodities—do not exist for those engaged in labor. The reward comes to those who *own* the means of production. For Marxist feminists, it is this form of oppression, the structure of class, to which all other forms of inequity are linked. Capitalism then is the reason for female oppression. Many Marxist feminists also link capitalist oppression to other spheres such as race, class, and sexual identity, which are all subordinated in the interest of capital gain. Marxist feminists would view women's oppression in exponential terms, because capitalism oppresses women, often based on gender, race, and class. Like radical feminists (and in contrast to liberal feminists), Marxist feminists tend to be skeptical about the chances of achieving substantive change by working within "the system."

Marxist feminist perspectives were also well represented in early publications in feminist anthropology. One of the most widely cited articles from that time period is anthropologist Gayle Rubin's "The Traffic in Women: Notes on the 'Political Economy' of Sex," which has been called "a tour de force of Marxism, structuralism, and Freudo-Lacanian theory, [as it] draws on analogies with political economy to hypothesize a universal 'sex-gender system.'"[24]

Socialist Feminism is an elaboration of Marxist feminism, but primarily with regard to the need to integrate a historical materialist analysis. A historical materialist perspective interrogates the causes of societal change and the development of society by examining the economic system that operates at particular moments. Socialist feminists depart from the Marxist focus on class oppression as the sole or primary way to view society. Rather, they argue that gender and class operate simultaneously creating particular forms of oppression and privilege for women and men in different classes. Socialist feminists view the intersection of sexism, racism, and classism as forms of oppression that need to be addressed concurrently. The solution they propose is socialism, a societal organization that encourages more social ownership rather than individual ownership, resulting in cooperative and more socially and economically equitable management of the economy.

◅◅⋓ SPOTLIGHT ⋓▻▻

Gayle Rubin's Influence

Photo Credit: Michael Rosen.

Gayle Rubin *completed her PhD in anthropology from the University of Michigan and now teaches there in anthropology and women's studies. She is best known as a feminist and queer activist and theorist of sex and gender politics. Along with "The Traffic in Women," discussed in this interview, her influential 1984 article, "Thinking Sex: Notes for a Radical Theory of the Politics of Sexuality," argues that there were different systems of stratification, and that certain kinds of sexual oppression (such as that of gay people) were not necessarily or uniquely attributable to gender stratification. Although Rubin's work was influenced by Karl Marx's work on class oppression, she argues against a sort of "theoretical mono-mania"—a single theory of everything (Marxism, feminism, etc.), or a single set of primary causal relationships at the root of all social problems. In this interview with Christa Craven, she addresses the legacy of she addresses the legacy of her article "Traffic in Women" for feminist ethnographers:*

I think it is important for emerging scholars to understand what questions earlier generations were trying to address, and what tools were available with which to tackle them. "Traffic in Women" emerged out of a very specific time and set of circumstances. Second Wave feminism was trying to establish the legitimacy of very basic claims to improved social status for women, and for its demands to redress a whole panoply of political and economic grievances. This was in the context of very pervasive assumptions that women were intrinsically different from men in ways that justified impaired civil status, lesser pay and other economic limitations, and a punitive sexual double standard. Male privileges—and their access to better jobs, more respect, greater physical mobility, and a vast range of personal and sexual services—were largely unquestioned. So intellectually, one of the pressing tasks was to dismantle the ideologies that reinforced these durable structural liabilities based on gender.

As for academic disciplines at the time, anthropology was probably among the more progressive, not only in terms of gender but also race and class (for which many anthropologists had been considered subversive and harassed during the course of the twentieth century). But it was still riddled with sexism and male privilege, both in its social relationships and substantive contents. So as Second Wave feminism took hold in the field, one task was a kind of ground clearing to challenge these assumptions. Another was efforts to collect more primary data on women cross-culturally to redress the skewed ethnographic focus on males. And another was to construct alternative theoretical frameworks and generate new models for human societies and behavior that did not project assumptions from the mid-twentieth-century United States onto the rest of human history.

CC: What drew you to Marxist critique in your analysis of "the political economy of sex," and how have you found it useful in your subsequent work on sexuality?

GR: The tool kit with which to approach all these issues was limited, although feminist anthropologists were extremely creative in figuring out how to use the existing intellectual resources of the field to do so. One of these was Marxism, which was then enjoying a kind of political and intellectual renaissance in parts of US academia. Women's Liberation largely grew out of what was then the "New Left," in which many strains of Marxism were percolating. But in addition to its political aspects, Marx's oeuvre was one of the great bodies of early social science analysis. Many of the basic concerns of emerging late-nineteenth-century social science—especially anthropology and sociology—were generated as various thinkers attempted to understand social stratification and how it operated in different times and places. Marx had always been among the most important of these. Moreover, there was actually a lot of Marx embedded within anthropology already, although not always explicitly or in recognizable forms. One problem with Marx, however, is that his work also tended to be treated as a rigid set of canonical beliefs, rather than as a collection of supple theoretical tools. So those of us working with Marx had to disentangle what was useful from accretions of stale and often mandatory dogmas. In some ways, this intellectual project was parallel to the political project of the differentiation of Second Wave feminism out of the New Left. Women's Liberation owed a great deal to the social and intellectual movements of the period, but had to establish its own claims, analytic frameworks, and organizational structures. My work at the time was part of this broader process.

Black Feminism emerged in the 1970s in response to white feminist efforts that failed to incorporate the simultaneous struggles for Black liberation in the civil rights movement. In England, Black feminism was the term used to include Asian and African women as a way to capture the fact that women from these locations had been subjected to colonization in their countries of origin and to racism in England. A Black feminist perspective is usually linked to socialist feminism in that it pushes for political analyses that incorporate race, gender, and class oppression along with heterosexism, as intersecting or intersectional issues. Black women's political participation—from abolition and suffrage movements to efforts for reproductive justice—have always engaged with intersectional analysis and resulting politics, even when organizers did not identify explicitly as feminists.

One of the most important—and enduring—outcomes of the Black feminist framework is the Combahee River Collective Statement, a document that lays out the importance of attending to sexism, racism, classism, and heterosexism as part of political organizing. Many feminists have drawn upon this statement as inspiration for intersectional scholarly work. An influential Black feminist thinker was Audre Lorde, whose creative writing, activism, and scholarship have influenced two generations of feminist scholars, artists, and activists. Lorde's contributions are the result of her complex analyses of systems of oppression and the relevance of her work on sexism, racism, heterosexism, classism, and imperialism that resonate both inside and outside the academy. Her work provides a grammar that gives durability to theorizing across disciplines and has contributed to Black feminist, literary, queer, and postcolonial theories and transnational feminisms.

🧠 ESSENTIAL

Excerpt from the Combahee River Collective Statement

The Combahee River Collective *was a group of Black, lesbian, socialist feminists in Boston who gathered from 1974 to 1980. The Combahee River Collective Statement, excerpted below, was inspired by abolitionist Harriet Tubman's leadership in the Combahee River Raid in South Carolina on June 2, 1863, during the Civil War, which freed 750 slaves. This statement exemplifies the commitment of many feminist ethnographers to combatting oppressions based not only on gender but also on multiple axes of inequality.*

Above all else, our politics initially sprang from the shared belief that Black women are inherently valuable, that our liberation is a necessity not as an adjunct to somebody else's but because of our need as human persons for autonomy. This may seem so obvious as to sound simplistic, but it is apparent that no other ostensibly progressive movement has ever considered our specific oppression as a priority or worked seriously for the ending of that oppression. Merely naming the pejorative stereotypes attributed to Black women (e.g., mammy, matriarch, Sapphire, whore, bulldagger), let alone cataloguing the cruel, often murderous, treatment we receive, indicates how little value has been placed upon our lives during four centuries of bondage in the Western hemisphere. We realize that the only people who care enough about us to work consistently for our liberation are us. Our politics evolve from a healthy love for ourselves, our sisters and our community which allows us to continue our struggle and work.

This focusing upon our own oppression is embodied in the concept of identity politics. We believe that the most profound and potentially most radical politics come directly out of our own identity, as opposed to working to end somebody else's oppression. In the case of Black women this is a particularly repugnant, dangerous, threatening, and therefore revolutionary concept because it is obvious from looking at all the political movements that have preceded us that anyone is more worthy of liberation than ourselves. We reject pedestals, queenhood, and walking ten paces behind. To be recognized as human, levelly human, is enough.

We believe that sexual politics under patriarchy is as pervasive in Black women's lives as are the politics of class and race. We also often find it difficult to separate race from class from sex oppression because in our lives they are most often experienced simultaneously. We know that there is such a thing as racial-sexual oppression which is neither solely racial nor solely sexual, for example, the history of rape of Black women by white men as a weapon of political repression.

Source: Moraga, Cherríe, and Gloria Anzaldùa. *This Bridge Called My Back: Writings of Radical Women of Color*. New York: Kitchen Table: Women of Color Press, 1983, 212–213. (This source is also available full text on multiple websites, such as http://circuitous.org/scraps/combahee.html.)

"Third World," Postcolonial, and Transnational Feminisms were emboldened in the 1980s by the critical work of Black feminists. Postcolonial feminist theorists began to critique Western feminist analyses of "Third World" women in homogenizing and derogatory ways without considering the context of their lives. Postcolonial and transnational feminist theorist Chandra Talpade Mohanty's groundbreaking essay from 1991, "Cartographies of Struggle: Third World Women and the Politics of Feminism," defines "Third World" as including Black, Latino, Asian, and Indigenous peoples in the United States, Europe, and Australia, as well as those from Latin America, the Caribbean, sub-Saharan Africa, South and Southeast Asia, East Asia, South Africa, and Oceania.[25] Although the terminology of "Third World" has given way to other articulations, and postcolonial feminism is used less frequently than transnational feminism among contemporary feminists, the history of the terms contributes to understanding the importance of the sustained influence of feminist perspectives that have emerged outside of a primarily white, Global North, colonialist framework. Closely aligned with Black feminism, postcolonial feminism emerged as a critique of Western feminists and postcolonial theorists, drawing critical attention to the impact of colonialism and imperialism on gendered oppression.

Several factors ushered in what has become known as transnational feminism, as distinct from the international women's movement from the 1970s, which was organized around the principle that "sisterhood is global"—a phrase coined by Robin Morgan in the 1980s. The general idea is that all women are linked through a *common bond of being women*. However, most transnational feminists vehemently resist a universalized vision of feminist solidarity. Rather, they address the intersections between nation, race, gender, sexuality, and economic exploitation in relation to global capitalism. A transnational feminist approach questions the inequities that have resulted from centuries of colonialism and racism, as well as new forms of inequalities as a result of globalization. As the theme for the 2020 National Women's Studies Association conference underscores, transnational feminism has "contributed immensely to decentering Western, especially US, scholarship and generated new forms of anti-racist, anti-imperialist, and decolonial feminist [practice and knowledge production] that cross national boundaries."[26]

ESSENTIAL

Excerpt from "Under Western Eyes Revisited" by Chandra Talpade Mohanty

Born and raised in India, **Chandra Talpade Mohanty** *received her PhD in education from the University of Illinois at Urbana-Champaign and is currently a distinguished professor of women's and gender studies at Syracuse University. She became widely known as a postcolonial feminist scholar after the 1984 publication of "Under Western Eyes: Feminist Scholarship and Colonial Discourses," which she wrote as a graduate student. Subsequent publications included* Feminism Without Borders: Decolonizing Theory, Practicing Solidarity *(2003) and numerous coedited volumes including* Third World Women and the Politics of Feminism *(1991),* Feminist Genealogies, Colonial Legacies, Democratic Futures *(1996),* Feminism and War: Confronting US Imperialism *(2008), and* Feminist Freedom Warriors *(2018). She is the cocreator with Linda Carty of the Feminist Freedom Warriors Video Archive:* http://feministfreedomwarriors.org. *The following excerpt is Mohanty's reflection on her first publication, which highlighted the colonization of the experiences of so-called Third World women within western feminist theory.*

Photo Credit: F.T. Reid.

I wrote "Under Western Eyes" to discover and articulate a critique of "Western feminist" scholarship on Third World women . . . I also wanted to expose the power–knowledge nexus of feminist cross-cultural scholarship expressed through Eurocentric, falsely universalizing methodologies that serve the narrow self-interest of Western feminism. As well, I thought it crucial to highlight the connection between feminist scholarship and feminist political organizing while drawing attention to the need to examine the "political implications of our analytic strategies and principles." I also wanted to chart the location of feminist scholarship within a global political and economic framework dominated by the "First World." My most simple goal was to make clear that cross-cultural feminist work must be attentive to the micropolitics of context, subjectivity, and struggle, as well as to the macropolitics of global economic and political systems and processes. . . .

After almost two decades of teaching feminist studies in U.S. classrooms, it is clear to me that the way we theorize experience, culture, and subjectivity in relation to histories, institutional practice, and collective struggles determines the kind of stories we tell in the classroom. If these varied stories are to be taught such that students learn to democratize rather than colonize the experiences of different spatially and temporally located communities of women, neither a Eurocentric nor a cultural pluralist curricular practice will do. In fact, narratives of historical experience are crucial to political thinking not because they present an unmediated version of the "truth" but because they can destabilize received truths and locate debate in the complexities and contradictions of historical life. [This approach suggests] the complexities of the narratives of marginalized peoples in terms of relationality rather than separation. These are the kinds of stories we need to weave into a [discussion of] feminist solidarity [which focuses] on mutuality and common interests. . . . It requires one to formulate questions about connection and disconnection between activist women's movements around the world. Rather than formulating activism and agency in terms of discrete and disconnected cultures and nations, it allows us to frame agency and resistance across the borders of nation and culture.

Source: Mohanty, Chandra Talpade. "'Under Western Eyes' Revisited: Feminist Solidarity through Anticapitalist Struggles." *Signs: Journal of Women and Society* 28, no. 2 (January 1, 2003): 222–223.

Postmodern Feminism developed in the 1980s out of a critique of ideological **binaries**. This form of feminism argues against binarisms as the primary organizing structure of society, such that categories like male/female or Black/white need to be rethought. Postmodern feminists draw on the intellectual legacies of theorists, such as Hélène Cixous, Simone de Beauvoir, Jacques Derrida, Franz Fanon, Michel Foucault, Luce Irigaray, Julia Kristeva, and Jacques Lacan, in an attempt to deconstruct and blur the boundaries of binaries to critique structures that dominate our ways of thinking. In other words, there are many ways of being "a woman," which makes the man/woman binary useless. How can there be an essence or an essential way of being if there are, in fact, a range of ways of being? Postmodern feminism was a key influence on feminist ethnography in the 1980s, in part because postmodern feminists view the use of language and writing as crucial. The primary technique employed by postmodernists is discourse analysis with attention paid to the fact that discourse and language are neither neutral nor objective. While masculinist language can reinforce the dominant social order, postmodern feminists believe that feminist/feminine approaches to writing promote alternative ways of seeing.

THINKING THROUGH . . .

Feminisms

In addition to the forms of feminisms highlighted in this chapter, there are many perspectives that have augmented and deepened this work, as well as new perspectives that continue to emerge. Among them are feminisms specific to particular identities (such as Crip Feminism or Transfeminism), religious and cultural traditions (such as Jewish Feminism or Asian Feminism), and forms of feminisms linked to movements (such as abolitionist, environmental and LGBTQI+ struggles). Select one of these feminist perspectives (or another) to identify its contribution to the lineage of feminist ethnographic production.

Conclusion

In this chapter, we have provided a general overview of feminisms that we see as most significant in their contribution to the emergence and production of feminist ethnography. We recognize that there are other feminist perspectives that have influenced particular feminist ethnographers. In the next chapter, we focus on the lineage of feminist ethnography, providing a window into how various feminisms contributed to women's entré into ethnography in the 1800s and ultimately the development of feminist ethnography as a practice in the late twentieth century.

THINKING THROUGH . . .

Feminist Perspectives and Key Texts

Identify a contemporary social issue, such as same-sex marriage or birth control, and apply what you have read to analyze the issue from two feminist perspectives. Write a brief comparison of how feminists with these different leanings might understand and approach the contemporary issue.

Suggested Resources

Angela Y. Davis (2011 [orig. 1981]) *Women, Race, & Class.*
bell hooks (1984) *Feminist Theory: From Margin to Center.*
Emi Koyama (2001) "The Transfeminist Manifesto," https://eminism.org/readings/pdf-rdg/tfmanifesto.pdf.
Judith Lorber (2011) *Gender Inequality: Feminist Theories and Politics*, 5th Ed.
Cherríe Moraga and Gloria Anzaldùa (1983) *This Bridge Called My Back: Writings of Radical Women of Color.*
Nancy A. Naples, ed. (2020) *Companion to Feminist Studies.*
Jennifer Nelson (2003) *Women of Color and the Reproductive Rights Movement.*

Notes

1 Before Common Era (BCE) is commonly used by anthropologists as an alternative, secular naming of the Christian Calendar. See Robin Patric Clair's "The Changing Story of Ethnography," in *Expressions of Ethnography*, ed. Robin Patric Clair, 1992.
2 Henry R. Schoolcraft (1793–1864) was one of the first in the United States to publish information in an ethnographic style. Schoolcraft was a geographer and ethnologist who studied Native Americans. Married to a woman who was part Ojibwa, he learned the language and began documenting Indian lore. Franz Boas, a German anthropologist, contributed to the further development of ethnography in the late 1800s. Boas's students, who included Margaret Mead, Ruth Benedict, Zora Neale Hurston, and Ruth Landes, among others, dominated the field of ethnography in the early 1900s.
3 Friedrich Engels, *The Conditions of the Working Class in England*, 1845; Flora Tristan, *Promenades dans Londres*, 1840.
4 Beverly Skeggs, "Feminist Ethnography," in *Handbook of Ethnography*, 2001, 428.
5 The panel "Interdisciplinary Perspectives on Feminist Ethnography & Activism" was organized by Christa Craven, moderated by Dána-Ain Davis, and included Nancy Naples, Lynn Roberts, Rosemarie Roberts, and Alisse Waterston at the 2014 Annual Meeting of the National Women's Studies Association.
6 Betty Freidan, *The Feminine Mystique*, 1963.
7 South African History Online, "Charlotte (née Manye) Maxeke," Text, February 17, 2011. http://www.sahistory.org.za/people/charlotte-n%C3%A9e-manye-maxeke.
8 Jennifer Nelson, *Women of Color and the Reproductive Rights Movement*, 2003.

9   Jael Miriam Silliman et al., *Undivided Rights*, 2004.

10   "Third World" was a term that referred to nonwestern "developing" countries. See the section in this chapter on Third World Feminism for more detail.

11   Audre Lorde, "The Master's Tools Will Never Dismantle the Master's House," in *Sister Outsider: Essays and Speeches*, 110–114. Berkeley, CA: Crossing Press, 1984 (originally presented as comments at the 1979 Second Sex Conference on a panel titled "The Personal and the Political").

12   Susan Stryker, *Transgender History*, 2017 (orig. 2008).

13   David Valentine, *Imagining Transgender*, 2007.

14   Eric Marcus, "Stonewall Revisited," in *Independent Gay Forum*, 1999; David Valentine, *Imagining Transgender*, 2007, 45.

15   Janice G. Raymond, *The Transsexual Empire: The Making of the She-Male*, 1979.

16   Riki Anne Wilchins, *Read My Lips*, 1997.

17   We use the terms Native American, Aboriginal, and Indigenous not to summarily lump together women, but in Medicine's article, she uses all three.

18   Beatrice Medicine, "Native American (Indian) Women: A Call for Research," *Anthropology and Education Quarterly*, 1988.

19   Adrienne Asch and Michelle Fine, "Shared Dreams: A Left Perspective on Disability Rights and Reproductive Rights," in *Radical America,* 1984.

20   Jennifer Baumgardner and Amy Richards, *Manifesta: Young Women, Feminism and the Future*, 2000.

21   The term BDSM includes erotic practices such as bondage, discipline, sadism, and masochism.

22   Emi Koyama, "The Transfeminist Manifest" in *Catching a Wave: Reclaiming Feminism for the Twenty-First Century*, 2003 (orig. 2001). Also available at: https://eminism.org/readings/pdf-rdg/tfmanifesto.pdf.

23   The term Crip is a reclamation of the derogatory term "cripple" by disability rights activists. It is meant to be inclusive of people with a broad range of physical and psychological differences.

24   Micaela di Leonardo and Roger Lancaster, "Gender, Sexuality, Political Economy," *New Politics*, 1996.

25   Revisiting her initial work, in *Feminism Without Borders,* Mohanty (2003) later rejected the term "Third World" in favor of "Two-Thirds World" to highlight the social majority of those in the "Third World" or "Global South" and move away from misleading geographical and ideological binarisms. As discussed further in chapter 3, we follow the more recent usage of the terms "Global North" and "Global South" by transnational feminists.

26   National Women's Studies Association Call for Proposals 2020, "The Poetics, Politics, and Praxis of Transnational Feminisms."

CHAPTER 2

Historicizing Feminist Ethnography

In this chapter you will explore the early formation of feminist ethnography. The questions below will help you identify how feminist ethnography was used as a "corrective" to earlier studies by and about men, and explain the range of contributions feminist ethnography has made for social issues:

- Who were some of the early contributors to feminist ethnography?
- How did feminist ethnography mature between the 1920s and 1960s?
- What impact did the women's movement of the 1960s have on the next phase of feminist ethnographic production (1960s–1980s)?
- What are the contributions of feminist ethnography from the 1990s through the present?

Spotlights in this chapter:

- Florence Babb on the Impact of *Woman, Culture, and Society* and *Toward an Anthropology of Women*
- Louise Lamphere on the Legacy of *Lamphere v. Brown*
- C. Riley Snorton on Feminist Anthropology and Trans Studies
- Lee Baker on Feminist Histories

Essentials in this chapter:

- Alice Fletcher and Francis LaFlesche, *The Omaha Tribe*
- Zora Neale Hurston, *Mules and Men*
- Esther Newton, "Too Queer for College" in *Margaret Mead Made Me Gay*
- Gina Pérez, "Methodological Gifts in Latina/o Studies and Feminist Anthropology"

You will also be **Thinking Through . . .**

- Restudying Culture
- Faculty Composition at Your Institution
- Critiques and Reviews of an Ethnography

Attention to issues of gender and inequality has a long history in some disciplines. For example, extending back to the early 1900s, anthropology and sociology have foregrounded concerns with social, political, and economic inequities and power differentials. In the previous chapter, we discussed the Second Wave of feminism and the women's movement of the 1960s and 1970s. During that time, feminists viewed women's oppression as the thread connecting women's experiences across the globe. Yet if one was searching for research on women's lives, there was little to be found. Feminist ethnography emerged out of an effort to correct women's absence from scholarship. Much of the previous **androcentric,** or male-centered, research focused primarily on understanding culture, history, and everyday life from men's perspective. So, the question many asked was: Where was women's point of view?

The beauty of working in the present is that one can go back in time and rethink scholars' interpretations, which were limited by the contexts and ideologies of the time. In that sense, the development of feminist ethnography is not a simple story. There are twists and turns. For example, sometimes the people identified in the **canon** as feminist ethnographers may not have used the label "feminist" to describe themselves. In some cases, a person may have identified as a feminist who conducted ethnography but may not have used what contemporary feminist ethnographers would consider to be a feminist methodology.

There are several ways to sort out any history. One can focus on particular people or categorize particular moments, such as musical periods of Rhythm and Blues (1940s–1950s), Funk (1960s), Deep Funk (late 1960s), Hip-Hop (1970s), and NeoSoul (1980s–1990s). Usually the categories roughly correspond to particular dates. This is called **periodization.** This chapter periodizes anthropological contributions to feminist ethnography; that is, it is divided into particular portions of time. Below, we use anthropologist Kamala Visweswaran's periodization, which she devised in her 1997 article "Histories of Feminist Ethnography" in the *Annual Review of Anthropology.* She proposes four time periods (1880–1920, 1920–1960, 1960–1980, and 1980–1996) as "rough approximations, not absolute chronological markers" of feminist ethnographic production.[1] It may be useful to connect the histories of feminist ethnography to the eras discussed in chapter 1, to get a sense of how the development of feminist ethnography intersects with the sociopolitical and historical contexts in which those moments are situated. To assist with this, see the timeline of key dates and periods in feminism and the development of feminist ethnography at the front of the book.

Who Were Some of the Early Contributors to Feminist Ethnography?

To understand the history of what became feminist ethnography, we begin by looking at several female anthropologists who were influential in the social sciences and innovative in their scholarship on women. Many of these scholars represent a generation of women ethnographers, who given the privileges of whiteness and wealth were able to attend university and work at a time when Victorian mores proscribed more restrictive roles for women. These women were among those who viewed themselves as achievers but were in many ways still constrained by the parochial conventions of women's expected roles.[2]

Edward B. Tylor, one of the founding figures of British anthropology, viewed women's contribution to anthropology as merely an addition to male anthropologists—not as one that could be legitimately produced on their own. He appears to have come to this conclusion while visiting James and Matilda Coxe Stevenson, the first ethnographers sent by the Bureau of American Ethnology to visit Zuni Pueblo in New Mexico in 1884.[3] In Tylor's estimation, some of the best results for anthropological work occurred when male anthropologists teamed up with their wives, who could collect information from women, a group to which the male anthropologist typically had little access.[4] Thus, women's role as anthropologists was viewed as something to be achieved through marriage, not formal training. Ironically, by Tylor's own admission, he recognized a different ethnographic production when the team of researchers was "male and female."

Indeed, Matilda Coxe Stevenson's (1849–1915) work took place primarily with Zuni women, in an effort to better understand domestic life and children's experiences. There are two ways in which one may consider Stevenson as part of a feminist ethnographic tradition. She was the first woman to study the American Southwest, albeit initially as an adjunct to her husband's work. An interesting point to consider in this discussion is, in whose interpretation was she an adjunct? Tylor's? James Stevenson's? Ours? Additionally, if we cast feminist ethnographic production in terms of prioritizing gender as a category of analysis, then Stevenson's work offers one of the earliest examples, as she was the first American ethnologist to acknowledge the cultural importance of women and men.[5]

Whereas Stevenson fit the mold described and proscribed by Tylor, she did not have a PhD and she was the wife of the anthropologist. By contrast, Alice Fletcher (1838–1923) offers a different experience of a female ethnographer during this period the Victorian era. Fletcher pursued archeology late in life and ultimately lived with and studied the Omaha Indians of Nebraska. By 1889, she was living on the Nez Percé reservation with Jane Gay, a childhood friend and presumed lover. Working on Indian policy for the Bureau of Indian Affairs, like many of her era, Fletcher developed and helped to implement controversial land reform policies on Indian reservations. Fletcher was a founding member of the American Anthropological Association in 1902. As was the case with Stevenson, gender was a significant category of analysis for Fletcher and she ultimately lived and studied among several Native groups, including Sioux women on the Rosebud Reservation. Her commitment to autonomy and gender equity may be viewed through her work with the Women's National Indian Association, where she—well ahead of her time—introduced the concept of microloans (small loans enabling the purchase of land and homes). Her achievements may be considered part of the history of feminist ethnography for several reasons, including that she was not married and carried out research as an independent woman unattached to a male anthropologist. Fletcher also supported women. One of her assistants on the Rosebud Reservation was Susan LaFlesche, an Omaha woman and the sister of Francis LaFlesche, a longtime collaborator of Fletcher's. Fletcher helped Susan LaFlesche secure a loan to attend medical school, which allowed her to become the first Native American doctor in the United States.

ESSENTIAL

Excerpt from *The Omaha Tribe* by Alice Fletcher and Francis LaFlesche

Courtesy of the National Anthropological Archives, Smithsonian Institution via Library of Congress.

Alice Fletcher *was trained with anthropologist Frederic Ward Putnam at the Peabody Museum of Archaeology and Ethnology, Harvard University. She was made assistant in ethnology at the Peabody Museum in 1882. She served as president of the Anthropological Society of Washington and was the first woman president of* *the American Folklore Society in 1905. She also served as vice president of the American Association for the Advancement of Science.* **Francis LaFlesche** *was the first professional Native American ethnologist (Omaha). He worked for the Smithsonian Institution and served as Alice Fletcher's translator and researcher. Fletcher and LaFlesche's book was based on twenty-nine years of study, and many consider it the most comprehensive study ever written about a Native American group.*

Avocations of Women

The avocations of women all pertained to the conservation of life. She transmuted the raw material provided by the man into food, raiment, and shelter; the home was a product of her labor and all its duties belonged to her.

Bringing the wood for the fire was a part of a woman's task. For this purpose she used the burden strap; the broad band was worn across the chest and the long thongs were used to tie the wood in a bundle at her back . . .

The care of the garden has already been mentioned. This was the principal outdoor work of the women, not that their labors were otherwise confined to the house, for during warm weather everything that could be done out of doors was performed under a shade set up outside the dwelling. Cooking, sewing, and the eating of meals all took place under this temporary structure.

Source: Fletcher, Alice Cunningham, and Francis A. LaFlesche. *The Omaha Tribe*, Volume 2. Bison Book Edition reproduced from the 27th Annual Report of the Bureau of American Ethnology to the Secretary of the Smithsonian Institution, 1905–1906. Washington: Government Printing Office, 1911, 339–340.

Many would argue that one of the most influential female ethnographers of her time during the early 1900s was Elsie Clews Parsons (1875–1941). Parsons was born into a wealthy New York family. She obtained her MA and PhD at Barnard, where she trained under the tutelage of evolutionary sociologist Franklin H. Giddings. His theoretical leanings were evident in her first work, *The Family* (1906), which discusses the family as a social structure, focusing on familial and marriage patterns. While the theoretical focus of the work has been critiqued, Parsons also became known for her controversial advocacy that women and men should enjoy "trial marriage, divorce by mutual consent, access to reliable contraception, independence and elasticity within relationships, and an increased emphasis on obligations to children rather than to sexual partners."[6]

Her feminist inclinations are most apparent in her work examining how marriage, the family, religion, and social mores act to constrain women. A self-identified feminist, Parsons wrote a text unpublished during her life, *Journal of a Feminist*, in which she argued for women's liberation.[7] Increasingly, she became interested in anthropology and was Franz Boas's first female student,[8] going on to conduct an ethnographic study at Zuni and Laguna.

Parsons was involved with various political groups and participated in a number of organizations composed of upper-middle-class and wealthy women who scorned the subservient role ascribed to motherhood (yet many reinscribed certain forms of subservience by hiring domestic help). While opposing the constraints women experienced, Parsons simultaneously universalized male dominance, and it is for the latter that she has been critiqued. However, she has been widely praised by later scholars for her patronage of other female anthropologists, probably more than any other person. Parsons funded the research of many women, including Ester Goldfrank, Ruth Bunzel, and Ruth Benedict.

In contrast to Parsons, ethnographer Daisy Bates, born in Ireland in 1863, did not identify herself as a feminist, but her research was important because she addressed culture, household, and family. Her major contribution was in the area of kinship systems in Australia among Aborigines.[9] She articulated a new understanding of kinship systems in the early 1900s, which was only parenthetically acknowledged by Alfred Radcliffe-Brown, a well-known social anthropologist from Britain who claimed "the discovery of the Kariera system by myself in 1911."[10] Bates later accused Radcliffe-Brown of stealing her idea. Based on the timing of her research (several years prior to Radcliffe-Brown's) and his admission that he had access to her work prior to his, her claims seem quite plausible. While she was critiqued for her maternalistic attitude toward her informants, exemplified by the title of her book *My Natives and I*[11]—an impulse not that different from other Victorian-era US-based anthropologists—Bates's near absence from the anthropological record illustrates how women's intellectual contributions have been obscured.

Recovering the histories of all female anthropologists and ethnographers is beyond the scope of this textbook, but a final anthropologist we wish to highlight, who also remains largely hidden in the annals of anthropological history, is Eslanda Goode Robeson, an African American anthropologist. Although she was not a contemporary of the women discussed above, Robeson was born in 1895, the Victorian era—the time during which Stevenson, Fletcher, Parsons, and Bates were conducting research. Robeson, a chemist, journalist, activist, and scholar, was married to actor, athlete, and activist Paul Robeson[12] and received her degree in anthropology from the London School of Economics under Bronislaw Malinowski. Historian Barbara Ransby authored the book *Eslanda: The Large and Unconventional Life of Mrs. Paul Robeson*,[13] which chronicles Robeson's contributions as an antiracist, anticolonial intellectual who advocated women's rights on an international level are an important addition to the hidden histories of the field.

These women represent—although not exhaustively—both the origins and the development of early feminist ethnography and activism. Some could be challenged for the ways they universalized women's circumstances and because some of them fostered mother/child-like dynamics with their informants. Yet we celebrate them for contributing to the development of feminist ethnography, problematizing patriarchy, supporting or living a version of women's autonomy, and contributing to a feminist intellectualism and institutionalization of the category gender as a legitimate field of inquiry. A charitable interpretation might position some of them as having had feminist sentiments or inclinations, although they were unable to achieve the kind of democratic intellectualism that allowed them to embrace class or racial differences. What these women did in studying Native Americans in the Southwest, Aboriginal groups, and challenging racism and colonialism, respectively, was to open up intellectual dialogues about social structure and patriarchy, as well as forge a path for women ethnographers to be visible and recognized.

How Did Feminist Ethnography Mature between the 1920s and 1960s?

The previous section points out that the antecedents for the intellectual project of feminist ethnography began in the late nineteenth century and the turn of the twentieth century. While that time period serves as foundational, it was during the forty-year period from the 1920s through the 1960s that female ethnographers elaborated on earlier work and themes, and more feminists engaged in ethnography and attended to gender issues in their scholarship. This literature reflects a formal articulation of purpose and perspective, highlighting the rethinking of the categories sex and gender, ethnographic work by and with Indigenous women, stylistic innovations, and narrations of race through the lens of gender.

During this time, there was a robust production of ethnographies by and about women. Although many of these authors did not explicitly identify as feminists, some aimed to correct the androcentric bias that had existed in earlier ethnographic work, an important thread in the trajectory of feminist ethnography. Their work positioned gender as a central category of analysis and, as Visweswaran points out, "oscillated between the empiricist assumptions of Tylor and Parsons (studying women for a complete picture of society) and vindicationist approaches that sought to refute cultural or gender stereotypes."[14]

Societal shifts in thinking about sexuality opened the door for women to begin studying sexual behavior and same-sex sexuality during the early to mid-1900s. Social scientists across the disciplinary spectrum came to understand a range of sexual practices as "normal," and feminist ethnographers took up these issues with vigor. Anthropologists Gladys Reichard and Ruth Benedict adopted more inclusive language to describe sexual behaviors than previous writers. In political science, Katherine Bement Davis, the first female Commissioner of Corrections in New York, who also worked at the Bureau of Social Hygiene, facilitated a study of sexual practices, frequency, and interest in the early 1900s.

Anthropologist Margaret Mead, well known for her work on adolescence and sexuality, is most often identified as one of the first feminist ethnographers. Ironically, this is not because she claimed that label for herself (she did not), but because of the major contribution (although subject to criticism) that she made to elaborating on the difference between sex and gender and her analysis of gender as socially constructed. Her first major work was *Coming of Age in Samoa* in 1928, challenging the notion of a universally difficult adolescence. Her later work took up the subjects of childbirth and child-rearing norms, and she was often called the "popularizer" of anthropology (most often as a critique), because of her regular column in the popular women's magazine *Redbook* and her work with high-profile childcare experts, such as Dr. Spock.

There were also a number of women who identified as feminists prior to attending university who continued the tradition of conducting work with Native groups, such as the Pueblo (Ruth Benedict), Navajo (Ruth Benedict and Gladys Reichard), and Piman (Ruth Underhill). They worked with female informants contributing to the nascent scholarship on women across different cultures. Ruth Underhill's *Papago Woman* in 1934,[15] for example, was the first substantial document on a Southwestern Indian woman. In the late 1930s, Phyllis Kayberry, who conducted ethnographic research with Aboriginal women in Australia—resulting in her book *Aboriginal Woman*[16]—used her work to challenge negative stereotypes about Native women by presenting the significance of Aboriginal women's contributions to societal development and organization.

Some scholars engaged in writing ethnographies that were stylistically innovative toward these ends. Ethnographic work was published in various forms, including novels, autobiographies, life histories, and travel narratives. Trained under Boas, Zora Neale Hurston was the first Black student at Barnard College in the 1920s and graduated in 1928 with a BA in anthropology. Her contributions have often been minimized in the discipline, but she has been widely recognized for her work as a novelist, journalist, and playwright. A variety of factors contributed to this trend—not the least of which was the racism that permeated the discipline at the time. In addition, at a time when ethnographic research focused primarily on Native North Americans in the United States and non-Western cultures, Hurston's ethnographic work centered on her hometown of Eatonville, an African American community in Florida, although she also drew from her fieldwork on the African diaspora in Haiti and Jamaica.

Hurston remains well known for her prolific contributions to literature, particularly the novel she is best known for, *Their Eyes Were Watching God* in 1937, and *Mules and Men* in 1935, the first major work on Black folklore by an African American.[17] In this text, Hurston blends genres and voice using a unique narrative style to document songs, conversations, and slave tales in African American communities of Eatonville and Polk County, Florida, and New Orleans, Louisiana. Anthropologist Graciela Hernández, in her article "Multiple Mediations in Zora Neale Hurston's *Mules and Men*," argues that Hurston's work elevates folklore to a form of literature, weaving it with ethnographic narrative.[18]

🧠 ESSENTIAL

Excerpt from *Mules and Men* by Zora Neale Hurston

Courtesy of the Library of Congress, New York, World-Telegram & Sun Collection.

*The following excerpt offers a beautiful example of **Zora Neale Hurston's** attention to African American folklore, language, and culture, and is evocative of her unique narrative style.*

I thought about the tales I had heard as child. How even the Bible was made over to suit our vivid imagination. How the devil always outsmarted God . . . When I was rounding Lily Lake I was remembering how God had made the world and elements and people. He made souls for people, but he didn't give them out because he said:

Folks ain't ready for souls yet. De clay ain't dry. It's de strongest thing Ah ever made. Don't aim to waste none thru loose cracks. And then men got to grow strong enough to stand it. De way things is now, if Ah give it out it would tear them shackly bodies to pieces. Bimeby, Ah give it out.

So folks went round thousands of years without no souls. All de time de soul piece, it was setting 'round covered up wid God's loose raiment. Every now and then de wind would blow and hist up de cover and then de elements would be full of lightning and de winds would talk. So people told one 'nother that God was talking in de mountains.

Source: Hurston, Zora Neale. *Mules and Men*. New York: Harper Perennial Modern Classics, 2008 [orig. 1935], 3.

Also trained under Boas, Ella Deloria wrote the novel *Waterlily* in the 1940s based on her ethnographic research that chronicled Dakota Sioux life prior to American expansionism and **settler colonialism** (see more on this in chapter 6).[19] Deloria's fictional work presented the contributions of Great Plains women. Exemplifying the devaluation of both stylistic innovation and gendered analysis, Deloria's fiction was not published until 1988, over a decade after her death.

Feminist anthropologists are noted for illuminating and reflecting upon their own gendered and raced positions to narrate or mediate issues of race in the mid-twentieth century. Hortense Powdermaker in *After Freedom* (1939) examines how race and gender confounded her research in Mississippi, exploring her role as a white woman interviewing "negro" men. Ruth Landes's *City of Women* (1947), based on fieldwork from 1938 to 1939 in Bahia, Brazil, describes the challenges of negotiating sexist and racial ideologies as a white woman both in the United States and at her field site. A cadre of women of color feminists, such as Johnetta Cole, Vera Green, Diane K. Lewis, and Niara Sudarkasa (born Gloria Marshall) trained as ethnographers in anthropology programs in the 1950s and 1960s. Cole and Sudarkasa moved into important leadership roles in the academy over the next few decades: Green contributed significantly to human rights work, and Lewis conducted pivotal analyses reinterpreting sex role socialization in Black families. By the end of this period, anthropology had gained more of a public face and contributed to movements for sexual freedom, civil rights, antiwar organizing, and the burgeoning women's movement.

What Impact Did the Women's Movement of the 1960s Have on the Next Phase of Feminist Ethnographic Production? (1960s–1980s)

Ethnographies by and about women written during the 1960s and 1970s were produced in part as a result of the women's movement of this time, the Second Wave of feminism discussed in chapter 1. In the 1960s, feminist ethnography became part of the larger challenge that feminism posed to **positivist** social research, in which researchers presume to approach the setting logically, objectively, and with predetermined criteria for measurement. But feminist philosophers of science, such as Sandra Harding and Donna Haraway, have challenged these notions as *always* situated and have critiqued positivism as reproducing a privileged perspective. One of the major accomplishments attributed to feminist ethnography is that it validated the epistemological importance of women's contributions to society. Feminist ethnography first sought to do research about women, by women, and for women. It was organized around the belief that women were universally oppressed by patriarchy—a central tenet of cultural feminism during the 1970s—that is, the systems of power that stabilized men's control over social, economic, and political life. In the 1960s and 1970s, feminist ethnography came to involve "giving voice" to marginalized groups whose experiences had rarely been represented or understood. This notion was not without critique, in that it reinforced a hierarchy of the researcher over the researched, and assumed a sort of victimhood and lack of **agency** among marginalized women.

In anthropology, where ethnography had become most common, this meant that the anthropological record had to be corrected and the missing story of women had to be included. At first, this "corrective project" was the result of research that had been conducted by the wives of male anthropologists, who told the stories their husbands did not. Later the corrective took on a new agenda, revisiting the fieldsites where men had done their research, but had omitted a gender, race, and/or class analysis.

THINKING THROUGH . . .

Restudying Culture

Many anthropologists have restudied topics that offer a different, more holistic gender, race, and class analysis of the subject. Can you identify an early ethnographic work (1800s–1950s) that is limited in its view and does not account for gender, racial, ethnic, sexuality, or class dynamics? Then identify a later ethnographic text that attempts to correct the absence of those dynamics. (One good example of the concept of corrective is the revision of Bronislaw Malinowski's *Argonauts of the Western Pacific* (1922) done by Annette Weiner in her 1988 restudy, *The Trobrianders of Papua New Guinea*, which offered a gender analysis of the Trobrianders.)

Women's experiences as ethnographers also became an important subject during this time, particularly as more and more women trained in ethnography and entered the field. Anthropologist Peggy Golde's groundbreaking collection *Women in the Field: Anthropological Experiences*, published in 1970, was among the first to address "subjective aspects of field work," particularly how gender can directly or inadvertently affect the ethnographic process. With chapters by pioneering female anthropologists, such as Ruth Landes, Ernestine Friedl, and Margaret Mead, the volume highlighted the vulnerabilities, misconceptions, and possibilities for North American women conducting ethnography in various contexts.

Two other texts stand out as foundational from the 1970s: *Woman, Culture, and Society* edited by Michelle Rosaldo and Louise Lamphere (1974) and *Toward and Anthropology of Women* edited by Rayna (Rapp) Reiter (1975). Both volumes attempted to answer questions about women's status cross-culturally. *Woman, Culture, and Society* grew out of a course taught at Stanford University in 1971 where various faculty gave lectures and was organized around three explanations about women's status: structural analysis, cultural analysis, and psychological analysis.[20] Some critics viewed the volume as essentialist because it had "Woman" in the title, which seemed to mark that there was only one way in which a woman could be a woman. The issue of whether scholars could make broad or universal claims about the category of woman created tension both within and beyond feminist anthropology.

Toward an Anthropology of Women addressed similar concerns but came at those issues from a distinctly Marxist feminist perspective. This collection emerged from a student-initiated women's studies course at the University of Michigan for which—in an effort to find relevant readings—Reiter (Rapp) and Norma Diamond solicited colleagues to write pieces, which became the "backbone of the network in *Toward an Anthropology of Women*."[21] The intentions of the text were very clear; in the introduction, it states that the goal of the volume was to help feminists in the struggle against sexism and inequality through an examination of how women experienced equality and inequality cross-culturally. The chapters place women at the center of analysis and locate the origins of women's subordination and oppression in capitalism, and they consider how various cross-cultural data inform analyses of the resulting inequities. For example, anthropologist Karen Brodkin Sacks's work explores state and class formation as instrumental in creating unequal spheres in which women and men operate. What is crucial about both texts is that they set the stage for the many directions that subsequent women in anthropology have taken, as well as led to a robust feminist inquiry in ethnography more broadly.

Many of the contributors to these volumes were also active in the burgeoning Women's Movement in the United States and Britain. As Louise Lamphere recalls in her reflection on the relationship between theory, ethnography, and activism in feminist anthropology during the 1970s:

> Through participating in demonstrations for women's liberation, legislative hearings on abortion rights, and especially consciousness raising (CR) groups, women anthropologists came to the view that "the personal is political" and began to bring a feminist sensibility to their research and teaching as well as to their own personal lives. At this stage, activism in the public sphere brought changes to anthropology, but feminist advocacy on issues of importance to women (abortion rights, child care, job discrimination, etc.) tended to be segregated from anthropological endeavors or at least treated through conventional research methodologies . . .
>
> [For instance,] in Boston, Bread and Roses, a socialist-feminist ("politico") organization, advocated for a broad range of changes in women's lives from equality in the workplace, to control over their bodies, and free child care. Michelle Rosaldo joined a Bread and Roses CR group composed of Radcliffe graduates in October 1969. She later participated in another group at Stanford. I joined a small group at Brown that emerged from our chapter of the New University Conference (NUC), a university and college-based anti-war organization and from activities that grew out of the Brown campus-wide May 1970 strike. We shared an interest in addressing our personal concerns in relation to men and to the larger power structure; these CR groups offered us a safe environment for exploring such issues.
>
> Female anthropologists in Michigan and New York were also part of similar CR groups. In Michigan, Rayna Rapp and Gayle Rubin joined a consciousness-raising group that had spun off from "Resistance," the draft resistance and anti-war movement group active on the University of Michigan campus. In New York, the Ruth Benedict Collective (RBC), brought together senior anthropologists (June Nash, Eleanor [Happy] Leacock, and Ruby Rohrlich-Leavitt), recent PhDs, and graduate students, including Leni Silverstein. In its early years (1969–1971), some of the 25 or so anthropologists in the RBC met in small consciousness-raising groups that provided personal, intellectual and professional support.[22]

☙ SPOTLIGHT ☙

Florence Babb on the Impact of *Woman, Culture, and Society* and *Toward an Anthropology of Women*

Florence Babb *received her PhD in anthropology from the State University of New York (SUNY) at Buffalo and is the Harrington Distinguished Professor of Anthropology at the University of North Carolina at Chapel Hill. She has conducted ethnographic research in Peru, Nicaragua, Mexico, and Cuba. She is the author of* Between Field and Cooking Pot: The Political Economy of Marketwomen in Peru *(1989, revised edition 1998),* After Revolution: Mapping Gender and Cultural Politics in Neoliberal Nicaragua *(2001), and* The Tourism Encounter: Fashioning Latin American Nations and Histories (2011). *Her most recent book is* Women's Place in the Andes: Engaging Decolonial Feminist Anthropology *(2018), and she is working on a companion ethnography,* Scaling Differences: Place, Race, and Gender in Andean Peru.

I was a student during the 1970s. It was a really important time for me. I went to grad school in 1974; that was the year when Michelle Rosaldo and Louise Lamphere's book came out (*Woman, Culture, and Society*). A year later Rayna Rapp Reiter's book came out (*Toward an Anthropology of Women*). To this day I still remember discovering those books on the bookshelves. I found the first, Rosaldo and Lamphere, at our bookstore the summer before I started grad school at SUNY Buffalo. And the following year I was doing research in Cornell University's archives, and I discovered Rayna's book at the campus bookstore. Both of them were hugely important to my thinking during that time—as they were for so many others. I have to say that those readings were very inspiring to me in my own work. I was bringing together strands of feminist theory and feminist studies along with my anthropology. And in fact Bill Stein, my advisor, helped make me a charter subscriber to the feminist journal *Signs*. So I would say that he was a feminist influence as well, along with Liz Kennedy, another key mentor. And as you know, during the mid-1970s it was the beginning of the UN conferences on women and attention to gender and development. I was going with that current, and my MA project in the mid-1970s was on gender and development.

Importantly, ethnographers of this time were also deeply influenced by the feminist fiction of the 1970s, including writers such as Toni Morrison (author of *The Bluest Eye* in 1970 and *Song of Solomon* in 1977), Maxine Hong Kingston (author of *Warrior Woman* in 1976), and Alice Walker (author of *Meridian* in 1976).[23] As Asian and Asian American literary scholar Karen Su writes in her chapter on ethnographic authority in *Feminist Fields: Ethnographic Insights*, "[The position of] ethnic women writers parallel the positions of 'native' women anthropologists. [They have] had to write under the constraints of the 'ethnographic gaze.'"[24] Some ethnographers were inspired by the different representations of women's experiences in literary works, leading them to analyze the challenges that they, as scholars, faced having "ethnographic authority" and exploring the importance of translating cross-cultural experiences.

Other collections of writing contributed to rethinking the different ways that women lived their lives. They raised questions about how women related to other women, to themselves, and to society. One of the most important collections that influenced feminists and feminist academics was the 1981 edited volume, *This Bridge Called My Back: Writings by Radical Women of Color*, which has become "one of *the most* cited books in feminist theorizing."[25] *This Bridge Called My Back* provided an important challenge to white feminists who drew upon the idea of sisterhood to make claims of solidarity. The volume brought together women who were Native American, Latina, Chicana, Asian, and Black, not only creating one of the most profound examples of writing about how it feels to be non-white but also serving as a major factor in the creation of women of color coalitions. One of the most notable moments for feminists in the 1980s was the international conference "Common Differences: Third World Women and Feminist Perspectives," held in 1983. This conference was organized by a multiracial, international group of women and one of the first times that women of color and white women in the United States and women from what we would now call the Global South, but then was referred to as the Third World, came together around their common differences. The conference fundamentally challenged the definition of feminism to include a much broader concern with equity.[26]

The Chicana movement also emerged in the 1970s, responding to female and maternal archetypes that limited Chicana women's agency. According to feminist educator and historian Barbara J. Love's book *Feminists Who Changed America 1963–1975,*[27] the Comisión Femenil Mexicana Nacional was founded in 1970 to address issues of concern to Chicana women and initially focused on ending the compulsory sterilization of women. By 1985, they had expanded their scope to include issues related to teenage girls involved in the criminal justice system. It was this kind of organizing that contributed to academic production on and by Chicana women. For instance, anthropologist M. Patricia Fernández-Kelly examined the gendered and human rights dimensions of multinational manufacturing in Cuidad Juarez on the US-Mexico border, where maquiladoras, or assembly plants, exist. Her book, *For We Are Sold, I and My People,*[28] uncovers the realities of "Third World women's" exploitation in manufacturing plants.

In the 1970s and 1980s, several ethnographies drew from dependency theory and gendered analyses of women's labor. For example, anthropologist June Nash's influential ethnography *We Eat the Mines and the Mines Eat Us: Dependency and Exploitation in Bolivian Tin Mines*[29] is but one example of the role she played in establishing gender as a crucial analytic for scholars of Latin America. Later, feminist ethnographers who did work in Latin America, such as anthropologist Kay Warren, documented gender roles among Indigenous communities in the Andes and Peru. Political scientist Susan Bourque (with Kay Warren) wrote *Women of the Andes: Patriarchy and Social Change in Two Peruvian Towns,*[30] offering an analysis of women's subordination.

Through the 1980s we find tremendously diverse efforts and scholarship shaping the production of feminist ethnography. But it was not a simple path toward gaining respect for feminist analysis. In fact, it was a rough and challenging road. Because of the projects and feminist commitments that women had, some were denied tenure, and others were unable to secure a full-time teaching job for many years.

🦪 ESSENTIAL

Excerpt from "Too Queer for College" by Esther Newton

Esther Newton *received her PhD in anthropology at the University of Chicago in 1968. She is now an emeritus professor at Purchase College, SUNY, and retired term professor of women's studies at the University of Michigan. Her first book,* Mother Camp: Female Impersonators in America *(1972), was the first major anthropological study of a homosexual community in the United States. Her second ethnographic book,* Cherry Grove, Fire Island: Sixty Years in America's First Gay and Lesbian Town *(1993), documented the* *changing dynamics of the beach resort Cherry Grove, one of the oldest and most visible predominantly LGBT communities in the United States. Most recently, she published a collection of essays, her "intellectual autobiogra-phy," Margaret Mead Made Me Gay (2000) and My Butch Career: A Memoir (2018). In the following excerpt from "Too Queer for College," Newton dis-cusses the challenges she faced not only as a butch lesbian in the field but also as a feminist, and among feminists:*

In 1968, after I got my first job, I became a passionately committed femi-nist. . . . The movement also attracted many straight women. Some have been staunch allies; others have capitulated under straight male pressure to get rid of the queer perspective my person and my work have represented.

I was denied tenure on my first job. The rejection felled me like a dumb ox. The process was secret, but privately and as a favor, the woman department head told me some people had trouble with my "personality." There was also a question about my "commitment to anthropology." It was like the menacing encounter I'd had with the college dean [who had threatened Newton with expulsion as a graduate student after seeing her in a phone booth with a friend, who ironically was not even her lover]: You're doing something wrong and I won't say what, but we *know* about it.

[Ultimately, Newton was also denied tenure at her second job, with the committee citing "feminist bias" in her work. More savvy and sophisticated, however, Newton fought and won her tenure case. Shortly afterward, she felt comfortable "coming out" on her job, as well as writing about her experi-ences as a butch lesbian feminist in academia.]

Source: Newton, Esther. "Too Queer for College: Notes on Homophobia 1987." In *Margaret Mead Made Me Gay: Personal Essays, Public Ideas*, 1st Edition, 219–24. Durham, NC: Duke University Press Books, 2000, 221.

Probably the most well-known and successful case against employment dis-crimination by a feminist ethnographer—a female faculty a female faculty member in the 1970s—was that of anthropologist Louise Lamphere. She was denied tenure by her all-male senior colleagues in the department of anthropology at Brown University in 1974. She filed a **Title VII** Sex Discrimination Case in 1975 that the university settled out of court, awarding her tenure in 1977. The case also required Brown to enter into what became known as the Lamphere Consent Decree, which governed the university's faculty hiring and tenure decisions between 1977 and 1992, and promoted a significant increase in women on the Brown faculty.[31] Upon her retirement from the University of New Mexico (where she took a position in 1986), Lamphere sought to preserve the legacy of feminist scholarship at Brown by ensuring that courses on gender and sexuality would be accessible to students; she created the Louise Lamphere Visiting Assistant Professorship in Gender Studies, a two-year rotating teaching and research position in both the Brown Anthropology Department and the Pembroke Center for Teaching and Research on Women. Marking the fortieth anniversary of the lawsuit's filing in 2015, the Pembroke Center hosted an exhibition and two-day conference, "The Legacy of *Louise Lamphere v. Brown University*." Lamphere was awarded an honorary degree in May 2015.

SPOTLIGHT

Louise Lamphere on the Legacy of *Lamphere v. Brown*

Louise Lamphere *received her PhD from Harvard University and is a distinguished professor emeritus from the University of New Mexico. She also received an honorary degree, a Doctor of Humane Letters (L.H.D.), from Brown University in 2015. In addition to her early contributions to feminist anthropology through* Woman, Culture, and Society *(1974), she coauthored* Sunbelt Working Mothers: Reconciling Family and Factory *(1993) with Patricia Zavella, Felipe Gonzales, and Peter B. Evans, and coedited* Situated Lives: Gender and Culture in Everyday Life *(1997) with Helena Ragoné and Patricia Zavella. Her most recent book* Weaving Women's Lives: Three Generations in a Navajo Family *(2007).* Three Generations in a Navajo Family *is the result of five decades of fieldwork and collaborative scholarship. We had the pleasure of speaking with Lamphere about her experiences with her legal case against Brown and its legacy. When Lamphere met with her Department Chair in May 1974 and discovered that she was being denied tenure, she was shocked:*

Photo Credit: Margaret Randall.

I was pretty shaken. I was very committed to my career and thought I had excellent qualifications. It was like a rug had been pulled out from under me. I didn't know how to respond when he told me that my teaching was "poor but not so much worse than others" and that my research on women was "theoretically weak." A man would have gotten angry, but, like many women, I felt angry but with a dose of self-doubt. I thought, "Maybe my Chair was right, maybe I wasn't good enough." Still when I left his office, I felt I had to do something. [Ultimately, Lamphere filed a lawsuit.]

The reason I was able to make an impact was that it became a Class Action suit. It took a year to certify the class, but ultimately three other women who had worked at Brown, including two who had also been denied tenure, joined the suit. If I had filed an individual lawsuit, I would have had to prove discrimination by the Department. Brown University could have said, "We'll give you a cash settlement, and you can go away." And that's what happened with a batch of these [kinds of cases] because any lawyer will tell you that most cases get settled out of court. The way they get them settled is to say, "We'll pay you this," and by that time, you're so tired you don't pursue further action.

The one thing that's good about discrimination law is that if the University or the Company loses, then they do have to pay the lawyers. Of course, the other thing is that you might have to pay their legal fees if you lose, so it's a risk. I had what I would consider to be a perfect storm. I had lots of information from the Anthropology Department's correspondence. I was the first woman to come up for tenure in Sociology and Anthropology. The man that came up the year before me . . . had fewer publications than I did. And of course, they claimed that the standards were being raised because they were in this terrible financial crush because of the decline of oil prices in 1973 and the heating bills were escalating. They were creating a staffing plan that they put into effect in about 1973. The law is a little [fuzzy on this. Some contended] that you couldn't raise the standards without telling anybody, suddenly in the middle of somebody's probationary period. I don't know how that would have played out in court. They could have argued, "Well, we had to raise the standards." And I would have said, "You didn't tell me!" and [laughter]. I had a stronger case than the last male [who received tenure in anthropology], because that's the way a lot of cases went. You sort of compared yourself to other men in equal positions, and if they had fewer publications than you did, then you could make a case for discrimination.

Despite the success of my case, it became harder to win these cases after the 1980s, when the burden of proof was shifted from the institution to the plaintiff. One of the things about Title VII, in the beginning, was that the burden of proof was with the university or the company or whatever, so they had to prove that they didn't discriminate. When they re-did the law they shifted the burden of proof to the plaintiff, so that meant that the person has to show that the university did discriminate. That's very hard. The burden of proof is where the toughest deal is. You know, I can say, "Prosecute somebody for a murder!" The burden of proof is on the state to prove that the person did it. In these civil cases, they can go either way, depending on how the law is written. . . .

You can tour Brown Universities exhibit on Lamphere's case virtually here: http://www.pembrokecenterexhibits.org/the-lamphere-case.

In light of these legal changes, the conflation of research and identity work in the academy continues to plague young feminist scholars, especially as denials of tenure and promotion are typically couched in language about "fit" with the program or institution. In an article in the journal *Cultural Anthropology*, anthropologists Tami Navarro, Bianca Williams, and Attiya Ahmad underscore this point, especially its relevance for women of color faculty.[32]

> Invocations of diversity made in many university mission statements, and the attention now paid to critical race and gender studies within disciplines such as anthropology would suggest that this is a new moment—a different time in which the academy has presumably ended explicit racism and begun seriously addressing questions of inclusion and exclusion. . . . We argue that despite these seeming improvements, the difficulties experienced by female faculty of color have not only continued, but have intensified in recent years. We partly tie this change to the increasing corporatization of the academy, particularly the decline in tenure-track appointments in favor of non-secure, contract-based positions. . . . Female professors of color . . . are confronted with students' preexisting raced, classed, and gendered understandings of what constitutes a "professor" (Agathangelou and Ling 2002). These understandings often come to light in student evaluations, which institutions take more and more seriously given their increased dependence on tuition and their focus on student satisfaction. In these evaluations, disappointed students who feel they have been cheated out of a "real" (i.e., neutrally positioned/ objective/white male) professor, often vent their frustrations. To compound these difficulties, women of color (WoC) continue to shoulder disproportionate amounts of affective labor in the academy, work that goes systematically unrecognized and remains undervalued. Finally, the conflation of WoC with their research agendas— that is, the assumption that these scholars are necessarily speaking from a "native" position—continues to be a problem for female anthropologists of color.[33]

Navarro, Williams, and Ahmad suggest not coddling or holding the hands of faculty of color—as they say, it is "an insulting notion, at best"—but rather making practical suggestions like hiring scholars of color in clusters so that they can support one another, connecting junior WoC with senior mentors for early feedback on publications, and offering opportunities for coteaching that can illuminate racialized and gender dynamics in the classroom, as well as foster interdisciplinary engagement among students and faculty. What is clear from this article, and our interviews with a variety of feminist ethnographers, is that—as we so often document in feminist ethnographic work in a variety of communities—equity has yet to be achieved in the academy, and the important work that feminist faculty began in the 1970s must continue into the future.

THINKING THROUGH . . .

Faculty Composition at Your Institution

Locate the most recent edition of the American Association of University Professor's (AAUP) Faculty Salary Survey (this is conducted biannually and searchable data can be found at the Chronicle of Higher Education's website, www.chronicle.org). Search the data for your college or university. Compare salaries for female and male faculty across salary ranks. (In the United States, assistant professors are often called "junior faculty"; once a faculty member receives tenure—when they are asked to stay at the institution in a permanent position—they are associate professors and may become full professors, the highest rank for faculty, based on further scholarly achievements.)[1] Consider also the number of full time versus part time or adjunct faculty. What gender disparities does your research suggest?

[1]*For more information, go to:* https://www.aaup.org/.

What Interventions Came Out of Feminist Ethnography from the 1990s Through the Present?

By the 1990s, feminist ethnographic production had grown and matured across various intellectual terrains. This scholarship included, but was not limited to, feminist ethnographies produced by women of color offering new epistemological narratives, the incorporation of gender analyses in global and transnational processes, research exploring the complexities of various domains of gender including masculinity and LGBTQI+ experiences.

From the 1990s until the present, feminist theorizing and feminist ethnographic production have been robust, having been influenced by social movements, tensions that arose within the feminist community in earlier decades, as well as economic shifts. Although we will cover ethnographic work from this period in many of the subsequent chapters, here we highlight feminist ethnography in these recent decades more broadly.

We start with the progressive scholarship by women of color, which had at its core an articulation of **intersectionality**. Conceptually, an intersectional analysis argues that all categories of identity and existence operate at the same time in a person's experience of oppression and subordination. It is a framework that gets used in many different ways—by scholars across many academic disciplines, as well as by institutional entities and the nonprofit sector to prop up diversity and inclusion.[34] One simple, yet instructive, example of an intersectional analysis can be found in exploring the Twitter responses to Nina Davuluri, who became the first contestant of Indian descent to win the Miss America contest in 2014. The aftermath was not unlike the racist backlash Vanessa Williams experienced when she was the first African American contestant to win. Following Davuluri's win, tweets appeared that misidentified her as Muslim or Arab and suggested that a terrorist or "Miss Al-Qaeda" won. These oppressive comments exemplify how racism, sexism, and xenophobia operated at the same time against Davuluri becoming the contest winner. The hate-filled response to her win and the ways in which people analyzed that hatred is an example of an intersectional analysis accounting for how race, nationhood, and gender operate to demonize groups of people. On what basis was she despised more? Because she was a brown woman? Because she was presumed to not be a citizen of the United States? It was none of these in isolation, but rather the intersection of them.

It became clear that the analytic category of gender as the dominant way in which women's experiences were both researched and produced was insufficient; thus women of color's scholarship became crucial during this time. We flag the broad ways in which work by women of color created a scholarship that influenced the production of feminist ethnography. This is accomplished by focusing on the frameworks and interdisciplinary critical perspectives offered by women of color scholars and writers.

Women of color scholars in the 1980s and 1990s not only acknowledged differences among women but also produced scholarship that "reshaped basic concepts and theories of the discipline," according to sociologists Bonnie Thornton Dill and Maxine Baca Zinn.[35] The Inter-university Research Group Exploring the Intersection of Race and Gender was the site of discussion and comparative research on women of color and members of the group used the analytic framework of intersectionality to explain both their lives as women of color scholars and the exclusion of women of color in research. *Women of Color in U.S. Society*,[36] edited by Dill and Zinn, was instrumental in showing how the lives of women of color are structured by race, class, and gender hierarchies. Importantly, these dynamics were analyzed and written by women of color. Another scholar noted for using intersectional analysis was anthropologist Patricia Zavella, whose ethnography *Women's Work and Chicano Families: Cannery Workers of the Santa Clara Valley*[37] merges Chicana labor history with the canning industry in California. The ethnography explores a range of workplace and kin networks, in which Chicana women circulate and strategize their survival. Psychologist Aída Hurtado's *The Color of Privilege: Three Blasphemies on Race and Feminism*[38] offers a different assessment of intersectionality as a response to critiques of Second Wave feminist essentialization of women. Hurtado makes the argument that women of color's responses to feminism are orchestrated not so much by the differences between women, but rather by the differentially subordinate relationship women have with white men. Anthropologist Leith Mullings's *On Our Own Terms* explores the racial and gendered difference in order to theorize women's work in the family, community, and wage labor. In this collection of essays, Mullings reveals how her own experiences serve as a foundation from which she can analyze inequalities in the lives of African American women drawing from her over two decades of ethnographic engagement. Finally, sociologist Yen Le Espiritu's book *Asian American Panethnicity: Bridging Institutions and Identities* was the first to explore the conflicts and benefits of the construction of Pan-Asian identities in the mid-1990s.[39]

Postcolonial feminist theorizing, like women of color theorizing, became central to feminist ethnography as a corrective to the orientation of feminist thinking based on Western experience. The intersection between globalization, gender, and labor is underscored in ethnographies such as Aihwa Ong's *Spirits of Resistance and Capitalist Discipline: Factory Women in Malaysia.*[40] Ong's ethnography demonstrates the assertion of global capitalism on culture, the economy, and gender in South East Asia. Anna Lowenhaupt Tsing's *In the Realm of the Diamond Queen: Marginality in an Out-of-the-Way Place* analyzes gender, power, and the politics of identity among Meratus Dayaks, a marginal and marginalized group in the Indonesian rainforest.[41] These and other works from the 1980s and early 1990s paved the way for more feminist ethnographic attention to the gendered effects of globalization.

ESSENTIAL

Excerpt from "Methodological Gifts in Latina/o Studies and Feminist Anthropology" by Gina Pérez

Gina Pérez *is a Professor in the Department of Comparative American Studies at Oberlin College. She received her PhD in anthropology from Northwestern University. Before coming to Oberlin, Pérez was a research associate at the Center for Puerto Rican Studies at Hunter College, CUNY. Pérez is the author of the award-winning* The Near Northwest Side Story: Migration, Displacement, and Puerto Rican Families *(2004), coeditor of* Beyond El Barrio: Everyday Life in Latina/o America *(with Frank Guridy and Adrian Burgos Jr., 2011), and author of* Citizen, Student Soldier: Latina/o Youth, JROTC and the American Dream *(2015).*

In the 1980s feminist anthropologists conducted pioneering research focusing on women and work, and women and development, as well as gender and the international division of labor. Studies by feminist anthropologists that focused on global division of labor were an important reminder of the ways in which local economies, gender ideologies, kin relations and household arrangements are shaped by global capital and uneven power relations among nations. Lynn Bolles' work in Jamaica, for example, demonstrated how Jamaican women workers, their local communities and households were shaped by International Monetary Fund structural adjustment programs, reminding us that what happens in local communities is indelibly shaped by global forces. Helen Safa's research on shifting gender relations in Puerto Rico highlighted how industrial policy and industrialization programs had a profound impact on shifting gender relations on the island. This analytical framing shares much with critical new directions in Latina/o studies scholarship employing a transnational lens for understanding gender, sexuality, cultural production and community development among Latina/o communities in the United States. In addition to the pioneering work of Juan Vicente Palerm, Patricia Zavella, Carlos Velez-Ibanez and Lynn Stephen, such scholarship has inspired a new generation of anthropologists whose work explores the various dimensions of transnationalism in the lives of migrants both in the United States and abroad. . . .

Finally, as Rayna Rapp noted in her contribution to this series, feminist anthropology is simultaneously found at the place where theory and practice meet. The scholarly, political and activist engagements defining feminist anthropology also inform Latina/o Studies scholarship, like Leo Chavez's work on the impact of immigration reform on immigrant communities; Ana Ochoa O'Leary's research highlighting migrant women's border crossings and the gendered experiences of border enforcement; as well as Latina/o anthropologists concerns with increasing militarization of Latina/o communities and shifting notions of citizenship. Luis Plascencia's investigation of the implications of posthumous citizenship for Latin American immigrant soldiers and Ana Yolanda Ramos Zayas' work exploring issues of citizenship and notions of "deficient citizenship" among Puerto Rican youth are examples of the continued salience of anthropological praxis in this post 9-11 world. My own work within Puerto Rican communities reflects many of these methodological questions and commitments. My first book provides a gendered reading of Puerto Rican migration and transnational practices, and locates the lives of Puerto Rican women and their families within the historical political economies of San Sebastian, Puerto Rico and Chicago. A particularly striking finding within my work was how military service often served as an important survival strategy for many poor and working-class Puerto Rican families and how a growing number of Puerto Rican and Latina/o youth participate in a growing number of JROTC[1] programs in American public high schools. The expansion of JROTC is concomitant with an explicit targeting of Latina/o youth for military service, and in both instances a powerful discourse of the military's ability to provide discipline for "at risk" youth, including young women at risk of becoming unwed mothers, justifies millions of dollars of government spending to support such efforts. Feminist and Latina/o scholarship in anthropology deeply inform my work, strengthen my methodological approaches and provide invaluable analytical tools in order to pursue anthropological research that seeks not only to continue to raise new questions about how research should proceed, but also how to use our research to build a more just world.

Source: Pérez, Gina M. "Methodological Gifts in Latina/o Studies and Feminist Anthropology." *Anthropology News* 48, no. 7 (October 1, 2007): 6–7.

[1] JROTC stands for the Junior Reserve Officers' Training Corps and is designed to ostensibly teach high school students the value of citizenship, personal responsibility, self-esteem, and community service, among other characteristics that seem to be important to the U.S. Army. It states that its mission is "to motivate young people to be better citizens."

Significant political events, such as the end of the Cold War in 1989 and the Soviet Union's collapse in 1991, further influenced the work of feminist ethnographers on globalization. On the one hand, some believed that with the end of "Communist threat," the United States would be the dominant superpower able to espouse and spread values of democracy, free markets, and peace. Others argued that there emerged a much greater potential for ethnic, political, and economic conflict. Economic shifts, such as the consolidation of **economic liberalism** and the signing of the North American Free Trade Agreement (**NAFTA**) in 1992, brought about divisions of labor and new economic and political arrangements.

The outcome of these new arrangements influenced the gendered dimensions of the international division of labor. For example, anthropologist Carla Freeman's *High Tech and High Heels in the Global Economy: Women, Work, and Pink-Collar Identities in the Caribbean*[42] discusses how processes of transnationalism impact Afro-Caribbean women's lives in Barbados. Economic liberalism and issues related to gender are the subject of such work as *After Revolution: Mapping Gender and Cultural Politics in Neoliberal Nicaragua*[43] by anthropologist Florence Babb, who examines agrarian reform on the lives of working class and poor women in Nicaragua.

Another significant influence on feminist ethnography during the 1990s and beyond was the interventions offered in LGBT and queer scholarship. We do not mean to suggest that all scholarship on LGBTQI+ issues exemplifies feminist thinking, but many scholars who do fieldwork in LGBTQI+ communities define themselves as feminist. This research contributed significantly to the feminist ethnographic enterprise in that it moved theorizing away from a gender-specific domain. In other words, rather than solely a focus on women, queer scholarship pushes forward analyses that examine differentially and differently gendered bodies. We limit our discussion primarily to the influences of queer ethnographers who articulate a feminist perspective in their work, acknowledging that much queer theory and early queer ethnographic inquiry was dominated by (white) male scholars.

It was only in the mid-twentieth century that ethnographic research began to focus explicitly on homosexuality, bisexuality, and transgender experiences. The first book-length ethnography on gay and transgender life was *Mother Camp: Female Impersonators in America* published in 1972 by anthropologist Esther Newton.[44] This classic text had no contemporaries until the later part of the 1970s and early 1980s when Deborah Goleman Wolf and Gilbert Herdt published *The Lesbian Community* and *Guardian of the Flutes: Idioms of Masculinity: A Study of Ritualized Homosexual Behavior*,[45] respectively. Evelyn Blackwood's *The Many Faces of Homosexuality: Anthropological Approaches to Homosexuality* was groundbreaking in 1986 because it was the first collection to examine diverse manifestations of homosexuality in various historical periods and across a variety of non-Western cultures.[46]

By the 1990s there were a number of theoretically sophisticated ethnographies examining LGBTQI+ issues. For example, anthropologist Kath Weston's *Families We Choose: Lesbians, Gays, Kinship* looks at the ways sexuality and identity reframe the biological meanings of family.[47] Anthropologists Ellen Lewin and William Leap coedited a volume considering the debates around gay and lesbian ethnography, with a focus on the positionality of the ethnographer, *Out in the Field: Reflections of Lesbian and Gay Anthropologists*.[48] Lewin's influential ethnography *Lesbian Mothers: Accounts of Gender in American Culture* and her edited collection *Inventing Lesbian Cultures in America*[49] also contributed to broader understandings of how female sexuality is shaped by culture, and the imagined communities that lesbians create. Further, Blackwood's feminist ethnographic study of tombois and femmes in Indonesian lesbi communities since the late 1980s was revolutionary in its attention to female desire and masculinity.[50]

The range of queer ethnographic scholarship produced in the late 1990s and early 2000s has been influential in moving scholars into directions of inquiry that interrogate the possibilities and limitations of queer theory, as well as among communities that were previously neglected in ethnographic research. For example, anthropologist Erica Lorraine Williams, in her ethnography *Sex Tourism in Bahia: Ambiguous Entanglements*,[51] points out that queer theory was important in her methodological, data collection, and interpretive choices—allowing her to question assumptions that all of the women involved in Brazilian sex tourism were straight. When we interviewed her, she explained how feminist ethnography benefits from the insights of queer ethnography:

> The literature on sex work was very heterosexual: American men, locals, Dominican women. But I saw more than that going on in Bahia. I really pushed back against having to be focused on just straight women. For example, one of the women I talk

about who identified as a lesbian and had a female partner, but in her sex work she had relationships with older European men. Just because people are sex workers does not mean they are straight. I found Black Queer studies, for example E. Patrick Johnson and Jafari Allen, to be a rich literature.

Likewise, Surinamese-Dutch anthropologist Gloria Wekker's *The Politics of Passion: Women's Sexual Culture in the Afro-Surinamese Diaspora* challenged Western stereotypes about identity-based sexuality in her study of the mati work among women in Suriname.[52] Wekker's ethnography examines the complex and historically constituted creation of family among working-class women that goes beyond **consanguinity**, or relation by blood, and beyond the choice of hetero- or homosexual family making. Wekker's reflexive discussion of her relationship with one of her informants, Mis' Juliette, also marks an important moment in queer feminist ethnography when, as Wekker writes, "It behooves us who do (cross-cultural) sex research to be transparent, accountable, and reflective about our own sexualities."[53] In the twenty-first century, there has been a proliferation of interdisciplinary scholarship on sexuality both within and outside North America. Here we underscore an example of the interrogation of Black queer experiences. As Shaka McGlotten and Dána-Ain emphasize in their edited collection *Black Genders & Sexualities*,[54] too often the Black body is a site of pathology, difference, and hypersexualization. Yet a central goal of many collections and ethnographies is to move the conversation about Black genders and sexualities beyond merely normative heterosexualities toward critical approaches to activism and performativity within the field of Black queer studies. African American Studies scholar Marlon M. Bailey's *Butch Queens Up in Pumps: Gender, Performance, and Ballroom Culture in Detroit* provides a combination of ethnography and memoir chronicling how over three decades of ballroom culture have provided a space of resistance for many Black gay men, a space where people who are marginalized build alternative communities.[55]

🏵 SPOTLIGHT 🏵

C. Riley Snorton on Feminist Anthropology and Trans Studies

C. Riley Snorton *received his PhD from the University of Pennsylvania Annenberg School for Communication with graduate certificates in Africana studies and women, gender, and sexuality studies and is a professor of English Language and Literature at the University of Chicago. He is the author of* Nobody Is Supposed to Know: Black Sexuality on the Down Low *(University of Minnesota Press, 2014) and* Black on Both Sides: A Racial History of Trans Identity *(University of Minnesota Press, 2017), winner of the Lambda Literary Award for Transgender Nonfiction and an American Library Association Stonewall Honor Book in Nonfiction.*

One might chart the relationships between and among feminist anthropology and trans studies in terms of bibliography or perhaps by tracing their geneaologies, or even still by attending to interanimating questions or overlapping methods. This approach gets us closer to thinking about the enduring legacies of feminist anthropology for trans studies in a consideration of how feminist anthropology thinks transly.

Analytically, feminist anthropology (and trans studies) critically reflects on the locations from which to articulate political worlding. This is an impulse and a gesture—that is, it is both a force and an articulation of the importance of situating the political stakes of a figure, event or idea in relation to the world. . . . One might find evidence of this in Zora Neale Hurston's reflections on language and drama . . . and it extends to contemporary studies of shapeshifting and cultural politics. . . . A key animating impulse in feminist anthropology that subtends trans scholarship and politics is its theorization of language and performance—of life, and how we've come to know it—in relation to necessity.

It is also important to note the influence of queer theory on spaces beyond solely or ostensibly LGBTQI+ communities. Anthropologist Margot Weiss's *Techniques of Pleasure: BDSM and the Circuits of Sexuality* explores San Francisco Bay Area's pansexual BDSM community (which included mostly heterosexual men and bisexual, lesbian, and heterosexual women, including two transwomen).[56] Weiss argues against the notion that BDSM is inherently transgressive. Rather, she highlights how economic shifts contribute to the development of commodity-oriented sexual communities, predicated on the eroticization of gendered, racialized, and national inequalities. Understanding sexuality as a circuit, she connects sexual desire and pleasure to the reproduction of raced and gendered social norms. Weiss's work offers an important intervention in the possibilities for the incorporation of queer theory into feminist ethnography.[57]

A final important thread in this discussion has to do with how masculinity has been mapped onto feminist thinking and ethnographic production over the past few decades. Anthropologist Matthew Guttman's *Meanings of Macho: Being a Man in Mexico City*,[58] for instance, pluralizes the meaning of Mexican masculinity thereby challenging the stereotypical legacy of machismo. Sociologist C. J. Pascoe's *Dude, You're a Fag: Masculinity and Sexuality in High School* addresses youth sexuality and masculine identities, including female masculinity.[59] Medical anthropologist Marcia Inhorn's work since the 1990s, and most recently in *The New Arab Man: Emergent Masculinities, Technologies, and Islam in the Middle East*, has addressed masculinity in the context of new reproductive technologies and infertility.[60] Another recent example is an article by Osmunco Pinho, "Ethnographies of the Brau: Body Masculinity and Race in the Reafricanization in Salvador,"[61] which explores masculinity as it is racially constructed. Outside of anthropology we can look to geographer Rashad Shabazz, who works on masculinity and spatiality. In particular, he examines categories of race, gender, and class and how they are mapped, considering how power is located spatially and what forms it takes. Shabazz's work is articulated within a feminist framework, as he enters into his "discussion of masculinity through the prism of Black feminism."[62] His historical ethnography charts the "architecture of black masculinity," through maps, memoirs, and historical documents, as well as analyzing contemporary texts and spatial relationships.

One of the things we wish to underscore in this text is that regardless of the gender identity of the ethnographer or whether their topic centers on analyses of women or gender, it is the feminist sensibility—the commitment to attending to previous feminist scholarship, and both respond to and integrate the complexities of feminist intellectual influences—that produces feminist ethnographic inquiry.

In our interview with anthropologist Lee Baker, whose work focuses primarily on the history of anthropology, he discusses the importance of the feminist perspective and avoiding tokenism.

SPOTLIGHT

Lee Baker on Feminist Histories

Lee Baker *received his PhD in anthropology from Temple University and currently serves as Dean of Academic Affairs and Associate Vice Provost of Undergraduate Education at Duke University. He is the author of* From Savage to Negro: Anthropology and the Construction of Race, 1896–1954 *(1998),* Life in America: Identity and Everyday Experience *(2003), and* Anthropology and the Racial Politics of Culture *(2010). Although Baker's work has focused on the history of anthropology, not feminist ethnography per se, we were struck by the significant influence of feminist ethnography on his writing, no matter what the subject. Baker began his interview by recounting the tremendous influence of feminist and womanist ethnographers on his work, although he recognized that his position as a Black male historian of anthropology meant that he had to take feminist and womanist approaches to his work very deliberately.*

My work is informed politically by a particular subject position, a perspective even, and I try to embrace that. What's a little different for me is that I don't have a community. It's just dead white guys who I do research on . . . For me, then, I think about my readers, that's my community, and I want to make sure that students who are reading the history of Anthropology understand that it was not just a bunch of dead white guys, but that there were plenty of women and underrepresented folks. Lots of people contributed and moved the discipline forward in important ways. That's why my more recent work on Margaret Mead is important because Margaret Mead played a huge role in the fight against racism. While you can be critical of Margaret Mead, especially her crusade of population control that leaned toward eugenics, what she did with regard to bringing the American Association for the Advancement of Science together with the American Anthropological Association was very significant. She was pivotal in the way she organized the scientific societies to figure out that there was no difference between the races, which was an important support for Civil Rights leaders. . . . There were a lot of scientists that were trying to say that IQs were different for different races, that they are really different species, and so that "race science" got recycled again in the mid-1960s, right in the middle of the Civil Rights Movement. But it was Margaret Mead, as a woman, who organized with all the men.

My feminist perspective is committing to really hunting down and uncovering herstory, the history when women had a big impact, but . . . don't have a large footprint in the historical record. I think you have to work harder, at least for me, when you're doing historical work. You have to dig deeper, because if you just research the usual suspects and the stuff that's been written before, you are going to just reproduce a sexist, heteronormative history.

It is particularly important though to avoid tokenism. . . . It's not like "Oh I found a couple of women, and throw them in there" . . . but you dig a little deeper and go into sources that are not the more traditional ones and start making connections. . . . It takes a lot of work to tell history from an empowering perspective.

Conclusion

Clearly, although feminist ethnography began as a project by, for, and about women, it has transitioned into broader explorations of gender and sexuality through a feminist lens. The theoretical sophistication evidenced in the historical trajectory of feminist ethnography elucidates important connections to intersectional, critical race, and queer scholarship. For us, the importance of writing this chapter was to uncover some of the complex, and often hidden, histories of those who contributed to feminist ethnography. We can look back to critique this canon, but also to make meaning of the contemporary articulations of the field. This history is not finite, but it is a beginning. We offer you our set of **interlocutors**, those who shaped our thinking about feminist ethnography, as a starting point from which to engage as you begin to grapple with contemporary feminist ethnography.

THINKING THROUGH . . .

Critiques and Reviews of an Ethnography

Whenever a scholar publishes their work, they open themselves to critique. This often serves as an elaboration of key issues in their discipline (or the disciplines of those reviewing their work). We have mentioned many ethnographies in this chapter, but did not have the space to discuss them in depth. Read one of these ethnographies—preferably on a topic or time period of particular interest to you. Make note of the theoretical, methodological, and/ or ethical issues that the ethnographer emphasizes. Then find at least three book reviews written about the ethnography. What critiques do they level? Do they engage in debate on topics in the book? Are they in agreement, or do you see differences of opinion across the reviewers?

Suggested Resources

Evelyn Blackwood and Saskia Wieringa, eds. (1999) *Same-Sex Relations and Female Desires: Transgender Practices Across Cultures.*

Michaela di Leonardo, ed. (1991) *Gender at the Crossroads of Knowledge: Feminist Anthropology in the Postmodern Era.*

The Latina Feminist Group (2001) *Telling to Live: Latina Feminist Testimonios* (especially chapters by Patricia Zavella, Iris López, and Ruth Behar).

Ellen Lewin (2006) *Feminist Anthropology: A Reader.*

Henrietta Moore (1989) *Feminism and Anthropology.*

Notes

1 Kamala Visweswaran, "Histories of Feminist Ethnography," *Annual Review of Anthropology*, 1997, 594.

2 There were also many individuals who moved across gender boundaries, such as Herculine Barbin, an intersex French individual who was designated female at birth but later considered male after an affair with a woman and physical examination; George Sand, who was born Armandine Aurore Lucille Dupine; and many others who have gone unacknowledged.

3 Zuni is a significant site in the development of professional anthropology and the location of field-work for Franz Boas's and other prominent anthropologists' students, such as Ruth Benedict and Elsie Clews Parsons.

4 Nancy O. Lurie, "Women in Early American Anthropology," in *Pioneers of American Anthropology*, ed. June Helm, 1966.

5 Nancy J. Parezo, "Matilda Coxe Stevenson: Pioneer Ethnologist," in *Hidden Scholars*, ed. Nancy J. Parezo, 1999.

6 Desley Deacon, *Elsie Clews Parsons*, 1997, xii.

7 Elsie Clews Parsons, *The Journal of a Feminist*, 1994.

8 Many consider Franz Boas the "Father of American Anthropology."

9 Antoinette T. Jackson, "Daisy M. Bates: Ethnographic Work among the Australian Aborigines." Unpublished Paper, 1998.

10 A. R. Radcliffe-Brown, "The Social Organization of Australian Tribes," *Oceania*, 1930, 46.

11 Daisy Bates (edited by Peter J. Bridge), *My Natives and I*, 2004.

12 As a student at Columbia Uniersity's school of law, Paul Robeson supported himself by playing professional footbal on the weekends. His career began as a lawyer, but racism intervened and, with the support of his wife, Eslanda, pushed him to the stage. He is most well known for his roles in *The Emperor Jones* by Eugene O'Neill and *Show Boat*, during which he sang "Ol' Man River," his signature song. His political passions included antiracism, anti-imperialism, and communism.

13 Barbara Ransby, *Eslanda: The Large and Unconventional Life of Mrs. Paul Robeson*, 2013.

14 Kamala Visweswaran, "Histories of Feminist Ethnography," *Annual Review of Anthropology*, 1997, 602.

15 Ruth Murray Underhill, *Papago Woman*, 1985 [orig. 1936].

16 Phyllis Mary Kaberry, *Aboriginal Woman*, 2004 [orig. 1939]. See also Christine Cheater, "Kaberry, Phyllis Mary (1910–1977)," in *Australian Dictionary of Biography*. Accessed October 4, 2015. http://adb.anu.edu.au/biography/kaberry-phyllis-mary-10654.

17 Zora Neale Hurston, *Their Eyes Were Watching God*, 2013 [orig. 1937], 3; *Mules and Men*, 1978 [orig. 1935].

18 Graciela Hernández, "Multiple Mediations in Zora Neale Hurston's *Mules and Men*," *Critique of Anthropology*, 1993.

19 Ella Cara Deloria, *Waterlily*, Reprint edition, 1988.

20 Louise Lamphere, "Anthropologists Are Talking about Feminist Anthropology," *Ethnos*, 2007.

21 Ibid., 415.

22 Louise Lamphere, "Feminist Anthropology Engages Social Movements: Theory, Ethnography and Activism," in *Mapping Feminist Anthropology in the Twenty-First Century*, edited by Ellen Lewin and Leni M. Silverstein, 2016.

23 Toni Morrison, *The Bluest Eye*, 1999 [orig. 1970] and *Song of Solomon*, 2014 [orig. 1977]; Maxine Hong Kingston, *The Woman Warrior: Memoirs of a Girlhood among Ghosts*, 2010 [orig. 1976]; Alice Walker, *Meridian*, 2011 [orig. 1976].

24 Karen Su, "Translating Mother Tongues: Amy Tan and Maxine Hong Kingston on Ethnographic Authority," *Feminist Fields*, 1999, 34.

25 Rebecca Aenerud, "Thinking Again: *This Bridge Called My Back* and the Challenge to Whiteness," in *This Bridge We Call Home*, eds., AnaLouise Keating and Gloria E. Anzaldúa, 2002, 71.

26 Chandra Talpade Mohanty, Ann Russo, and Lourdes Torres, eds., *Third World Women and the Politics of Feminism*, 1991.

27 Barbara J. Love, ed., *Feminists Who Changed America, 1963–1975*, 2006.

28 Maria Patricia Fernández-Kelley, *For We Are Sold, I and My People*, 1984.

29 June Nash, *We Eat the Mines and the Mines Eat Us*, 1979.

30 Susan Bourque and Kay Warren, *Women of the Andes*, 1981.

31 "Exhibit—The Lamphere Case: The Sex Discrimination Lawsuit That Changed Brown | Pembroke Center for Teaching and Research on Women." Accessed June 4, 2021. https://www.brown.edu

/research/pembroke-center/archives/christine-dunlap-farnham-archives/louise-lamphere-v-brown
-university/exhibit-lamphere-case.

[32] Tami Navarro, Bianca Williams, and Attiya Ahmad, "Sitting at the Kitchen Table: Fieldnotes from Women of Color in Anthropology," in *Cultural Anthropology*, 2013.

[33] Ibid., 443–44.

[34] There are different genealogies of intersectionality. Legal scholar Kimberlé Crenshaw coined the term intersectionality in her widely read 1991 article "Mapping the Margins: Intersectionality, Identity Politics and Violence Against Women of Color." She later gave a TED Talk, "The Urgency of Intersectionality," that encouraged continued efforts to bear witness to and speak out against prejudice. Scholars in several different disciplines have explored the histories and debates surrounding intersectionality, including sociologists Patricia Hill Collins and Sirma Bilge's *Intersectionality*, 2016, political scientist Ange-Marie Hancock's *Intersectionality: An Intersectional History*, 2016, and Jennifer C. Nash's *Black Feminism Reimagined: After Intersectionality*, 2019.

[35] Bonnie Thornton Dill and Maxine Baca Zinn, *Women of Color in U.S. Society*, 1994, 3.

[36] Ibid.

[37] Patricia Zavella, *Women's Work and Chicano Families*, 1987.

[38] Aidá Hurtado, *The Color of Privilege*, 1997.

[39] Leith Mullings, *On Our Own Terms*, 1997; Yen Le Espiritu, *Asian American Panethnicity*, 1993.

[40] Aihwa Ong, *Spirits of Resistance and Capitalist Discipline*, 1987.

[41] Anna Lowenhaupt Tsing, *In the Realm of the Diamond Queen*, 1993.

[42] Carla Freeman, *High Tech and High Heels in the Global Economy*, 2000.

[43] Florence Babb, *After Revolution*, 2001.

[44] Esther Newton, *Mother Camp*, 1972.

[45] Deborah Goleman Wolf, *Lesbian Community*, 1979; Gilbert Herdt, *Guardians of the Flutes*, 1981.

[46] Evelyn Blackwood, *The Many Faces Of Homosexuality*, 1986.

[47] Kath Weston, *Families We Choose*, 1991.

[48] Ellen Lewin and William L. Leap, eds., *Out in the Field*, 1996. See also their subsequent volumes: *Out in Theory*, 2002, and *Out in Public*, 2009.

[49] Ellen Lewin, *Lesbian Mothers*, 1993; and Ellen Lewin, ed., *Inventing Lesbian Cultures in America*, 1996.

[50] Evelyn Blackwood, "Tombois in West Sumatra: Constructing Masculinity and Erotic Desire," in *Cultural Anthropology*, 1998; and later, Evelyn Blackwood, *Falling Into the Lesbi World: Desire and Difference in Indonesia*, 2010.

[51] Erica Lorraine Williams, *Sex Tourism in Bahia*, 2013.

[52] Gloria Wekker, *The Politics of Passion*, 2006.

[53] Ibid., 134.

[54] Shaka McGlotten and Dána-Ain Davis, *Black Genders & Sexualities*, 2012.

[55] Marlon M. Bailey, *Butch Queens Up in Pumps*, 2013.

[56] Margot Weiss, *Techniques of Pleasure*, 2011.

[57] It would be impossible to name all of the innovative queer feminist ethnographies that have emerged over the past two decades—for some of the highlights, see the Association of Queer Anthropologist's (AQA) Ruth Benedict Prize winners (http://queeranthro.org/awards/), the proceedings of the Yale University Queer Anthropologies conference in 2015 (http://lgbts.yale.edu/event/conference-queering-anthropology), the proceedings of the "Queer Kinships and Relationships" Conference organized by the Institute of Psychology, Polish Academy of Sciences, in Zalesie Mazury, Poland (http://queerkinship.systemcoffee.pl), and the special issue of *lambda nordica*, a journal of LGBTQ Studies in Sweden on Queer Kinship and Reproduction (Ulrika Dahl and Jenny Gunnarsonn Payne, eds., "Special Issue: Kinship & Reproduction," *lambda nordica*, 2014).

[58] Matthew Guttman, *The Meaning of Macho*, 1996.

[59] C. J. Pascoe, *Dude, You're a Fag*, 2011.

[60] Marcia C. Inhorn, *The New Arab Man*, 2012.

[61] Osmundo Pinho, "Ethnographies of the Brau: Body, Masculinity and Race in the Reafricanizatin in Salvador," *Estudos Feministas*, 2006.

[62] Rashad Shabazz, *Spatializing Blackness*, 2015.

CHAPTER 3

Debates and Interventions in Feminist Ethnography

In this chapter, you will examine debates in feminist ethnography from the 1980s through the present by considering the following questions:

- Who should be claimed as a feminist ethnographer?
- Can there be a feminist ethnography?
- How have feminist ethnographers approached the insider/outsider dilemma?
- What is the role of citational politics in feminist ethnography?
- Can an ethnographer's personal experience be a part of a study?
- How involved or engaged should a feminist ethnographer be?

Spotlights *in this chapter:*

- Shannon Speed on Fieldwork and Identity
- Christen A. Smith on Citing Black Women
- Laura Mauldin on the Impact of Life Experiences
- Brenna McCaffrey on the Political Stakes of Feminist Ethnography
- Mary L. Gray on the Labor of Feminist Ethnography

Essentials *in this chapter:*

- Linda Tuhiwai Smith, *Decolonizing Methodologies*
- Judith Stacey, "Can There Be a Feminist Ethnography?"
- Nancy A. Naples, *Feminism and Method*
- Patricia Zavella, "Feminist Insider Dilemmas"
- Sara Ahmed, *feministkilljoys*, "Making Feminist Points"

*You will also be **Thinking Through . . .***

- An Intellectual Genealogy
- What Would a Feminist Ethnographer Do?

The histories of feminist ethnography have included several debates and interventions. In this chapter we present, in roughly chronological order, issues as they have influenced research and production in the field of feminist ethnography. Beginning with the emergence of feminist ethnography as a field in the 1970s, scholars have questioned whose voices should be claimed from the historical canon. In the 1980s feminist ethnographers queried, in the context of concern about power inequities in feminist ethnography (and feminist research more generally):

Can there even be a feminist ethnography? Feminist ethnographers became active in debates about what Patricia Zavella in the 1990s called the insider/outsider dilemma. Another significant concern in the 1990s was citational politics—that is, whose work is being cited more or less often than others. Yet citational inequities continue into the twenty-first century. Finally, debates over activist scholarship have emerged in many fields over the past few decades, and feminist ethnographers have been instrumental in these discussions.

Who Should Be Claimed as a Feminist Ethnographer?

Early in the feminist ethnographic enterprise, as we noted in the last chapter, the cadre of feminist ethnographers that emerged in the 1980s and 1990s struggled to "reclaim" earlier female researchers who had inspired the development of this field, but may not have identified their work as "feminist." Generally, women scholars of the early and mid-1900s did not use the word feminist in the titles of their work, although their work contributed to feminist goals and some participated in feminist movements. Conceptually, women's scholarship, especially in anthropology, was organized around traditional subjects such as family, politics, religion, and subsistence. However, those traditional anthropological inquiries, when viewed through the lens of women's roles represented a deliberate departure from earlier studies focused on men. We also see evidence of a convergence of gender politics and scholarship in what anthropologist Micaela di Leonardo has called the "bibles" of feminist anthropology: Michelle Rosaldo and Louise Lamphere's edited collection *Woman, Culture, and Society* and Rayna (Rapp) Reiter's *Toward an Anthropology of Women*.[1] These texts formed the underpinnings of Second Wave feminist anthropology, and in both, the authors of the various chapters theorize and analyze women's lives. Yet it took nearly fifteen years after the publication of both collections for the Association for Feminist Anthropology to be established in 1988.

Feminist ethnography came into existence in the context of struggle and it was not an easy road. In order to contextualize this history, we first want to take into account cross-cultural examples of the types of challenges faced in gender-based research. For example, in areas such as Southern Africa, particularly Namibia—where Dána-Ain worked with Richard Lee, Ida Susser, and Karen Brodkin—research on gender is often commissioned by **donor agencies** or governments. What this meant at the time was that gender-based research was guided by funders' interests, a situation that can compromise an ethnographer's research agenda. Additionally, feminist ideology, theory, and practice have developed differentially. In other words, feminist ethnography did not necessarily correspond to the timeline of the emergence of feminism in the West. For example, as discussed in chapter 1, if one uses suffrage as a marker for the emergence of feminist thinking and organizing and thus writing, the development of feminist ethnography was (and remains) uneven in light of this differential political positioning. Finally, although not limited to women in the global South, but certainly important there, while women may be involved in political organizing, they may not necessarily consider themselves feminists. For example, consider the Committees of the Mothers of the Disappeared across Latin America in the 1970s. During this time, right-wing military and paramilitary dictatorships, which governed much of Latin America, used tactics such as "forced disappearances" of people who opposed their regimes. As this issue surfaced as a global concern, many Latin American women were at the forefront of the movement against state-sanctioned violence, highlighting their roles as mothers, wives, sisters, grandmothers, daughters, and aunts of disappeared men, but not necessarily counting themselves as feminists. Consequently, we must recognize that some scholars have strategically avoided the term "feminist," viewing it as a Western imperialist and elitist term. Yet other scholars, including an advocate for Indigenous feminist research Linda Tuhiwai Smith, have directly challenged Western feminist attitudes toward "the Other" and proposed alternative forms of feminist knowledge gathering.

🧠 ESSENTIAL

Excerpt from *Decolonizing Methodologies: Research and Indigenous Peoples* by Linda Tuhiwai Smith

Photo Credit: University of Waikato.

Linda Tuhiwai Smith *is a professor at Te Whare Wānanga o Awanuiārangi in New Zealand. She is the author of* Decolonizing Methodologies: Research and Indigenous Peoples, *which is now in its third edition. She has been recognized internationally for her work on Indigenous research and Kaupapa Māori. Below is an excerpt from the introduction of* Decolonizing Methodologies, *and Smith discusses the fifteen-year anniversary of her book in a YouTube video,* "Decolonizing Knowledge," *offered as a suggested resource at the end of this chapter.*

From the vantage point of the colonized, a position from which I write, and choose to privilege, the term, "research" is inextricably linked to European imperialism and colonialism. The word itself, "research," is probably one of the dirtiest words in the indigenous world's vocabulary. When mentioned in many indigenous contexts, it stirs up silence, it conjures up bad memories, it raises a smile that is knowing and distrustful. It is so powerful that indigenous people even write poetry about research. The way in which scientific research is implicated in the worst excesses of colonialism remains a powerful remembered history for many of the world's colonized peoples. It is a history that still offends the deepest sense of our humanity. Just knowing that someone measured our "faculties" by filling the skulls of our ancestor with millet seeds and compared the amount of millet seed to the capacity for mental thought offends our sense of who and what we are. It galls us that Western researchers and intellectuals can assume to know all that is possible to know of us, on the basis of their brief encounters with some of us. It appalls us that the West can desire, extract and claim ownership of our ways of knowing, our imagery, the things we create and produce, and then simultaneously reject the people who created and developed those ideas and seek to deny them further opportunities to be creators of their own culture and own nations. It angers us when practices linked to the last century, and the centuries before that, are still employed to deny the validity of indigenous peoples' claim to existence, to land and territories to the right of self-determination, to the survival of our languages and forms of cultural knowledge, to our natural resources and systems of living within our environments.

> This collective memory of imperialism has been perpetuated through the ways in which knowledge about indigenous peoples was collected, classified and then represented in various ways back to the West, and then, through the eyes of the West, back to those who have been colonized.
>
> *Source*: Smith, Linda Tuhiwai. *Decolonizing Methodologies: Research and Indigenous Peoples* (Second Edition). London: Zed Books, 2012 (orig. 1999), 1.

Smith proposes explicitly Indigenous research projects, such as Claiming, Testimonies (which she links to *testimonios*, the Latin American tradition of narratives of collective memory), Intervening, (Critical) Reading, Writing and Theory Making, Gendering, Envisioning, Networking, and Sharing Knowledge among Indigenous people from throughout the world.[2] Smith also highlights New Zealand Māori scholar and lesbian activist Ngahuia Te Awekotuku's set of ethical responsibilities that researchers have to Māori people, based on the code of conduct for the New Zealand Association of Social Anthropologists, which in turn is based on the American Anthropological Association's Code of Ethics.

1. *Aroha kit te tangata* (a respect for people).
2. *Kanohi kitea* (the seen face; that is, present yourself to people face to face).
3. *Titiro, whakarongo . . .* (look, listen . . . speak).
4. *Manaaki kit te tangata* (share and host people, be generous).
5. *Kia tupato* (be cautious).
6. *Kaua e takahia te mana o te tangata* (do not trample over the *mana* of people).
7. *Kia mahaki* (don't flaunt your knowledge).[3]

We began this section by asking who should be claimed as feminist. But maybe the question is not who should be considered a feminist, but rather who and what has contributed to feminist knowledge production and in what ways? Reframing the question this way suggests that feminist knowledge production can rely on contributions by people who do not necessarily claim or are able to claim being feminists. Nor does making the claim have to be linked to individual feminist declarations. Like the example of the Māori Code of Ethics above, which embodies a set of principles, the same may be said for other principles and theories such as critical race, disability, and queer studies.

Can There Be a Feminist Ethnography?

A central question raised in the 1980s by sociologist Judith Stacey and anthropologist Lila Abu-Lughod is whether there can even be such a thing as a feminist ethnography.[4] It may well be accurate that the relationship between feminism and ethnography can be "awkward," as anthropologist Marilyn Strathern has emphasized.[5] Strathern questions whether feminist research is capable of transforming anthropology. Some contemporary scholars would agree with anthropologist Kamala Visweswaran that ethnography is not inherently feminist, in the sense that it could avoid all inequity between researcher and participant.[6] But, like many other contemporary feminist ethnographers, we believe ethnographic research is not a project that feminists should give up. For instance, feminist ethnography has charted new terrain on the challenges of power dynamics within fieldwork. This impels us (and others) not to abandon our work, but to approach it with heightened care and awareness.

Stacey's now-classic article "Can There Be a Feminist Ethnography?" raised questions about feminist ideals of equity in the research encounter at a vital point in the development of feminist principles for research and ethnography. Stacey challenged the notion that feminist ethnography was somehow egalitarian—that there could be fewer, if any, power distinctions between the researcher and her informant because of women's shared identity *as women*. As Stacey saw it, feminist ethnography is faced with several problems: that of interventions, the inherently unequal relationship with informants, and feminist reporting quandaries.[7] One of Stacey's arguments was that contradictions exist between feminist principles and feminist ethnography. Although one goal of feminist ethnography is to produce nonhierarchical, collaborative research, the data a feminist ethnographer collects can compromise a participant's integrity.

Stacey argued that the feminist ethnographic process places subjects in a position of exploitation because the lives, loves, and tragedies they share with a researcher are "ultimately data, grist for the ethnographic mill, a mill that has a truly grinding power."[8] Her point was that despite the equitable intentions of feminist ethnography, there are numerous fieldwork experiences that generate a conflict of interest and emotion between the ethnographer and the participant because of *the things that we cannot tell*. To illustrate, Stacey describes a situation in which she cultivated a close relationship with two women who were key informants. The first of the two women shared very personal information about the second: although the second woman was married and a fundamentalist Christian, at the time of her conversion just prior to being married, she was in a closeted lesbian relationship with the first. The awkward situation for Stacey was twofold. First, there was the potential betrayal to both women if she shared the "intimate" information publicly in her book. Second, the conundrum raised the possibility of being inauthentic as a researcher if Stacey did not.

🧠 ESSENTIAL

Excerpt from "Can There Be a Feminist Ethnography?" by Judith Stacey

Judith Stacey *received her PhD in sociology from Brandeis University and is an emeritus professor of New York University's Department of Social and Cultural Analysis. In addition to her classic article on feminist ethnography, excerpted here, Stacey is the author of* Brave New Families: Stories of Domestic Upheaval in Late-Twentieth-Century America *(1990) and* Unhitched: Love, Marriage and Family Values from West Hollywood to Western China *(2011).*

Although there is no uniform canon of feminist research principles, and many lively debates about whether there should be, and, if so, what one should contain, still it is possible to characterize a dominant conception of feminist research currently prevailing among feminist scholars. Most view feminist research as primarily research on, by, and especially for women and draw sharp distinctions between the goals and methods of mainstream and feminist scholarship. Feminist scholars evince widespread disenchantment with the dualisms, abstractions, and detachment of positivism, rejecting the separations between subject and object, thought and feeling, knower and known, and political and personal as well as their reflections in the arbitrary boundaries of traditional academic disciplines. Instead most feminist scholars advocate an integrative, trans-disciplinary approach to knowledge which grounds theory contextually in the concrete realm of women's everyday lives. . . .

Ethnography emphasizes the experiential. Its approach to knowledge is contextual and interpersonal, attentive like most women, therefore, to the concrete realm of everyday reality and human agency. Moreover, because in ethnographic studies the researcher herself is the primary medium, the "instrument" of research, this method draws on those resources of empathy, connection, and concern that many feminists consider to be women's special strengths and which they argue should be germinal in feminist research. Ethnographic method also appears to provide much greater respect for and power to one's research "subjects" who, some feminists propose, can and should become full collaborators in feminist research. . . .

[Yet] precisely because ethnographic research depends upon human relationships, engagement, and attachment it places research subjects at a grave risk for manipulation and betrayal by the ethnographer. . . . [Additionally,] ethnographic method appears to (and often does) place the researcher and her informants in a collaborative, reciprocal quest for understanding, but the research product is ultimately that of the researcher, however modified or influenced by informants. With very rare exceptions it is the researcher who narrates, who "authors" the ethnography. In the last instance an ethnography is a written document structured primarily by a researcher's purposes, offering a researcher's interpretations, registered in a researcher's voice. Here too, therefore, elements of inequality, exploitation, and even betrayal are endemic to ethnography. Perhaps even more than ethnographic process, the published ethnography represents an intervention into the lives and relationships of its subjects.

Source: Stacey, Judith. "Can There Be a Feminist Ethnography?" *Women's Studies International Forum* 11, no. 1 (1988): 21–24.

Stacey advocates that ethnographers remain humble about the limitations of their work and that "partially feminist" projects are important when the benefits outweigh the drawbacks. Performance scholar E. Patrick Johnson adopts this notion of a "partially feminist" project in his ethnography *Black. Queer. Southern. Women.: An Oral History*.[9] As a male ethnographer, he emphasized the importance of expressing vulnerability with the women he engaged with through the collection of oral histories. He was also mindful of what performance ethnographer Dwight Conquergood called the "skeptic's cop-out"—the refuge of cowards and cynics—a position that forecloses dialogue completely by claiming that differences are too great to understand.[10] Rather, Johnson felt compelled not only to initiate a dialogue with interlocutors whose experiences differed from his own but also to "create a living archive of black women's sexual history in the South," a topic that has received little attention in academia.[11]

Nearly twenty years after Stacey's germinal article, Dána-Ain revisited Stacey's questions in "Border Crossing: Intimacy and Feminist Activist Ethnography in the Age of Neoliberalism."[12] The motivation for reengaging with the self-revelatory narrations that women shared with her during oral and life history interviews was to explore how those self-disclosures could be understood in terms of power, as articulated by Stacey, and within the context of **neoliberalism**. The question became, what insights did feminist ethnography generate about the relationship between intimacy (or self-disclosure) and neoliberalism? In revisiting her research, she realized that Black women who were battered and needed public assistance had expectations of her. Dána-Ain faced having to decide whether to reciprocate after women shared their desperate needs and some very personal details about their lives. Whereas one of Stacey's concerns was that there was an unequal relationship between researcher and informant because of our power to use women's stories as we saw fit, Dána-Ain dealt with women mobilizing their stories to get something from her to mitigate their experiences of scarce resources. And while Stacey was concerned about what not to say for fear of betraying women's "secrets," the women Dána-Ain interviewed were more likely to *want* her to share their stories with people in powerful positions, who they believed might be able to facilitate helping the women access housing and services they required. Women's interests in having their lives narrated by the researcher to people they presumed had power differed across race. No white woman requested that Dána-Ain share her experiences with others, because access to resources was differently situated across race, ethnicity, and citizenship status.

Writing during the same period as Stacey, Lila Abu-Lughod's article—also titled "Can There Be a Feminist Ethnography?"—critiqued feminist ethnographers who assume a universal "women's experience" that erases power differentials between the most privileged ethnographer and her research subjects.[13] Abu-Lughod's work was a response to radical feminists, such as Robin Morgan, who argued in the introduction to *Sisterhood Is Global* that a latent global women's culture exists that could be activated by women examining their common experiences with patriarchal oppression.[14] The majority of contemporary feminist ethnographers join Abu-Lughod in rejecting this claim. In *Feminism and Method*, for instance, sociologist Nancy A. Naples frames feminist ethnography as emerging from diverse perspectives, as well as the unique personally, politically, and academically significant experiences of feminist ethnographers.

Following debates over whether there could even be a feminist ethnography, which were largely resolved through increased attention to power differentials in research (albeit with the admission that this would always be imperfect), feminist ethnographers have continued to debate the limitations of some theoretical proclivities guiding ethnographic research and their ensuing outcomes. One such debate has been over the theoretical frameworks of **postmodernism** and **poststructuralism**, which in broad strokes seek to shift away from what is perceived as reductionist generalizations, to analyses that reveal fluidity and **polyvocality**, analyses that could have multiple, contestable meanings. A popular cultural example of polyvocality can be seen in performer Janelle Monáe's album *The Electric Lady*,[15] where Monáe uses her music to showcase a powerful consolidation of **Afrofuturism** and **cyberfeminism**. To get a sense of how she accomplishes exemplifying polyvocality through music/gender/feminism/race/technology, look at the multiple levels of meaning in the videos from her album.

ESSENTIAL

Excerpt from *Feminism and Method* by Nancy A. Naples

Photo Credit: Don Levy.

Nancy A. Naples *received her PhD in sociology from the Graduate Center, City University of New York, and holds degrees in education and social policy. She is a professor of Sociology and Women's, Gender and Sexuality Studies at the University of Connecticut, as well as author of* Grassroots Warriors: Activist Mothering, Community Work, and the War on Poverty *(1998) and* Feminism and Method: Ethnography, Discourse Analysis, and Activist Research *(2003); coeditor of* Women's Activism and Globalization: Linking Local Struggles and Transnational Politics *(2002) and* Border Politics: Social Movements, Collective identities, and Globalization *(2014); and editor of* Companion to Feminist Studies *(2020). She has also served as president of Sociologists for Women in Society (2004) and is the recipient of the Sociologists for Women in Society's 2011 Distinguished Feminist Lecturer award.*

Feminist theoretical perspectives were developed in the context of diverse struggles for social justice inside and outside the academy. In their various formulations, feminist theories emphasize the need to challenge sexism, racism, colonialism, class, and other forms of inequalities in the research process. . . . Like many feminist scholars, I address questions in my research that are simultaneously personally, politically, and academically significant. From my earliest memories I have been concerned with understanding and fighting inequality and injustice. Not surprisingly, my academic work focuses on examining the reproduction of, and resistance to, inequalities in different communities, as well as identifying strategies that foster social and economic justice. My growing sensitivity to the formal and informal ways domination is manifest in different research settings helped me negotiate discrimination, sexual abuse, and the relations of ruling that infuse my own life. In light of my activist goal of challenging inequality in all its complex guises, I was drawn to feminist efforts to conduct research that minimizes exploitation of research subjects.

Source: Naples, Nancy A. *Feminism and Method: Ethnography, Discourse Analysis, and Activist Research*. New York: Routledge, 2003, 13.

One of the main critiques feminist ethnographers have leveled against the "post-" discussions within academia is that they are depoliticized, offering little (if any) analysis of power, race, class, and gender dynamics. A major corrective to that work is Micaela di Leonardo's *Gender at the Crossroads of Knowledge: Feminist Anthropology in the Postmodern Era*.[16] Expanding upon previous work in feminist anthropology that had focused primarily on sociocultural analyses of gender, di Leonardo's volume is grounded in the political economy across all four subfields within anthropology, including archaeology, biological anthropology, and linguistic anthropology. Although authors were influenced by postmodern debates, such as an enhanced attention to reflexivity, they contended that material realities cannot be disconnected from the ways that meaning and knowledge are constructed. Specifically, the collection emphasizes how knowledge production is always political, as well as historically embedded in political, economic, and social processes. Di Leonardo offers one of the most comprehensive discussions of feminist anthropology's history from the 1970s through the 1990s, when feminist texts proliferated.

From the 1980s onward, the increasing engagement with reflexivity and attention to relations of power in the research encounter lead feminist ethnographers to (re)consider their own identities as "insiders," "outsiders," and often both in their fieldwork. The position of the ethnographer vis-à-vis the research participants involves not only their own position in terms of how they perceive themselves but also how participants respond to and perceive them—which can include many different experiences even within a single community or field site.

How Have Feminist Ethnographers Approached the Insider/Outsider Dilemma?

The insider/outsider dilemma concerns the researcher's relationship to those being studied. Specifically, it suggests that an "outsider" might lack strategic knowledge of those under investigation and presumes that the "insider" knows the perspective of the group under study. This debate is concerned with whether being an outsider "guarantees" a more objective view or interpretation of the group or situation under investigation. Is the insider/outsider dichotomy a definitive way to understand the researcher/researched relationship? Does the insider role establish legitimacy for the researcher? Does being familiar with the group make it easier to interview or conduct extended fieldwork with them?

Earlier discussions of this debate were framed as emic versus etic perspectives. An emic perspective is that taken by a researcher who is part of the community being studied, or the perspectives of those within the community. Alternatively, an etic perspective assumes that a researcher is not part of the community being studied. Another question is: To what degree can an ethnographer become immersed in a community given their (assumed) group membership? Another way the insider/outsider debate has been cast is in terms of the problems posed for researchers who straddle both an insider and an outsider role.

Ethnographers have discussed the pros and cons of this issue at length. For instance, being an insider may help the researcher understand the contexts in which people do things because they know the history of the community and the meaning people give to some aspects of life. They are able to explain, describe, and interpret their experiences with a degree of authority. Another benefit may be that the researcher knows participants, and having access to individuals within the community can facilitate the research process. Yet some suggest that knowing "too much" about a community or an individual's circumstances creates bias in the data one collects, and how one interprets it. This last point leans toward the view that being an outsider is advantageous because the researcher is presumed to have more distance and is therefore capable of being more objective. One question to ask, however, is whether it is possible to maintain strict objectivity throughout any research project. And why is objectivity considered an advantage? Most feminist researchers, including feminist ethnographers, would argue that all scholarly inquiry is subjective—in the questions we choose, how we gather data, as well as our positions as we encounter participants in fieldwork.

A further critique of the feminist insider/outsider dilemma is that it sets up a dichotomy related to a researcher's position that is too simplistic, emphasizing that one is either *only* an insider *or* an outsider. This construct suggests there is a degree of absoluteness in sameness or difference. Let us presume that you are a Senegalese ethnographer conducting research among Senegalese factory workers. The insider/outsider construct could ostensibly position you as a person who would be successful in conducting research among Senegalese workers employed in a groundnut/peanut oil factory *because* you are Senegalese. Or the insider/outsider construct could locate you as a person who might be biased in your data collection *because* you are Senegalese. What if more detail was available? For instance, what if you were a university-educated Christian from a Wolof-speaking community and most workers were poor, Muslim Wolofs who had not completed elementary school? The presumed similarity of a Wolof-speaking researcher and participants in your research would obscure the fact that there are differences among Senegalese that can create more research challenges than opportunities.

Anthropologist Patricia Zavella wrote about a similar problem in her now-classic 1993 article, "Feminist Insider Dilemmas: Constructing Ethnic Identity with 'Chicana' Informants."[17] Here, she reflects on research she conducted with cannery workers in California. As a Chicana woman, Zavella initially saw herself as an insider who had participated in the Chicano movement. Being part of the movement meant acknowledging pride in pre-Columbian heritage and celebrating **mestizo** culture, as well as rejecting the influence of Spanish colonizers. But instead of identifying as Chicana, most of her informants identified as Spanish or Spanish American, and Zavella struggled with what she perceived as their self-identification with colonizers in contrast to her own sense of politicized identity.

🧠 ESSENTIAL

Excerpt from "Feminist Insider Dilemmas" by Patricia Zavella

Photo Credit: Lily Pinedo Gongai.

Patricia Zavella *recently retired from the University of California, Santa Cruz, after over three decades of teaching in the Latin American and Latino Studies Department. She is the recipient of Career Achievement Awards from the American Anthropological Association's Committee on Gender Equity in Anthropology, the Society for the Anthropology of North America, and the Association of Latina and Latino Anthropologists. Her latest book is* The Movement for Reproductive Justice: Empowering Women of Color Through Social Activism (2020). *In her 1993 reflection on her first book,* Women's Work and Chicano Families: Cannery Workers of the Santa Clara Valley, *published in 1987, Zavella reflects on how ethnic and political identity became a key issue she grappled with as a Chicana feminist.*

My Chicana feminism itself was an example of "outsider within" status. Framed by larger historical forces and political struggles, identifying myself as a Chicana feminist meant contesting and simultaneously drawing from Chicano nationalist ideology and white feminism—being an insider and outsider within both movements and ideologies. It was only in retrospect, when I came to understand how Mexican American women informants from New Mexico constructed their ethnic identity in very different ways, that I realized I needed to deconstruct and problematize my own sense of Chicana feminism so that I could "see" the nuances of ethnic identity among my informants. . . . In retrospect, my expectations were naive, for the [people I sought out] were predominantly middle-aged, seasonal cannery workers who were being displaced by cannery equipment in the Santa Clara Valley. These women (and men) were acutely conscious of my privileges as an educated woman, and assumed I had resources that as a poverty-stricken graduate student I did not have . . . .

My cannery research experience challenged my Chicana feminist perspective, but more in terms of the gender politics within "the movement," and how class consciousness was framed in daily life. It was only in retrospect that I came to see the importance of ethnic identification with different political strategies. My shortsightedness was in tune with the field at the time.

Source: Zavella, Patricia. "Feminist Insider Dilemmas: Constructing Ethnic Identity with 'Chicana' Informants." *Frontiers: A Journal of Women Studies* 13, no. 3 (1993): 53-76, 56-58, 60.

While hindsight always gives us a broader vision, what Zavella pinpoints in this final remark is that we are *all* products of our own training, and the historical moment within which we come to fieldwork. None of us can avoid using language, ideas, and perspectives that will later seem outdated or naive.

This example makes it clear that shared membership in a group does not automatically mean there is complete sameness within that group. There are also times when a researcher is mistaken by those they encounter for being "one of us" when, in fact, that relationship is contested. As a postdoctoral researcher conducting African feminist ethnography in Angola, Selina Makana found that her Kenyan identity *and* coming to her research from an elite US university created competing misperceptions of her identity. Depending on the circumstance, some Angolans wanted to claim her as "one of us"—either as an Angolan or with shared history as Africans—which others were profoundly surprised that she was not a white researcher or journalist. While initially disheartening for Makana when she felt that it questioned her legitimacy as an African researcher, she ultimately found it a sobering reminder that the way most of the people she encountered had experienced research was with white, Western researchers on short-term visits.

Likewise, not being a member of a group does not denote complete distinct identities. It seems interesting that the poles of this discussion are set in an absolutist way, offering a narrow range of experience and understanding. Anthropologist Kirin Narayan highlights in her widely read article "How Native Is a 'Native' Anthropologist?"[18] that **hybridity**—being both insider and outsider—reveals the challenge of the native/anthropologist dichotomy. When anthropologists return to study their culture of origin, particularly in postcolonial contexts where their communities were colonized, colleagues often problematically position the "native" anthropologist's knowledge as authentically "native." Assuming that the ethnographer is automatically an insider obscures the relations of privilege that they may have as an outsider as well, particularly vis-à-vis their education and/or class status.

Feminist ethnographers, indeed researchers in general, typically recognize the fluidity and complexity of human experience and know that the spaces between the poles of insider and outsider are far more complicated. This is demonstrated in the experiences of ethnographers whose positionality is ambiguous, which also has pros and cons. One researcher, for instance, a communication studies scholar Anastacia Kurylo who studies interpersonally communicated stereotypes says that she is "visually ambiguous." The fact that she could be a member of a variety of ethnic or racial backgrounds means she could be viewed as an insider. However, among some groups she would also be perceived as an outsider. Kurylo thinks that having an ambiguous cultural identity makes people cautious about saying anything they might deem "too offensive" out of fear that they will insult her. She also points out that even ambiguous positionality can be useful, because if people do not identify her as a minority, then they may be less cautious about describing stereotypes.[19]

The experience of feminist geographer Lorena Muñoz in her research on Latina street vendors is also instructive in this debate. During an interview, Muñoz told a participant, Herminia, that she was also "gay" and noticed a profound change in Herminia's demeanor toward her. In fact, Herminia had many questions for Muñoz about how her family responded to her sexuality and whether she had a partner, and she admitted, "*Huy si hubiera sabido esto desde antes, te hubiera invitado a mi casa desde hace mucho* [Well, if I had known that from the beginning, I would have invited you to my house a long time ago]."[20] Ultimately, Muñoz notes that her "queer" feminist identity often conflicted with her identity as a "cross-border Chicana." Her ability to speak Spanish with a "Mexican" accent had initially positioned her as a community member with many of the vendors, although she notes that it took her longer to establish relationships with vendors from Central America. Yet identifying herself as "queer," as someone who usually "embodied [a] straight Chicana immigrant identity" in heteronormative spaces, became not only a potential barrier but also an opening to multiple ways of seeing the lives of the women she studied.[21]

With regard to the conundrums that arise in the insider/outsider debate, Shannon Speed notes that

> a fundamental premise of participant observation—anthropology's primary ethnographic research method—is that viewing a culture from an outside perspective allows one to "see" aspects of its workings that for insiders are naturalized and thus invisible. At the same time, the presumption that prolonged field work and some measure of cultural participation is needed to get inside of a cultural context in order to understand it, is also built into the discipline.

ꙮ SPOTLIGHT ꙮ

Shannon Speed on Fieldwork and Identity

Dr. Shannon Speed *is a tribal citizen of the Chickasaw Nation of Oklahoma. She is Director of the American Indian Studies Center (AISC) and Professor of Gender Studies and Anthropology at UCLA. Her ethnographic work has been primarily in Mexico and in immigration detention facilities in the United States, on topics including Indigenous politics, human rights, neoliberalism, gender, Indigenous migration, and activist research. Speed has published* *seven books and edited volumes, including her most recent award-winning book,* Incarcerated Stories: Indigenous Women Migrants and Violence in the Settler Capitalist State (2019)*, and a volume coedited with Lynn Stephen titled* Heightened States of Injustice: Activist Research on Indigenous Women and Violence. *Speed is the Past President of the Native American and Indigenous Studies Association (NAISA).*

The question of emic and etic, or insider and outsider, perspectives is crucial to the anthropological undertaking of ethnographic research. A fundamental premise of participant-observation—anthropology's primary ethnographic research method—is that viewing a culture from an outside perspective allows one to "see" aspects of its workings that for insiders are naturalized and thus invisible. At the same time, the presumption that prolonged fieldwork and some measure of cultural participation is needed to get inside of a cultural context in order to understand it is also built into the discipline. A variety of critical perspectives have been brought to bear on these premises, perhaps most notably feminist critiques challenging the bipolar nature of the insider/outsider dichotomy and simultaneously occluding and reinscribing the relations of power between researcher and researched.

One important line of this critique has highlighted the fundamental arrogance of presuming that a researcher can or should come from outside to tell the people involved what they are actually doing, rather than what they think/say they are doing (most often a Western, first-world academic deciding the "truth" of what non-Western/non-first-world/less formally educated people are doing). This led to a period of reflection on "home work" by "insider" ethnographers—many of them feminists of color—working with/in their own communities, however defined. Yet home work also generated contradictions and tensions, as researchers confronted their own "outsider-ness" as their university educations altered their positionalities within their communities, and many struggled to rectify theoretical frameworks learned in academia with the lives of their friends and family members as research "subjects." Following on the insights this work provided, feminist ethnographers have been interested in exploring the ways in which one is simultaneously an insider and an outsider, and how different aspects of these relational concepts come to the fore in different moments.

These insights were crucial for me as an Indigenous feminist ethnographer. As a tribal citizen of the Chickasaw Nation, I am a Native American, though tribal belonging in the United States brings its own complex set of insider/outsider issues based on enrollment, residence, language ability, blood quantum, and phenotype, just to name a few. The fact that I grew up in Los Angeles and my Anglo-leaning phenotype have led some to question my right to claim insider status as a Native American. These questions—at least the ones I took seriously—came from a "people of color" perspective which rightly noted that I do not suffer racial bias as a person of color. Due to the history of imposed assimilation and colonization of this country, the fact is that many Native Americans who have legitimate relationships with their tribal nations do not "look Indian," particularly to non-Indians bearing their own unexamined stereotypes about what an Indian looks like. However, at least for the federally recognized tribes (another can of worms), tribal sovereignty dictates that tribal governments have the right to define their membership, not the racial-stereotype bearing general public. That said, while my tribal membership was clear, my field research relationships in Oklahoma were likely to raise significant issues of difference and my perspective could hardly be simply defined as an "insider" one in this regard.

These blurrings of the dichotomous line between insider and outsider became even more muddied when I decided to shift my field research to Chiapas, Mexico, where an important Indigenous uprising was occurring. I was drawn there because, as a Native person, I was interested in Indigenous oppression and Indigenous rights, and because I saw the tremendous shared experience of oppression and resistance of Native peoples that the Zapatista movement embodied. Nevertheless, to arrive in Chiapas and present myself to communities of impoverished Maya as "one of them" or our experience as one of "shared oppression" would have been incongruous. The racial privilege I enjoy based on my phenotype in the United States was amplified in Chiapas, where as a gringa (person from the United States) and a güera (white girl), as well as a university researcher in a context where few Indigenous people have access to a university, I was as alien as anyone else stepping into those communities. The extraordinary levels of poverty, marginalization, and violence that characterize the lives of Indigenous communities of Chiapas are not part of my experience or that of most Chickasaws. I do not wish to underestimate the poverty and violence suffered by Native communities in the United States, which in some cases approximates that of the Mayan communities of Chiapas, but in this case it would have been preposterous for me to assert an insider positionality. Yet my research was inevitably shaped by my own perspective as an Indigenous person and my experience as a Native American in a distinct context. Indeed, my analysis of identity formation, the role of different states and social movements in relation to Indigenous identity, and the ways these played out for Indigenous women, was undoubtedly a product of my own positionality as a Native researcher, though many I worked with never identified me as such.

I venture this brief reflection on my field experience to support the fundamental feminist insight that dichotomies such as insider/outsider, based in the first instance on positivist impulses to codify social reality, simplify to a point of occluding most of what is interesting about a given social situation. As positionalities, insider and outsider are fluid and porous categories and are experienced differently by people at distinct points in time and as they move through different subject locations. Most important, attempts to impose insider/outsider distinctions can do violence to our research subjects by masking the power differentials and experiential differences between the researcher and the researched.

Many of the questions that emerged around insider/outsider concerns during the 1980s coincided with the intervention of **feminist standpoint theories.** Feminist standpoint theorists, such as sociologist Dorothy E. Smith, claim that knowledge is socially situated: the knowledge that one has is affected by where they stand (their subject position) in society.[22] Sociologist Patricia Hill Collins emphasizes that marginalized groups are socially situated in ways that make it more possible for them to be aware of things and ask questions than it is for nonmarginalized groups and that research should be particularly focused on power relations and begin with the lives of marginalized people.[23] Among feminist standpoint theorists, the idea is that particular positions occupied by women and people without societal privileges are a good source of knowledge making because they have different views of a situation. Yet others have argued that understanding the powerful relations and structures which orchestrate one's life is but one way to survive the reality of being dominated or controlled. Standpoint has been an important theoretical position for feminists. However, critics have questioned an "automatic epistemic privilege" such that one's social location is enough to give one an advantage of knowledge. Instead, they argue that the standpoint of subordinated group members is achieved through history, economic status, and through the process of political consciousness.

What becomes clear is that a key aspect of feminist ethnographic inquiry is the interrogation of one's **positionality**—how one is situated in relation to participants in their work. Some feminist ethnographers rely on the position and experience offered by standpoint theory, which can serve as an important epistemological location. A significant aspect of standpoint theory is the role **reflexivity** plays in guiding the critical review of the feminist insider/outsider dilemma. This requires that researchers position themselves in terms of the research being conducted, by identifying who they are, as well as a critical reflection on their relationship to the project or community. As cultural geographer and creative writer Richa Nagar and feminist historian Susan Geiger caution:

> A widespread engagement with reflexive practices by feminist ethnographers has generated rich dialogues about the methodological and epistemological dilemmas endemic to fieldwork, as well as the challenges associated with identity politics as they affect academic, interpersonal, institutional, and intellectual relationships. Such reflexivity, however, has mainly focused on examining the identities of individual researchers rather than on how such identities intersect with the institutional, geopolitical, and material aspects of their positionality. . . . Producing knowledge across social divides in ways that are explicitly committed to a transformative politics necessitates that researchers rethink reflexivity, identity, and positionality, as well as the ends toward which these notions are deployed.[24]

Nagar and Geiger advocate for a "speaking-with approach"—both in fieldwork engagements and in subsequent intellectual and political productions—that grapples with the identities and relationships that are situated, negotiated, and often shifting during ethnographic encounters. This nuanced approach to reflexivity and identity is what we invite feminist ethnographers to engage in in the subsequent chapters.

What Is the Role of Citational Politics in Feminist Ethnography?

A crucial part of conducting any feminist ethnographic project is developing a feminist intellectual genealogy. Who you read and *how* you read that material is a significant part of how one develops, organizes, and embarks upon a project. This background can encourage you first to ask questions informed by a feminist sensibility and perspective, and then to choose research methods that will allow you to collect the information most necessary to answer them. Many of those interviewed for this book acknowledged the important intellectual debts they owe to other feminist scholars, as we have done in the previous chapters. They are also keenly aware of the need to prepare for new projects by reading the work of feminist scholars to think through the subject and to frame their projects.

In his book on race, gender, and revolution, *¡Venceremos? The Erotics of Black Self-making in Cuba*, anthropologist Jafari Allen draws on the influence of Black feminist scholars to address how some Cuban women he interviewed engaged in liberatory actions and organizing but did not necessarily identify as "feminist":

> As Barbara Smith reminds us "Black women were never fools, we could never afford to be" (1998: xxvii). That is, black women's participation, from the abolition and suffrage movements to anti-lynching activism, civil rights efforts, and HIV prevention, for example, has had long and deep engagement in intersectional analysis and action. The same is true for Cuban women, whether or not they used the term "feminist." In "A Black Feminist Statement" the Combahee River Collective, including Smith, connects socialist political activism in transnational communities of black women with the most intimate and personal political areas of everyday life. Moving precipitously beyond the sort of feminism that Espín [a participant in Allen's study] and others eschew, this speaks directly to the current struggles and triumphs of my Cuban respondents and friends.[25]

Allen's work exemplifies how one can draw from a Black feminist vocabulary to analyze a range of gendered experiences. His strategy illustrates that we can connect our participants to those we cite, generating parallel as well as integrative voices, which can be a key facet of feminist scholarship.

Although the issue of citational politics is not restricted to gender, it has been well documented that publications with women authors (whether as sole authors or coauthors) are cited less frequently than those attributed to male authors.[26] Anthropologist Lynn Bolles stresses that African American women's publications are significantly undercited by other scholars, including feminists.[27] It is important to keep in mind that who we cite—and, equally important, who we do *not* cite—shapes our projects in important ways.

As a brief personal aside, Lynn Bolles and her work on citational politics was a crucial reason that Christa entered the field of anthropology. When Christa went to her first American Anthropological Association conference as an undergraduate in 1995, the first panel she attended was a retrospective honoring the twenty-year legacy of the feminist anthropological canons, *Toward an Anthropology of Women* and *Woman, Culture, and Society*. It was there that she heard Bolles deliver a paper in which she strategically cited only women of color to underscore the ways in which their work was so often omitted from the (feminist) anthropological canon. It was an epiphany of sorts when Bolles shifted the focus from critiquing whom we do not cite (though certainly acknowledging the importance of this) to becoming actively engaged with locating diverse scholarship in order to influence our work and knowledge development.

Taking up the issue of citational practice, anthropologist Christen A. Smith launched the Cite Black Women campaign in 2017. Her goal was to ensure that we generate ideas and knowledge in the context not only of our own life experiences, as feminists have long argued, but also in relation to the scholars, activists, and others who influence our work.

SPOTLIGHT / ESSENTIAL*

Christen A. Smith on Citing Black Women

Christen A. Smith *is a Black feminist anthropologist, social justice advocate, founder of Cite Black Women, and Associate Professor of Anthropology and African and African Diaspora Studies at the University of Texas at*

Austin. Her work focuses on the gendered dimensions of anti-Black state violence and resistance in the Americas, particularly Brazil. She is the author of Afro-Paradise: Blackness, Violence and Performance in Brazil *(2016), which uses the lens of performance and performance theory to chronicle Black Brazilians' experiences with police violence in Salvador, Bahia, and the dialectic between this violence and the state's construction of Bahia as an exotic space (afro-paradise).*

*Editors' Note: We designated this textbox as both a Spotlight (interview) and an Essential (excerpt) because our engagement with Christen A. Smith defies traditional scholarly convention. Rather, it embodies how ideas become actions—ones that often have a far greater impact than the originator imagined. We began to talk about highlighting Smith's work on Cite Black Women at a conference in 2017 when we purchased Cite Black Women t-shirts. That conversation evolved into a lively email exchange and we shared a portion of that in the first edition. In May 2021, what began as an "oral history" about why Smith started the Cite Black Women became a part of her introductory remarks as the guest editor of a Special Issue on the Cite Black Women in Feminist Anthropology. *Here is that iteration:*

Photo Credit: Jozzu Freitas.

There has been a total disregard when it comes to recognizing and respecting the intellectual property of Black women. For centuries, people have been content with erasing us from mainstream bibliographies, genealogies of thought, and conversations about knowledge production. The university has exploited Black women's labor, appropriated our ideas, and refused to give us the appropriate credit for our work. In "Telling the Story Straight," Lynn Bolles notes, "If the citation wars have meaning in the modern academy . . . then in both short and long runs African American scholars are/will be faceless and voiceless."[1] Citation as a practice allows us to engage with voices so often silenced or left behind. As Barbara Christian argues, we have "more pressing and interesting things to do, such as reading and studying the history and literature of black women, a history . . . ignored [and] bursting with originality, passion, insight, and beauty."[2] Citing Black women is both feminist and antiracist, pushing back against the hegemony of white male heteronormativity in discourses of knowledge production. Within this context, citing Black women is a project of radical refusal with revolutionary possibilities.

In November 2017, I started Cite Black Women—a global campaign that pushes people to critically rethink the politics of knowledge production by engaging in a radical praxis of citation that acknowledges and honors Black women's transnational intellectual production. The project started on a whim— a simple idea born out of the frustration of having my work appropriated without credit by someone who I thought I could trust. Untenured and isolated, I sought the support of senior colleagues to no avail, and was forced to carry the pain of that experience around silently for years while working toward tenure. Fastforward: I got tenure and tried to put the experience behind me. Then, in 2017, I attended a conference where I saw passages from my book paraphrased without credit on the slides of a conference attendee. This was the straw that finally broke my silence. Incensed, I decided that I could no longer ignore the past. I decided to channel my anger and frustration into positive action. As a first step I made t-shirts that simply said "Cite Black Women" as a fun way to bring awareness and redirected the profits from this endeavor to support a grassroots community school I had been working with in Brazil (a space where I have collaborated and worked for two decades). I wanted to provoke a public conversation about the politics of citation by using the shirts to "interrupt" academic conference spaces. The t-shirts became a symbolic interruption of normal conference proceedings (panels, sessions, common spaces). The simple phrase provoked people to stop and think about the politics of race, gender, and citation and consider their citational practices in a fun, casual, yet public and provocative way. This tactic was one that I had learned from my work with performance artists in Brazil over the years. In the span of weeks, what began as a way to channel frustrated energy became an incredible success. Friends and colleagues, including *Feminist Anthropology* editor Sameena Mulla, encouraged me to expand beyond t-shirts to build an awareness campaign. The awareness campaign began on Twitter and Instagram with the handle @citeblackwomen and the hashtag #CiteBlackWomen. Cite Black Women began to solidify conceptually with the creation of five guiding principles in January 2018, the creation of #CiteBlackWomenSunday, the establishment of the Cite Black Women Collective and the launch of the Cite Black Women Podcast. Since then the collective has engaged the public on and off social media, through numerous conference panels, workshops, and other public engagements, like the 2019 Executive Session at the AAA: "Cite Black Women: Race, Gender, Justice and Citational Politics in Anthropology."

[The May 2021] special issue of *Feminist Anthropology* is the latest of these collective efforts to build a global movement to center Black women's thought. It is evidence that the small and simple idea I had has grown far beyond my nascent dreams of 2017. It is the fruit of the collective labor of Black women–especially the Cite Black Women Collective–and our allies inside and outside of the discipline of anthropology. The academic essays, creative poems and reflections included here present a holistic picture of the potential of the what the Cite Black Women project envisions.

Source: Smith, Christen A. "An Introduction to Cite Black Women." *Feminist Anthropology* 2, no. 1 (2021): 6–9.

[1] Lynn Bolles, "Telling the Story Straight" (2013), 63.

[2] Barbara Christian, "The Race for Theory," *Cultural Critique* (1987), 51.

Although Smith initially sought to influence academics, the Cite Black Women movement quickly expanded on social media platforms and was featured as a "Trending Topic" in the popular Black women's lifestyle magazine, *Essence*.[28]

As Smith articulated during the Cite Black Women conference panel at the American Anthropological Association conference in 2019,[29] her commitment to centering the undercitation of Black women in particular drew inspiration from the Combahee River Collective Statement: "If Black women were free, it would mean that everyone else would have to be free, since our freedom would necessitate the destruction of all systems of oppression." This includes other marginalized populations who have equally been erased from disciplinary canons, like Indigenous and non-white scholars from the global South. An important caveat that Sameena Mulla added during the panel is that in citing Black women—particularly those of us who are not Black ourselves—we must take care to avoid citational tokenism. Merely mentioning several well-known Black female writers does not meet the goals of this project. We must curate our discussion of Black women's scholarship with the same care that we would any other form of citation where we pay respect to scholars who have influenced our work. For non-Black people, it is also vital not to use the practice of citing Black women merely to increase the value of our own work. Engaging in a more equitable citational practice involved lifting up historically marginalized voices, stepping back, and promoting their work to others through our class papers, syllabi, presentations, and myriad other parts of our lives.

To curate a diverse bibliography, we suggest looking for sources not only published by major presses and searchable on Google Scholar:

- Look for publications outside of your discipline (such as Indigenous Knowledge Commons and check with your reference librarian)
- Look for nonacademic sources such as art exhibits, performances, and archives (such as the Herstory Archives)
- Explore fiction and memoir related to your topic
- Look for publications by scholars affiliated with organizations such as the Organization of Oral Historians, the International Union of Anthropological and Ethnological Sciences, Society for Disability Studies, and the Center for Intercultural Dialogue
- Look to your own community of feminist scholars and activists to offer suggestions
- Comb the bibliographies of others doing similar work

Ultimately, the onus is on each of us as feminist scholars and writers to make it *our business* to seek out, and incorporate, innovative research from scholars whose work is often ignored because of structural inequities. While we cannot "do it all" and find every citation that constitutes a politics of diversity, be "promiscuous" with your reading (h/t Margot Weiss). And remember, it is not just about locating the resources; it is about engaging deeply with them.

This allows us to produce the best (feminist) ethnographic work possible. In fact, we don't believe that this should only be a feminist project, but rather all scholars should look for diverse interlocutors as they approach their research. Anthropologist Elizabeth Chin (see *Spotlight* in chapter 5) once half-joked that we should have photos next to the authors' names in every work cited, reference, or bibliography. Although it is easy to challenge the politics of using visual identification—being both an imperfect way to identify people and problematic that people would need to be identified in any way—this would offer a startling "**taxonomy**" of how identity can, and so often does, shape those who are credited in scholarly work. Ultimately, citation is quite an effective "reproductive technology," as independent feminist scholar Sara Ahmed points out on her research blog, *feministkilljoys: killing joy as a world making project*.

We argue that being insistent about developing a diverse intellectual genealogy is key to feminist ethnography. But it need not be done in isolation. It should, in fact, involve reaching out to others who conduct similar work—whether they be peers in class, your professors, other feminist scholars you connect with through hearing campus talks, via social media, attending conferences, et cetera. It also involves looking at those you admire and seeing who they cite in their research: Who has influenced their thinking? Being attentive to the politics of citation is also an important reminder that feminists must broaden their intellectual circles of influence, which means making the work of historically marginalized authors more visible and valued. In that way, we contribute to revising and shaping broader ethnographic canons.

ESSENTIAL

Excerpt from "Making Feminist Points," on the *feministkilljoys* Blog by Sara Ahmed

Photo Caption: Feminist Killjoy Coloring Page by Heather Tovey (NerdLab YYC), Creative Commons.

Sara Ahmed *is an independent scholar and the author of seven single-authored books, including* Cultural Politics of Emotion *(2004),* Queer Phenomenology: Orientations, Objects, Others *(2006), and* The Promise of Happiness *(2010). She is the coconvenor of the MA in Gender, Media and Culture, the convenor of the Feminist Postgraduate Forum, and the director of the Centre for Feminist Research. She is currently writing a book,* Living a Feminist Life, *which draws on everyday experiences of being a feminist, particularly experiences of being a feminist killjoy, as a way of doing feminist theory. Ahmed is also the author of* feministkilljoys, *her research blog, where she wrote the excerpt below about the politics of citation:*

I would describe citation as a rather successful reproductive technology, a way of reproducing the world around certain bodies.

These citational structures can form what we call disciplines. I was once asked to contribute to a sociology course, for example, and found that all the core readings were by male writers. I pointed this out and the course convener implied that "that" was simply a reflection of the history of the discipline. Well: this is a very selective history! The reproduction of a discipline can be the reproduction of these techniques of selection, ways of making certain bodies and thematics core to the discipline, and others not even part.

I have noticed as well that these citational practices can occur even when the topic is one that feminists have written extensively about. I recently attended a conference in which there was a panel on reproductive justice, a topic that feminists have written rather extensively about, and two of the three papers were entirely framed around the work of male philosophers! Indeed men can even cite only men when critiquing male privilege. . . .

We are not just talking about citation within academic contexts. We are talking about what I think of as screening techniques: how certain bodies take up spaces by screening out the existence of others. If you are screened out (by virtue of the body you have) then you simply do not even appear or register to others. You might even have to become insistent, wave your arms, even shout, just to appear. And then of course how you appear (as being insistent) means you still tend not to be heard.

Source: feministkilljoys. "Making Feminist Points." *Feministkilljoys*, September 11, 2013. http://feministkilljoys.com/2013/09/11/making-feminist-points/.

> **THINKING THROUGH . . .**
>
> ## An Intellectual Genealogy
>
> Select a contemporary ethnographer and trace that person's intellectual gene-
> alogy. You should begin by researching the ethnographer's training (mentors,
> advisors, and dissertation committee members), as well as reading their work
> to see which theorists and other ethnographers that person cites. Do you see
> any of the trends noted above?

Can an Ethnographer's Personal Experience Be a Part of a Study?

We begin this section with the often-quoted feminist slogan: The Personal is Political. When it comes to feminist ethnographic research, this could not be truer. Feminist sociologists Dorothy E. Smith and Patricia Hill Collins have emphasized that
an individual's knowledge and opinions develop from one's experiences in different
social locations. One's perspective always involves multiple, intersecting factors.
Feminists have a long history of valuing personal experience, and how it informs
and often becomes part of our scholarship.

Feminist ethnographers often discuss personal aspects of their lives that motivated them to embark on particular projects, or compelled them to approach a
project in particular ways. Anthropologist Rayna Rapp, whose research centers on
gender, science, and technology studies, opens her feminist ethnography *Testing
Women, Testing the Fetus: The Social Impact of Amniocentesis in America* with
a chapter titled "How Methodology Bleeds into Daily Life," where she intimately
interlaces her own experience with prenatal diagnosis with those of participants in
her study, alongside a broader review of biomedical and feminist research on new
reproductive technologies.[30] Sharing those experiences can legitimate ethnographic
inquiry. But it can also highlight the differences that may become apparent because
of other aspects of identity and privilege. For Rapp, this necessitated having what
she calls an "open-ended methodology," meaning that she followed opportunities
to interview people on the "outer reaches" of her sample (which originally included
women undergoing—or opting out of—prenatal diagnostic tests), including disability rights activists, pregnant friends seeking advice, and a reporter sent to interview
Rapp about her research. In many settings, she noted, it became increasingly difficult to tell who was interviewing whom.

Sharing cultural connections with participants can also shape ethnographers'
experiences, sometimes in quite unexpected ways. Palestinian American anthropologist Lila Abu-Lughod has written about her experiences with what she calls "halfie
anthropology," fieldwork conducted by bicultural or multicultural anthropologists
who share a partial belonging with those involved in their research. In her first
book, *Veiled Sentiments: Honor and Poetry in a Bedouin Society*,[31] Abu-Lughod
discusses how she began her fieldwork among the Awlad 'Ali Bedouin in the Western Desert of Egypt in 1978 with her father as an intermediary.

Abu-Lughod's experience offers an important reminder of how our identities
as "insiders" and "outsiders," and all the shades of in-between that these seemingly exhaustive terms elide, always matter in the ethnographic encounter. It is our
job as feminist ethnographers to be attentive to positionality as we embark on our
research and discuss the inevitable (and sometimes multiple) impacts of our identity

in our writing. Abu-Lughod experience also reminds us that there is much that an ethnographer can learn about one's location through fieldwork—as she did about Bedouin understandings of gender and sexuality, the importance of family and community, and respectability—that can never be taught in books or even by previous ethnographers who do not share one's particular identity.

⚛ SPOTLIGHT ⚛

Laura Mauldin on the Impact of Life Experiences

Photo Credit: Michael Ian.

Laura Mauldin *is a sociologist by training and specializes in health/illness, disability, care and caregiving, and science and technology studies (STS). She is jointly appointed in Human Development and Family Studies and Women's, Gender and Sexuality Studies at the University of Connecticut. Students who work with her can expect to focus on the role of ableism and other interconnected systems of oppression and how they shape the various systems we have in place that provide healthcare-related services and care infrastructure for unpaid caregiving. She is the author of* Made to Hear: Cochlear Implants and Raising Deaf Children *(2016) and is currently writing a book on spousal caregiving supported by the Social Science Research Council. Here, Laura describes how she came to study disability and how growing up around deaf children influenced her scholarship.*

My first book, which was on mothers' experiences getting a cochlear implant for their deaf child and based on my dissertation, came directly out of my experiences growing up. I grew up in a large school district that served deaf students across the region. I am deeply indebted to the deaf students I went to school with who let me into their world. I was certainly curious about American Sign Language, but the larger driving force was that I could not imagine only being able to communicate with others who could sign. But the key here was that I assumed the onus was on all of us who didn't know it to learn it and include them, which is exactly what I did. And their willingness to be patient with me as I did so set the path of my life and I've garnered immense privilege as a hearing person who signs because of it. I eventually attended Gallaudet University (the only liberal arts university for deaf people in the world), and there I became so immersed in deaf culture that I began to need to pull myself out and understand where this community and its culture fit within larger society: How did this community form and what's its relationship to the broader category of disability? How is the culture that is steeped in pride in being deaf generated out of the power of medicalization and pathologization? And what role does technology have in shifting the boundaries of the deaf community and deaf experiences? These experiences morphed into sociological questions that drove my academic life, and ultimately my research for the first book. But these aren't the only experiences driving my research agenda: while in graduate school, my partner got cancer and became progressively sicker and more disabled. I was responsible for medication dosages and home infusions, among other things. She eventually passed away after years of my being her primary caregiver. My next project is on partners where at least one has a chronic illness; I'm interested in how they experience caring for each other and the role of medical technologies in their day-to-day lives. I feel I'm in a unique position to access these stories and to know what questions to ask. One thing that's become clear is the need to better account for how we process trauma while in the field, and the ways that care for ourselves and each other can be built into the work we do. While all of my work circles around the experiences of non-normative bodies, the role of medicine and technology in shaping our lives, it is all grounded in the life experiences I bring with me.

Life-altering events may also have significant impacts on the ways that feminist ethnographers are accepted (or not) in the field, as well as the ways they think about their work. For some, this has been a diagnosis of a life-threatening illness or the death of a parent or spouse. For anthropologist Elise Andaya, having children profoundly shifted her approach to analysis and writing her ethnography, *Conceiving Cuba: Reproduction, Women, and the State in the Post-Soviet Era*:

> Still childless when I conducted the bulk of this fieldwork, the fact of becoming a mother (twice over) during the long process of analysis and writing has inevitably meant that I have reread the material collected for this book in the context of my own U.S.-centered experiences of prenatal care, gendered labor and household economies, and the home/work balance, heightening my appreciation for both the difficulties and the benefits of mothering under Cuban socialism of the twenty-first century. This has also entailed grappling with a central tension: as a feminist, I applaud the Cuban state's commitment to the provision of services such as subsidized childcare and free and accessible abortion and prenatal care. Also as a feminist, however, I am compelled to critically examine the often unintended consequences of state policies as they shape women's lives in post-Soviet Cuba.[32]

For communications scholar Ahmet Atay, his identity as a queer diasporic Turkish Cypriot man and his use of the Internet to establish a diasporic community influenced his cyberethnography of diasporic masculinity. In *Globalization's Impact on Cultural Identity Formation: Queer Diasporic Males in Cyberspace*, Atay writes that self-awareness was integral throughout his study from choosing what to observe, what methods to use, what data to collect, and how to write about a cultural group that defied geospatial boundaries. Reflecting on his own identity, he writes:

> Reflexivity was a central part of my research process on diaporic queer bodies. In order to make sense of my own life and in-between experiences, I turned outwards to study cultural groups, particularly diasporic queer bodies, and their cultural identity formation through mediated forms, particularly through the Internet and cyberspace technologies. Therefore, I had to be constantly aware of my own positionality in this research. Understanding my reasons to select particular web pages and Internet-based social networks as part of my cyberfield, realizing how emotional and intellectual states interfered with my data collection, selection, and finally the writing process helped me to reflect on my own involvement in this research. For me, reflexivity became a way of finding my own voice in this research, while I

reflected on others who are similar and also different, in terms of lived queer diasporic experiences and positionalities.[33]

Feminist ethnographers' commitment to reflexivity may also extend to the relationship an ethnographer has with particular participants. For example, Alisse Waterston describes her work, *My Father's Wars: Migration, Memory, and the Violence of a Century*, as "intimate ethnography," where she centers the narrative around his life (not her own, as an autoethnographic account would) through her interviews with him and those who knew him, archival research, and participant-observation in the areas he lived. As Waterston writes:

> The dual daughter-anthropologist role makes it difficult to place this book in an established genre. It is not just my father's biography, not just his narrated memoir; it is not about the anthropologist, not about the daughter, nor is it only about cultural framework or national histories or the violence that wreaked havoc during my father's lifetime. It is about all these things at once.[34]

Most contemporary ethnographers engage in some form of reflexivity in their work, though considering the ethics of fieldwork encounters in relation to an ethnographer's positionality has been important for feminist ethnographers with their attention to power and privilege. This is especially true for performance ethnographers such as Tami Spry who views autoethnographic performance as having personal, professional, and political emancipatory potential. For her, the body is evidence in the same way that experience is. The body becomes a site of "corporeal literacy"—in other words, the body can be read or engaged with as a text. Thus personal experience factors profoundly in her autoethnographic performance, which is shaped through self-reflection of her reality. Thus, personal experience factors stridently in autoethnographic performance. Spry says:

> Investigators analyze the body for evidence, the body as evidence, the body of evidence. But evidence, like experience, is not itself knowledge; like evidence, experience means nothing until it is interpreted, until we interpret the body as evidence. For a performative autoethnographer, the critical stance of the performing body constitutes a praxis of evidence and analysis. We offer our performing body as raw data of a critical cultural story. So, when I perform "Ode to the Absent Phallus," a performative autoethnography of sexual assault, the audience not only sees my body as evidence of an assaulted body, they also see my body performing a reflexive critique upon dominant cultural notions of victim and survivor contextualized in that place and in that time. If autoethnography is epistemic, then the evidence of how we know what we know must reside in the aesthetic crafting of critical reflection upon the body as evidence.[35]

How Involved or Engaged Should a Feminist Ethnographer Be?

There have been ongoing debates about positivist expectations that ethnographic work must be objective and neutral rather than humanistic that, for some, would certainly foreclose being an engaged scholar. Feminists have disputed the accusation that their position sacrifices objectivity. And many feminist ethnographers are engaged in research that is linked to their identities and experiences, which plays a formative role in their research project. Here, Brenna McCaffrey reflects back on her position as a feminist ethnographer and reproductive justice activist, and how that influences the way she pursues her research and activist work.

SPOTLIGHT

Brenna McCaffrey on the Political Stakes of Feminist Ethnography

Photo Credit: Peter Nicholson.

Brenna McCaffrey *earned her PhD in Anthropology at the Graduate Center, CUNY. Her interdisciplinary research explores the interaction of feminism and biomedicine within the fields of sexual and reproductive health. Her current project uses ethnography to ask how the abortion pill is changing medical, social, and political understandings of abortion and reproductive justice in Ireland. McCaffrey comes to this project informed by her experiences as a daughter of young working-class parents, an advocate for self-managed abortion, and a white American woman of Irish descent.*

ES: How has feminist ethnography has impacted the direction of the work that you do? How do you utilize a reproductive justice framework in your research process as a white researcher?

BM: My research has been driven by the premise that access to full reproductive justice is essential for feminist liberation. I think all feminist anthropologists have a mission statement like this, a sense of the political stakes of their research that guides them. My interest in abortion as one aspect of reproductive justice is no accident: abortion is important to me because of my identity and experiences, the same way it was for the white women who centered abortion in Second Wave US feminism. Those feminists failed to address how the value of reproduction was stratified by race and class, and we can learn from their mistakes! Our identities will always inform our research questions, methodologies, and experiences in fieldwork. But white feminist researchers particularly have a responsibility to center race and other forms of oppression when designing research projects, especially those concerning reproduction.

ES: How has the recent legalization of abortion in Ireland influenced the way that you think about reproductive justice?

BM: Studying reproductive justice outside of the United States forces us to account for different social contexts of racialization and class politics. It can call attention to local forms of reproductive justice that may have their own histories. The right to have and raise children in safe environments was threatened for generations of families in Ireland who were poor, non-white, or deemed "deviant" in their gender expression or sexuality. Mothers were separated from their children, who were put up for adoption with wealthy American families, while women were punished in workhouses like the Magdalene Laundries. These issues are only now being understood through the language of "reproductive justice," but advocacy around these issues precedes and informs contemporary abortion-centric reproductive rights activism in Ireland.

*This interview was conducted by Emery Stewart (a Women's, Gender, and Sexuality Studies graduate of the College of Wooster), who drew on insights from Brenna's doctoral research on the abortion pill in Ireland for her own undergraduate thesis on moral dilemmas over abortion in US and Irish contexts.

In sociologist Ann Oakley's critical discussion of feminism and the social sciences, she challenges the feminist case against quantitative methods in favor of qualitative methods and argues that positivism is ultimately a search for social facts that predict behavior.[36] The adequacy of positivist social science is guaranteed by objectivity, the absence of bias, and distance or removal of the researchers' values and experiences to ensure validity of the knowledge being understood and produced. Oakley is suggesting that positioning the debate as one of positivism versus antipositivism takes away the gray area where positivist research, such as quantitative research, may be useful to activists and/or activist-scholars. She advocates the value of mixed-methods research, since creating a dichotomy between quantitative and qualitative approaches shuttles away the possibilities for one, and reifies the other.

A further feminist challenge to positivism are ethnographers who work to decenter their own perspectives and work to lift up the voices of others. Disability justice activist and performance artist Leah Lakshmi Piepzna-Samarasinha felt this acutely when she approached editors about her book of essays, *Care Work: Dreaming Disability Justice*, and was told she must present herself as "the expert." Her response became a central feature of the book:

> [I] want to be very clear: I am one writer and performer in a sea of sick and disabled QT/BIPOC [queer trans*, black, indigenous, people of color] people who are doing work in many ways all the time—as writers and activists, and as everyday folks who are keeping themselves and other people alive. I do not want this to be "the" book on disability justice. This book is one in a garden of books that I invoke to become more abundant.[37]

In some cases though, there are dangers to lifting up others' voices, as well as one's own. There is a danger in becoming seen as "the voice"—whether purposeful or not—on topics that are deemed controversial by constituencies both in and outside academia.

ᨒ SPOTLIGHT ᨑ

Mary L. Gray on the Labor of Feminist Ethnography

Mary L. Gray *is a senior principal researcher at Microsoft Research and an associate professor in the Media School at Indiana University. She maintains a faculty position in the Luddy School of Informatics, Computing, and Engineering with affiliations in Anthropology and Gender Studies at Indiana University. Gray, an anthropologist and media scholar by training, focuses on how people's everyday uses of technologies transform labor, identity, and human rights. Her books include* Out in the Country: Youth, Media, and Queer Visibility in Rural America *(2009) and* Ghost Work: How to Stop Silicon Valley from Building a New Global Underclass *(2019). In 2020, Gray was named a MacArthur Fellow for her contributions to anthropology and the study of technology, digital economies, and society.*

Last month [in 2015] someone sent me an email, cc'ing it to the entire faculty of the Media School, my home academic department. The person addressed it to me because I had been in the newspaper talking about LGBTQ issues and they wanted my peers and university administration to know their contempt for me as a scholar and the institution that supported such work. It was a screed about how homosexuals should not have legal rights and people like me should never be allowed to teach. I responded to the individual and the entire faculty, acknowledging the email and letting the person know that I would contact them directly. I then emailed the Media School faculty and asked that they not engage with the person, fearing that someone might decide to take on this hater and I would be left to clean up the mess. People have no idea what you have to deal with when you take a position as an activist ethnographer. Vitriolic emails like this are the clearest reminder of the cost that comes with being public. While they can be personally hurtful, they also underscore the yawning divide between those of us who can imagine being targeted by hatred and peers who cannot. But the experience can also be validating, showing others the need for our work. Another challenge may be the added weight if students identify with you and see you as a safe harbor on campus for issues around sexuality, race, and class. But we also run the risk of becoming the tokenized, resident person for whom both faculty and students rely on for support. So much happens through the bodies of scholars doing this work. It's not measurable and we don't feel entitled to ask for support. Peers who do work that is not as politically charged struggle to understand the vitriol and political work that activist scholars take on.

Additionally, Mary L. Gray underscores the labor associated with doing feminist work, particularly research that does not stem from a positivist framework, from within the academy. This labor, she argues, needs to be visible because, for some, it is just as fundamentally important and part of an academic's praxis as the other roles a researcher plays. Any ethnographer's research stands the chance of being misinterpreted, but when one has a long-term engagement or commitment to a community, those stakes may be higher.

What we find in Gray's case is that a scholar runs the risk of becoming the laser focus of a disaffected group or person who now have a place to deposit their hostility. This may make some scholars question the practicalities of being an engaged scholar. But Gray's commitment to activist work and public scholarship is an important intervention that calls into question the idea of positivist neutrality that is so often expected in knowledge production. But if a feminist researcher is committed to being an activist and does not claim neutrality, does that mean the scholarship is compromised? What does being "neutral" accomplish for a researcher? Is neutrality even possible in the context of feminist critiques of positivist research? For many feminist ethnographers, writing about these issues and debates has become a crucial part of their ethnographic work.

And for some feminist ethnographers, such as anthropologist Faye V. Harrison (see *Spotlight* in chapter 4), engagement remains central to their work, not "an appropriated buzzword."[38] Deeply influenced by feminist and Pan-Africanist scholars Louise Lamphere, George Houston Bass, St. Clair Drake, Bridget O'Laughlin, and Michelle Rosaldo, Harrison has challenged the lines between activist engagement and academic production throughout her career. In an interview with Gina Athena Ulysse, Harrison envisions a field that centralizes engaged scholarship:

> Those of us who wish to align our scholarly endeavors with activism, advocacy, policy reformation and reaching wider audiences should be encouraged to do so.

Moreover, the organizational means should exist to facilitate those pursuits. I don't want my students and my son, who is also a cultural anthropologist, to replicate the disciplinary alienation and negation that generations before them experienced. I'm working toward the anthropology I optimistically envisioned when all those years ago, I decided that I wanted to be an anthropologist when I grew up.[39]

Toward this end, Harrison's 1991 classic *Decolonizing Anthropology: Moving Further Toward an Anthropology for Liberation* was a key theoretical intervention in the field, emphasizing the political responsibility of intellectuals to interrogate "race and class disparities, which anthropologists are too prone to neglect or ignore . . . with gender to assume their rightful place at the center of political as well as theoretical deliberation."[40] Harrison's goal was and continues to be encouraging more ethnographers to become committed to liberating the discipline and engaging in scholarly inquiry aimed at transformation and liberation.

Conclusion

As with all decisions in practicing and producing feminist ethnography, it is crucial for the feminist ethnographer to critically think through their engagement. Exploring some of the debates and deliberations in feminist thinking and feminist ethnography offers a window into how raising questions and engaging in debate and deliberation can destabilize what may be considered resolved. One can certainly argue that feminist theorizing and feminist ethnography have grown from these debates. The questions we raise among ourselves and what influences our understandings of knowledge production can contribute to a feminist ethnographic literacy. In the following chapters, we take up some of the methods, methodologies, and styles of production that feminists have used to pursue these goals.

THINKING THROUGH . . .

What Would a Feminist Ethnographer Do?

Identify a feminist ethnographer among the faculty at your school or at another school who you can interview in person, via online chat, or phone.[1] Develop a set of questions that will allow you to explore how they became a feminist ethnographer and how they situate themselves with regard to one (or more) of the debates above. Some of the things you want to be sure to find out are: What is their discipline? How did they come to identify themselves as a feminist ethnographer? Who influenced their thinking about feminism? What does being a feminist or feminist ethnographer mean to them? How does being a feminist influence their research? Write a short essay discussing the feminist ethnographer's perspectives on the field. Ideally, you can share these, and note comparisons, with other class members.

[1] *If they are unavailable, email questions, but understand that written responses are far less dynamic than verbal interactions.*

Suggested Resources

Begoña Aretxaga (1997) *Shattering Silence: Women, Nationalism, and Political Subjectivity in Northern Ireland.*

Decolonizing Knowledge: A Conversation between Dr. Linda Tuhiwai Smith, Dr. Michelle Fine, and Dr. Andrew Jolivette on community-based research within Indigenous communities (2013) https://www.youtube.com/watch?v=7lb7edhWghY.

Maynard Maynard (2013). (Orig. 1994). *Researching Women's Lives from a Feminist Perspective.*

Richelle D. Schrock (2013) "The Methodological Imperatives of Feminist Ethnography," in *Journal of Feminist Scholarship.*

Kamala Visweswaran (1994) *Fictions of Feminist Ethnography.*

Notes

1 Micaela di Leonardo, "Introduction: Gender, Culture and Political Economy: Feminist Anthropology in Historical Perspective," in *Gender at the Crossroads of Knowledge*, 1991, 7; Michelle Rosaldo and Louise Lamphere, eds., *Woman, Culture, and Society*,1974; Rayna Reiter (now Rapp), *Toward an Anthropology of Women*, 1975.

2 Linda Tuhiwai Smith, "Twenty-five Indigenous Projects," in *Decolonizing Methodologies*, 2012, 143–164.

3 Ngahuia Te Awekotuku and Manatu Maori, *He Tikanga Whakaaro: Research Ethics in the Maori Community*, 1991.

4 This section is adapted from Dána-Ain Davis, "Border Crossing: Intimacy and Feminist Activist Ethnography in the Age of Neoliberalism," *Feminist Activist Ethnography,* eds. Christa Craven and Dána-Ain Davis, 2013.

5 Marilyn Strathern, "An Awkward Relationship: The Case of Feminism and Anthropology," *Signs: Journal of Women and Society*, 1987.

6 Kamala Visweswaran, *Fictions of Feminist Ethnography*, 1994.

7 Judith Stacey, "Can There Be a Feminist Ethnography?" *Women's Studies International Forum*, 1988, 26.

8 Ibid., 24.

9 E. Patrick Johnson. *Black. Queer. Southern. Women.: An Oral History*, 2018. Greensboro: University of North Carolina Press.

10 Dwight Conquergood. "Performing as a Moral Act: Ethical Dimensions of the Ethnography of Performance," 1985, 8.

11 Ibid., 13.

12 Dána-Ain Davis, "Border Crossing: Intimacy and Feminist Activist Ethnography in the Age of Neoliberalism," in *Feminist Activist Ethnography,* eds. Christa Craven and Dána-Ain Davis, 2013.

13 Lila Abu-Lughod, "Can There Be A Feminist Ethnography?" *Women & Performance: A Journal of Feminist Theory*, 1990.

14 Robin Morgan, *Sisterhood Is Global*, 1996, 1.

15 Janelle Monáe, *The Electric Lady*, Wondaland Arts Society and Bad Boy Records, released 2013.

16 Micaela di Leonardo, ed., *Gender at the Crossroads of Knowledge*, 1991.

17 Patricia Zavella, "Feminist Insider Dilemmas: Constructing Ethnic Identity with Chicana Informants," in *Feminist Dilemmas in Fieldwork*, ed. Diane L. Wolf, 1996.

18 Kirin Narayan, "How Native Is a 'Native' Anthropologist?" *American Anthropologist,* 1993.

19 Anthothy Naaeke et al., "Insider and Outsider Perspective in Ethnographic Research," Proceedings of the New York State Communication Association, 2011. Available at: http://docs.rwu.edu/nyscaproceedings/vol2010/iss1/9.

20 Lorena Muñoz, "Brown, Queer and Gendered: Queering the Latina/o 'Street-Scapes' in Los Angeles," in *Queer Methods and Methodologies*, 2010, 55.

21 Ibid., 60.

22 Dorothy E. Smith, *Writing the Social*, 1999.

23 Patricia Hill Collins, *Black Feminist Thought*, 2009.

24 Richa Nagar and Susan Geiger, "Reflexivity, Positionality, and Languages of Collaboration in Feminist Fieldwork," in *Muddying the Waters: Coauthoring Feminisms across Scholarship and Activism*, 81–89. Urbana, Chicago, and Springfield: University of Illinois Press, 2014.

25 Jafari Allen, *¡Venceremos?: The Erotics of Black Self-making in Cuba*, 2011, 117.

26 Virginia Dominguez, Matthew Guttman, and Catherine Lutz, "Problem of Gender and Citations Raised Again in New Research Study," *Anthropology News*, 2014.

27 Lynn Bolles, "Telling the Story Straight: Black Feminist Intellectual Thought in Anthropology." *Transforming Anthropology*, 2013.

28 Tanya A. Christian, "Trending Topics," *Essence* (April 2018).

29 Executive Roundtable, "Cite Black Women: Race, Gender, Justice and Citational Politics in Anthropology" (organized by Christen Smith), American Anthropological Association Annual Meetings, Vancouver, British Columbia, November 2019. Participants included Christen A. Smith, Antoinette T. Jackson, Erica L. Williams, Bianca C. Williams, Dána-Ain Davis, A. Lynn Bolles, Christa Craven, and Sameena Mulla.

30 Rayna Rapp, *Testing Women, Testing the Fetus: The Social Impact of Amniocentesis in America*, 1999.

31 Lila Abu-Lughod, *Veiled Sentiments: Honor and Poetry in a Bedouin Society*, 1999 [orig. 1986].

32 Elise Andaya, *Conceiving Cuba*, 2014, 22.

33 Ahmet Atay, *Globalization's Impact on Cultural Identity Formation*, 2015, 54–55.

34 Alisse Waterston, *My Father's Wars: Migration, Memory, and the Violence of a Century*, 2014, xv–xvi.

35 Tami Spry, "Bodies of/as Evidence in Autoethnography," 2009, 583.

36 Ann Oakley, "Gender, Methodology and People's Ways of Knowing: Some Problems with Feminism and the Paradigm Debate in Social Science," *Sociology*, 1998.

37 Leah Lakshmi Piepzna-Samarasinha, *Care Work: Dreaming Disability Justice*, 2018, 26.

38 Gina A. Ulysse, "Faye V. Harrison and Why Anthropology Still Matters," in *The Huffington Post*, 2013.

39 Ibid.

40 Faye V. Harrison, *Decolonizing Anthropology: Moving Further Toward an Anthropology for Liberation*, 1997 [orig. 1991], 9.

CHAPTER 4

How Does One *Do* Feminist Ethnography?

This chapter covers the process of developing and doing a feminist ethnographic research project. You will learn how to design a feminist methodological approach to, and employ a variety of methods in, a feminist ethnographic project by examining the following questions:

- How should a feminist ethnographer choose a topic?
- What methods have been useful to feminist ethnographers?

Spotlights *in this chapter:*

- Elisabeth Engebretsen on Choosing Methods and Shifting Knowledge
- Class of 2021 Undergraduates on Fieldwork during a Pandemic
- Tracy Fisher on Using Oral/Life History to Address Feminist Ethnographic Questions
- Whitney Battle-Baptiste on Historical Archaeology and Literary Fiction

Essentials *in this chapter:*

- Faye V. Harrison, "Feminist Methodology . . ." in *The Gender of Globalization*
- Naisargi Dave, *Queer Activism in India*
- Caroline C. Wang and Mary Ann Burris, "Photovoice"

You will also be ***Thinking Through . . .***

- Three Options to Explore Methodological Possibilities
- Word Cloud Magic!

This chapter explores the creation of a feminist methodology and the kind of methods that feminist ethnographers can use to carry out their research. In part, it offers a "how to" guide with the goal of introducing you to basic principles and methods that have been useful to ethnographic researchers and fruitfully employed by feminist ethnographers. Yet this is also a theoretical chapter, in the sense that conducting ethnography involves far more than the successful application of particular research methods. In fact, as visual sociologist Alison Rooke notes in her ethnographic project exploring the interconnections of spatiality and subjectivity for working-class lesbian and bisexual women in Britain, "Ethnography [including feminist and queer ethnography] is undoubtedly methodologically untidy."[1]

By focusing on methods and methodology, this chapter also invites you to imagine (and possibly develop) your own project, consider how to create feminist research questions, choose research methods suitable for a feminist ethnographic project, and begin to think through how choices about method and methodology influence the production of feminist ethnography. As you read this chapter, remember that many examples and issues will resurface in subsequent chapters (and we'll return to a few briefly introduced before). Indeed, it is ultimately the ways that feminist theory and methodology can contribute to scholarly aims and activist possibilities for feminist ethnography that we hope you will engage in as you move through the rest of this book.

In order to do this, differentiating between one's research methodology and one's methods is essential. Developing a feminist methodology—a body of methods that allows us to create knowledge by engaging with feminist theoretical and ethical perspectives—is the crux of getting at the business of *doing* ethnography. Anthropologist Faye Harrison emphasizes that methods themselves are neither inherently feminist nor nonfeminist. However, they offer important tools to aid in gathering data that is then subject to feminist analysis and interpretation. It is important to remember that two ethnographers could use the very same methods—say, participant-observation and in-depth interviews—to study prostitution but approach it from very different theoretical and methodological orientations. Thus, it is *how* a feminist ethnographer utilizes and contextualizes various methods that enable them to contribute to feminist ethnographic research.

🧠 ESSENTIAL

Excerpt from "Feminist Methodology . . ." by Faye V. Harrison

Faye V. Harrison *received her PhD from Stanford University in 1982 and currently teaches in anthropology and African American studies at the University of Illinois at Urbana-Champaign. Harrison is the editor of* Decolonizing Anthropology: Moving Further toward an Anthropology for Liberation, *originally published in 1991 with a second edition published in 2010, and author of* Outsider Within: Reworking Anthropology in the Global Age *(2008). She discusses the importance of not conflating method and methodology in "Feminist Methodology as a Tool for Ethnographic Inquiry on Globalization" in* The Gender of Globalization: Women Navigating Cultural and Economic Marginalities *(Nandini Gunewardena and Ann Kingsolver, 2007), winner of the 2011 Society for the Anthropology of Work Book Prize. Expanding on philosopher Sandra Harding's distinction between epistemology, method, and methodology in her classic 1987 edited collection* Feminism & Methodology,[1] *Harrison writes:*

Methods are specific procedures, operations, or techniques for identifying and collecting the evidence necessary to answer research questions. In and of themselves, they are not feminist or non-feminist. Therefore, there are no "feminist methods" per se. However, there are "feminist methodologies," because methodologies articulate conceptual, theoretical, and ethical perspectives on the whats, whys and hows of research and the production of knowledge. . . . Methodologies provide the philosophical or logical rationale for the links researchers make among theory, pragmatic research strategies, evidence, and the empirical world. . . . A feminist methodology clues us in on which combination of methods is likely to be most suitable for meeting the pragmatic and ethical objectives of a feminist research project. . . .

Although ethnography is typically characterized principally in terms of qualitative methods, its methodological repertoire may indeed include quantitative techniques, particularly those appropriately and meaningfully triangulated with the styles and procedures that are ethnography's traditional cornerstones—participant-observation and various kinds of intensive interviewing. . . .

We might even claim that ethnographic methodologies cover the range of research theories that consider experience-near participant-observation or participatory-immersion approaches central to the process of asking researchable questions, finding the best answers by some combination of techniques, and producing new layers of knowledge from analyzing and theorizing the research results. . . . [In this way,] ethnography has been conceptualized and deployed as a feminist methodology.

Source: Harrison, Faye V. "Feminist Methodology as a Tool for Ethnographic Inquiry on Globalization." In *The Gender of Globalization: Women Navigating Cultural and Economic Marginalities*, edited by Nandini Gunewardena and Ann Kingsolver, 23–31. Santa Fe, NM: School for Advanced Research Press, 2007, 25.

[1] Sandra G. Harding, *Feminism and Methodology*, 1987, 2–3.

In our interview with anthropologist Cheryl Rodriguez about her research on the gendered dimensions of community activism in relation to lowincome housing, she, too, discussed the methodological approaches to her work as what makes it explicitly feminist. She notes:

First of all, I rely on the work of feminist thinkers. Sometimes that feminist thinker is not necessarily an ethnographer, but that person's theoretical perspective can contribute in some way to my own thinking and to what I am trying to accomplish. The first thing is the literature, being grounded in feminist literature. And then in terms of methodology, I just think that many of us, even those who don't call themselves feminists, have tried to transform what we think of as ethnographic work into a much kinder, gentler, more compassionate type of research where we understand our role as researchers and where we know that we are in the way. We know that we are changing things just by being there. In other words, [we must think] about the implications of our presence as researchers. Because our work involves situating ourselves in some place, in some institution, [that] affects people's lives. Typically, we are not just sitting in a room—we are not supposed to be anyway—just making stuff up. So for me, my methodology is about self-awareness and being caring, and understanding the threatening aspects of my asking questions and having a real solid sense of what I am trying to get at.

As a part of this awareness, it is important for feminist ethnographers to think carefully about how they refer to those who participate in their research. It should already have become apparent (we hope) that when it comes to the language that feminist ethnographers employ, our words, their histories and connotations, and their (sometimes multiple) meanings matter deeply. Ethnographers have referred to those who participate in their research in many different ways: as subjects, informants, participants, contributors, respondents, interpreters, interlocutors, and those with whom they had especially close relationships as key informants, gatekeepers, coauthors, and collaborators. Although we do not wish to anoint any one of these terms as appropriate for all feminist ethnographic projects, we do believe that thinking through the meanings and connotations of each is important as we consider research topics and develop our methodological choices. For instance, what type of relationship do you hope to develop with those who participate in your research (this may be different for short- and long-term projects)? Does the term you choose suggest a hierarchical relationship between you, the researcher, and the researched (is this your intent? could inequities be minimized?)? How much shared work does the term suggest? Are those involved in your research prepared to make this commitment of time and energy? What connotations might the term have outside of your discipline, and outside of academia? For instance, "respondent" and "subject" have a long history of use in psychology to describe those who fill out surveys or are involved in experiments—will your research aim to replicate, or differ from, such studies?

We choose to use "participant," a more neutral term, acknowledging that feminist ethnographers have used others in their publications (and we maintain their usage when citing or referring to their work). Beyond naming those involved in our ethnographic work, how we phrase and frame our research questions and how we describe and implement our methods (i.e., contemporary feminists avoid terminology like "giving voice to" those in their research) should be subject to the same types of preliminary interrogation as we begin our projects. It is beyond the scope of this text to discuss all of these possibilities, but the points we wish to emphasize here are that (a) feminist ethnographers must think about language to describe their research *as they design their study* and (b) as feminist ethnographers approach their writing, it is important to explain how and why particular choices were made (or why and how changes occurred during or after the research encounter).

Doing feminist ethnography requires significant practice, and how methods are employed is (or at least should be) a result of reading about the experiences of many previous ethnographers. Their pitfalls and successes have influenced the ways that these methods have been practiced over time. In our interview with sociologist Jennifer Bickham Mendez, for instance, she likened the methodological process for each feminist ethnographer to practicing yoga: it is a life-long exploration, and what it looks like—what comes easily and what is particularly challenging—will be different for each person.

How Should a Feminist Ethnographer Choose a Topic?

Choices about where and with whom to conduct research are necessarily riddled with basic and sometimes mundane questions: Where do you live or have the ability to travel? What will it cost to go to your research site and what funding is available for your research? Do you know people in the community you hope to access? How might your identity, your personality, your similarity and/or difference to those you will interact with impact your research? What potential logistical challenges may arise? Are there ethical challenges can you foresee in your fieldwork? Are there precautions you can take ahead of time to mediate these concerns?

Beyond these basic questions (relevant for any ethnographic project), feminist anthropologist Margery Wolf says, "Choosing a research topic sounds rather like a chapter title in an elementary methodology textbook, but it could also be one in a book of feminist ethics."[2] Indeed, feminist researchers have a long history of challenging inequalities—both in their application of research methods and through their research objectives. A principal priority in feminist ethnographic work, since its inception, is to honor what is important to the people you are working with. This is true both in terms of topic and how they participate in your work.

In the following *Spotlight*, Elisabeth Engebretsen discusses the way she developed her methodology for her feminist ethnographic work with queer Chinese women, and how it ultimately shifted her "Western" assumptions about gender and sexuality as a Norwegian ethnographer trained in Europe and the United States.

Feminist ethnographers often engage in projects reflecting particular political commitments or develop research agendas that highlight gender dynamics/issues and intentionally employ methods in feminist ways. In some cases, a feminist ethnographer may be asked by a community or organization to work on a particular project. Remembering what makes an ethnographic project feminist is when it is in the hands of a feminist someone who pays attention to gender and power dynamics—who is intentional in their research design and draws from previous feminist scholarship to conduct feminist ethnography. It is also true that a person may shape a feminist project on a topic that does not have an inherently feminist focus. For instance, anthropologist Matthew Gutmann's now-classic discussion of changing male identities and practices with respect to fathering, sexuality, housework, alcohol, violence, and the cultural history of machismo in *Meanings of Macho: Being a Man in Mexico City* offered a feminist approach to gender images, practices, and beliefs about *machismo*. The topic of masculinity or *machismo* could be approached from many perspectives—indeed, it has often been approached from a decidedly patriarchal perspective—but the theoretical insights and analytical techniques Gutmann employed, as well as collaborative methodologies such as returning to participants with their initial answers to questions and continuing discussions, mark his approach as a feminist one.[3]

🕊 SPOTLIGHT 🕊

Elisabeth Engebretsen on Choosing Methods and Shifting Knowledge

Photo Credit: Uni You.

Elisabeth Lund Engebretsen *received her PhD in anthropology from the London School of Economics and Political Science in 2008. She is an Associate Professor at the Centre for Gender Studies in the University of Stavanger, Norway. Engebretsen is the author of* Queer Women in Urban China: An Ethnography *(2014), coeditor of* Queer/Tongzhi China: New Perspectives on Research, Activism and Media Cultures *(2015), the* Sexualities *special issue titled* Anthropology's Queer Sensibilities *(2018), and the forthcoming volume* Transforming Identities in Contemporary Europe. *Engebretsen is editor-in-chief of the* Lambda Nordica *journal.*

The methodological specifics of my work have been shaped by the fact that lesbianism was and is relatively invisible in Chinese society and homosexuality remains taboo even though it is not criminalized as such. In my initial study, I wanted to focus specifically on women because there was, at the time, no work being done on "queer women"; Chinese homosexuality was by default focusing on men. Few women were "out," and managing confidentiality—also within community settings—was essential. Conventional interviews, focus groups, and other structured research methods would not have worked in this context. Instead, I came to rely on unstructured, semi-casual conversations with women in social and community spaces of their choice. I did eventually conduct and digitally record fifteen semi-structured interviews, but they served a complimentary function. As I came to know more people and get a sense of the concerns that shaped their everyday lives, I revised my initial topic guide to focus on three broad themes: (1) personal life, including intimate experiences and sex, romantic relationships and desires, and the process of coming to terms with same-sex desires; (2) negotiating family and social life, including marriage pressure and children; and (3) community experience, including activism and politics. Whereas I initially imagined my research to concern identity politics and activism, I learned from my research participants about the ways that broader issues shape queer lives. This insight profoundly altered my understanding of how to study sexual and gender subjectivities transnationally, relativized my "Western" knowledge of these matters, and it continues to inform my work.

Feminist ethnographers must also consider the desires of participants regarding how they engage with ethnographic work. At times, feminist ethnographers develop collaborative projects that fully involve participants in designing, implementing, analyzing, and producing research. At other times, feminist ethnographers make strategic choices to involve participants (or select participants) in generating questions for the project, reading and discussing interview **transcripts** (typed copies of recorded interviews), participating in focus groups for data analysis, et cetera. Many feminist ethnographers have considered the benefits and the challenges of collaborative work. When anthropologist Karen Brodkin Sacks conducted fieldwork with African American hospital workers for her book *Caring by the Hour: Women, Work, and Organizing at Duke Medical Center*, for instance, she positioned her work as part of a feminist and radical tradition:

> Feminist ethnography takes sides and challenges the idea that there is a privileged, objective, and neutral point of view, that observer and observed, analyst and subject are unrelated. Among other things, this involved sharing my interpretations with activist workers and submitting prepublication drafts for criticism. Each of these activities had its own consequences, and facing them with more or less success has in turn shaped the final work. To ask those with whom I was working to share in my research was easier and democratic in theory than it was in practice. Such participation demands more work from people than the most thoughtful interview. It also contains a hidden constraint: that the co-analyst [must] either approach the issues guided by my assumptions and questions, or challenge them.[4]

Another example of choosing a topic with collaborative intention is Swedish anthropologist Ulrika Dahl's collaborative "femme-on-femme" ethnographic research. What she terms a "femme-inist" ethnography calls into question "the dichotomy between the theorizing academic and her 'informants'."[5] Her collaborative ethnography with gender variant queer visual artist Del LaGrace Volcano, *Femmes of Power: Exploding Queer Femininities*,[6] provides an example of feminist efforts to include participants as coresearchers and coproducers of research, as both objects and subjects of research.

Through sharing many moments of making images with femmes, I was able to follow how collaboration works in the production of representation, and learn about the intimacy of photographic art and about the mutual trust that is required in order to produce a carefully framed image with many layers. Through "participant-observation" in the photographic sessions, I gained a tremendous respect for the femmes who were willing to partake in the project and for the labour it takes to make images under what at times were rather difficult conditions of cold, rain, snow, crowd intervention and so on. In many cases, the very production of the image turned into a public spectacle, which in and of itself contributed to the reconfiguration of public representations of femininity.[7]

In an effort to create a collaborative "queer archive," Dahl includes performative and written work by the authors, performers, and artists that she researches into her publications.[8]

Ultimately, there is no one "right" way to make choices about a topic, research design, or potential collaboration in feminist ethnographic projects. But feminist ethnographers must be deliberate in thinking through the relationships they hope to build with participants, as well as attending to the power dynamics inherent to social research. There is no completely equitable ethnographic encounter (see chapter 3 on Debates), but we believe that feminist ethnographers should work toward as balanced an exchange as possible with those involved in their research. Florence Babb, who conducts her anthropological work in Latin America and the Caribbean (see *Spotlight* in chapter 2), says she actualizes her feminist practice by spending sufficient time with a group of people to build a relationship and trust, enabling her to deepen her understanding of their lives and of the questions she wants to address in her research. It is important, she argues, to remain flexible so that she can revise her research plans as things move along, taking her cues from the people she is working with and remaining mindful of their differences. Babb points out that these may or may not be feminist methods:

> I think they reflect my desire to respond to those I work with and to try to produce work that they would deem worthy of their time and collaboration. I make an effort to be sensitive to differences of power between myself and my collaborators, and seek out individuals who might not be the customary spokespeople in their communities. Women and others who may be socially marginal are often central to my interest.

What Methods Have Been Useful to Feminist Ethnographers?

Feminist ethnographers can use traditional and/or experimental methods. These typically include participant-observation—often considered the hallmark of ethnographic research—and many have integrated life history and in-depth interviewing, surveys, the analysis of archival or cultural materials, participatory research, and interpretive communities in their work. In fact, **mixed-methods** approaches, using several research methods together for a particular project, are common in feminist ethnographic work. Many feminist ethnographers, such as anthropologist Leith Mullings in her article "African American Women Making Themselves: Notes on the Role of Black Feminist Research," have made compelling arguments for blending feminist ethnographic approaches, including participant-observation and in-depth interviewing, with multidisciplinary collaborative community research, particularly toward political aims and efforts to shape public policy.[9] Mullings worked with anthropologist Alaka Wali on their book *Stress and Resilience: The Social Context of Reproduction in Central Harlem*. They partnered with the New York Urban

League's Harlem Birth Right project, which sought to understand and combat the high rates of infant mortality in the Harlem Community. By partnering with the project, Mullings and Wali included community members in the design of questions and methods and in the implementation of the ethnographic research.[10] The result is that the book incorporates the voices of women in the community who document their own experiences in words and participatory engagement with the study.

Ultimately, however, it is the feminist practice of paying attention to power differentials that should guide methodological choice. As the quote by Faye V. Harrison in the first *Essential* in this chapter underscores, research methods themselves are neither feminist nor nonfeminist. They offer us tools through which to collect data and are used in a variety of scholarly projects. Rather, it is our methodology—the rationale we create for the links we make among feminist theory, our research strategies and ethical decisions, the data we collect, and its relevance to the world—that marks our research as feminist ethnography. Nevertheless, the choices we make to utilize and/or combine specific methods are critical to the success of feminist ethnographic research and should be both pragmatic and political. Pragmatically, we must ask ourselves: What methods will give us the data we need to answer our research questions? What limitations exist for particular methods and will this undermine our research goals? What possibilities are there for combining methods (and perhaps collaborating with other researchers and/or participants) to broaden the net we cast for data that can inform our project?

In this section, we introduce some of the most common ethnographic research methods, particularly those that have been used in innovative or particularly effective ways by feminist ethnographers. Our list of methods is not exhaustive, but there really are a limited number of ways to collect data. Feminist methodologies, however, can deeply influence how we *use* those methods. For example, interviewing is one ethnographic method. A feminist interpretation of that technique might result in the researcher allowing interviewees to ask them questions, as Christa did with LGBTQ people in her interview-based project on **reproductive loss**, such as miscarriage and adoption loss. The project grew out of her desire to make more resources available for LGBTQ families. Christa began each interview by telling participants that they were also welcome to ask her questions about her experience as a queer woman who had a second-trimester loss. Another example is when Dána-Ain conducted interviews with battered women. Acknowledging their difficult circumstances and experiences, she was open to conducting the interviews in nontraditional ways. One woman did not want to tell the story of her life on tape, so, instead, she drew a timeline. Another woman wanted to be given the questions so she could answer them in the privacy of her own space with Dána-Ain's recorder.

What we do here is offer an overview of several key methods and at least one practical example of their use by a feminist ethnographer. You may explore this further in the *Thinking Through . . .* activity listed at the conclusion of this chapter.

Participant-Observation

Participant-observation is the most common method employed in ethnographic fieldwork. It involves intensive involvement with a group of people over an extended period of time (often a year or more). Ethnographers take detailed fieldnotes and frequently conduct informal interviews during participant-observation. They often pair this method with others, such as in-depth interviewing, life history, or surveys. Although some journalists have adopted the term participant-observation to refer to spending a few days or a week with a group, most scholars find this usage problematic, since the goal of participant-observation is to gain a deep and intimate familiarity with a community. Many students conduct what some professors call "mini-ethnographies" over the course of a semester-long class.

Participant-observation is often considered the mainstay of cultural anthropology, but is also commonly used in sociology, communication studies, social psychology, religious studies, and human geography, among other disciplines. Some critics have argued that participant-observation is merely an "awareness" of things around you, but participant-observation relies upon detailed, recorded observations and reflection upon one's own participation in ways that allow for the collection of a large body of data for ethnographic analysis. Anthropologist Aimee Meredith Cox describes engaging in her work as what she calls an "observing participant," underscoring the intention with which one approaches a project, and the longevity that allows for physical relationships to develop.[11]

🧠 ESSENTIAL

Excerpt from *Queer Activism in India* by Naisargi Dave

Naisargi Dave *earned her PhD in anthropology at the University of Michigan and now teaches in anthropology and the Centre for South Asian Studies at the Asian Institute at the University of Toronto. She is the author of* Queer Activism in India: A Story in the Anthropology of Ethics *(2012). The following excerpt discusses the questions and process that led to her participant-observation.*

There is no one setting from which to write an ethnography of lesbian activism in India: queerness has a way of moving about. Gay lovers escape oppressive regimes, lesbians run away from small towns, women leave their villages to become men, hijras move to the city, and nonresident Indians come looking for their roots, perhaps founding an NGO while they are at it. But this is not just an ethnography of the movement of people and things; it is also an ethnography of how queer people came to be, how they imagine, transform, and are transformed. These are questions that require both physical location and conceptual mobility. My methodology was thus multi-sited. I accompanied activists as they traversed the network of their associations across India and also conducted short periods of research on my own in Bangalore, Bombay, and Pune. My place of everyday engagement, though, was Delhi. . . .

I lived and conducted fieldwork in this remarkable city between December 2001 and December 2003. My work began smoothly through a snowballing of acquaintances. . . . I made friends and accompanied them to meetings, or gay nights at a local club. I could soon move comfortably through this world on my own.

I write in this book not only about my friends, but about people whose work I believe in. As a queer woman, these are also the people who have made my own life fuller, easier, and better. To write critically in such a context has been a source of trouble—for my conscience and, occasionally, my relationships . . .

Although I have strived to be careful and accurate, and to honor my relationships of care and politics through a practice of critical solidarity,[1] my perspective, like anyone's, remains utterly partial. As I say again later on, I spent more time, and shared more deeply with some than others. Often this was rooted in politics—I was drawn, for example, toward groups with strong feminist connections and, sometimes rather conflictingly, with feminists who sought radical, explicit queer transformations. An ethnographer with different priorities, passions, and education who sat through the same meetings as I did at the same period in history would surely have tracked different debates and offered other conclusions.

Source: Dave, Naisargi N. *Queer Activism in India: A Story in the Anthropology of Ethics.* Durham, NC: Duke University Press, 2012, 21–22, 26–27.

[1] Sharad Chari and Henrike Donner, "Ethnographies of Activism," *Cultural Dynamics*, 2010.

Feminist ethnographers conduct participant-observation in many ways. The following excerpt offers an example of multisited participant-observation in anthropologist Naisargi Dave's research on queer activism in India.[12] She describes how she carried out her research and how the relationships that ethnographers forge can complicate, but also deepen, our research. Although this method has most often been used in person, for the past few decades some ethnographers have turned to virtual communities for fieldwork. And with the advent of COVID-19 in 2020, many projects moved online unexpectedly and researchers—including students working on undergraduate and graduate theses—have probed the benefits and drawbacks of digital fieldwork.

In the early aughts, anthropologist Tom Boellstorff was among the first to conduct fieldwork entirely virtually, within an online community. In his groundbreaking virtual ethnography *Coming of Age in Second Life: An Anthropologist Explores the Virtually Human*,[13] he argued that ethnographers need to take the spaces of virtual communities, and their inhabitants, seriously, conducting fieldwork in much the same way as ethnographers do so in the "actual" world. Boellstorff set aside time for fieldwork at regular intervals, developed a presence in Second Life, and interacted with other participants in much the same way as an ethnographer would do in any field site. For Boellstorff, this means he was particularly attentive to the ways that power and inequities form in virtual locations, as well as ways in which they reflect, replicate, or challenge those that participants may experience in "actual" worlds. Although he never made an effort to meet any participants outside of their virtual community, his own virtual experience (as well as theirs) reflected "a complex transaction between the designers [of virtual worlds], who have certain goals and desires about what people will do, and the denizens of the virtual worlds themselves who exercise individual and collective agency."[14] His analysis focused on themes such as personhood, intimacy, community, and inequality in virtual communities.

Ethnographic Interviewing

In the same way that participant-observation is more than just "awareness" of people, things, and settings an ethnographer encounters, ethnographic interviewing is more than just asking a predetermined set of questions. Interview questions are usually generated from ethnographic fieldwork that involves other methods, such as participant-observation and informal interviewing. Further, ethnographers conduct open-ended interviews, in the sense that they frequently depart from predetermined questions to get more information using probes, such as "Can you tell me more about that?" when a participant strays from the focus of the ethnographer's questions to more specific ways: "I heard you sigh when you spoke about that. Can you share more about why?" In many cases, ethnographic interviews become more like conversations than one-sided questioning, and the ethnographer frequently learns more about their projects by fielding questions from participants in this context. Going "off-topic" also allows ethnographic interviews to delve further into things that are important to participants. Feminist ethnographers have found this useful as a guide to how their project unfolds and what elements of it become central to their analysis.

Claire Sterk's *Tricking & Tripping: Prostitution in the Era of AIDS* has become a "classic" ethnography on prostitution and drug use in the 1980s and 1990s when HIV/AIDS was becoming a pandemic.[15] Trained as both a sociologist and a medical anthropologist in the Netherlands, Sterk engaged in participant-observation over ten years, ultimately conducting in-depth interviews with 180 women. This is a *far* greater number of interviews than most ethnographic projects, which oftentimes rely on between 25 and 50, and sometimes ethnographers write their accounts primarily about a single individual. The sheer quantity of interview data Sterk collected underscores the importance of this method to her project. Particularly since Sterk left the field daily (versus an ethnographer who lives with a population for extended periods of time), she found it essential to collect in-depth stories from the women she met during fieldwork to get a fuller picture of their lives. In her ethnography, she quotes extensively from many participants—sometimes including two or three excerpts per page—which serves her goal of humanizing the women she interviewed, in contrast to many dismissive portrayals of prostitutes' lives. Utilizing direct quotes also allows participants to speak for themselves, versus an analytical paraphrase by the ethnographer. Of course, the ethnographer is usually the one choosing the excerpts (though not always), so it is important to always be thinking about how an ethnographic account is shaped, even if the words of participants make up the bulk of it.

Ethnographic interviewing often takes place during fieldwork and ethnographers frequently find that the political and cultural contexts of our interlocutors (and ourselves) have unexpected influences on our research. While all research is marked by its particular historical moment, when ethnographic research occurs in the context of catastrophic events—such as political conflict, resistance, or natural disasters—these issues are likely to have significant impacts on research projects. In the following *Spotlight*, we focus on the challenges and possibilities that came about for student researchers during the global COVID-19 pandemic. The restrictions on mobility, restructuring of care and work responsibilities, and the fears and losses that often accompany global and local crises impacted researchers in many different ways. Some had to leave fieldsites, others faced funding and logistical constraints, and some had to abandon projects (and sometimes degrees) all together. Most researchers had to shift their plans in some ways—but for many, this also required a shift of ideological assumptions about ethnographic fieldwork. While some were able to use technology to continue participant-observation, many had to rely on (digitally mediated) ethnographic interviewing or surveys to complete their studies, or abandon ethnographic research all together. Especially for those with strict timelines, like undergraduates working on senior theses, which typically involve just a few months of research, the effects of the pandemic were particularly profound. Those of us who teach and advise student research projects got to witness students respond in real time and grapple with ethical complexities that many more established scholars were able to avoid by postponing fieldwork, requesting extensions on grants, or shifting to different projects. Graduate and undergraduate students lived the realities of the pandemic through their ethnographic fieldwork in very immediate and tangible ways. Here we home in on several undergraduate students who navigated completing their degrees—which required an undergraduate thesis—while maintaining their commitments to feminist, queer, anti-racist, and decolonial approaches to ethnography.

ꙮ SPOTLIGHT ꙮ

Class of 2021 Undergraduates on Fieldwork during a Pandemic

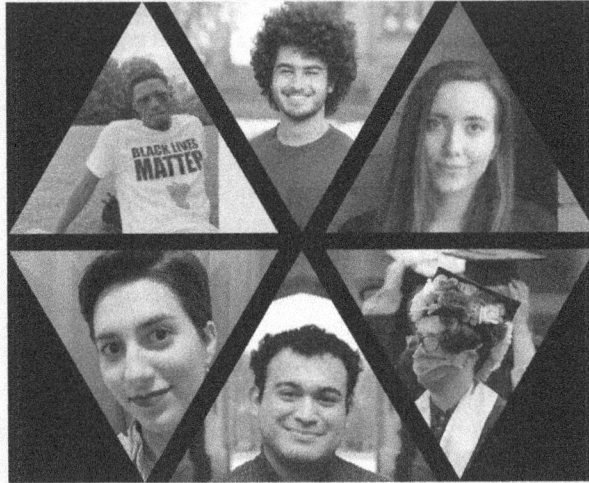

Clockwise from top left: Perry Worthey, saeed husain, Hannah Lane-Davies, Hayden Ruairí Nolan, César Oswaldo López, and Ella Lang.

saeed husain, Hannah Lane-Davies, Ella Lang, César Oswaldo López, Hayden Ruairí Nolan, and Perry Worthey *all earned their BAs at the College of Wooster in 2021 (with a mix of majors and minors in Anthropology, Education, Environmental Studies, Sociology, and Women's, Gender & Sexuality Studies). They came to college in rural Ohio from across the United States—Kalamazoo, Michigan; New York City; Atlanta, Georgia—and Karachi, Pakistan, with the intention of conducting fieldwork to complete a required senior thesis.[1] Christa had the opportunity to work with some of them as primary advisor on their theses (meeting once a week throughout the 2020–2021 academic year) and others less formally through conversations about their projects that continued from previous courses.[2] We connected on masked socially distant walks around campus and via video chats from multiple locations—from their dorm rooms and college libraries to their childhood bedrooms and the homes of family and friends who needed care and support during the pandemic. After graduation, I sent them this question: How did approaching ethnography with commitments to feminist/ queer/antiracist/decolonial ethnographic approaches influence how you shifted your research as a result of the pandemic? The conversations that ensued were a powerful reminder of how the pandemic—as well as research intertwined with social justice work—deepened many of our commitments to shifting the balance of power in ethnographic research.*

Most of these students found their research topics shifting—not necessarily to an entirely different focus, but the questions they posed changed. They became centered on what were now more salient issues: the effects of the pandemic on marginalized communities; the intense toll that studying and working remotely has taken on LGBTQ+ mental health; the global reverberations of antiracist organizing that intensified after the murder of George Floyd, Breonna Taylor, and so many others; and the intensified care obligations felt most acutely by female caregivers—particularly women of color/BIPOC women already engaged in professional carework—as schools, daycares, and some eldercare facilities shut down.

Most students had to shift their fieldwork plans from focusing on a single, geographically bounded community to include a broader range of participants across many different "fieldsites." As a Black man in the United States, **Perry Worthey** knew his thesis would focus on the Black Lives Matter movement. But the pandemic forced him to conduct much of that research from his dorm room rather than at the protests he had envisioned forming the basis of his research. This shift brought him into contact with BLM activists BLM activists from throughout the world who shared many of his own goals.

Similarly, **César Oswaldo López** shifted his research site from Atlanta to recruit "any queer Central American in the United States." He enjoyed the opportunity to connect with a broader range of participants but found that the necessity of virtual interviews made it much more difficult to gauge emotional and physical cues when he was "not able to observe participants' body language beyond the borders of our cameras." This made him more intentional about his approach to participants' agency and active consent, particularly when they entrusted him with sensitive or traumatic experiences they had had with family and family life. As he explained, "this topic was really close to home for me. It's what drove me to it but it also meant that it was emotionally draining at times and made it difficult to process . . . [especially] amid the pandemic, when folks were forced to stay distant from relatives or closer to home, my conversations with participants were a lot more salient/difficult in [this] moment." He ended up writing at length about the significance of participants' long pauses, deep breaths, fractured responses, fidgety hands, watery eyes, and cracked voices.

Other students also found themselves approaching research from a trauma-informed lens, understanding (sometimes from their own experiences or from witnessing others') that the pandemic has caused not only physical and emotional trauma from being sick and losing loved ones but also intense mental exhaustion and extreme loneliness that impacted researchers, as well as those we ask to participate in our research. For instance, **Hayden Ruairí Nolan** chose to shift from the in-depth interviews they had planned to conduct with queer, transgender, and nonbinary people who had grown up in small towns in the United States South to a survey-based methodology that drew experiences from the Midwest and other areas as well. Although they were conscious that this posed limitations because responses were less detailed than the in-depth stories they had imagined collecting in interviews, they also recognized the challenges potential participants were facing—many of whom were now living at home with unsupportive relatives—that made asking for a conversational virtual or phone interview unethical in this context. The geographical breadth of the responses also allowed for comparative reflection on the experiences or queer, transgender, and nonbinary people in different rural areas.

saeed husain's research focused on Sikh art collectors of Indian descent. Having been raised as a Muslim in Pakistan, he felt the research was particularly important in promoting more unity between descendants of nations and religious traditions that had so often been in conflict. They found commonality in a decolonial approach to museum work and ethnographic research:

> Colonial anthropology was conducted with a depleted sense of humanity and [reliance on] economic inequities. During my research I limited how many times I would contact someone, and how long/complex I needed my messages to be. Even at the time of interviews, I needed to give my interlocutors the space they required for changing times or cutting interviews short. This will be a practice that I will continue [in graduate research and beyond], since the ethnographer is often researching from a greater place of privilege.

He also noted the ethical dilemmas that came up when the lines between personal communications and research ties became increasingly unclear during the pandemic. While some social media platforms require public profiles, others restrict access only to "friends." Many students (and participants in their research) use social media for both personal and professional purposes, often intermingling photos of themselves with friends or family and posts about upcoming professional talks or links to content related to their work. Some found themselves unsure about whether participants' "informed consent" should extend to such contexts, as well as more informal means of communication like text and WhatsApp messages and chats. While social media platforms have been a powerful tool for activism in the last decade, the pandemic markedly increased their usage and students found minimal professional guidance on ethnographic work on social media. husain linked this to the colonial logic of assuming research will take place on private property, often on colonized land. The public-private distinction in virtual spaces is also shaped by this logic, as well as the vagaries of accessibility and stratification of infrastructure that allows (or doesn't allow) particular types of access.

Several students were struck by how conducting interviews (and, in some cases, participant-observation) in digital spaces allowed for different kinds of interactions. When participants were in a space where they felt comfortable, like the familiarity of their room or even their bed, "the often-casual nature of the locations of both participants and [the researcher] during interviews [were reminiscent] of ongoing pandemic-era conversations about working from home, and particularly from bed." In her interviews with birth workers, including midwives, obstetricians, doulas, and social workers, **Hannah Lane-Davies** drew on the work of queer disability justice scholar Leah Lakshmi Piepnza-Samarasinha, who writes about working from their bed: "Draped in pillows, red and plum sheets, surrounded by good art to look at, curtained by plum sari fabric. This is my place of power, the fulcrum, the place everything emerges from."[3] As Lane-Davies asks, "What does it mean for us to normalize this behavior, cultivating an affect of coziness [in the context of research]? How might working from bed be a form of care? If meeting people where they are is a feminist practice, how might intentional, consensual digital interactions follow a feminist praxis?"

In this vein, multiple students felt that their research became more collaborative because of the pandemic, even though they were initially concerned it would be less so. In her study of the materiality of clothing, **Ella Lang** had initially planned to take photographs of participants and their clothing during in-person interviews but shifted to asking them to provide photographs that guided their video interviews:

> An unexpected result of this unanticipated change was that participants became more like collaborators because of their increased involvement in the project, which was important to me in lessening the hierarchical relationship between researcher and participant. Additionally, the inclusion of photos draws attention to the form, color, and texture of the garment, which highlights its materiality for readers and for me, since we were not able to touch the garment personally.

In this way, Lang and other student-researchers also sought to make their projects more reliant on sensory experiences that move beyond the written page and enter into more public-facing initiatives. Lang created a companion website with a creative mix of photos and text that encouraged viewers to experience the project in a multidimensional and multisensory format. husain felt that the pandemic had reaffirmed, and ultimately strengthened his commitment to public, activist scholarship. Having served as a student member of academic hiring committees, he felt that academia needs to place "greater emphasis on continued engagements (activist or otherwise) [that an ethnographer] has made with the communities that they have worked with, rather than scores of academic papers behind paywalls." Most found that the pandemic reinforced the need for ethnographers to work *with* communities and make their work more accessible to audiences beyond academia.

Some also shared their disappointment that they were not able to engage in the more hands-on activist work they had intended. As Lane-Davies shared, "especially as someone with academic privilege, I wanted to show up and demonstrate commitment in ways that couldn't happen without in-person gatherings." But post-graduation, several have already found themselves returning to that work. Lane-Davies offered this as her biggest take-away:

> I didn't get to be as involved as I wanted to in the context of my research, so I guess now I'm just doing it in the context of the rest of my life! I wanted to experience praxis and I initially felt like the pandemic took that opportunity away. But I still built the skills and now have the ability to use them in different ways. Actually, that says a lot about the applicability of ethnographic work beyond academia!

[1] While completing their senior theses, they were also involved in organizing that contributed to the sense of community on campus during a particularly trying senior year, including work with the Amnesty International, Black Student Association, First-Generation Student Organization, Noor (Wooster's Muslim student association), Organization of Latin American Students, the Sexual Respect Coalition, Sociology & Anthropology Club, Student Government, the Queer Student Union, as writers for the student newspaper, *The Wooster Voice*, and as performers in various music and dance productions. Most stressed that these connections and camaraderie were instrumental as they completed their research, particularly in the ways they kept conversations about ethical commitments centered throughout.

[2] You can find more information on their theses in The College of Wooster's I.S. (Independent Study) Database: https://www.wooster.edu/academics/research/is/database/.

[3] Leah Lakshmi Piepzna-Samarasinha, *Care Work: Dreaming Disability Justice*, 2018, 145.

Oral History/Life History

A style of ethnographic interviewing that is often associated with feminist ethnography is what many historians and archaeologists call "oral history" and many social researchers term "life history" interviewing. This method involves multiple planned interviews with individuals, during which they are encouraged to document key moments or a particular aspect of their lives that has developed over their life course. Many ethnographers begin with in-depth interviewing of various community members but encounter a particular individual whom they believe can accurately or eloquently capture experiences within a culture or community.

Probably the best-known ethnography featuring extensive life history interviewing is *Nisa: The Life and Words of a !Kung Woman* by anthropologist Marjorie Shostak. Although Shostak interviewed many !Kung San women in the Kalahari desert of Botswana about "what being a woman meant to them and what events had been important in their lives," she developed a particularly close bond with a middle-aged woman she calls Nisa.[16] Nisa was an accomplished storyteller, and over the course of fifteen interviews conducted during a two-week period, and six more during a second fieldwork trip four years later, Shostak amassed nearly thirty hours of recorded interviews in the !Kung language that produced hundreds of pages of literal translations once transcribed. Although Shostak focuses on Nisa's life story in her ethnography, she notes that it is just one view of !Kung life, because Nisa's interview represented only 8 percent of the total hours she spent conducting interviews with !Kung women. Drawing from her participant-observation and interviewing, Shostak begins each chapter with an overview of !Kung life to contextualize Nisa's stories. Nisa's stories are then included verbatim, though organized by Shostak to flow chronologically. *Nisa* has been widely read in introductory Cultural Anthropology courses, and is one of the books that has continued to popularize feminist ethnographic approaches since its publication in 1981. Shostak wrote a second book based on later interviews with Nisa as Shostak was battling breast cancer in the 1990s, *Return to Nisa*, which was published posthumously in 2000.[17] The poignancy of this second book, especially Nisa's efforts to heal Shostak's cancer through a traditional !Kung ceremony, offers a moving example of the power of life history to teach readers about unfamiliar cultural and political contexts.

The politics of memory and whose stories are valued is a critical question that anthropologist Tracy Fisher poses in producing life histories.

🦅 SPOTLIGHT 🦅

Tracy Fisher on Using Oral/Life History to Address Feminist Ethnographic Questions

Tracy Fisher *earned her PhD in anthropology from the Graduate Center, City University of New York (CUNY). Fisher's work is situated at the intersections of Feminist, Gender, and Sexuality Studies, Critical Race and Ethnic Studies, Black Diaspora Studies, and Anthropology. She takes a feminist intersectional approach to explore the ways in which people of different racial-ethnic backgrounds have actively transformed racial meanings, and, how they struggle to build transracial-ethnic gendered solidarities within specific political-economic and sociocultural contexts. She is the author of* What's Left

of Blackness: Feminisms, Transracial Solidarities, and the Politics of Belonging in Britain *(2012) and a coeditor of* Gendered Citizenships: Transnational Perspectives on Knowledge Production, Political Activism, and Culture *(2009).*

I am interested in life histories and oral histories as feminist ethnographic methods. I find life histories and oral histories fascinating. People can have recollections, but in the (re)telling of events, situations, and circumstances, they can recreate, reshape, and interrupt history and normative narratives. Thus, life histories and oral histories can disrupt master narratives, while at the same time serve as important sources of knowledge. Life histories and oral histories can illuminate people's every day experiences shaped by race, class, gender, and sexuality. The key is to couple these histories—because they have value and meaning—with other methods so one can obtain the most accurate interpretations of an event or history. The data gathered from life histories or oral histories can fill in the gaps that may occur by using a different ethnographic method. There are lots of different methods that one can employ to gather data, but the key for me is the kinds of questions one asks, the methodologies.

The kinds of questions asked in feminist projects are marked by their connection to justice-based visions for transformation. For example, what kind of power is embedded in gender? What are the ways in which we can challenge systems of knowledge and knowledge production? How can we talk about an oppositional consciousness? Can we imagine a world free from gendered racial and sexual exploitation and oppression? How might we imagine liberation and freedom in the broadest sense? What new tools are needed to combat inequality and injustice in the context of globalization?

Collecting **demographic information**—like gender identity, race, ancestry, nationality, religious background, or age—can be useful to provide nuance to individual examples, as well as provide a broader sense of the characteristics of a community or population. What is key to ethnographic research is finding out how a participant identifies themselves. Often, these details are shared in the course of an interview or oral history. But researchers frequently find it useful to have a list of characteristics they identify as important to gather information on that they can ask if that information is not offered by the participant at other times. Like ethnographic methods more broadly, you should choose strategically what things you will ask about, and think carefully about how you will ask for them. Sometimes gathering information about sexual orientation, income, age, and so on is just plain nosy. Researchers need to think ahead of time about *why* they want particular information and, during fieldwork, whether they need to make adjustments to what and how they are asking for it. Ultimately, we must balance several things: (1) we often cannot go back and collect demographic data after our initial encounter (so a researcher needs to gather most of that information "in the moment," during fieldwork or interview encounters), (2) ethnographers have a complicated colonial history of asking for information that participants did not wish to give (think of kinship studies gone awry when it was not culturally appropriate for people to give the names of ancestors), and (3) people's individual conceptions of their identity may not match how the ethnographer understands them. There is no one "right" way to gather pertinent information for a study, but thinking strategically about it and making changes to your approach when appropriate are key features of feminist ethnographic research.

In Christa's study on LGBTQ experiences with reproductive loss, conversations about identities sometimes stretched longer than some of my initial questions. Yet they proved helpful to understanding not only the differences among individual experiences but also the diversity of LGBTQ reproductive experiences. She chose to ask questions about gender identity, sexual orientation, relationship status, number of children, and so on at the conclusion of my interviews, rather than what is more typical in survey research of asking them at the beginning, so that they aren't overlooked by a respondent and can be used to code and analyze data that may differ for different populations. There were several reasons for this choice. One is that because this topic is a difficult one and since participants had prepared to talk about loss, she wanted to let them tell their story without a lot of preceding considerations. Also, most participants did not know her prior to meeting for our interview. Questions regarding gender identity, sexual orientation, race, and religion are often fraught with tension for LGBTQ people, sometimes stemming from negative experiences with previous researchers, healthcare professionals, and others. Similarly, sociologists have stressed that demographic questions about socioeconomic class (such as "what kind of work do you do?") can "immediately create social distance and distrust" on the part of participants.[18] She decided that after our discussions during interviews, participants could better choose what to share with her, or choose to omit, for the purposes of the study. Her goal in gathering this data was to provide context and nuance to stories from participants and to present **descriptive statistics** on the overall demographic picture of the fifty-four LGBTQ people interviewed, which ultimately challenged popular assumptions that LGBTQ family-making occurs only among white, wealthy, urban gay and lesbian couples.[19]

Whatever the particular decisions of the feminist ethnographer, they must be sensitive to cultural and community norms, designed to collect only data that the researcher sees as necessary for the project, and attentive to how people see their own identities (even if the researcher also wants to combine groups, like Black and African American, to indicate broader statistical trends).

Survey

The use of survey research—a predetermined set of questions that are given to a particular sample of a population—is by no means unique to ethnography. In fact, applied statistics and survey research have long dominated government censuses, health and marketing research, political and public opinion polls, and academic fields like psychology, political science, and quantitative sociology. Yet many ethnographers have found surveys a useful complement to fieldwork in order to offer a broader picture of the communities and groups they study. Some feminist ethnographers have also adopted the use of surveys with strategic political intent. Anthropologist Iris López, for instance, used a combination of participant-observation, survey, and interviews in *Matters of Choice: Puerto*

Rican Women's Struggle for Reproductive Freedom.[20] She used quantitative data on Puerto Rican women's reproductive health strategically to make the experiences of individuals and communities with sterilization more likely to be heeded by policy analysts and other academic researchers concerned with "scientific objectivity." For instance, as a result of her survey, López was able to document that 47 percent of Puerto Rican women in Brooklyn whom she surveyed were surgically sterilized, one of the highest rates of sterilization in the world. Although generating quantitative data is not typical of most ethnographic research, in this case, it served as a useful mechanism to demonstrate the importance of López's interview data in documenting trends among the women she interviewed.

A second example, where survey was central to an ethnographic project, is sociologist Mignon Moore's *Invisible Families: Gay Identities, Relationships, and Motherhood Among Black Women.*[21] Moore paired her survey with long-term participant-observation, attending social gatherings among Black lesbians in New York for twelve months before beginning formal fieldwork. After an additional twelve months of participant-observation, during which she hosted weekly dance parties, she administered a fourteen-page survey. Although survey response rates vary greatly, it is a testament to Moore's long-term involvement with the community and the trust she was able to build that participants returned 100 of 131 surveys, an impressive response rate of 76 percent. Moore used these surveys, along with other methods, to gain insight into the ways that Black women negotiate sexuality, family, and identity, and they guided the questions she then generated for individual interviews and focus groups around key topics, such as gender identity and religion. Surveys in and of themselves can never replace the ethnographic emphasis on close interactions with communities and individuals, but these examples show the utility of survey both to complement and to aid in generating additional data for feminist ethnographic studies.

Analysis of Cultural Material

The analysis of cultural materials spans a wide array of possible records, including archives, museum collections, and caches of virtual material, to name but a few. What is important is that cultural materials are different from other ethnographic data, in that someone other than the ethnographer collects them. They can represent an individual's collection or an historical record made to preserve particular information. Ethnographers frequently look at archival materials for what they can reveal about the group they are studying—history, changes over time, cultural norms (which may also change over time), representations of particular groups or actors. It is important to consider not only who compiled the materials but also for whom they were/are intended. Some cultural materials may be promotional (for instance, in advertising for a political candidate) or critical in nature (e.g., an op-ed piece). Additionally, keep in mind that cultural material of any kind, but particularly those collected digitally (for instance, through data capture), can be overwhelming to any researcher! It is important to develop meticulous labeling and categorization when preparing cultural materials for analysis.

Many feminist ethnographers employ cultural materials in their analyses, and one example is anthropologist Catherine Lutz and sociologist Jane Collins's *Reading National Geographic.*[22] The authors engaged in participant-observation at the National Geographic headquarters conducted extensive interviews with editors, photographers, and writers and provided a detailed history of the publication.

However, the bulk of their analysis centers on a systematic analysis of the photographs in the magazine and their captions (how they are presented to the reader). Lutz and Collins used extensive coding to categorize photos. They enlisted a group of graduate students to **code** all photos that included people by skin tone: black, bronze, and white. Some photos included multiple people or could not be categorized, but overall there was 86 percent agreement among themselves and their coders. They were also particular about choosing their timeframe for analysis, 1950–1986, citing key historical changes as a result of social movements. Ultimately, their analysis addresses the ways that the "ethnic other" is created in the pages and how race and gender are presented to exoticize Black people and "civilize" whites.

One of the biggest logistical challenges of analysis of cultural materials is to narrow down one's sources but still come away with meaningful results that can elucidate cultural patterns accurately. While Lutz and Collins, and their team of graduate researchers, were able to analyze over 400 full issues of *National Geographic*, let's use a similar project as an example to consider how a student ethnographer might further narrow their focus if they had less time and resources. Ethnographers aiming to look at changes in the representation of gender and race over several decades might choose to analyze all magazines from a single year of publication at regular intervals (i.e., 1951, 1961, 1971, 1981, or 1950, 1955, 1960, 1965, etc.). Alternatively, if a researcher aimed to look at changes over a shorter period of time (say, a single decade), they might look at the publication during a single month—to account for seasonal changes that might be affected by holidays or special issues—of each year (such as every March edition between 1965 and 1975). The bottom line is that any good ethnographer assessing inequities or prejudice in their analysis must find ways to systematically categorize their materials for meaningful analysis.

Social Media Research

A particular kind of cultural material that merits further discussion is social media. Since the early aughts, the popularity (and sometimes dissolution) of interactive online platforms like MySpace, Facebook, RenRen, Instagram, Twitter, Snapchat, Tic Tok, Weibo, and WhatsApp have become ubiquitous as a way to create and share textual and visual material with virtual communities. Social media platforms have been lauded as spaces for expansive connections with real and/or online communities and have served important roles in grassroots activism (think: Arab Spring, antigovernment protests across the Middle East in the early 2010s, and the intensification of the Movement for Black Lives in 2020–2021), as well as communication (and marketing) for a wide range of constituencies, including governments, political candidates, corporations, entrepreneurs, and nonprofit organizations. Social media is also frequently demonized for the negative influences of cyberbullying and the propensity for "addiction" to the constant stream of new information, shares, and "likes."

Whatever your take on its efficacy, social media can provide a tremendous amount of content for ethnographic research. Marketing expert Robert Kozinets coined the term **netnography** in 1995 to refer to collecting data from public conversations on a broad range of digital communication networks for ethnographic analysis.[23] Others have described the application of ethnographic methods to the digital landscape as virtual ethnography, digital ethnography, cyberethnography, and the linguistically unwieldy webnography. Whatever the moniker (and there are heated debates about what terminology to use), researchers have increasingly begun to focus on the collection of textual, graphic, photographic, audio, and video data that may then be used for content analysis, as the basis for interviews, and sometimes analytic techniques to reveal patterns and trends in **"big data"** (large data sets) on human behavior and interactions. Netnography has become ubiquitous in consumer research across a broad range of industries, such as gaming franchises, tourism, and healthcare. It has also drawn disciplines where ethnography is common—anthropology, education, geography, sociology, etc.—into conversation (and sometimes collaboration) with researchers in library and information sciences and computer science. Analyses of this kind can be shaped by, augment, and in some cases replace in-person participant-observation and other ethnographic data-gathering.

Importantly—especially from a feminist ethnographic perspective—ethical debates about how, when, where, and by whom digital data is used have occupied nearly as much scholarly attention as the methods for collecting and analyzing it. Researchers encountering digital media—with its multiple entry points and non-linear organization—are faced not only with an abundance of possible data and pathways of access but also questions about privacy and **informed consent**, which is typically a written (or sometimes oral) agreement when a person who participates in research gives permission to the researcher to use quotes, stories, photos, or other information in their research and publications. Many digital platforms involve multiple interlocutors who view, read, comment, "like," repost, skim, curate, lurk, and leave at different intervals and frequencies. Questions about what is public or private become particularly blurred with platforms that support public profiles and personal social networks. These are by no means new concerns for feminist ethnographers (think about how you might handle that spot-on insight from a family member who walked through the kitchen while you were recording an interview but never consented to being part of your research?). Yet digital mediums do not, as some utopian visionaries suggest, neutralize the power imbalances inherent in all social interaction, and thus all ethnographic inquiry.

In her research on digital repositories of Black life (and death), like the TransAtlantic Slave Trade Database, historian and digital humanist Jessica Marie Johnson explains:

> Bias is built into the architecture of digital technology. The digital, like any tool, institution, or system across society, from law and medicine to the academy, will be radical or transformative only to the extent that researchers, programmers, designers, hackers, and users make an effort to dismantle the residue of commodification that is slavery's legacy in the New World. Invoking black digital practice draws attention to the many ways users, content creators, coders, and programmers have worked ethical, intentional praxis into their work in pursuit of more just and humane productions of knowledge. Because blackness is most often constructed in proximity to bondage and the rise of Atlantic slaving, black digital practice uses the commodification of blackness during the slave trade as a reference point, building sites, projects, organizations, and tools that resist and counteract slavery's dehumanizing impulses.[24]

When viewed as a reference point, rather than an end in and of themselves, these archives—in this case of slave ship manifests replete with biometrics and racist nomenclatures and other historical accounts created by slave traders—can stimulate critical and potentially radically transformative discussions. For instance, the numerical data (and computational analysis of it) made available through public, accessible, searchable databases demonstrated that enslaved African women and youth were brought to the Americas by slave traders in much larger numbers than previously assumed. This has inspired research into the significance of their contributions to Black life and struggles against the brutalities of slavery.

Ethnographers have increasingly joined coalitions of humanists and social scientists like #transformDH, which describes itself as "an academic guerrilla movement seeking to (re)define capital-letter Digital Humanities as a force for transformative scholarship by collecting, sharing, and highlighting projects that push at its boundaries and work for social justice, accessibility, and inclusion."[25] Feminist ethnographers have also contributed to the skepticism about the radical "democratizing" possibilities of digital technology—in terms of both who has access to it and how technology has a long history of being used as a tool for control and systematic discrimination.[26]

Here we offer two examples of feminist ethnographic inquiry involving Twitter, a public-facing platform which allows users to share images along with 280 characters (a number that doubled in 2017 for non-Asian languages from the original 140). Sociologist Latoya Lee utilizes Twitter as a source of ethnographic data in her analysis of Black Twitter as a medium that can be used to disrupt and resist. However, education scholar James Popham and criminologist Latasha VanEvery argue that Twitter can also become an environment that replicates stereotypes.

Lee examines how Black Twitter—over 40 percent of users are young African Americans—deployed hashtags and "textual poaching" to resist degrading narratives of Black and Brown bodies. Informed by participant-observation, Lee tracked how hashtags such as #ICantBreathe, #DangerousBlackKids, and #AliveWhileBlack began to "trend" on Twitter within hours of news reports of the murders of Mike Brown, Eric Garner, Jordan Davis, Trayvon Martin, Tamir Rice, and Renisha McBride. Lee took twenty-four-hour snapshots after the first usage of each hashtags to see how often and with what frequency messages were retweeted, which tweets were picked up by popular Twitter users, and what was picked up by mainstream media. One moment Lee highlights, for instance, followed the 2014 conviction of the Detroit man who claimed to have "feared for his safety" when he shot Renisha McBride on his porch after she was in a car accident and came to his home for help. After the trial, the Associated Press tweeted, "Suburban Detroit homeowner convicted of second-degree murder for killing woman who showed up drunk on porch." The response was almost immediate. Black Twitter countered the suggestion that McBride was at fault with viral sarcastic tweets like "#APHeadlines millions of Africans complain after free cruise to the Americas; slave traders find them 'ungrateful'" and "Children flee tourist locations in Latin America in hunt for government handouts and comfy beds in deportation centers. #APHeadlines." Lee describes this as the creation of a digital homespace, a collective exercise in which users create their own communities to express adoration or frustration with specific media content, exposing racial bias in mainstream news coverage.[27]

A second example shows how viral tweets, particularly images, can perpetuate stereotypes. Popham and VanEvery examine how Indigenous protest was portrayed on Twitter during 2016 protests at Standing Rock, North Dakota, against the Dakota Access Pipeline (DAPL), an over 1,000-mile underground oil transport system funded by the US government. In this case, Popham and McEvery used ethnographic content analysis of the social media commentary that accompanied an image of a figure on a horse against the backdrop of law enforcement officers who are flanked by military-style vehicles. This image was widely shared within a few days of its first appearance on Twitter, and the authors highlight how the captions carried colonial undertones, such as paternalism and archetypal labeling. The authors argue that the public consumption and relabeling of this image via social media shifted attention away from the justice issues that precipitated the protests toward consumable narratives that replicate Indigenous stereotypes and gain public significance by accumulating shares and likes.[28]

In thinking about how to use social media as a site of ethnographic data collection, one can track the frequencies of hashtags in real time and conduct archived searches on particular hashtags using the advanced search tab with various filters on platforms like Twitter. Researchers can also use more advanced text analysis software, like Voyant (a free, **open-source** application: https://voyant-tools.org/), to create visual representations of data, like when particular hashtags are used together (see discussion of Moya Bailey's research on #girlslikeus in the next chapter).

Ethnohistory

Ethnohistory combines ethnographic work with historical analysis. It is used by ethnographers tracing the history of communities in many disciplines, as well as a common technique among historical archaeologists. It produces a cultural history by examining—but moving beyond—existing historical records, such as documents and archives. Ethnohistory often includes an analysis of folklore, archaeological materials, music, language, museum collections, and may incorporate life history interviews. As Lee Baker discussed in chapter 2 on historicizing feminist ethnography, uncovering historically marginalized voices is challenging and can require intensive work for the feminist ethnographer. One must also consider how these power differentials play out, not only in social interactions but also in how materials were produced, and for what audiences.

A poignant example of the use of ethnohistory in feminist ethnography is Janice Boddy's *Civilizing Women: British Crusades in Colonial Sudan*, which examines British efforts to eliminate Sudanese practices such as female genital cutting (FGC, which some also term female genital mutilation or FGM) through health and education projects. Boddy draws on a broad range of archival sources to produce a nuanced ethnohistorical context for her analysis, including government materials published by British midwives and teachers, advertisements, novels, memoirs, and both scholarly and popular histories, especially during the period from 1920 to 1946, when British colonial efforts were most intense. The second half of her book relies on her participant-observation among Arab Sudanese women in Hofriyat conducted in the 1970s and 1980s to analyze the effects of post-coloniality on notions of agency, Islamic piety, and gender identity. Ultimately, she underscores that feminism is not a homogenous movement, nor do Sudanese women all agree about circumcision. She argues that those who oppose FGC must move beyond a framework of judgment toward one of mutual respect, attentive to the social and historical contexts of African lives. Further, they must consider the work of Sudanese feminists who address FGC not in isolation but alongside issues of reproductive health more generally, as well as the negative effects of structural adjustment on food security and health services. The power of ethnohistory as a primary method in Boddy's work is that it offers important context for what is often construed by international anticircumcision activists and politicians as merely a contemporary ethical and cultural debate.

As a second—quite different—example of the use of ethnohistory, we include an interview with feminist historical archaeologist Whitney Battle-Baptiste, who, although she does not conduct ethnography, has found feminist ethnographic approaches essential to her historical archaeological analysis. Battle-Baptiste's work pays particular attention to the intellectual legacy of African American literary fiction as it directly documents the lives of African Americans. While some historical documents exist from this time period, they are written primarily by white men and some white women; there is little recorded in African American women's voices. Thus, although literary fiction is not typically incorporated into archaeological analysis, in reconstructing the past, fictional accounts shape Battle-Baptiste's feminist analysis and interpretation in important ways. Feminist archaeologists have long critiqued the androcentric focus of the archaeological record,[29] but Battle-Baptiste's attention to contemporary ethnographic work on African Americans as well as historical literary fiction offers new methodological possibilities for feminist ethnographic approaches within archaeology.

In her book *Black Feminist Archaeology*, Battle-Baptiste delves into how she utilized a Black feminist framework to conduct her archaeological research.[30] In addition to the literature of Zora Neale Hurston, she drew upon Black literary fiction writers Toni Morrison and Gayl Jones. Her analysis is also informed by feminists including the Combahee River Collective, Audre Lorde, and feminist anthropologists, such as Johnetta Cole, Irma McLaurin, Lynn Bolles, and Maria Franklin, among others. The point of her methodological approach is to use a Black feminist framework as a lens to examine race, class, and gender in the past. Battle-Baptiste's reading and engagement with Black feminist theory, ethnography, and literature shaped her interpretations of the domestic sphere of both female and male enslaved Africans. In this case, it influences research questions and opens up spaces to generate new theories. As new interpretations of a site become possible, different ways of viewing the space are inevitable. Battle-Baptiste's work inspires an expanded interpretive lens. For example, one could go to an archaeological site of an antebellum home and ask questions such as: Did the homes of women of African descent mimic the consumption patterns of white women? What Battle-Baptiste's discussion demonstrates is how a methodological strategy of engaging with Black feminist texts activates the conceptual framework or methodology (as Harrison discusses earlier in this chapter) that she draws upon to develop her project.

🜏 SPOTLIGHT 🜏

Whitney Battle-Baptiste on Historical Archaeology and Literary Fiction

Whitney Battle-Baptiste *describes herself as "a Black Feminist (who happens to be an archaeologist)." She received her PhD in anthropology at the University of Texas, Austin, in the African Diaspora Program and now teaches anthropology at the University of Massachusetts Amherst, where she was recently named director of the W. E. B. Du Bois Center. A historical archaeologist of African and Cherokee descent, she has done fieldwork at Colonial Williamsburg, the Hermitage, the W. E. B. Du Bois homestead, and other sites in the Southern United States and the Bahamas. She is the author of* Black Feminist Archaeology *(2011), which argues for the centrality of the tenets of Black feminist thought in reshaping contemporary historical archaeology.*

Battle-Baptiste began the interview by highlighting how archaeologists are typically concerned with "materials and landscapes. In historical archaeology, we move back and forth between artifact and . . . oral histories." She started her work during the 1990s when there was a disciplinary move toward public archaeology. As she emphasizes, however, "Public archaeology was still about taking the knowledge as an expert and presenting it to the public. So it is still a presentation, a distance model." When she began her own research, she admits that she "was still using that archaeological tool kit that separates you from living people because we are dealing with the past," but she soon began to see the intersections of her work and Black women's fiction. Zora Neale Hurston was an important influence: "It was through [her] fiction that I began to open my eyes and see that Black women were writing in ways that seemed relevant [to the materials I was researching]."

Literary fiction became increasingly important to her project.

"Because I started out looking at slavery and plantations I did not have the benefit of talking with women or being a participant-observer in a particular society or culture or place. . . . I didn't have the people to speak to, but I still had to figure out how patriarchy worked in a society that is different [for those that were] captive people. How is it different? How is gender functioning in these spaces? Because captive African men are not benefiting from patriarchy in the same ways white land-owning men are. Even though I don't have people to speak to, that's where I look to literature, I hate the term but, at the neo-slave narrative of how people who are remembering the past [are constructing it]."

*This interview was conducted by Ishan Gordon as part of her final project for Dána-Ain's course "Feminist Ethnographies" at the Graduate Center, CUNY.

Participatory Research

Many feminist ethnographers engage with participants before, during, and/or after their research, and discuss these decisions in their publications. They often seek guidance on issues of importance to the community and/or return transcriptions of interviews to participants for edits, comments, and to inspire further conversation. Some also engage in analysis with participants. Sociologist Shulamith Reinhartz describes collaborative research as a model "Designed to create social and individual change by altering the role relations of people involved in the project. . . . Differences in social status and background give way as shared decision-making and self-disclosure develop."[31] We would argue, in the spirit of Judith Stacey, that while this may be the *ideal*, collaborative researchers must be especially attentive to these relationships and reflect critically on their limits.

One collaborative strategy that has been used productively by feminist ethnographers is **Participatory Action Research (PAR)**. PAR aims to better understand a community not only through participation in it (as all ethnographers do) but also through working collaboratively with participants to make social change. PAR is predicated upon collaborative reflection and collectively inquiry. One example is education scholar Patricia Maguire's research with a group of battered women in Gallup, New Mexico, which she chronicles in *Doing Participatory Research: A Feminist Approach*.[32] Maguire draws on educator and philosopher Paulo Freire's emphasis on learning as a dialogical process,[33] working with formerly battered women in a cycle of reflection and action with the intention of moving forward after living with abusive partners.

An innovative example of PAR was orchestrated by faculty and students in the social psychology program at the Graduate Center, City University of New York. The project examined the impact of access to college classes in prison on women and their children, ultimately assessing the outcomes after their release from prison. The report, "Changing Minds: The Impact of College in a Maximum-Security Prison," is recognized as the basis for supporting the College in Prison movement and is a powerful example of feminist ethnography using a participatory, multi-method approach with the goal of creating social change.[34]

One genre of PAR is photovoice, a technique that has been used by feminist ethnographers to engage with participants to record and reflect upon their community. After participants take photos centered on a particular theme or topic (which may simply be about their lives), photographs are often displayed publicly or to small groups to promote critical dialogue about challenges and concerns they face. Additionally, photovoice—through photographs and critical responses by participants— may be used to lobby policy makers or others in positions of power. Public health researcher Caroline C. Wang's provocative work, "Worker Self-Narrative through Photography" (http://photovoicechina.com/), drew from participants who experienced common challenges in Chinese factories, such as low worker morale, lack of job satisfaction, and poor communication among workers and between workers and management. Wang presented these stories publicly and engaged with companies to improve the conditions for workers.

ESSENTIAL

Excerpt from "Photovoice" by Caroline C. Wang and Mary Ann Burris

Photo Credit: University of Michigan School of Public Health.

Photovoice was developed by **Caroline C. Wang** *from the department of health behavior and health education at the University of Michigan School of Public Health. Initially, Wang and her research partner* **Mary Ann Burris** *used the method in 1992 as a way to empower rural women in the Yunnan Province of China and to influence the policies and programs that affected them. Photovoice has become widely used in participatory research to promote participant engagement and empowerment. The following is an excerpt from "Photovoice: Concept, Methodology, and Use for Participatory Need Assessment" (1997):*

Photovoice is a process by which people can identify, represent, and enhance their community through a specific photographic technique. It entrusts cameras to the hands of people to enable them to act as recorders, and potential catalysts for change, in their own communities. It uses the immediacy of the visual image to furnish evidence and to promote an effective, participatory means of sharing expertise and knowledge. In previous instances, we have called this methodology photo novella. But the terms photo novella, foto novella, and photonovel have also been commonly used to describe the process of using photographs or pictures to tell a story or to teach language and literacy. . . .

Photovoice has three main goals: (1) to enable people to record and reflect their communities' strengths and concerns, (2) to promote critical dialogue and knowledge about important community issues through small and large discussion of photographs, and (3) to reach policymakers. In line with these goals, people can use photovoice as a tool for participatory research.

Source: Wang, Caroline, and Mary Ann Burris. "Photovoice: Concept, Methodology, and Use for Participatory Needs Assessment." *Health, Education & Behavior* 24, no. 3 (1997): 369.

The possibilities for photovoice and PAR in feminist ethnography are exciting and something that has become popular in recent years. Another example of a feminist ethnographic project that includes photovoice was the New York State Scholar Practitioner team directed by anthropologist Leith Mullings.[35] In 1996, the W. K. Kellogg Foundation developed a multiyear initiative that sought to understand the effects of welfare reform and health care in five states across the country: Wisconsin, Florida, Washington, Mississippi, and New York. Working with community members and employees of community-based organizations in Harlem and the Lower East Side of New York, the team invited people to use a camera to capture their community on film. This approach had the effect of allowing people to record and reflect on their community's strengths and concerns as they related to the passage of the Personal Responsibility and Work Opportunity and Reconciliation Act (PROWORA) of 1996. It promoted critical dialogue and knowledge about personal and community issues. One team member facilitates group discussions with photographers to develop captions and analyze the meaning of the images as they related to the impact of welfare policy on people's lives and to reach policy makers. The flexibility, innovation, and emphasis on participation that characterize this methodology made it ideal for the New York State Scholar Practitioner team to use as a strategic engagement with community participants.

Taking up Wang and Burris's use of photovoice, applied anthropologist Beth Uzwiak directs Story Collaborative, a research consulting firm located in Philadelphia. As part of her work, she often facilitates civic engagement and community-based research projects in the city, including Fairmount Park Conservancy's community catalyst residency in the Strawberry Mansion neighborhood of North Philadelphia. Location, in this case, was essential to Uzwiak's project. While its history is largely unknown outside of the neighborhood, many of the Black musicians and athletes who have roots there are quite familiar—influential figures like John Coltrane, Nina Simone, Jill Scott, Meek Mill, Dawn Staley, Muhammad Ali, and Joe Frazer. As Uzwiak explained,

> For decades, the fallout from de-industrialization, redlining and disinvestment and the consequences of racialized criminalization has shaped outside perceptions of the neighborhood as "blighted" and dangerous. Now, residents face economic pressures as "re-development" efforts unfold, from new housing construction to a multibillion-dollar Audubon bird sanctuary recently opened in the adjacent Fairmount Park.

Uzwiak's goal was to bring Strawberry Mansion's rich legacy to the fore while documenting the structural conditions and policies that have conspired to create hardship for residents.

Uzwiak collaborated with local artist collective Amber Art & Design and Fairmount Park Conservancy to launch a photovoice project as part of a **cultural** asset mapping process in the neighborhood to identify key cultural resources that could be incorporated into community planning. As part of an artist residency at the historic Hatfield House, she used ethnographic and art-based research methods to build relationships and create an enduring platform for neighbors' interests and needs to be heard.

> Along with curating a series of events and exhibitions showcasing local artists and musicians, we conducted 35 life history interviews detailing residents' experiences in the neighborhood. We complemented this data with two years of participant observation, informal interviews and several youth-led interactive roundtables recording input from more than 20 young people. Along with sharing memories of civil rights activism and cultural milestones—including when Stevie Wonder performed at the local high school, residents shared experiences of racism and marginalization, including anger at extractive engagement projects which serve to generate tokenistic participation for institutions rather than redirect resources to community-based entities.

From this data, they collaborated with residents to design a deck of playing cards celebrating local figures and places of significance. The cards were used to inspire dialogue with residents about future visions for the neighborhood. Uzwiak also designed the curriculum for a summer photography camp for local youth and developed a locally sourced historical curriculum for the camp using interview data. Community elders led fieldtrips, sharing neighborhood histories with youth, who used digital cameras to document local sites. Youth then curated and installed an exhibit of photos and videos at the conclusion of the camp and created "recording stations" to document residents' memories of living in the neighborhood. Uzwiak recalls that

> through the engagement process, we collaborated with residents to identify and create pathways for structural parity, moving from a process of documenting and circulating local assets to identifying areas where residents could increase participation and decision- making within local institutions with the goal of creating a more equitable development process, and restructuring how institutions partner and collaborate with community-based entities.

Interpretive Communities

All ethnographers engage in some form of thematic analysis of the data they collect, which involves the identification of recurrent themes. Narrative analysis using texts, such as transcriptions of interviews and cultural materials, can allow the ethnographer to construct a story from the data that can be a useful way of presenting it to an audience. How ethnographers locate such themes, however, has generated important conversations among feminist ethnographers. Creating interpretive communities is one strategy that some feminist ethnographers use, allowing them to be direct conversation with research participants.

When research participants are involved in analysis, they assist in shaping the ethnographic project by identifying themes that are salient and meaningful, often encouraging researchers to rethink, revise, and develop new thematic frameworks. Dána-Ain's book *Black Battered Women and Welfare Reform*,[36] for instance, benefited immeasurably from the interpretive community she formed among some participants to consider themes that were emerging in her research. In this case, Dána-Ain gave copies of oral history interviews back to the women for both approval and ideas about emerging themes. One theme that several women identified was how they use talking to get resources (such as apartments, jobs, and housing). Because several women noted the same phenomenon, Dána-Ain expanded upon this theme in her work, calling it "Speech Acts," which became a subtopic in one of the chapters of her ethnography.

In her new book *Reproductive Injustice: Racism, Pregnancy, and Premature Birth*,[37] Davis examines Black women's experiences of racism during medical encounters during their pregnancies and after the births of premature infants. In the absence of an activist organization that Dána-Ain could work alongside that would hold her work accountable, she developed a variation of her earlier use of an interpretive community. She drew from the expertise of four reproductive justice activists and scholars by forming a reproductive justice interlocutor team. While they did not conduct interpretive analyses of the data, over the course of eight years, the team members regularly conferred with Dána-Ain—pointing her to sources, assisting her in thinking through the ethical implications of the research on premature birth and neonatal intensive care units, connecting her with informants and providing insights into the theoretical framing of the project.

Interpretive communities may also be a collective endeavor undertaken by scholars committed to fostering feminist ethnographic work *among themselves*. For instance, the collection *Interpreting Women's Lives: Feminist Theory and Personal Narratives* began as a collective project among scholars in the Personal Narratives Group, a research group affiliated with the Center for Advanced Feminist Studies at the University of Minnesota in 1984. The interdisciplinary group met to facilitate and coordinate feminist scholarship and conduct research that placed personal narratives at its core. As a result of meeting regularly over several years, the group of historians, anthropologists, and literary scholars implemented several related projects: co-teaching courses on women's autobiography, organizing a conference on autobiography, biography and life history, and eventually publishing *Interpreting Women's Lives*. As they write in the introduction:

> [Ongoing] discussions . . . made us increasingly aware that we were seeing women's personal narratives from new perspectives. We were repeatedly reminded of the importance of the narrator's own self-definitions as they talked about their lives, in contrast to the definitions imposed by interpreters of personal narratives and by the narrators' own society. The importance of the political and institutional contexts of both the narrator and the interpreter of a personal narrative became increasingly obvious. We began to question the relationship between the form of a narrative and the interpretation of the life story told. These issues exemplify our own intellectual transformation.[38]

Conclusion

Whatever methods or analytical techniques you choose, our aim in this chapter is to have gotten you thinking critically and creatively about the research process. Inevitably, just like two ethnographers could do research in the same area and have very different experiences based on their positionality and the topics that interest them, ethnographers use the methods and analytical techniques outlined above in very different ways, and often toward very different ends. Our intent is to get you thinking about and experimenting with a variety of possibilities and reflecting on how to choose the methods that will be most fruitful for your project. Indeed, the feminist practice of being attentive to marginality and reflecting critically upon power differentials within the research context is an important first step toward conducting feminist ethnography.

THINKING THROUGH . . .

Three Options to Explore Methodological Possibilities

1. Select any one of the methods discussed above. Using three or four different sources, prepare a brief critical discussion of how a range of researchers have utilized that method. The focus of this assignment is for you to understand the possibilities for, but also limits and critiques of, particular methods.
2. Read a feminist ethnography of your choice and take note of what methods the author uses, how they explain their methodology, and their strategies for analysis. Write a brief essay summarizing their methods, the challenges they faced, and what methods you might consider using if you were working on the same research topic.
3. Select a topic that you are interested in—maybe incarceration, Black Lives Matter, access to birth control, heritage studies, whatever you like. Then, in a brief essay, discuss first your methodological strategy and how at least three of the methods described would be effective (or not) in researching your topic.

THINKING THROUGH . . .

Word Cloud Magic!

Don't think this takes the place of more substantive data analysis (such as manual coding or qualitative data analysis programs) . . . but creating a word cloud can provide you with a "first run" of thematic coding through visual representation of text data. Word clouds are typically used to depict the importance of single words or phrases based on font size and/or color. Take a previously written paper or data you have collected (say, interview transcripts, digitized archival materials, data collected on social media or online forums, or typed fieldnotes) and upload it into a word cloud generator, such as WordCloud.com, WordArt.com, or Abcya.com. You can use the resulting visualization to see what major words are most prevalent in your text, and it may help you create a title or even an analytical focus!

Suggested Resources

Rae Bridgman, Sally Cole, and Heather Howard-Bobiwash, eds. (1999) *Feminist Fields: Ethnographic Insights.*

D'Lane R. Compton, Tey Meadow, and Kristen Schilt, eds. (2018) *Other, Please Specify: Queer Methods in Sociology.*

Amin Ghaziani and Matt Brim, eds. (2019) *Imagining Queer Methods.*

Sharlene Nagy Hesse-Biber (2014) *Feminist Research Practice: A Primer.*

Nancy A. Naples (2003) *Feminism and Method: Ethnography, Discourse Analysis, and Activist Research.*

Michelle Téllez (2005) "Doing Research at the Borderlands: Notes from a Chicana Feminist Ethnographer," *Chicana/Latina Studies.*

Diane L. Wolf, ed. (1996) *Feminist Dilemmas in Fieldwork.*

Any of the feminist ethnographies profiled in this chapter would also make for useful further reading.

Notes

1   Alison Rooke, "Queer in the Field: On Emotions, Temporality and Performativity in Ethnography," in *Queer Methods and Methodologies*, 2010, 28.
2   Margery Wolf, *A Thrice Told Tale*, 1992, 124.
3   Matthew C. Gutmann, *The Meanings of Macho*, 1996, 9.
4   Karen Brodkin Sacks, *Caring by the Hour*, 1988, vii.
5   Ulrika Dahl, "Femme on Femme: Reflections on Collaborative Methods and Queer Femme-inist Ethnography," in *Queer Methods and Methodologies*, eds. Kath Browne and Catherine J. Nash, 2010, 145.
6   Ulrika Dahl and Del LaGrace Volcano, *Femmes of Power*, 2009.
7   Ulrika Dahl, "Femme on Femme" 2010, 156.
8   Ibid., 161, 174.
9   Leith Mullings, "African American Women Making Themselves: Notes on the Role of Black Feminist Research," *Souls*, 2000, 21.
10 Leith Mullings and Alaka Wali, *Stress and Resilience*, 2001.
11 Aimee Meredith Cox, *Shapeshifters*, 2015, 31–32.
12 Naisargi Dave, *Queer Activism in India: A Story in the Anthropology of Ethics*, 2012.
13 Tom Boellstorff, Bonnie Nardi, Celia Pearce, and T. L. Taylor, eds. *Coming of Age in Second Life*, 2015 (orig. 2008).
14 Tom Boellstorff, ed., *Ethnography and Virtual Worlds*, 2012, 1.
15 Claire Sterk, *Tricking & Tripping: Prostitution in the Era of AIDS*, 2000.
16 Marjorie Shostak, *Nisa*, 1981, 7.
17 Marjorie Shostak, *Return to Nisa*, 2000.
18 Mignon Moore, "Challenges, Triumphs, and Praxis: Collecting Qualitative Data on Less Visible and Marginalized Populations," 2018, 177.
19 Christa Craven, *Reproductive Loss: Challenges to LGBTQ Family-Making*, 2019.
20 Iris López, *Matters of Choice: Puerto Rican Women's Struggle for Reproductive Freedom*, 2008; see also, Iris López, "Negotiating Different Worlds: An Integral Ethnography of Reproductive Freedom and Social Justice," in *Feminist Activist Ethnography: Counterpoints to Neoliberalism in North America*, eds. Christa Craven and Dána-Ain Davis, 2013.
21 Mignon Moore, *Invisible Families: Gay Identities, Relationships, and Motherhood Among Black Women*, 2011.
22 Catherine Lutz and Jane Collins, *Reading National Geographic*, 1993.
23 Robert Kozinets, *Netnography: Doing Ethnographic Research Online*, 2009.
24 Jessica Marie Johnson, "Markup Bodies: Black [Life] Studies and Slavery [Death] Studies at the Digital Crossroads," *Social Text*, 2018, 65–66.
25 #transformDH Collective, "About #transformDH," transformdh.org/about-transformdh/.
26 Tom Boellstorff, Bonnie Nardi, Celia Pearce, and T.L. Taylor, eds. *Ethnography and Virtual Worlds: A Handbook of Method*, 2012. See also, Safiya Umoja Noble's eye-opening study *Algorithms of Oppression: How Search Engines Reinforce Racism*, 2018.
27 Lee, Latoya A. "Black Twitter: A Response to Bias in Mainstream Media," 2017, 26.
28 James Popham and Latasha VanEvery, "Representing Indigenous Protest on Twitter: Examining the Social Media Dialogue that Accompanied a Single Image of the DAPL Protests at Standing Rock," 2018.
29 Joan M. Gero and Margaret Conkey, eds., *Engendering Archaeology*, 1991; Janet Spector, *What This Awl Means*, 1993.
30 Whitney Battle-Baptiste, *Black Feminist Archaeology*, 2011.
31 Shulamit Reinharz, *Feminist Methods in Social Research*, 1992, 181.
32 Patricia Maguire, *Doing Participatory Research*, 1987.
33 Paulo Freire, *Pedagogy of the Oppressed*, 2000.

34 Michelle Fine et al., "Changing Minds: The Impact of College In a Maximum-Security Prison," A Collaborative Research Project by the Graduate Center of the City University of New York and the Women in Prison at the Bedford Hills Correctional Facility, 2001.

35 CUNY Graduate Center, PhD Program in Anthropology, "The Impact of Welfare Reform on Two Communities in New York City," W. K. Kellogg Foundation, 2003.

36 Dána-Ain Davis, *Black Battered Women and Welfare Reform: Between a Rock and a Hard Place*, 2006.

37 Dána-Ain Davis, *Reproductive Injustice: Racism, Pregnancy, and Premature Birth*, 2019.

38 Personal Narratives Group, *Interpreting Women's Lives: Feminist Theory and Personal Narratives*, 1989, 12.

CHAPTER 5

Challenges for Feminist Ethnographers

In this chapter, you will investigate how to address challenges in fieldwork and the production of feminist ethnography by considering the following questions:

- What logistical constraints arise in feminist ethnographic research?
- How do ethical concerns shape the research encounter?
- How can we assess the (potential) impacts of feminist ethnography?

Spotlights in this chapter:

- Elizabeth Chin on Envisioning a Feminist IRB Process
- Loretta J. Ross on Working with Former Skinhead White Supremacists
- Tanya Erzen on the Politics of Reciprocity and Mediation
- Kiersten Downs on "Feminist Curiosity" and Stamina
- Sandra Morgen on Movement Building

Essentials in this chapter:

- Aren Z. Aizura, "Following as Method" in *Mobile Subjects*
- Delores Walters, "Cast among Outcastes" in *Out in the Field*
- Maya J. Berry, Claudia Chávez Argüelles, Shanya Cordis, Sarah Ihmoud, Elizabeth Velásquez Estrada, "Toward a Fugitive Anthropology: Gender, Race, and Violence in the Field"

You will also be **Thinking Through . . .**

- Difficult Ethnographic Experiences
- Ethical Dilemmas

Ethnography is a challenge. It is a challenge for a number of reasons, not the least of which is that it is difficult to define. Ethnography has historically been both the process and the product of anthropology and other disciplines. Ethnographic research is often conducted to capture and tell the stories of people's lived experiences. As such, it can—among other things—be helpful in challenging stereotypes. An ethnographic project may also be used to examine the interconnectedness of communities or peoples to broader structures and processes, especially (though not exclusively) by residing in communities for extended periods of time and presenting data through the eyes of those living there. Questions regarding how one engages in long-term involvement with a community are germane to any study, but particularly when a feminist ethnographer is attentive and reflexive about power relationships that may emerge within (and beyond) the research encounter.

Nearly every social science discipline has a Code of Ethics within their professional organization(s) that offer guiding principles for conducting research (see a partial list in the Suggested Resources). Although professional organizations are not **adjudication boards**, meaning that they do not prosecute or punish members, they do investigate breaches of ethics on the part of researchers and, in some cases, remove the researcher from the organization. The primary goal of such codes is the welfare and protection of the individuals and groups that researchers study. Central issues are **confidentiality**, keeping the identity of participants from being disclosed beyond the researcher, and **informed consent**, confirmation that participants are taking part in the study willingly and not being coerced to participate.

For feminist ethnographers, however, ethical concerns go far beyond those described in the disciplinary Codes of Ethics, such as the debates over inequities in the research encounter detailed in chapter 3. For example, the issue of ethics and the **Institutional Review Board** (IRB) process is one that both interdisciplinary scholar Moya Bailey and anthropologist Elizabeth Chin have pointedly critiqued.

In *Misogynoir Tranformed: Black Women's Digital Resistance*, Moya Bailey utilizes digital media as a form of collaborative construction. Through collaborative construction, she makes the "emotional and uncompensated labor" of the community she creates visible through blogging and inviting people to respond to work that she is producing about them.[1] For instance, in Bailey's analysis of the attacks on trans women of color through social media sources, she sought to ensure that her inquiries about trans advocate Janet Mock's Twitter hashtag #girlslikeus were welcome. She reached out to Janet Mock directly via Twitter to see if she was interested in Bailey researching the tag. Although Bailey was pleased that Mock welcomed her research on the hashtag, she still wanted to provide the opportunity for Mock to decline participating in the project and for others who had used the #girlslikeus hashtag to have agency as part of the project. Bailey did so as part of her commitment to an ethical feminist research practice. Bailey highlights the irony that "trans women of color are not understood as one of the vulnerable communities identified by the IRB that assesses the potential harms of academic research on those researched."[2] While Bailey acknowledges that the intentions of the IRB are necessary, broadly, to ensure that research conducted at institutions that receive federal resources does not cause harm to participants, she questions the paternalism of IRBs, particularly when doing work in the digital domain. Our ethical obligations require forethought that extends far beyond what we submit to an IRB.

In "The Neoliberal Institutional Review Board, or Why Just Fixing the Rules Won't Help Feminist (Activist) Ethnographers,"[3] Chin encourages feminist ethnographers to actively challenge the level of scrutiny IRBs often place on feminist research and their uneven application of restrictions—often judging projects, like feminist ethnography, which contest positivist research aims, more harshly. Chin's polemic argues that feminist ethnographers should challenge the structural role of the IRB as it reinforces the neoliberal transformation of the academy. In our interview with Chin, she reflected on the possibilities of a feminist IRB.

What we explore in this chapter are some of the challenges that have emerged out of our reading of feminist ethnographic texts and the interviews we conducted with feminist ethnographers. We take up concerns about the particular gendered dimensions of being in the field, ethical concerns that move far beyond the IRB, the politics of doing research with groups with which you are not politically aligned, how feminist researchers approach issues of reciprocity with participants, and consider the potential for broader contributions of feminist ethnographic work.

✨ SPOTLIGHT ✨

Elizabeth Chin on Envisioning a Feminist IRB Process

Elizabeth Chin *is an anthropologist whose practice includes collaborative ethnography with children, performative knowledge production, and a range of writing experiments. She is the author of* Purchasing Power: Black Kids and American Consumer Culture *(2001) and* The Consumer Diaries *(2016). She is Editor-in-Chief of* American Anthropologist.

In my imagination the IRB would use feminist principles to do its work. The review process would be a dialogue engaging the members of the IRB with the researcher and, if possible, including representatives of the group to be researched. Rather than being the closed and oppositional process that typifies IRB workings currently, the IRB would focus on supporting researchers in doing the most creative and ethically rigorous work possible. Indemnification of the institution, the current focus of most IRBs, would be strictly a by-product of the work, not its core. In my dream process, the expertise of the IRB members would be used to productively challenge researchers to consider the best interests of those participating in research, and could further assist researchers in accessing resources necessary to meet these interests in a timely and rigorous way. People would sit together and really talk about the work. At present, you submit an application and you get a decision; it's a kind of black box process and everybody hates everything about it. You have people from a variety of disciplines on these panels, but too often people are imposing their own disciplinary values onto other people and this is especially difficult for feminist ethnographers who tend to use methods that stray quite significantly from the positivist approaches used in the best-funded of the social sciences, much less in the hard sciences and in medicine. It's a problem, of course, to assert that because we're "down with the people" we can skirt things like informed consent, but the problem for many of us is that the very form of informed consent—particularly a piece of paper covered with legalistic writing—inserts itself as a kind of violence into the delicate and intimate relationships we form in the field. We need other ways to communicate to people about what we are doing and what the implications are. Now that I work in a design department, I can imagine visual ways to explain our work and to get consent. Perhaps there are other media and technologies we could develop that would allow us to effectively communicate our research while securing the safety and dignity of our interlocutors all at the same time satisfying institutional needs.

Just as important as securing informed consent, feminist researchers must also be attentive to **informed refusal**. We asked homebirth midwife and nursing educator Hakima Tafunzi Payne, known to her community as Mama Hakima, about how informed refusal impacted both the reproductive healthcare she provides and her work as the founder and Chief Executive Officer of Uzazi Village, a nonprofit organization dedicated to eliminating outcome inequities in maternal and infant health in Black and Brown communities in Kansas City, Missouri. Mama Hakima stresses that informed refusal—whether in healthcare settings or research contexts—must be preceded by the same informing process as consent but that it emerges out of the fact that too often community members are denied the right to consent *or* refuse treatment because they are told that there will be a consequence impacting their health. One of her concerns is that particular groups of people, in this case Black birthing people, are often subjected to research or health interventions that have not been adequately explained. For example, she says, "African-American women often cannot explain why they had a cesarean or labor induction, and don't know exactly what diagnosis prompted the treatment they received. Or they cannot detail the stream of events that led to emergency interventions." In other words, people should be given all of the information they need so that they have the power to refuse to engage in research or treatment with as much integrity as they should have to give their consent.

The importance of informed refusal is that in terms of research or health care, the power of decision-making or even veto-power should rest in the hands of the person or people most directly impacted. People can and should be apprised of what they are consenting to and should have the option to refuse participation—be it a research study or a healthcare treatment. Essentially accepting that some people may choose to refuse allows feminist researchers to hold space for the fact that consent and refusal are rights rooted in basic human respect, autonomy, and self-determination.

What Logistical Constraints Arise in Feminist Ethnographic Research?

Although conducting research in a community for an extended period of time was a prerequisite for early ethnographers, some contemporary researchers do not live with the people they study. For feminist ethnographers, it is important to think about how and where we can best collect data for feminist analysis. All ethnographers face logistical concerns, including access to a site and the constraints of **geopolitics**. Geopolitics includes such issues as diplomacy, security, global economics, financial markets, and sometimes civil disruption. The following is one example of a feminist ethnographer (who we do not name to protect her identity) who faced logistical constraints that ultimately compromised her ability to conduct research.

> [A feminist ethnographer] who conducted dissertation fieldwork in a Middle Eastern country was forced by her home institution (an Ivy league University) to create a relationship with an IRB in her host country. This requirement is indeed best practice and uncontested by the American Anthropological Association (AAA) on principle. The problem was that in her host country there was no such thing as the IRB, but there was a highly repressive political regime. My colleague had arrived in her host country intending to conduct research on women and politics. As her work progressed, her interlocutors told her over and over again that the real thing she needed to look into was sexual revolution. In the meantime, members of her host country IRB were spying on her and those with whom she spoke. What her home institution had failed to account for was that the host country might not have an understanding of ethics commensurate with that in the United States. My colleague was forced to conduct a huge amount of "red herring" research in order to protect her research subjects; needed to send her field notes via encrypted FTP to her advisor; and kept an entire computer full of field notes utterly unconnected to her project. The host country ultimately placed her under house arrest for six weeks, bringing her field research to a close.[4]

Others, such as graduate school colleagues Maya J. Berry, Claudia Chávez Argüelles, Shanya Cordis, Sarah Ihmoud, and Elizabeth Velásquez Estrada (see *Spotlight* later in this chapter), used blogging as a way to keep track of each other's whereabouts during fieldwork, when other means of communication were unsafe or impractical.

Safety concerns are important for all ethnographers to consider—in terms of a researcher's well-being and the accessibility of a research site, as well as the ethnographer's comfort level sharing details about aspects of their life. Yet most of the writing on the dangers and difficulties associated with ethnographic research assume the researcher is, and remains, healthy and able-bodied throughout.[5] This poses particular challenges for ethnographers with visible and invisible disabilities, but the ways our bodies and identities shape our research encounters are important for all feminist ethnographers to think about before, during, and following fieldwork. This work must go deeper than simplistic distinctions between what may be visible to others and what may remain hidden. For instance, a researcher's chronic illness or disability—much like one's race, gender, or age—may be discernable by some research participants, misidentified by others, or go largely unacknowledged.

Anthropologist Candice Bradley's experience conducting fieldwork in western Kenya with insulin-dependent, Type I diabetes is an instructive example. Diagnosed shortly before beginning her doctoral fieldwork, she found that she had to learn to do fieldwork differently than she had been taught, adjusting the rhythms of her participant-observation and interviewing to the fluctuations of her blood sugar. Bradley laments initially becoming a "super-crip,"[6] one who tenaciously pursued her research, but also put herself in danger by subscribing to ableist assumptions about how fieldwork is "supposed" to be done. Her sage advice is relevant to all of us:

> [Ethnographic] fieldwork is an occupation of workaholics, a model that may have contributed to what we now know is a devastatingly high rate of injury, illness, and death in the field. People who are tired whether or not they have a chronic illness, are at more risk for infection and accidents. . . . [Ethnographers] working away from home should try to plan a "normal" working day with reasonable performance expectations that include time for relaxation.[7]

Writing about our bodily experiences—including how they are impacted by health status and disability as they are influenced by race, ethnicity, nationality, gender, sexuality, et cetera—is an important reminder of the plurality of individuals who engage in feminist ethnographic work, both as researchers and those who participate in our fieldwork.

Some researchers with visible impairments have found that, like other visible aspects of identity, they can assist in building rapport with some participants. Health science researcher Felicity Boardman notes that her use of a wheelchair frequently generated rapport with participants who felt an affinity with her during interviews for her study on attitudes toward prenatal testing for genetic disease, but she had concerns that it could inhibit interactions with nondisabled participants. She found that she preferred to conduct interviews via phone or on digital platforms so that she could choose whether and how much to disclose about her disability.[8] Her experiences also expose the fallacy of all-too-common assumptions that researchers with a disability only participate in disability studies research—much like the frequent expectations that if an ethnographer identifies as LGBTQ+, they must study sexuality.

Whatever the research topic, the slipperiness of categories like "visible" and "invisible" also belie complexities like the challenges of the insider/outsider dichotomy discussed in the previous chapter. Lindsey Brown's experience as a researcher with epilepsy, which is usually described as a "hidden disability," demonstrates this complexity. During her in-person interviews about patient consent and the limits of anonymization in medical records, the presence of her assistance/service dog—wearing his unmistakable bright yellow jacket—became a point of connection (especially for those who liked dogs) but also prompted uninvited questions about her health status (many assumed that she was blind or d/Deaf) that sometimes distracted from the focus of her research. Similarly, for communication studies scholar Laura Ellingson, for instance, the disclosure of her identity as a cancer survivor was a point of connection with oncology patients when she conducted ethnographic research in a medical facility. However, she also found that her visible knee brace had the undesired effect of marking her as a patient participating in the study to other members of the research team.[9]

These researchers' experiences also prompt ethical and personal dilemmas that all researchers should consider, especially feminist ethnographers seeking to normalize candid discussions about researcher's identity and experiences. Is there an ethical imperative to disclose (particular) aspects of our identities to participants? Does whether that identity relates to one's research topic matter? Will participants feel betrayed if they learn later that an ethnographer is "exposed" as being not who they may have imagined them to be? How much should be disclosed, when, and should it be the same with all participants? What about times when disclosing one's identity may feel unsafe? These are questions that all ethnographers have to grapple with to some degree, and it is likely that additional, unanticipated dilemmas will emerge during the process of research.

Logistical constraints can also impact an ethnographer's methodological choices as they relate to the choice of fieldsite(s). For Dána-Ain's project on Black women who were battered, she did not live at the shelter where she worked because it was not feasible to do so; it was a shelter, after all, and the available beds were for staff, not researchers. In other cases, informants' mobility or multisited fieldwork means that it may not be possible to participate with and observe people in a single setting. Christa, for instance, could not have lived in every community that had midwives in Virginia. Instead, she traveled to multiple communities for weeklong stints to conduct interviews and participant-observation and met many homebirth activists multiple times at legislative hearings in Richmond and at activist meet-ups throughout the state.

It has also become more commonplace that researchers will no longer spend years in a single location doing research, but that an ethnographic project may be of a shorter duration, involve research across a range of locations, and involve cultural material from archives (formal and informal) that document mobility across geographical and other borders. For instance, cultural studies scholar Aren Z. Aizura traces not only the geographical paths of people seeking gender reassignment surgery (GRS) in Thailand but also the textual spaces where trans and gender nonconforming people have documented that mobility.

🧠 **ESSENTIAL**

Excerpt from "Following as Method" in *Mobile Subjects: Transnational Imaginaries of Gender Reassignment* **by Aren Z. Aizura**

Aren Z. Aizura *earned a PhD in cultural studies from the University of Melbourne and now teaches in Gender, Women and Sexuality Studies at the University of Minnesota. Aizura's interdisciplinary research explores* *gender reassignment surgery tourism in Thailand and elsewhere published in* Mobile Subjects (2018), *he is coeditor (with Susan Stryker) of* The Transgender Studies Reader 2 (2013). *Aizura's current research project works across medical anthropology and transnational studies to investigate the transnational circulation of new terminologies to describe gender variant and gender nonconforming people, particularly within global human rights discourse, nongovernmental aid, and public health.*

Photo Credit: Otto Ramstad.

Following as Method

I trace the intersections between geographical mobility and trans and gender nonconforming life across a dozen categories of texts and their discursive frameworks, including literary texts, films, autobiographies, historical documents, photographs, online journals, corporate employment policy, trans employer/employee handbooks, and others. I am most concerned with narratives that circulate about trans mobilities within trans and gender nonconforming cultural productions. Self-made accounts form an archive of trans cultural production that has existed between the cracks of the sexological, medical, legal, and academic discourses that produce trans and gender nonconforming bodies and practices as the objects of a rational scientific-juridical gaze.

Alongside these discursive formations I have adapted ethnographic methods from anthropology and cultural studies: interviews, field observation, autoethnography, and the obsessive collection of anecdotes from friends, relatives, fellow researchers, and random strangers about trans mobility. These research methodologies are unrepentantly and ambitiously interdisciplinary. I undertook extensive fieldwork in Thailand and Australia between 2006 and 2009, [but] multisited ethnography does not begin and end at a cross-cultural analysis that assumes comparison between regions, nations, or communities as the central hermeneutic. Particularly in relation to anthropologies of sexuality and gender, focusing on cross-cultural analysis means that translation of sex/gender/sexuality systems attains a rhetorical importance that supersedes other modes of analysis. Even if that translation involves tracing the historical shifts of such systems, the very historicity invoked means making an assumption of past stability. For example, to trace transnational GRS markets is irreducible to a discussion of identity categories or sexual practices, although GRS markets exist in the forms they do precisely because of contradictions and inconsistencies among sex, gender, and sexuality system. . . .

Source: Aizura, Aren Z. *Mobile Subjects: Transnational Imaginaries of Gender Reassignment.* United Kingdom: Duke University Press, 2018, 14–16.

Ultimately the issues raised above reflect shifts in the practice of ethnography responding to ways in which the temporal (time) and spatial (space) conditions of ethnography have changed, as well as traditional disciplinary assumptions. The challenges for all ethnographers include questions such as: Is what one observes typical of what happens in this culture or context? What if we only view people in one part of their lives (e.g., if we only view them at work, but not at home or in leisure time)? Do we miss something? Can we access information to help us better understand mobility by moving between multiple physical or textual locations?

Cultures and communities transform in relation to global and political processes, which can pose challenges for both the initiation and the continuation of ethnographic research projects. Anthropologist Andrea Queeley conducted her research in Cuba among the descendants of early twentieth-century migrants from the English-speaking Caribbean to Cuba.[10] They were attracted to move there because of heavy US economic investment. The children and grandchildren of those original immigrants had initiated a revitalization of the West Indian organizations that their parents and grandparents had established between the 1920s and 1950s but had been closed down due to the revolution. Queeley wanted to examine the dynamics around that revitalization. One challenge she faced was the inability to continue her research because the state of Florida passed a statute in 2008 that no faculty or students at Florida public institutions could travel or use state funds to travel to any country on the list of "Terrorist Sponsoring Nations." Although faculty throughout Florida waged a campaign to dispute the legislation, it did not result in a policy change. Queeley was informed that she would be unable to use any funds to go to conferences in Cuba or travel to Cuba. Further, outside grants (those that were not from the university where she worked) could not be used for travel to Cuba either. In this case, the challenge was that Queeley was unable to continue her research due to geopolitics. The United States has adjusted its relationship to Cuba, and as of January 2015 the US trade and travel restrictions were loosened, but new geopolotical complications brought on by the COVID-19 pandemic have continued to restrict access.

The global politics of mobility also revises the notion that all ethnographic research takes place in single "bounded communities." For example, although Dána-Ain primarily conducted her research with women who were battered in "Laneville," New York, some of the women she encountered were from all over New York State and some women had immigrated from Mexico and Europe. Thus, their histories of violence and survival were linked to multiple places. In one case, Drita, a sixty-year-old woman, had experienced a range of forms of violence. In her country of origin, Serbia, Drita's husband had beaten her for forty years. In sharing her oral history, Drita positioned the Yugoslav Wars from 1991 to 2001, which centered on ethnic conflict, as another form of violence that she endured, linking it to the violence she experienced at the hands of her husband. Finally, she and her husband left Serbia and came to the United States, where he continued to beat her, marking the reason she left him and came to the shelter. In this case, analyzing Drita's oral history had to take into account the multiple spatial locations that she had occupied. Consequently, understanding her cumulative incidents of violence had to be contextualized by the politics of Serbia, her immigration to the United States, and her ability to feel safe in upstate New York.

Going into the field posed a different kind of challenge for Delores Walters, a Black lesbian anthropologist, who describes what she had to deal with when she began her fieldwork on women, health care, and social reform in Yemen. Walters integrated her identification as a feminist and her desire to be "out" in the field as a lesbian into her preparation for fieldwork. Her reflection on the experience, and the challenge it posed for her, points toward one way in which feminist ethnographers may have to confront issues that more positivist researchers do not have to address.

🐚 ESSENTIAL

Excerpt from "Cast among Outcastes" by Delores Walters

Delores Walters *earned her doctorate in anthropology from New York University after researching an outcaste, African-identified group in Yemen in the 1980s. She also holds degrees in liberal studies, biology, and nursing. After teaching courses on diversity, cultural competency, and the Underground Railroad, she concluded her career as an educator/administrator at the University of Rhode Island serving in various capacities as director of recruitment and retention of faculty of color; associate dean for diversity; diversity consultant; and director of the Southern Rhode Island Area Health Education Center (sriAHEC) in the College of Nursing. She coedited* Gendered

Photo Credit: Sonya Pressley.

Resistance: Women, Slavery and the Legacy of Margaret Garner *(2013), an anthology with historian Mary E. Frederickson, winning an Afro-American Historical and Genealogical Society Book Award. Currently, she is researching her family history, conducting genealogy workshops and seminars on Margaret Garner. In this excerpt from her chapter in* Out in the Field: Reflections of Lesbian and Gay Anthropologists, *she discusses the challenges of being "out" in Yemen.*

In the summer of 1982, my partner at the time and I left the United States for nearly two years, most of which was devoted to conducting fieldwork in what was then known as the Yemen Arabic Republic. . . . One of the pressing questions for those about to embark on fieldwork is how to conduct or maintain one's personal life. To a group of graduate students who inquired how I managed, I remarked that I had taken my personal life with me. These students, whom I encountered at an American Anthropological Association meeting on my return from the field in 1984, were somewhat in awe at such a novel idea. I am not sure whether it was the public statement about having a same-sex partner in the field that was mildly shocking or the fact itself, because I know that among my sympathetic listeners there were other lesbians.

Anyone planning an extended stay in Yemen is required to pass a stringent security clearance. The question was how to get my partner, Lee, into the country. . . . Thus, one of my objectives when I visited Yemen the year before I began fieldwork was to determine whether a companion would be permitted to accompany me. Clearance through the proper Yemini authorities might be facilitated by a few options, according to my British and American colleagues, then resident in the country. Couldn't I claim that Lee was my mother? they asked. To which I replied, "right age, wrong color," because she is White and old enough to be my mother. Little did I know that when they met us Yemeni women all over the country would immediately assume that Lee was my mother because they observed an appropriate age difference for this to be possible and ignored the fact that she is fairskinned and blue-eyed while I, especially in the sunny climate of Yemen, am very brown. . . . Adoption was another option, but it would take too long and besides, my own mother would be eagerly awaiting my return. . . . Finally after exhausting all the possibilities, my colleagues and I simply inquired at the research center. I was assured that permission would be easily granted. Once we arrived in the country, I had only to write Lee into my project for their records. The way was clear for the two of us to work together as a team.

*This excerpt is dedicated to the memory of Lee Maher, who was my valuable assistant and partner in Yemen.

Source: Walters, Delores. "Cast among Outcastes: Interpreting Sexual Orientation, Racial, and Gender Identity in the Yemen Arab Republic." In Ellen Lewin and William L. Leap, eds., *Out in the Field: Reflections of Lesbian and Gay Anthropologists*, 58–59. Urbana and Chicago, IL: University of Illinois Press, 1996.

Sociologist Annette Lareau, who conducted one of the first **longitudinal** ethnographic studies on childhood education, contends that researchers should be open about the logistical and ethical challenges that we face—in order to help students cope with their own fieldwork challenges and develop better skills in the field. Lareau has written extensively about feeling "unsure"—at many times—during her research and offers reflective, practical suggestions on how she would deal with particular challenges differently in future research.[11] For instance, she found herself unable to take detailed fieldnotes during many of her participant-observation sessions at schools and with families in their homes. At first, she committed to writing detailed notes after each visit but frequently found that she did not have the time to complete them because of other obligations outside of her field site. She advises students to be aware of this when making decisions about note-taking and fieldnotes. Time—for researchers as well as the participants—is clearly an important practical consideration.

Several edited collections by feminist ethnographers have also sought to elevate the research process to more than a casual mention in an appendix or footnote. *Gendered Fields: Women, Men and Ethnography*, edited by anthropologists Diane Bell, Pat Caplan, and Wazir Jahan Karim, considered the influence of gender in the ethnographic fieldwork encounter by incorporating the experiences of international scholars, including geographers, historians, philosophers, and sociologists.[12] Sociologist Diane Wolf edited *Feminist Dilemmas in Fieldwork* about the complicated dynamics inherent in fieldwork, as well as for feminist ethnographers in the academy.[13]

Feminist ethnographers often study marginalized groups, those with less social, political, or economic power than themselves. Yet, in 1972, Laura Nader issued a clarion call for anthropology to reinvent itself and for researchers to "study up," given their unique position and focus on analyzing processes of power. In her still important article, "Up the Anthropologist: Perspectives Gained from Studying Up,"[14] Nader argues that we need to examine the operationalization of power where it is wielded. Nader asked, "What if . . . anthropologists were to study the colonizer rather than the colonized, the culture of power rather than the culture of the powerless, the culture of affluence rather than the culture of poverty?"[15] Given that there was already a lot of scholarship on disadvantaged populations, we had much to learn by putting a face on bureaucracy, institutions, and people who control lives of others. Nader's original call was for ethnographic studies of banks, realtors, law firms, insurance companies, manufacturing corporations, the communications industry, and government regulatory agencies—institutions at the center of capitalist processes leading to stratification. This appeal posed challenges, however. How was the ethnographer to gain access to bankers, CEOs, lawyers, and the like, who are often paid substantially for their time? Could the ethnographer offer critical perspectives on the workings of power without being silenced or sued?

Nader's call was answered by some feminist ethnographers and scholars such as former investment bank employee and anthropologist Karen Ho, who wrote *Liquidated: An Ethnography of Wall Street*, which addresses financial crises and booms, connecting the values and actions of investment bankers to the construction of markets and the restructuring of US corporations.[16] Political theorist Cynthia Enloe, in her book *Seriously! Investigating Crashes and Crises as If Women Mattered*,[17] points out the importance of examining the gendered politics of institutions and notes that patriarchal privileging can be understood when one investigates women's experiences of how masculinity operates. According to Enloe, Ho's ethnography, which she situates as a feminist text, scrutinizes masculinity within the context of institutional power. Also, anthropologist Melissa Fisher's ethnography *Wall Street Women* examines the first cohort of women in finance and explores how they enacted market feminisms by incorporating tenets of liberal feminism, such as equal rights, into Wall Street institutions and practice.[18] Fisher faced challenges doing this work of studying up. In our interview with Fisher, she noted that "when you're looking at elites, there's an issue about . . . your relationship with powerful people." Arguably, ethnography, and feminist ethnography in particular, presumes a degree of authority over those whom researchers study. This is especially evident if one is studying people who occupy subordinate social spaces. Yet this asymmetrical relationship is either neutralized or inverted in a number of circumstances, such as with Fisher and Ho. Fisher's book was innovative because no one had previously followed a group of elite women over a long period of time. Fisher and Ho's work raise a question: If one goal of feminist ethnography is to reduce power differentials through the possibilities of cocreating the ethnography, how is that transformed when the power dimensions of your work are reversed? For instance, if an ethnographer were to coauthor a publication with a CEO or president of an organization, they might be significantly constrained in what and how they could write.

Finally, in the vein of studying up, anthropologist Sandra Morgen and social welfare scholar and activist Mimi Abramovitz probe what we might call an "up issue" in *Taxes Are a Woman's Issue: Reframing the Debate*.[19] One of the significant challenges that they faced was that no one, including feminists, had paid attention to taxes regarding their gendered dimensions and consequences. Morgen and Abramovitz show how the US tax system, supported by the Internal Revenue Service (IRS), was created in—and still caters to—ideals of men as breadwinners with stay-at-home wives. In response to the challenge of addressing a complex tax policy system, their goal in writing this book was to demystify the tax system, foster tax literacy through accessible writing, and draw women more substantively into debates surrounding tax reform. In so doing, they make a complex system legible to readers. Although making complex systems comprehensible has been the intent of many ethnographers, what is notable here is that these authors include the demystification of political, legal, and economic systems as fundamentally essential for their vision of feminist ethnographic inquiry.

🧠 **ESSENTIAL**

Excerpt from "Toward a Fugitive Anthropology: Gender, Race, and Violence in the Field," by Maya J. Berry, Claudia Chávez Argüelles, Shanya Cordis, Sarah Ihmoud, Elizabeth Velásquez Estrada

Photo Credit: Ahmed Ghappour.

Claudia Chávez Argüelles, *Assistant Professor, Tulane University*
Elizabeth Velásquez Estrada, *Assistant Professor, University of Illinois Urbana-Champaign*
Sarah Ihmoud, *Assistant Professor, College of the Holy Cross*
Shanya Cordis, *Assistant Professor, Spelman College*
Maya J. Berry, *Assistant Professor, University of North Carolina at Chapel Hill*

The coauthors' convergence was made possible by the Diaspora and Activist Tracks in the Anthropology Department at the University of Texas at Austin, which came to be known as "The Austin School." Those tracks (which formed in the 1990s and ran until roughly 2017) were led by a critical mass of faculty, first housed in Anthropology and later with stronger affiliations in African and African Diaspora Studies and Latin American Studies at UT Austin, whose research agendas, methodologies, and pedagogical commitments were shaped by "the critical turns" within the discipline since the 1960s which squarely critiqued its colonial legacy and sought to reshape the relationship between anthropological knowledge production, power, and liberatory struggles for social transformation. Although largely marginalized within the anthropology department, for the coauthors, the training received in the Diaspora and Activist Tracks was, and continues to be, a privilege and a challenge. As a collective of Black, Brown, Indigenous, mestiza, and/ or queer cisgender women, they decided to confront the paradox of how they had each individually abided by what seemed to be an unspoken code of silence around their own experiences of racialized gender violence even while simultaneously espousing feminist and decolonial principles in their politically engaged research endeavors. They found not only strength but also great clarity through the process of collectively writing from differently situated standpoints in terms of race, sexuality, geographic locations, and national origin during various stages in the doctoral research and dissertation writing process. This collective exploration led to the publication of "Toward a Fugitive Anthropology: Race, Gender, and Violence in the Field" (Cultural Anthropology, 2017). Little did they know that the ideas introduced in the essay would coincide with a seismic shift in the public debate about violence against women encapsulated in the United States by the hashtag #MeToo.

We write this essay as black, brown, indigenous, mestiza, and/or queer cisgender women trained in the United States in the tradition of decolonial and activist anthropological praxis, whose research centers on marginalized, disenfranchised, and oppressed communities in the global South. Occupying gendered-as-female bodies, which were interpellated in racialized and sexualized ways, punctuated a process of embodied pedagogy during our fieldwork experiences. Our experiences with racialized gender and sexual violence compelled us to question the pervasiveness of dominant logics within activist research in relationship to our own fieldwork in El Salvador, Cuba, Palestine, Mexico, and Guyana.

. . . We refuse the emblematic racially privileged male anthropologist and the aforementioned assumptive logics of doing ethnographic fieldwork, both of which undergird the discipline's implicit masculinist "shut up and take it" mentality in reference to gendered violence in the field . . . . Being marked as racialized women inevitably shaped our research projects and the lines of inquiry we pursued during fieldwork. By engaging with our complex positionalities, our critical examination of activist methods builds on feminist ethnography to envision avenues for social transformation while recentering our physical, mental, and spiritual bodies in our methodological and epistemological toolkits. Our experiences call up the following questions: How do our gendered racial positionalities inflect the research process, and how can we push activist research methods to be accountable to the embodied aspects of conducting research in conflict zones, colonial contexts, and/or conditions of gendered and racialized terror? How can we produce feminist ethnography through activist research in a context of subordination and violence against women? Finally, how does our involvement in patriarchal relationships, as marked but relatively privileged women, affect local dynamics, the knowledge we produce, and our methodologies?

Source: Berry, Maya J., Claudia Chávez Argüelles, Shanya Cordis, Sarah Ihmoud, and Elizabeth Velásquez Estrada. "Toward a Fugitive Anthropology: Gender, Race, and Violence in the Field." *Cultural Anthropology* 32, no. 4 (November 20, 2017): 537–565, 537–538, 540.

Each author follows with an ethnographic vignette from their individual fieldsites to engage these questions. Collectively, they advocate a fugitive approach to ethnographic practice—one that emerges from subjugation to challenge dominant heteronormative and colonial narratives. What does this notion of fugitivity mean to you in the context of your discipline and research opportunities?

How Do Ethical Concerns Shape the Research Encounter?

Clearly, ethical concerns can—and do—arise in all research projects. Feminist ethnographers often have an awareness of such issues because of the attention they pay to gendered dynamics in the research encounter, which we frequently reflect upon in our writing. *Women Fielding Danger: Negotiating Ethnographic Identities in Field Research*, edited by sociologist Martha Huggins and anthropologist Marie-Louise Glebbeek,[20] addressed a range of logistical and ethical issues faced by feminist ethnographers across a range of disciplines, including anthropology, criminology, Latin American Studies, literary criticism, political science, psychology, sociology, and Women's and Gender Studies. The collection explores female ethnographers' experiences with threats of physical violence, the emotional toll of difficult fieldwork experiences, and the influence and negotiation of gender, as well as nationality, ethnicity, caste, and class, on ethnographic research. Authors also address ethical dilemmas, such as choices to conceal aspects of their identity, concerns about placing local interlocutors in danger through their research, conducting research with groups that the ethnographer does not respect or support (such as torturers or paramilitary members), and protecting sensitive field data. The question of ethics raised in these instances poses a significant quandary for ethnographers who study sensitive or controversial topics.

Depending upon the location of fieldwork, scholars may find themselves in situations when they observe something horrific or have participated in an event sanctioned by the community, or person being studied, with which they disagree. Deciding whether to participate is often fraught with tensions about acceptance in the field and concerns about maintaining respect within one's discipline. Ellen Gruenbaum's fieldwork in Sudan that resulted in the ethnography *The Female Circumcision Controversy: An Anthropological Perspective*[21] drew her into complex emotional and ethical territory. Gruenbaum draws on five years of fieldwork to demonstrate the deep embeddedness of female circumcision in Sudanese cultural traditions and to critique simplistic (often feminist) Western efforts to summarily eradicate the practice. Gruenbaum's participant-observation spanned many events and spaces, but the one she reflects on most profoundly was when she observed a girl's genital surgery with a midwife she had come to know well. Despite planning to limit herself to observation in this setting, she found herself helping to hold the child steady for xylocaine injections.[22] Although this situation was ethically complicated (not to mention unexpected) for the ethnographer, those in the community saw it as part of her engagement with a cultural practice they deeply valued. This is a particularly shocking (for most Western readers) example of the ways that ethnographers often encounter unexpected events in their research. Part of the writing process for feminist ethnographers is to reflect upon these experiences, consider the ethical implication, and pay attention to how power manifests in the situation.

Ethical concerns begin as we start to conceive our projects and continue far beyond our fieldwork into our choices about writing, continued involvement with the people and communities we study, and our responses in the event of controversy that emerges from our research. People with various political perspectives conduct research of all types, even research that may seem to be counter to the researchers' politics. In this vein, imagine doing a research project that is at odds with your political perspective. For example, picture being a feminist who favors reproductive freedom and conducting research on right-wing pro-life efforts. Or how would it feel to study with people whose politics you disagree with? What might it be like to study racist groups if you are antiracist?

Anthropologist Faye Ginsburg, who wrote the ethnography *Contested Lives: The Abortion Debate in an American Community*,[23] faced a significant dilemma regarding her work. For this project, Ginsburg conducted research with pro-choice and pro-life activists in Fargo, North Dakota. Doing this ethnography forced her to confront what it meant to be a feminist engaged in this kind of study, as well as her decision not to share her convictions about the debate with either participants or her academic colleagues. She writes that a "native's point of view" is fine when the "native" is from someplace else. It is another thing to describe the worldview of informants when they are from the same place as the researcher and when they are presumed to be the enemy. Ginsburg was accused of having "gone native" and becoming a right-to-life advocate. Ultimately, her largely pro-choice academic colleagues struggled more with her decision than her participants, who were more comfortable with her role of neutrality.[24] In a project such as this one where participants have a wide range of beliefs about a subject, it is possible for the finding to be endorsed by all the members of the study group?

THINKING THROUGH . . .

Difficult Ethnographic Experiences

Free Write and Conversation: Given what you have read in this textbook thus far, what tools do you think a feminist ethnographer should draw upon to navigate these situations? Do Gruenbaum and Ginsburg's experiences exemplify situations where you think an intervention must or should occur? Why or why not?

In her recent article, "Trying to Be a Vulnerable Observer: Matters of Agency, Solidarity and Hospitality in Feminist Ethnography," anthropologist Tine Davids reveals that she struggled with the dilemma of having a different political perspective than her informants.[25] Her research explored elite Mexican women's engagement in politics. Davids reexamined the difficulty she had conducting research with right-wing, female politicians. She found herself rethinking the idea of feminist solidarity with someone whose politics diverged from her own. Focusing on Marina, whose political sympathies Davids found troubling, she wondered how the concepts of "vulnerable observer" (a term coined by Ruth Behar) and cultural diversities are managed in such a situation. Davids's commitment to feminism and her willingness to deploy a reflexive stance allowed her to listen and hear Marina's voice differently. By examining her own biases, Davids analyzes the processes whereby she opens herself up to locate agency in Marina's conservatism. What comes through in this reflexive analysis is that understanding the researcher's context as part of narrative interpretation is important, as is revisiting one's work to face interpretive challenges or differing perspectives. Davids suggests that in opting to critically examine our own roles and relationships to power in the construction of feminist research, we should make ourselves vulnerable and be hospitable to our informants. In this case, we must take risks in opening up our emotional door to strangers that could be "unsafe," instead of only opening our emotional door to those we already know. In other words, we can easily show or feel solidarity to those with which we agree. Managing interpretations of differing perspectives, Davids suggests that we integrate hospitality into our conceptualization of solidarity.

In some cases, researchers may choose to make their potentially conflicting identities or perspectives known to the communities they study. Others working from the assumption that an absolute eradication of bias is both impossible and unnecessary opt instead to critically examine their own roles and relationships to power in the construction of feminist research.

This was the case with feminist sociologist Kathleen Blee, author of *Women of the Klan: Racism and Gender in the 1920s.*[26] In her work on women in the Klan, Blee indicates that she had very little difficulty interviewing women who had been members of the Ku Klux Klan in Indiana in the 1920s. She points out that it was very easy to develop a rapport with her informants, in part because she was from Indiana and has white skin. Blee's initial recruitment of participants did not indicate her own political leanings opposing the Klan. In fact, it was her similarity to her informants that led them to assume that she had the same worldview they did. Blee also admitted she was prepared to hate her informants, in part because of her own progressive politics. Instead, she found the women "interesting and intelligent." Although **cultural relativism,** the idea that a culture must only be judged within its own cultural context, is the stated goal of most ethnographers, this is not the same as **moral relativism,** often taken to mean that we should tolerate all cultural behaviors even when we disagree with them. It is important for feminist ethnographers to reflect on these challenges as they aim to gain a greater understanding of the communities they research.

Reproductive justice activist Loretta Ross's work with former white supremacists also offers an illuminating example. While Ross is not a feminist ethnographer, she has contributed to shaping national conversations about injustice and **reproductive justice,** a term that she coined along with eleven other women in 1994, attending a conference sponsored by the Illinois Pro-Choice Alliance and the Ms. Foundation for Women. Because her work dovetails with that of feminists and feminist ethnographers, such as sociologist Kathleen Blee, political scientist Marlene Gerber Fried, and others, we include her here. While her work researching hate groups was difficult, she felt that it was important to know how the "other side" thinks and works.

🕊 SPOTLIGHT 🕊

Loretta J. Ross on Working with Former Skinhead White Supremacists

Loretta J. Ross *is an Associate Professor at Smith College. She is an activist, public intellectual, and scholar. She started her career in activism and social change in the 1970s, working at the National Football League Players' Association, the DC Rape Crisis Center, the National Organization for Women (NOW), the National Black Women's Health Project, the Center for Democratic Renewal (National Anti-Klan Network), the National Center for Human Rights Education, and SisterSong Women of Color Reproductive Justice Collective, until retiring as an organizer in 2012 to teach about activism. Her most recent books are* Reproductive Justice: An Introduction, *cowritten with Rickie Solinger, and* Radical Reproductive Justice: Foundations, Theory, Practice, Critique. *Her forthcoming book is* Calling In the Calling Out Culture: Detoxing Our Movement *due out in 2022. She has been quoted in the* New York Times, Time, *the* Los Angeles Times, *and the* Washington Post, *among others. Her website is www.LorettaJRoss.com.*

I worked at the Center for Democratic Renewal (CDR), formerly known as the National Anti-Klan Network, from 1990 to 1995 as their program director. One of my jobs was to work with people who had been in the hate movement who were seeking to defect. The challenge for me was working with the perpetrators instead of victims. That wasn't the first time I had to deal with this transposition. Back in the 1970s at the DC Rape Crisis Center, I worked with men who were incarcerated because they had raped women. But they were Black men, so it felt like I was working with a portion of our community who were in jail. When I had to work with ex-neo-Nazis and Klansmen, they were not my "community." So it was a major paradigm shift that I didn't think I could handle.

My boss at the time was Rev. C.T. Vivian, who was an aide to Rev. Martin Luther King. He said to me, "If you ask people to give up hate, then you must be there for them when they do," which I didn't necessarily want to hear. This led to me working with CDR's Research Director Leonard Zeskind and participating in the de-programming of people who had been in the hate movement. It was wonderful to work. It blew my mind and made me rethink how I viewed people who had been in the hate movement. I tended to think of them as people who were like roaches who only came out in the dark. And because they practiced the politics of hate, they didn't have human rights that I needed to respect. But working with them humanized them for me. I no longer could maintain the anger I felt toward them individually or as a group. I began to feel sorry for their particular combination of fear and envy that propelled them into hate groups.

Someone who stood out for me was Floyd Cochran in 1992. He and I ended up together on the *Jerry Springer Show* as part of a road tour for Floyd to apologize for his previous behavior as a Nazi. Floyd was a national spokesman for the Aryan Nations, and when his second child was born with a cleft palate, his Aryan brothers told him his child was defective and needed to be put to death. Aryans believe in a so-called "human perfectability." Floyd's epiphany was realizing that these people did not have his best interests at heart. He left the compound and asked CDR for help. (See "Up from Hatred," *Los Angeles Times*, http://articles.latimes.com/1997/aug/10/magazine/tm-21338.)

With the assistance of churches and other antiracists, CDR had a sort of underground railroad for people defecting from the white supremacist movement. People leaving these movements often do so with knowledge about crimes the group has committed, so they need protection. We've helped people who had to leave home in the dead of the night. There is no government program designed to help them reestablish a new life. Many want to leave. Some turn state witnesses, but most don't; they just want out.

Floyd's most painful story was that he had recruited two skinheads from Allentown, PA. Their last name was Freeman. These two brothers were churchgoing boys who became members of the Aryan skinhead movement. One evening, they came home and killed their entire family—mother, father, and eleven-year-old brother. They were caught and convicted of murder. Floyd never confessed to any crimes he personally committed, but he did feel responsible for the murder of the Freeman family. (See *New York Times*: "2 Skinhead Brothers Charged with Killing Family Members," http://www.nytimes.com/1995/03/03/us/2-skinhead-brothers-charged-with-killing-family-members.html.)

Let's be clear, a lot of teen boys can be attracted to hate movements, not necessarily because of the ideology, but because they are bullied. When they join racist groups like skinheads or neo-Nazi groups, it is as a counter to being bullied. That was Floyd's experience. He became a Nazi because he was a rather small guy getting bullied; it was not the ideology of Nazism—he barely understood that as a teenager. A lot of people don't understand the psychological impulses that can cause people to join hate groups.

I never felt particularly unsafe doing this work until after the Oklahoma City bombing on April 19, 1995, by white supremacist and militia member Timothy McVeigh. After I was in some interviews in national newspapers, the Texas Militia managed to make contact with my mother, who was wheelchair-bound, suggesting that they wanted to talk to her about me. This tricked her into revealing a lot of personal information about me because my mother tended to brag about her children. They invited my mother to a meeting of the militia to prove that they weren't part of a racist movement, as I had said in the newspapers. When I called her on Mother's Day to ask if she received the flowers I sent, she told me she had had a two-hour phone call with the Texas Militia. Her number was unlisted, so this definitely scared me. It wasn't personally threatening to me, but it was a not-so-veiled warning to me through my family.

Sometimes, identifying the "other side," however, can be difficult in projects that engage with activist movements. In Christa's research with midwifery advocates, for example, organizers frequently disagreed upon strategies to forward their cause. It would have been impossible to agree with, or support, each position. Christa had to bow out of particular debates—for instance, what type of licensure or certification the government should provide to midwives, a subject well beyond her area of expertise—and discuss other debates and conflicts in her published work.

Other feminist ethnographers have found that studying groups with which they are not in agreement offers insights into their other research. For instance, anthropologist Srimati Basu became interested in studying the Indian MRM (Men's Rights Movement) following her feminist work on violence against women, in part because of the contradictions she saw in their opposition to the Indian feminists she had come to know. From the outset of this research, she realized that studying a group that one does not support "disturbs the methodological dream of radical mutual disclosure and transformation." Rather, like Loretta Ross, she had fears about her privacy and safety in ways that hadn't occurred to her with previous research.

I have no sympathy for the MRA [Men's Rights Activists'] accusation that feminists encourage wives to "misuse" law, nor in rationalizing or excusing any confessions of violence, but I was interested in documenting the experiences and ideologies which ground anti-feminist discourse, as also in the diverse circumstances and locations which bring people to the movement. I had little recourse to evaluating the veracity of any alleged violence (on either side), but constantly had to push against many interlocutors' attempts to cast all gender-based violence statistics in doubt . . . I worried about being harassed and trolled, pondering the foolhardiness of seeking out people accused of violence, and the impossibility of trying to hide my identity from people who prided themselves on their dominance of Internet search engines.[27]

Although most of these fears ultimately did not come to pass, she found tensions between her role as a feminist ethnographer and her efforts to keep her distance from her new participants. This dissonance, however, allowed her a deeper understanding of the political and legal controversies around sexual assault, divorce, and women's right to inheritance.

Another particularly thoughtful engagement with writing about conflicts and controversies is American Studies scholar Tanya Erzen's book, *Straight to Jesus: Sexual and Christian Conversions in the Ex-Gay Movement*, which investigates the lives of men and women living at New Hope Ministry, a residential ex-gay program. Erzen spent eighteen months volunteering at New Hope while she conducted fieldwork.

Being uncomfortable is something that most ethnographers become intimately familiar with during—and, in Erzen's case, also following—fieldwork. Researchers who conduct studies that address traumatic events must find ways to address discomfort throughout their fieldwork, and frequently for audiences who read or hear about their work. Sociologist Doug Meyer conducted research on violence against queer people, a topic that has attracted media attention in recent years, though the focus has been primarily on white, middle-class men.[28] Meyer conducted forty-seven interviews with LGBTQ people who had experienced violence to show that misogyny (for women and transgender people) and racism (toward queer people of color) were significant factors that impact the forms of violence that LGBTQ people encountered, as well as their perceptions of that violence. Although Meyer does not offer "easy answers" for how a researcher should approach such work, in a subsequent blog post, he discussed developing the art of reading people as an interviewer "reading what people want to talk about and what they most certainly do not want to talk about."[29] These skills move far beyond a typical "Code of Ethics" aiming to protect research participants and they are equally, if not even more, important for feminist ethnographers aiming to conduct research on sensitive or controversial topics or populations.

🔊 SPOTLIGHT 🔊

Tanya Erzen on the Politics of Reciprocity and Mediation

Tanya Erzen *is Associate Research Professor in Religion and Gender and Queer Studies at the University of Puget Sound and director of the Crime, Law and Justice Studies program. Her most recent book is* God in Captivity: The Rise of Faith-Based Ministries in an Age of Mass Incarceration *(2017). She is also the author of* Straight to Jesus: Sexual and Christian Conversions in the Ex-Gay Movement *(2006), which received the Ruth Benedict Prize and the Gustave O Arlt award;* Fanpire: The Twilight Series and the Women Who Love It *(2012); and coeditor of* Zero Tolerance: Quality of Life and the New Police Brutality in New York City *(2001). She is a founder and faculty Director of the Freedom Education Project Puget Sound, an organization that provides college classes to women in Washington prisons and seeks to educate the public about educational access and incarceration. Below, Erzen discusses the challenges of working with a conservative movement.*

One of the really practical things that happened when I first started doing the ex-gay research was that I was trying to find a reason to actually be at the ex-gay ministry, especially as a woman around men. In graduate school, I had made money doing HTML webpage work, and [the ministry] needed somebody to help them with their website, and I remember asking Faye [Ginsburg, my dissertation advisor], should I volunteer in their offices, so I can actually be in the office every day that I'm there? And she said, "oh absolutely, you have to do this." I said, "but then I'm helping them to create their website" [for a cause I didn't support]. And she said, "but I think if you're explicit about that in your research, then that's okay."

The other was there's this whole piece that I don't think is always talked about in feminist ethnography around religion and especially in a community that is a proselytizing community that very much saw me as a person, well, at the time I was single. I had moved across the country by myself. The woman who ran the ministry with her husband said she saw herself in me at a younger age. And so there were all these strange dynamics with them feeling like they were taking care of me, but maybe hoping that in some way that this would alter me to a certain extent. I was sort of submitting myself to that process, even knowing it wouldn't happen.

I think that as time went on—and I spent a lot of time there—it became easier. I never hid my views. I mean, we were always respectful, but I never pretended to think otherwise. I was very clear, I'm only here because I want to really understand what sort of motivations and rationale [you have] and daily life of how a place like this functions. If I were interested in just bashing you, I don't have to do this. And I think they really respected that, just the commitment to spend time. The people who I ended up being closest to were in some ways more marginal to the ministry, and the people who were much more stalwart believers in the mission of the ministry as Christians, I always knew them, but I didn't have the rapport I had with other people.

[After publishing my research, sometimes I've felt like a] mediator. It was really stark when the book came out because I did a lot of live radio shows—unexpectedly, since I didn't have any experience with that. They had call-ins, and you'd get people saying, "why do you hate gay people?" And then the next caller would say, "why do you hate Christians?" . . . One other funny anecdote: the only time I was on TV was MSNBC, and the woman interviewing me, the anchor, I don't know who briefed her, but she introduces me, "It's Father's Day. Imagine your son says, 'Dad, Happy Father's Day, I'm gay.' Here's Tanya Erzen, a lesbian, a former lesbian who went through an ex-gay ministry to talk to us about her book." [laughter]

Also, I felt that initially when I would present about the work to academics, they felt I was too sympathetic to the group. When I gave a talk at [a prominent University in California, where I conducted my research, after] the book came out, one of the men in the book who lived there, and who I have remained close with, came to the talk, and in the Q&A he actually spoke up and identified himself to the audience. I knew he was planning to be there. It was a moment of the two worlds really colliding. There's always an expectation in those academic settings that the people [you research] aren't there, and yet here he was in that presence, and he actually now has a PhD. So, he started speaking back to that academic world. And that was a really interesting moment for me. It was very cordial, but it was really uncomfortable for some people in the audience. But I actually think it's good to be uncomfortable, and those moments can generate things that are important. I almost wish there was more of that.

Questions about whether—and how much—a feminist ethnographer should "give back" to participants are clearly a complicated one. Many feminist ethnographers want to avoid overburdening participants who often see a little direct benefit from ethnographic research. Some may see part of "giving back" as offering participants opportunities to contribute to, or collaborate, in research, such as reviewing interview transcripts. Participants might ask, "Why should I bother reading a transcript and discussing it with you when you'll just include what you want anyway?" Feminist ethnographers need to grapple with this question. What would you be willing to change in your writing based on a participant's comments? Are you willing to note where interpretations differ? How will including participant's perspectives benefit them?

Rarely will one find a completely equal research/participant encounter, as we discussed in chapter 3, despite the best intentions of the feminist ethnographer. In fact, researchers most often hold the pen (or wield the keyboard) and make critical choices—alongside publishers and editors—about what to include and not include in the ethnography. "Giving back" is not only about remuneration; it is also about having respect for the input of participants in your research. There are complicated logistics that often come with that goal. For instance, do participants have the time, finances, and technological ability to be in dialogue (literally or electronically) with you? Do they even care? We do think it is worth mentioning that sometimes our research matters more to us than it does to the people with whom we work.

The issue of what the researcher gives back in return for research participants' willingness to participate in our studies is one that does not have a clear cut answer and is challenging on many fronts. One may question whether it is appropriate, or even desirable, to "give back" in all instances of feminist ethnographic research. This poses complex questions for feminist ethnographers who research conservative movements, like those discussed above. Even if a researcher does determine that they wish to "give back" to participants, challenges remain in figuring out a culturally appropriate way to do so that is respectful of participants' time, expertise, and engagement in the project. On the one hand, typical research compensation, such as offering cash to entice people to participate in an experiment, is different from and may not acknowledge the extent to which many participants may become deeply involved in feminist ethnographic research. Participant-observation may span months, or even years, and some participants may contribute to multiple formal and informal interviews, or be involved in data analysis to varying degrees. Thus, the ways that a researcher might "give back" to individual participants are varied.

While one might offer financial payment, if available, many ethnographers find themselves contributing in other ways, such as buying a meal, assisting with living expenses, offering rides, or babysitting a participant's children might be meaningful gestures for those who offer time and expertise to one's research. Other times, an ethnographer may feel compelled to "give back" in the form of support for the organization they work with by grant writing, developing a website, or other volunteer work that fits their skill sets. Dána-Ain, for example, donated all the royalties from her book sales to the shelter where she conducted the research. Elizabeth Chin donated the royalties from her book *Purchasing Power: Black Kids, America and Consumer Culture* to a scholarship fund in New Haven, the site of her research.[30]

Many feminist ethnographers also hope to "give back" to the people, organizations, and communities with which they work by publishing their research beyond academic audiences with the hope of raising visibility of the issue or group. Contributing to public policy reports or evaluation, or writing op-eds or blogs for nonacademic publications can accomplish this. The challenges we face during fieldwork and the writing process often become the foundation upon which we make decisions about how to present and utilize our data toward a variety of ends. In fact, writing about the ethical concerns and challenges that arise in our research is crucial to feminist ethnographic writing, as we will discuss in the following chapter. Although there is no single "right" answer about how (or even whether) a researcher should "give back," it is a question that should be considered by all feminist ethnographers.

Often feminist ethnographers engage in research that is connected to broadbased social change, which they also see as a way of giving back to communities or organizations with which they work. Many would argue that ethnography, particularly feminist ethnography, has proven extremely useful in studying and moving forward the goals of social change movements. Ethnographic methods, such as oral history, are useful for capturing the development of a movement. The work of feminist ethnographers has been influential within movements, such as Occupy movements internationally, reproductive justice struggles, the battered women's movement, Black Lives Matter, prison reform efforts, domestic worker rights, and welfare rights movements, among others. In chapter 7, we offer detailed examples of how feminist ethnography has worked toward social change.

How Can We Assess the (Potential) Impacts of Feminist Ethnography?

We don't always know what the outcome of our research will be. In fact, we really never do. But feminist ethnographers need to think through the possibilities for impact prior to, and as we conduct, research. Some research can emerge from wishing we had contributed (more) to social change in the other aspects of our lives, in an effort to lead to a change in the future. This is the case for Kiersten Downs, a graduate of the University of South Florida in Applied Anthropology and veteran of the US Air Force. Her research addresses women veterans' experiences after they leave the service following the prolonged influence of military masculinity. She focuses on the challenges that she has faced implementing a feminist mixed-methods study, including an anonymous online survey, semi-structured interviews, and participant-observation to explore American women veterans' experiences reentering civilian life. In Downs's case, her aim is to break down the silences around sexism and gender discrimination in the military through her research.

ᵐᴰ SPOTLIGHT ᴰᵐ

Kiersten Downs on "Feminist Curiosity" and Stamina

Kiersten Downs *is an applied anthropologist, qualitative researcher, and veteran of the US Air Force and Air National Guard (2001–2009). She received her doctoral degree from the University of South Florida (2017) and also holds a graduate certificate in Women and Gender Studies from USF. In addition, she has an MS in Conflict Analysis and Resolution from Nova Southeastern University and a BA in Political Science from Binghamton University. Her doctoral dissertation research was a feminist ethnography exploring women veterans' experiences with integration into their communities after military service. She works with the Department of Veterans Affairs as a consultant and qualitative researcher specializing in health equity research for minority veterans, reintegration and transition services, and community-based research.*

Photo Credit: Devin Mitchell, Veteran Vision Project.

This photo was taken by Devin Mitchell, founder of the Veteran Vision Project. For me, this photo provides a glimpse of my personal experiences and military transition. It tells a story about the motivation behind my work as an applied anthropologist and an activist scholar. It has taken me years of reflection and intense devotion to higher education to even begin to understand my own experiences as a woman veteran within the complex web of American militarism. There is a part of me that wishes I would have done more to stand up against sexism and gender discrimination while I was still in the military. It has been really difficult to come to the realization that I was part of the problem by keeping quiet about what I was experiencing or observing taking place. But what I also now realize is that my own silence and the silence of others is a by-product of the gendered institution that we were or still are a part of.

Developing a "feminist curiosity"[1] takes stamina, and according to [international relations scholar] Cynthia Enloe it is not a quiet intellectual pastime. Publicly advocating for gender equity has always been an uphill battle. I realized very quickly that any woman serving in the military or any woman veteran who deliberately analyzes, critiques, and challenges power systems in this arena tends to become an instant target for those in opposition to advancing social justice. It is obvious especially in light of discussions focused on recent current events such as the two women that passed the Army's Ranger training along with highly politicized negotiations on expected regulation changes allowing women to serve in all combat roles, that women in today's military continue to provoke mixed responses. Even more interesting to me is the level of condescension coming from some of the men and even other women who were or are part of the military with regard to gender integration. I will elaborate on this latter notion as part of my research analysis.

Like so many other feminist scholars, I am a member of the population that I am researching. There is no way for me to get around the fact that I hold personal biases that likely influence my research. However, this closeness also serves as the motivating force which continues to drive me forward, when even at times the emotional stress of the work has led me to question my efforts in the field. Additionally, I have come to accept that this closeness will always draw criticism from those within academia who feel that we (feminist scholars) have strayed too far from what they understand to be an objective truth. My time in the service has probably aided in the development of my thick skin when it comes to dealing with those colleagues or contentious onlookers who do not hide an exaggerated eye roll the moment the word "feminism" is uttered in relation to social science research or, in my case, any work having to do with the military institution. I think it is fair to say that many of us doing this kind of work have experienced damaging and misogynistic rhetoric to a certain degree. I will be up front in saying that at times the continued negativity has gotten to me. Although a burden, it has not stopped me from moving forward with my work.

[1] Cynthia H. Enloe, *Globalization and Militarism: Feminists Make the Link*, 2007.

SPOTLIGHT

Sandra Morgen on Movement Building

Photo Credit: Robert Hill Long.

Sandra Morgen *received her PhD in 1982 from the University of North Carolina at Chapel Hill and became professor of anthropology at the University of Oregon, Eugene. Morgen began her career in academia as a doctoral student doing feminist ethnographic work studying the women's health movement in the United States. But it was a challenge because, in her own words, "there wasn't anything called feminist anthropology at that time." She is the author and editor of eight books, including* Women and the Politics of Empowerment *(1988), edited with anthropologist Ann Bookman;* Into Our Own Hands: The Women's Health Movement in the United States, 1969–1990 *(2002); and, as discussed earlier in this chapter,* Taxes Are a Woman's Issue *(2006), coauthored with Mimi Abramovitz. Below, Morgen discusses the role that feminist activist ethnography can have in social movements. After having spent a decade conducting research on the impact of welfare reform (the Personal Responsibility and Work Opportunity Reconciliation Act of 1996), she reflects on the success of that research in addressing the policies that made receiving assistance more difficult.*

Our research was part of a national feminist effort to question the mainstream narrative of the success of welfare "reform." We found that most former recipients of welfare continued to experience significant economic hardship and insecurity and struggled to balance low-wage, often inflexible paid employment with their and their children's needs, especially among families of color. Unfortunately, policy decisions were not being made on the basis of research, but on ideologies steeped in racist, sexist, and class-based assumptions.

In the advocacy work I was doing on welfare, I kept hearing women on welfare compared negatively to this "hard-working taxpayer." I realized how little we knew about tax politics or how taxes related to what are traditionally considered "women's issues." So I decided to study tax policy and politics. I coauthored a book with Mimi Abramovitz about women and national tax policy called *Taxes Are a Woman's Issue* and then began research on tax politics as expressed in ballot initiative campaigns in Oregon. I have done some advocacy within the research and policy communities to look at gender, race, and class as dimensions of tax politics. But also within the feminist community to see the importance of working on tax fairness for women, recognizing that tax fairness means very different things for women in different classes.

I think this kind of work expands what counts as feminist scholarship, a project women of color have been engaged in since the earliest days of feminism. I didn't study taxes because I had an intrinsic interest in tax policy. I did it because my advocacy experience around welfare came smack up against the question of taxes. Is this movement building? I hope it helps point to where progressive, feminist activism needs to be. Even when our scholarship isn't immediately connected to movement building, when it questions and changes paradigms, when it contributes to a feminist critical race, class-conscious way of looking at the world, it is part of the long process of movement building. I have come to believe that work should count as important politically, because we don't know what will build or aid the movements of the future.

In cases like what Sandra Morgen describes, feminist ethnography can contribute to social movement building. In fact, the passage of the 1996 Welfare Reform Bill by US president Bill Clinton led many scholars to examine the impact of the changes in welfare policy. As discussed earlier in this chapter, Morgen is one feminist scholar who spent a decade conducting research on the impact of welfare reform, particularly on women and mothers. That experience led her to shift her research and advocacy agenda far from her previous expertise, to studying tax policy and politics from a feminist perspective.

While at times feminist ethnographers' work is to contribute to the documentation of movement building, at others, a feminist ethnographer may seek to evaluate or critique a social movement. For instance, while Christa's research is supportive of efforts to enhance access to homebirth and legalize midwives, she is critical of the use of "consumer rights" language among middle-class, organizers, since this strategy can be dismissive of the experience of low-income women. During and following her fieldwork, this often meant having difficult—though also essential and constructive—conversations with activists, many of whom saw little reason to question consumer-based strategies that had proven useful in conversations with legislators. In some cases, these discussions contributed to the inclusion of advocacy strategies, such as highlighting the importance of midwives to improve access to prenatal care among low-income, rural populations. Yet scholarly critique—no matter how constructively intended—is always part of broader legacies of the marginalization of particular voices. The homebirth mothers and families Christa studied frequently bore the brunt of campaigns by powerful medical officials against midwives. In this charged context, her efforts to raise the volume of low-income women's voices within the movement were often met with skepticism. Christa wanted to encourage midwifery advocates to question "sisters in struggle" narratives because they overlooked racialized and socioeconomic disparities in care. For their part, many advocates worried that any questioning of organizing strategies would damage rather than strengthen the movement.[31]

As many researchers learn, once our research moves "off the shelf" (to borrow a phrase from Waterston and Vesperi's *Anthropology Off the Shelf: Anthropologists on Writing*[32]) and into popular consciousness, we relinquish control over how it is interpreted—and ultimately utilized—by both proponents and opponents of our aims. Thus, as well as thinking about how to "give back," we must also be conscious of how our research can be used by others, in support of, but also sometimes against our aims.

THINKING THROUGH . . .

Ethical Dilemmas

Select one of the issues or figures listed below. Conduct research on the topic. Then write an essay summarizing the ethical issues that you see in relationship to how the research was conducted and what you think a feminist ethnographic approach would have done differently.

- Henrietta Lacks
- Tuskegee Syphilis Experiment
- Stanford Prison Experiments
- Rigoberta Menchu
- Alice Goffman's "On the Run: Fugitive Life in an American City"

Conclusion

It is not always possible for an ethnographer to control the outcomes of their research, but it is essential for feminist ethnographers to consider what possibilities exist and what strategies they can use to anticipate what might emerge, both positive and negative. We also believe that looking back on this process is a worthwhile and fruitful endeavor for feminist ethnographers because it encourages not only personal reflection but also reflexivity within a field devoted to considering and reconsidering challenges as they continue to emerge.

Suggested Resources

Behar, Ruth (1996) *The Vulnerable Observer: Anthropology that Breaks your Heart.*
Boellstorff, Tom, Bonnie Nardi, Celia Pearce, and T. L. Taylor, eds. (2012) *Ethnography and Virtual Worlds: A Handbook of Method.*
Durban, Erin L. 2021. "Anthropology and Ableism." *American Anthropologist* 124 (4): 1–14.
Lewin, Ellen, and William L. Leap, eds. (1996) *Out in the Field: Reflections of Lesbian and Gay Anthropologists.*
Longman, Chia, and Tamsin Bradley (2015) *Interrogating Harmful Cultural Practices: Gender, Culture and Coercion.*
Sins Invalid (2019) *Skin, Tooth, and Bone: The Basis of Movement Is Our People: A Disability Justice Primer*, 2nd Edition.
The Feminist Ethnographer's Dilemma (September 24, 2011) a panel discussion featuring Orit Avishai, Lynne Gerber, and moderator Margot Weiss at the Barnard Center for Research on Women, http://bcrw.barnard.edu/videos/the-feminist-ethnographers-dilemma/.

World Council of Anthropological Associations Ethics Task Force: Working Paper Series: Ethics (2020), https://www.waunet.org/wcaa/working-papers/. A list of over 50 worldwide member organizations is available: https://www.waunet.org/wcaa/members/associations.

Ethics statements from US-based organizations that relate to ethnography include:

American Anthropological Association Principles of Professional Responsibility (1970 [2012]) https://www.americananthro.org/ethics-and-methods
American Political Science Association Guide to Professional Ethics (1989 [2012]) http://www.apsanet.org/portals/54/Files/Publications/APSAEthicsGuide2012.pdf
American Psychological Association Ethical Principles and Code of Conduct (1992 [2017]) https://www.apa.org/ethics/code
American Sociological Association Code of Ethics (2018) http://www.asanet.org/images/asa/docs/pdf/CodeofEthics.pdf
Association of American Geographers Statement of Professional Ethics (1998 [2009]) http://www.aag.org/cs/about_aag/governance/statement_of_professional_ethics

Notes

1. Moya Bailey, "#transform(ing)DH Writing and Research: An Autoethnography of Digital Humanities and Feminist Ethics," 2015; Moya Bailey, *Misogynoir Transformed*, 2021.
2. Ibid.
3. Elizabeth Chin, "The Neoliberal Institutional Review Board, or Why Just Fixing the Rules Won't Help Feminist (Activist) Ethnographers," in *Feminist Activist Ethnography,* eds. Christa Craven and Dána-Ain Davis, 2013.
4. Ibid., 210.
5. Candice Bradley, "Doing Fieldwork with Diabetes," *Cultural Anthropology Methods Journal,* 1997.
6. Bradley draws on anthropologist Robert Murphy's (1987) use of this term in *The Body Silent,* an autoethnographic account of his experience with a deteriorating spinal condition that led to paraplegia.
7. Bradley, "Doing Fieldwork with Diabetes," 1997, 7.
8. Lindsey Brown and Felicity Boardman, "Accessing the Field," *Social Science & Medicine,* 2011.
9. Laura Ellingson, "Embodied Knowledge: Writing Researchers' Bodies into Qualitative Health Research," *Qualitative Health Research,* 2006.
10. For more discussion for her research, see Andrea Queeley. "*Somos Negros Finos*: Anglophone Caribbean Cultural Citizenship in Revolutionary Cuba," in *Global Circuits of Blackness: Interrogating the African Diaspora,* eds. Jean Muteba Rahier, Percy C. Hintzen, and Felipe Smith, 2010.
11. Annette Lareau, "Common Problems in Field Work: A Personal Essay," Appendix to *Home Advantage,* 1989.
12. Diane Bell, Pat Caplan, and Wazir Jahan Karim, *Gendered Fields: Women, Men and Ethnography,* 2013.
13. Diane L. Wolf, ed., *Feminist Dilemmas in Fieldwork,* 1996.
14. Laura Nader, "Up the Anthropologist: Perspectives Gained from Studying Up," in *Reinventing Anthropology,* ed. Dell Hymes, 1972.
15. Ibid., 289.
16. Karen Ho, *Liquidated,* 2009.
17. Cynthia Enloe, *Seriously!* 2013.
18. Melissa Fisher, *Wall Street Women,* 2012.
19. Sandra Morgen and Mimi Abramovitz *Taxes Are a Woman's Issue: Reframing the Debate,* 2006.
20. Martha K. Huggins and Marie-Louise Glebbeek, eds., *Women Fielding Danger,* 2009.
21. Ellen Gruenbaum, *The Female Circumcision Controversy,* 2000.
22. Ibid., 57–58.
23. Faye Ginsburg, *Contested Lives,* 1998.

24 Faye Ginsburg, "Procreation Stories: Reproduction, Nurturance, and Procreation in Life Narratives of Abortion Activists," *American Ethnologist*, 1987.

25 Tine Davids, "Trying to Be a Vulnerable Observer: Matters of Agency, Solidarity and Hospitality in Feminist Ethnography," *Women's Studies International Forum*, 2014.

26 Kathleen Blee, *Women of the Klan*, 2008 (orig. 1991).

27 Srimati Basu, "Hiding in Plain Sight: Disclosure, Identity, and the Indian Men's Rights Movement," 2018, 120, 123.

28 Doug Meyer, *Violence against Queer People*, 2015.

29 Doug Meyer, "Researching Violence and Asking People to Describe Traumatic Experiences," accessed September 30, 2015. https://gendersociety.wordpress.com/2015/01/30/researching -violence/.

30 Elizabeth Chin, *Purchasing Power: Black Kids, America and Consumer Culture*, 2001.

31 Christa Craven, "Reproductive Rights in a Consumer Rights Era: Toward the Value of 'Constructive' Critique," in *Feminist Activist Ethnography*, eds. Christa Craven and Dána-Ain Davis, 2013.

32 Alisse Waterston and Maria Vesperi, *Anthropology Off the Shelf: Anthropologists on Writing*, 2009.

CHAPTER 6

Producing Feminist Ethnography

There are many ways to create, produce, and distribute feminist ethnography. This chapter will explore feminist ethnographic writing, film, performance, and other creative approaches by asking the following questions:

- How does one write feminist ethnography?
- What creative possibilities exist for writing and circulating feminist ethnography?
- How can we make feminist ethnography publicly accessible?
- How do feminist ethnographers engage in creative and artistic projects?

Spotlights *in this chapter:*

- Asale Angel-Ajani on Writing (Without Swagger)
- Harjant Gill on Film as a Powerful Feminist Medium

Essentials *in this chapter:*

- Kirin Narayan, *Alive in the Writing*
- Savannah Shange, *Progressive Dystopia: Abolition, Antiblackness and Schooling in San Francisco*
- The Sangtin Writers Collective and Richa Nagar, *Playing with Fire*
- Judy DeLoache and Alma Gottlieb, *A World of Babies*
- Gina Athena Ulysse, "My Jelly Platform Shoes" from *Downtown Ladies*

You will also be **Thinking Through . . .**

- Citational Politics, Revisited in the Age of #MeToo
- Experimental Design
- Developing Creative Ethnography

The most common form of producing and distributing feminist ethnography is through written accounts, which is where we begin this chapter. Traditionally, this takes the form of ethnographic monographs, a book-length manuscript dedicated to the ethnographic study of a single culture. The word "ethnography" is derived from the Greek word "ethnos" (people, ethnic group, and "graphein" to write, or be represented). Creative approaches to producing ethnography also have a storied history that we aim to uncover. Although not feminist in content, one may take a cue in the creative production of scholarly work from W. E. B. Du Bois's pageantry genre, which is an instructive dramatic narrative and is related to our discussion of representation. In *The Star of Ethiopia*, Du Bois had thousands of artists dramatize a spectacle on the fiftieth anniversary of the Emancipation Proclamation. There were only four productions in 1913, 1915, 1916, and 1925, in which the history of Blacks is performed in five parts.

Other examples of creative uses of scholarly material can be found in the work of ethnographers like Zora Neale Hurston, who wrote ethnographic fiction in the 1940s. In the 1980s, ethnographers pointedly interrogated the tradition of ethnographic monographs (intended for academic audiences) and scholarly articles written for academic journals. Feminist ethnographers were a lively part of these discussions and productions. As creative experimentation in ethnographic writing came center stage in the 1990s, feminist ethnographers began to publish more frequently in a variety of genres including fiction, memoir, poetry, collaborative blogs, and graphic novels. Feminist ethnographers also engage in performance art, dance, and other creative methods to showcase their ethnographic work, several of which we will highlight in this chapter.

This chapter offers examples of many forms of ethnographic production—aimed at inspiring you to think innovatively about your own work. We hope that the following discussion encourages you to think about ethnography in new and different ways, and to consider the potential of different approaches for generating research products. We advocate becoming adept (or at least trying your hand) at as many styles of writing and production of ethnographic work as possible. This allows for creativity and can also serve as an important dialogue with your professors about how to best express your work, possibly in multiple forms.

Writing and producing feminist ethnography is an important task, one that can ultimately influence who will come in contact with our work. As mentioned previously, Ruth Behar and Deborah Gordon's groundbreaking edited collection *Women Writing Culture* in 1995 demonstrated women's robust creative contributions to ethnographic writing. Ethnographers have used various writing styles from fiction to life history, and from critique to memoir. Scholars such as Elsie Clews Parsons, Ella Deloria, and Barbara Meyerhoff were largely erased from the canon, but their work demonstrated the breadth of what women had produced in written form since the 1800s. Feminist scholars, including Louise Lamphere, Dorinne Kondo, Paulla Ebron, and Geyla Frank, resuscitated the silenced innovations of those identified above. That said, innovative and creative approaches—and, we would underscore, engaging and accessible writing—can and should be a part of all (feminist) ethnographic work and we should be open to integrating creative and critical writing. We hope the examples offered here will serve as an inspiration and encourage creative thinking about even more novel approaches to circulating feminist ethnography within and beyond the classroom.

How Does One Write Feminist Ethnography?

Science fiction writer Octavia Butler reminds us that persistence is probably the most important determinant of a good writer:

> First forget inspiration. Habit is more dependable. Habit will sustain you whether you're inspired or not. Habit will help you finish and polish your stories. Inspiration won't. Habit is persistence in practice.
>
> Forget talent. If you have it, fine. Use it. If you don't have it, it doesn't matter. As habit is more dependable than inspiration, continued learning is more dependable than talent. . . . Cultivate habits that enable you to persist in finishing your work and improving it. Learn as you go and have fun.[1]

Writing is not always easy, no matter the genre. Feminist ethnography can be especially difficult because of the expectation to be politically, strategically, ethically, and reflexively engaged. We think that the more freedom and flexibility you give yourself to write badly (at least for your first draft . . . not the one you'll hand in to your professor!), the more enjoyable a process it can be. A fantastic short essay on this subject is Anne Lamott's "Shitty First Drafts"—a must read if you ever struggle with writer's block![2] In it, she reminds writers:

> Almost all good writing begins with terrible first efforts. You need to start somewhere. Start by getting something—anything—down on paper. A friend of mine says that the first draft is the down draft—you just get it down. The second draft is the up draft—you fix it up. You try to say what you have to say more accurately. And the third draft is the dental draft, where you check every tooth, to see if it's loose or cramped or decayed, or even, God help us, healthy.[3]

To facilitate writing—especially that challenging first draft—performance scholar D. Soyini Madison suggests what she calls a "Muse Map," something like a roadmap or outline but with the intention of being a guiding force versus merely charting the trajectory of a document. This can be simple or comprehensive, but the point is to have your ideas written down in broad strokes, or perhaps expressed artistically, so that when you approach that dreaded "blank page" your map can give you guidance and the freedom to engage in some "expressive irreverence," ideally bringing both confidence and joy to the writing process as a performative event itself.[4]

A classic take on experimentation with different styles of writing is anthropologist Margery Wolf's book *A Thrice Told Tale: Feminism, Postmodernism and Ethnographic Responsibility.*[5] In this book, Wolf, who also wrote the classic ethnography *The House of Lim: A Study of a Chinese Farm Family* in 1968,[6] offers the reader three texts that emerged from her ethnographic fieldwork in Taiwan during the early 1960s. They all center on the story of a young mother, Mrs. Tan, who begins to behave in a strange way that villagers attribute to a variety of possible causes: she is becoming a shaman possessed by a god, she is mentally unstable and in need of hospitalization, or she may be being manipulated by her lazy husband to gain community sympathy and financial support. Wolf notes that although this is a story that has undoubtedly been told numerous times by others who witnessed it, hers are the only written accounts of the events. She is wary of giving her observations unearned legitimacy and reminds us to be attentive to the power of writing—inscribing and publishing any story gives it a frozen quality. Wolf is also aware of how her own writing is in some senses polyvocal, incorporating multiple voices: villagers she interviewed, her Chinese research assistant, and her husband, who was also conducting fieldwork in the same location.

Wolf begins *A Thrice Told Tale* with a piece of fiction she wrote shortly after the incident in 1960 but never published. Although fictional, and experimental in form, Wolf notes that when she wrote it, she did not think of it as a feminist account. In fact, she highlights the challenges of returning to earlier work as a more experienced, and by then, in 1992, decidedly feminist ethnographer. She follows the fictional account with "raw" fieldnotes that she, her field assistant Wu Chieh, and her then-husband Arthur Wolf wrote as the events unfolded. Importantly, she notes, her husband came away with a very different interpretation of the events, despite writing many of the fieldnotes they all agreed upon regarding their accuracy. For Wolf, this makes a useful point: that part of ethnographic responsibility is to present events in a way that allows for multiple interpretations—even by different ethnographers conducting research at the same time.

Finally, Wolf concludes *A Thrice Told Tale* with her academic article from *American Ethnologist* in 1990, analyzing the events from her current perspective as a feminist ethnographer returning to an incident that occurred thirty years prior. A central point that Wolf makes is that ethnographic experience is—and should be—messy. We learn a great deal from challenging and sometimes unpleasant experiences. Her writing evokes this lesson as she demonstrates different styles of experimental/creative writing, polyvocality, reflexivity, and the differences between fiction and ethnography.

Most ethnographers do not have the occasion—or perhaps the inclination—to offer multiple, potentially competing versions of their work. Indeed, it is rare that we get to see an ethnographer's "raw" data or fieldnotes, except in the cases where formal interviews may be archived. In any piece of ethnographic writing, there are many details that are not present, many events that go unanalyzed, and many perspectives that are not emphasized. When most ethnographers begin to write, they sit down with pages and pages of fieldnotes, transcriptions, archives, and the like. It would be impossible to incorporate all the forms of data. The task of the ethnographer as a writer is to sift through that material and find stories, events, moments, and ideas that conjure up central aspects of their work. As the example of Margery and Arthur Wolf's different interpretations of the same events above reveals, even two ethnographers working on the same project will have different points of view about the events, and even within those events, different issues may interest them. This is where the importance of a feminist ethnographer's sensibility becomes important and can help sort through their data and begin the process of writing an ethnographic account.

An indispensable book on the process of ethnographic writing, authored by feminist anthropologist Kirin Narayan, is *Alive in the Writing: Crafting Ethnography in the Company of Chekhov*. Narayan introduces students to (as well as invigorates seasoned writers to reconsider) the ethnographic process of writing through reflecting on her own experiences authoring two ethnographies, a novel, and a memoir. Additionally, she shares how she was inspired by Anton Chekov, the Russian physician who wrote short stories and plays during the late 1800s, often based on his travels. Narayan weaves together additional examples from ethnographers and other "ethnographically inclined" nonfiction writers, interspersed with practical advice and targeted writing exercises. Notably, she highlights the significant overlap in style and form among ethnographic writing, creative nonfiction, memoir, biography, nature writing, travel writing, literary journalism, and cultural criticism. Indeed, there is much to be learned from reading, and experimenting, widely.

Taking up Narayan's attention to the power of well-chosen words, we argue that writing is not only a practical or even creative endeavor but also a political one. Indeed, an important political reason for writing feminist ethnography with care is so that people take your feminist concerns seriously. Toward this end, we take inspiration from a broad range of feminist writers—ethnographers, creative writers, journalists, et cetera—who write deliberately and purposefully. For Narayan, writing purposefully means making decisions like limiting freewriting in response to her prompts to under two pages. This strategy both enables and entices others to give you useful feedback, which is less likely if you offer them a long, rambling account. Good, concise writing also encourages people to listen to your argument.

Key to this endeavor of writing well is paying attention to grammatical choices and etymological histories. For instance, there are important feminist implications to consider when using passive voice, the sentence construction "(noun) (verb phrase) by (noun)" where the subject is acted on, rather than acting. Although some academic disciplines commonly use passive sentence construction (the natural sciences and psychology, for instance, as in "interviews were conducted"), ethnographers tend to favor "active voice" ("students conducted interviews") because it reveals who is doing the action. Feminist writers have long critiqued passive sentence construction regarding violence, such as "a woman was raped" or "a transwoman of color was murdered," because this grammatical construction can lead a reader to ignore, or a writer to obscure, the fact that someone performed the action.

As with all advice (whether with feminist intent or not), a writer needs to consider the appropriate use of the passive voice. For instance, the passive voice does not always hide meaning and can serve useful rhetorical functions. It can allow you to choose what or whom to put in the grammatical subject position. For instance, writing "Student activists were honored at the University" puts the focus on the students, rather than a sentence in active voice that focuses on who honored them, such as "University administrators honored student activists." Like any other grammatical structure or literary convention, if overused or adopted *in order to* hide meaning or harmful actions, it becomes problematic.

In some cases, passive voice may be used effectively when we do not know the agent of the action. For instance, when a writer does not know the identity of an alleged perpetrator, "a woman was raped" may be preferable to "someone raped a woman," because the latter construction privileges a vague perpetrator ("someone") over "the woman." Additionally, a statement like "a man was raped," in the passive voice, may actually draw attention to a problematic reality that many people believe that men cannot be victims of rape. In this case, passive voice can rhetorically be used toward the feminist goal of educating readers.

Choosing the words we use in our writing (and performance, filmmaking, etc.) also needs to be done attentively. For instance, groundbreaking scholarship is frequently referred to as "seminal," linking to the production of semen. In a figurative sense, seminal is often invoked to suggest that something is "full of possibilities," and "to disseminate" refers to the spreading or dispersal of (male) seed. The term "germinal" has been used by some feminists as an alternative, though acknowledgment for being the "original" does not carry the same weight as something that has become widely *used* by others.[7] In truth, sometimes there is not an effective or evocative word to use in place of those with gendered, racialized, colonial, ableist, or other harmful histories. Terminology often requires an explicit discussion. But in this case, we would argue that accolades like foundational, innovative, fundamental, or revolutionary (or germinal, in the sense that it is the seed from which later developments grew) offer compelling options that invoke different etymological legacies.[8]

Many feminist ethnographers also develop new terminology—or new ways of using terminology—to underscore their findings or convey the importance of particular uses of language to the communities they study. For instance, using local terms to describe gender and sexuality (among other Indigenous terms) has been critical in queer anthropology. Feminist and queer ethnographers have explored terminology to describe sexual identity, subject position, and practice in many cultural contexts: *toms* and *dees* in Thailand, *hijras* in India, *'yan daudu* in northern Nigeria, *lala* and *tongzhi* in China, Butch Queens in Detroit Ballroom culture, and Afro-Surinamese working-class women who do "*mati* work" (a practice—versus an identity—of rejecting marriage in favor of male and female sexual partners), among many others.[9] Emphasizing and reiterating Indigenous terminology in ethnographic writing also challenges readers to avoid Euro-American assumptions of sexuality and gender systems. Anthropologist Tom Boellstorff describes a process of "dubbing culture," where multiple terminologies exist in "awkward fusion," rather than one originating from the other. This provides a framework for examining the relationship between the English "gay" and Indonesian "*gay*" (and other terminology like "lesbian"/"*lesbi*" and "homosexual"/"*homoseks*").[10] In his writing on masculinities in *Filipino Crosscurrents: Oceanographies of Seafaring, Masculinities, and Globalization*, anthropologist Kale Fajardo adopts a different strategy. He opted *not* to italicize words in Tagalog and Filipino—which most style guides require—so as not to mark them as "foreign" and distinct from English. He frames this as a strategic choice to decolonize language in ethnographic writing.[11]

Consequently, we emphasize that all feminist writers, including ethnographers who are writing for academic or popular audiences, must make informed and strategic use of grammar to effectively convey the feminist issues we research and care about.

🧠 ESSENTIAL

Excerpt from *Alive in the Writing* by Kirin Narayan

Photo Credit: Shiela Reaves.

Kirin Narayan *has written extensively about the craft of ethnographic writing and her long-term fieldwork on religion, gender, and oral traditions in South Asia. She earned her PhD in anthropology from the University of California, Berkeley, and is currently a professor at the Australian National University. Her first book,* Storytellers, Saints, and Scoundrels: Folk Narrative in Hindu Religious Teaching (1989), *won the inaugural Victor Turner Prize for Ethnographic Writing and was cowinner of the Elsie Clews Parsons Prize for Folklore. Her many books include a novel and a family memoir. Her most recent ethnography is* Everyday Creativity: Singing Goddesses in the Himalayan Foothills *(2016). The following excerpt, highlighting her approach to writing with galvanizing prompts, is from* Alive in the Writing: Crafting Ethnography in the Company of Chekhov *(2012).*

Writing offers the chance to cultivate an attentiveness to life itself, and to enhance perceptions with the precision of words. Writing also potentially communicates images and insights to unseen circles of readers. . . . We all continually improve our ability to describe with vivid accuracy, to lay out ideas with clarity, to make every word count. Writing composed with craft touches readers on several levels—intellectual, emotional, and aesthetic—and the impact lingers longer than words dashed off. Whether in books, essays or articles, grant applications, reviews, letters of application, blogs, or editorials, well-chosen words gather the power to change others' minds and possibly the conditions of our own lives. At its best, strong writing can direct attention to suffering and injustice, deepen compassion and outrage, elaborate imaginative alternatives, and mobilize energies for action. . . .

The boldface prompts throughout the text are meant to initiate freewriting—uninterrupted writing that grows from whatever that seed suggests to you, and that you might later edit and refine. The exercises at the ends of the chapters, though, call for more polished pieces intended for others' eyes. For these exercises, I suggest just two double-spaced pages—not a line more—and here are my reasons. First, learning to write with brevity is a gift to overburdened readers, and especially if you're working as part of a group, a short piece is more likely to receive considered comments. Second, I believe that forcing oneself to be concise renews respect for language itself, for the weight of every word. (xi–xii)

[Throughout Narayan's text, simple prompts, such as "**Start with 'I am most curious about . . .' and write forward. (2 minutes)**" (21) build into more substantive exercises, such as:]

Begin narrating an event that dramatizes the central idea or issue you want to write about. Drawing on all of your senses, use vivid details to describe the people and the place as you follow what happened. For now, don't explicitly say what concept you're trying to illuminate; only show life in process. 2 pages. (22)

Source: Narayan, Kirin. *Alive in the Writing: Crafting Ethnography in the Company of Chekhov.* Chicago: University of Chicago Press, 2012, xi–xii, 21–22.

We also choose—with what we write about and how we write about it—to engage with particular issues and not others, highlight particular points of view, and center our accounts on matters that we find meaningful. For feminist ethnographers, it is particularly important to draw inspiration from both our intellectual genealogy and the feminist sensibility that comes from critical and meaningful engagement with fieldwork and making complicated decisions about what to include—and who is willing to be included—in an ethnography.

ESSENTIAL

Excerpt from *Progressive Dystopia: Abolition, Antiblackness, and Schooling in San Francisco* by Savannah Shange

Photo Credit: Sahar Coston.

Savannah Shange earned a PhD in Africana Studies and Education from the University of Pennsylvania, an MA in teaching from Tufts University, and a BFA from Tisch School of the Arts at New York University. She teaches anthropology at University of California, Santa Cruz. She is a Black queer feminist scholar who works at the intersections of race, place, sexuality, and the state. Her research interests include gentrification, multiracial coalition, ethnographic ethics, Black femme gender, and abolition. Her research has been published in Women and Performance, The Black Scholar, Transforming Anthropology, *and* The Feminist Wire.

"You can follow me, but I'm not gonna to talk to you."

That's what Tarika told me when I had asked her if I could shadow her classes. My first impulse was to cajole her with jokes and build rapport—surely, she *would* talk to me eventually. Or else I could have simply defaulted back to one of the other dozen or so Black girls with whom I had an easy bond, whose text messages bottlenecked on the screen of my phone, whose mothers' voices I knew by heart. But I bit my tongue, and in the interest of taking young people at their word, I assented and silently sat beside her, not only through the Beginning Spanish class that I spent a part of each day in, but also shuffling on through the halls to Algebra, Humanities, and Advisory period.

Even now, I know former Robeson staff who have Tarika's current number, and I have her Instagram handle. I heard from someone around the way that she did end up graduating from another SFUSD school, and I could ring her up with a few questions about that experience. I could slide in her DMs, or take her to In-N-Out for a follow-up interview next time I am in the Bay, but I won't. Built into the genre of ethnography is an expectation of narrative thickness, a rich tapestry of voices that leaves the reader satiated by the elegant rhythm of *I saw, she said, I saw, she said*. The "right" way to end this essay is with a pithy quote from Tarika, an emic insight that could stand in for twenty-odd pages of academic grandstanding and simultaneously give me cred as a community-accountable ethnographer who gives her research participants the last word. But to reach out to Tarika with the intent of hearing her perspective, even in the interests of a putatively liberatory ethnographic project, still demands access to Black girl interiority as the price to ride on the freedom train. If both the carceral and the decolonial engagement with young Black women rely on the same remedy—her performative transparency—then both political projects prioritize their pre-authored frameworks over Black girl self-determination.

Perhaps here I fail as an anthropologist, and the petticoat of my disciplinary drag is showing. But I sense there is more explanatory power in Tarika's agentic absence, in the opacity of not-knowing, than I would find tracking her down (*like a runaway*) and feigning a complete circle of analysis.

Tarika don't want me to find her.

Source: Shange, Savannah. *Progressive Dystopia: Abolition, Antiblackness and Schooling in San Francisco.* Durham, NC: Duke University Press, 2019, 119–120.

One way some ethnographers ensure that their work is meaningful to those who are part of the research is to engage in collaborative writing. Hence, an ethnographer can create an account that moves beyond polyvocality in the sense that multiple perspectives are incorporated, but toward an even greater engagement with the people and communities under study by integrating their voices into a final product. Collaborative work and authorship, although not inherently feminist, have been an important part of the history of feminist ethnography. Collaboration can be achieved in many ways—from coauthoring academic or popular pieces with a single participant to participatory action research that involves community members in drafting a policy brief. Collaborative writing can also help build feminist solidarity.

The collaborative writing endeavor we highlight here is the book *Playing with Fire: Feminist Thought and Activism Through Seven Lives in India*, written by the Sangtin Writers, a collective of women employed by a large **NGO (non-governmental organization)** in Uttar Pradesh, India, as activists in their communities. One of those writers is Richa Nagar, who, although she is clearly the impetus for bringing the text to academic audiences (by publishing the English version through a university press), joined the collective as a participant and cofacilitator, synthesizer, and editor of the collaborative writing that emerged in the journals of the activists between December 2002 and March 2004.

In all ethnographic writing, it is essential to be aware of intentionality and potential weaknesses. Enlisting the help of others—be they participants in our research, mentors, or peers—can often help us to see and reconsider our work in the context of different theoretical perspectives, ethical dilemmas, and authorial choices. A second example of collaboration is the Latina Feminist Group's *Telling to Live: Latina Feminist Testimonios*,[12] in which poets, oral historians, literary scholars, ethnographers, and psychologists reclaimed the notion of *testimonio*, or life story, to document their experiences as Puerto Rican, Chicana, Native American, Mexican, Cuban, Dominican, Sephardic, mixed-heritage, and Central American women within academia.

This textbook is also an example of collaborative writing, one that does not easily reveal the individual input of both Dána-Ain and Christa. Our process involved each being responsible for writing particular chapters and then each of us reviewing the other's chapter in turn. After writing this chapter, we reviewed, edited, changed, and debated content via phone, text, and email over thirty-five times! We continued to flesh out and enrich the chapters written by the other as we revised (actually, neither of us could tell you who wrote the initial draft without looking at our notes). With each modification, we conferred with each other about how the material should be presented and what should be included, edited, or omitted. In thinking about the arithmetic of this collaboration, ordinarily one might say that our division of labor was such that this book was written 50 percent by Dána-Ain and 50 percent by Christa. In fact, we feel it was written 100 percent by both of us, because of the collaborative writing process.

Collaborative feminist ethnographic work can also take the form of researchers publishing together about related projects. For instance, Swedish media studies scholars Jenny Sundén and Malin Sveningsson produced what they call a "twin ethnography" in *Gender and Sexuality in Online Game Cultures: Passionate Play*. They write:

> This book . . . develops two parallel stories. The two trajectories of the book are relatively independent, and can be read separately. Then again, there are multiple conversational points of both convergence and divergence between the two storylines, some of which will be made explicit in the collaboratively written closing chapter. In this sense, the chapters can also be read in tandem, guided by our cross-references between chapters as a going back and forth between the "straight" and the "bent," which provides a different reading experience. The first section of the book consists of the ethnography performed by Sveningsson on "straight" game cultures, and opens with the chapter "Go with Your Passion!" . . . The second section of the book consists of Sundén's ethnographic work on queer cultures of play.[13]

┌───┐
│   ✦ ESSENTIAL   │
└───┘

Excerpt from *Playing with Fire* by the Sangtin Writers Collective and Richa Nagar

The nine authors of *Sangtin Yatra/Playing with Fire*. Mishrikh, 2004.
Photo Credit: David Faust.

Richa Nagar's *antidisciplinary work in English, Hindustani, and Awadhi blends scholarship, creative writing, theatre, and activism to build alliances with people's struggles and to engage questions of ethics, responsibility, and justice. Her eight books include the award-winning trilogy* Playing with Fire: Feminist Thought and Activism Through Seven Lives in India *(2006),* Muddying the Waters: Coauthoring Feminisms Across Scholarship and Activism *(2014), and* Hungry Translations: Relearning the World Through Radical Vulnerability *(2019). Other works include the books* A World of Difference: Encountering and Contesting Development *(2009) and* Critical Transnational Feminist Praxis *(2010) and dozens of articles, essays, plays, and poems in leading academic journals and literary outlets. Nagar's writing has been translated into German, Italian, Korean, Mandarin, Marathi, and Turkish. She has worked closely with the Sangtin movement of farmers and laborers in India, and she has cocreated a multisited community theatre project* Parakh *and the online, open genre journal,* AGITATE! Unsettling Knowledges. *(For more information, see richa.nagar .umn.edu & agitatejournal.org.)*
    The section is titled "Blended, but Fractured 'We'":

The chorus of nine voices in *Playing with Fire* does not remain constant throughout the book. As one of us speaks, the second or third suddenly blends in to give an entirely new and unique flavor to our music. Our notes blend, disperse in ones or twos or sevens, and regroup. . . .
    The use of a blended "we" is a deliberate strategy on the collective's part, as is our decision to share quotes from the diaries in a minimal way. Rather than encouraging our readers to follow the trajectories of the lives of seven women, we braid the stories to highlight our analysis of specific moments in those lives. At the same time, our narrative evolves in the same dialogic manner that our journey did, and in the process, it seeks to open up spaces where the primary intended readers of the original book [the original version of the book, *Sangtin Yatra*, published in Hindi]—other NGO workers and members of the authors'

own communities—can insert their own narratives and reflections into the dialogue. We want to interrupt the popular practice of representation in the media, NGO reports, and academic analyses, in which the writing voice of the one who is analyzing or reporting as the "expert" is separated from the voice of the persons who are recounting their lives and opinions. One way we have chosen to eliminate this separation is by ensuring that our nine voices emerge as a chorus, even if the diaries of only seven of us are the focus of our discussions.

At no time is this unity meant to achieve resolution on issues of casteism, communalism, and hierarchy within the collective, however. From the outset, the desire that this journey be about "opening sealed boxes tucked away in our hearts" (chapter 1) translated into an assumption that issues of power hierarchies could be raised fearlessly only if there were no expectations of resolution. In other words, the blended "we" hinged on the trust and honesty with which each author could articulate her disagreements and tensions. Bitterness, anger, suspicion, and conflict within the collective produced as many tears in the journey as were produced by the pains and sorrows inflicted by "others." . . . Yet, as an alliance of transnational actors, we want the readers to be aware that the analysis and stances shared in the book are not merely a collection of individual stories but a result of a collective journey.

Source: Sangtin Writers Collective and Richa Nagar. *Playing with Fire: Feminist Thought and Activism through Seven Lives in India*. Minneapolis: University of Minnesota Press, 2006, xxxiv–xxxv.

Even when feminist ethnographers are not writing with a coauthor (or multiple coauthors), they often consult with communities of other scholars, activists, professionals, and/or participants in their fieldwork. No ethnographic writing is ever produced in isolation. We draw influences from those whose works inspire us, those whose works make us angry, as well as our contemporary communities that provide support, validation, and allow us to commiserate. Even as we have written this textbook—sometimes struggling when writing came slowly, erratically, or not at all—we have turned our attention to our acknowledgments that appear at the beginning of the book. Recalling and appreciating the influences on your writing, as well as who you want to emulate and write for, can be one of the best motivators when writing gets tough.

What Creative Possibilities Exist for Writing and Circulating Feminist Ethnography?

Much creativity goes into *any* expression of writing, including the evocative stories and theoretical innovations that are part of any well-written ethnographic monograph. In this section, we take up approaches to writing that differ from the classic ethnography in both style and form. For some writers, this may include poetry, creative art, photography, or other original elements in their ethnographic accounts. For others, it means reimagining how to engage with ethnographic data to create short stories, novels, plays, or even imagined childcare guides. Some experiment with parallel writing, and still others draw lessons from the reflexive turn in ethnography—the enhanced attentiveness to our position as feminist ethnographers and our effects on fieldwork—to produce intimate ethnographic accounts through memoir and autoethnography. In this section, we concentrate on creative written forms, and in the next we take up other innovative approaches to circulating ethnography beyond the printed page. The final subsection addresses the possibilities for making ethnography accessible to audiences beyond academia.

SPOTLIGHT

Asale Angel-Ajani on Writing (Without Swagger)

Asale Angel-Ajani *is a writer and professor at the City College of New York (CUNY) and serves as the director of the Women's and Gender Studies Program. Her novel,* A Country You Can Leave, *is forthcoming in 2022. She is the author of the nonfiction book* Strange Trade: The Story of Two Women Who Risked Everything in the International Drug Trade *(2010). She's held writing residencies at Tin House, Djerassi, Playa, VONA, and she is a recipient of grants from the Ford and Rockefeller Foundations. She has a PhD in Anthropology and an MFA in Fiction. In the following excerpt, Angel-Ajani addresses how the personal experience of having a parent who was involved in drug trafficking impacted the ways she approached writing her book.*

I first came to anthropology through my love of Zora Neale Hurston, mainly her ethnographies—*Mules and Men* and *Tell My Horse*. What I admired most was her ability to strike the balance between studying a particular culture and writing (with humor and without ego) about her place as the anthropologist observing it. She was the first feminist anthropologist that I read. What I learned from her and other feminist ethnographers was to value the stories that were undervalued and less likely to fit in a neat theoretical framework but also to constantly be questioning my personal stakes in the practice of writing and representation.

My book, *Strange Trade*, takes a more narrative approach that is perhaps more emotionally rooted than other books written by anthropologists. Even though there has always been a space for this kind of writing within the discipline, we have moved away from the value of storytelling for language that often obscures and only validates the insular world of the discipline. When we move away from more narrative approaches, we lose the possibilities to craft meaningful, transformative, powerful, informed ethnographies that cause us not to look away but to be there, present as readers as actors in the world and that lock on to our memories in the ways that only good stories do.

That said, there are many ways to write about drug trafficking and there are some really good books, important books that treat the subject differently than I do. Journalists like Misha Glenny, Moises Naim and Eric Schlosser have written very succinctly about organized crime and underground economies, including (but not exclusively) drug smuggling, covering the facts and figures and painting rich portraits. But what I found when I was teaching these books was that though the students loved them—I think in part because of the male swagger and exotic locations—they had a hard time remembering that stories of large drug busts or arms deals are peopled by individuals who all have complex reasons that drive their actions. As an anthropologist and a writer, I am always interested in how we choose to tell a particular story. I took a more intimate approach with my own work.

One thing we rarely discuss is an ethnographer's personal impulses to conduct the type of research that they do. Though it wasn't really on my mind while I was conducting fieldwork, my family, particularly my father, with his own history of drug smuggling, was easy and almost natural for me to write about, even though I knew I wanted to try to write a finely rendered account of the lives of Mary and Pauline as they shared them with me. What was difficult was writing about myself as the narrator of this story with emotional candor, which always means sharing vulnerabilities that never make anyone look like a hero. I wanted to be honest about the moral conflicts I faced, the feelings of inadequacy and the loneliness that I felt because I was living a kind of double life in Rome: one of the student and researcher and the other as a sidekick and confidant to a drug lord. At the time, I was not confident with either role. I guess you could say that I had no swagger.

What makes my work a feminist ethnography is the intention behind the writing and publishing of it. I wrote about my research with a much more narrative/literary style because the women who I worked with, who educated me and whose stories allowed me to go on and get a PhD and jobs I felt, should be able to recognize themselves in the pieces that I publish.

Fiction

Examples from early ethnographers—such as Zora Neale Hurston's powerful fiction in the 1920s and 1930s (read an excerpt in chapter 2)—show that ethnographers have long experimented with creative styles of writing about their research. Hurston's work was largely ignored in the academy when it was published, and despite later acclaim—most famously when writer Alice Walker placed a marker at Hurston's grave identifying her as "A Genius of the South" in 1973—Hurston's work remains most commonly assigned in literary courses, not in courses on ethnography. Although her work is recognized as experimental fiction, it also employs familiar ethnographic tropes. She draws on the rigor of ethnographic methods to legitimize her interpretations, as well as the theoretical insights of her mentors, such as Franz Boas, Ruth Benedict, and Margaret Mead. Hurston is also reflective about how her own position as an African American woman who grew up in Eatonville, Florida, one of the first all-Black towns incorporated in the United States, impacted her fieldwork and writing. She inspired subsequent writers of anthropological fiction to consider the power and politics of ethnographic representation, not only in the ethnographic monograph but also in fictional accounts that may use artistic license to depart from actual events or people.

The same is true of Ella Cara Deloria's novel *Waterlily*,[14] which was originally written in the 1940s but published posthumously in 1988—coinciding with the increased disciplinary interest in experimental ethnographic writing in the 1980s. Deloria, an anthropologist of European American and Dakota ancestry who studied with Boas and Benedict, engaged in twenty years of fieldwork studying the history and contemporary practices in Sioux culture before writing her novel that describes Dakota life before the US expansion into Sioux territory. Although the novel was shortened by half, following Benedict's suggestion to focus more centrally upon the plot, it has been heralded as far more compelling than an ethnographic report, but written with equal authority.[15]

In some cases, such as Laura Bohannon's *Return to Laughter: An Anthropological Novel*,[16] ethnographically inspired fiction has been published in lieu of an ethnographic monograph in an attempt to protect participants in ethnographic research. In fact, when the book was first published in 1964, it was credited to Elenore Smith Bowen, Bohannon's pseudonym. *Return to Laughter* chronicles the great difficulty, and at times cruelty, that ensued as an unnamed group in West Africa faced a devastating smallpox epidemic. Since the book is also autobiographical and reflective upon Bohannon's failings as a novice anthropologist, some critics have suggested that her decision to publish under a pseudonym was to protect her professional reputation. Yet concerns for protecting the anonymity of participants in her research, during a harrowing time for the Tiv in southeastern Nigeria, remain significant.

Another example of what one might call semifictional accounts is the "imagined childcare guides" produced in the two editions of *A World of Babies* written by psychologist Judy DeLoache and anthropologist Alma Gottlieb. Relying on the work of ethnographers in more than a dozen different societies between the two books, *A World of Babies* provides an engaging format to consider cultural beliefs about infancy and child-rearing. Each chapter imitates the style of Benjamin Spock's *The Common Sense Book of Baby and Child Care*, originally published in 1946, which remains in print after nine subsequent editions. Each chapter of *A World of Babies* is authored by an ethnographer writing as if they are imparting knowledge to new parents as a childcare expert in the given culture, such as a grandmother, midwife, or diviner.

ESSENTIAL

Excerpt from *A World of Babies* by Judy DeLoache and Alma Gottlieb

Photo of the authors in summer 2015, at Marbach Castle in Germany, where they were completing a fully revised, updated edition of *A World of Babies.*

Judy DeLoache *earned her PhD in psychology at the University of Illinois and is professor emerita of psychology at University of Virginia. Her specialty is early cognitive development, and she has published numerous books and articles on the topic.* **Alma Gottlieb** *earned her PhD in anthropology from the University of Virginia and has taught and had affiliations at many universities, including Princeton University, École des Hautes Études en Sciences Sociales in Paris, University of Leuven in Belgium, and Instituto Superior de Ciências Sociais e Políticas— Universidade Técnica de Lisboa in Portugal. She is Professor Emerita at the University of Illinois at Urbana-Champaign and is currently a Visiting Scholar in Anthropology at Brown University. Among other topics, her research addresses infancy and childcare among the Beng in West Africa and cross-culturally. In this excerpt, the coauthors describe the breadth and impetus for their creative writing project,* A World of Babies.

People living in different parts of the world and at different historical times hold diverse beliefs about the nature and nurturing of infants. This book celebrates that diversity. Each of its seven chapters is written as though it were an advice manual for new parents in a particular society. The seven societies we highlight include the Puritans of seventeenth-century Massachusetts and six contemporary societies: the Beng of Ivory Coast (West Africa), the Balinese of Indonesia, Muslim villagers in Turkey, the Warlpiri (an Australian Aborigine group), the Fulani of West and Central Africa, and the Ifaluk people of Micronesia. Although these seven by no means represent the range of societies worldwide, they are located on four different continents and differ substantially from one another in many ways. For example, three major world religions—the Judeo-Christian tradition, Islam, and Hinduism—as well as a variety of local religious traditions are represented. The residents of our societies earn their living in a variety of ways, from hunting and gathering to herding, fishing, and farming, to working in the tourist trade. Most important for our purposes, these seven societies represent a wide spectrum of beliefs and practices with respect to infants and they all differ radically from industrialized Western societies.

Furthermore, childcare practices differ even within these societies, since subgroups exist within every one. Moreover, all of the contemporary societies we include in this book have undergone significant social change in the course of this century, and, existing at the intersection of many local and international forces, they continue to undergo such change. In the United States today, for example, many Protestants share some child-rearing beliefs and practices with the Puritans while they adamantly reject many more. Within other societies too, many of the "old ways" are no longer followed—a fact no doubt approved by some of their members but deplored by others.

The world of babies is really many different worlds . . .

Source: DeLoache, Judy S., and Alma Gottlieb, eds. *A World of Babies: Imagined Childcare Guides for Seven Societies*. Cambridge, New York: Cambridge University Press, 2000, 2–4.

A World of Babies has become a mainstay in many academic courses on reproduction and has reached more popular audiences as a frequent gift to new parents.[17]

Parallel Writing

Although some (semi-)fictional texts, like *A World of Babies*, are preceded by academic analysis, other authors have engaged in parallel writing, juxtaposing two (or more) distinct texts, often on the same page. Political theorist Annemarie Mol's *The Body Multiple: Ontology in Medical Practice*[18] interrogates the numerous meanings of atherosclerosis, a disease described as the thickening of the arteries. On the upper half of each page, she documents her participant-observation in medical consultations and procedures and her interviews with doctors and patients at a Dutch university hospital. On the lower half, she writes in parallel text (made distinct by a different font, and presented as two columns) to reflect on related literature spanning philosophy, feminist theory, science and technology studies, anthropology, and sociology. Ultimately, the texts are in dialogue with each other, aimed at probing the multiplicity and situatedness of Western understandings of disease.

Another compelling example is educator Patti Lather and psychologist Chris Smithies's *Troubling the Angels: Women Living with HIV/AIDS*.[19] The book weaves the authors' experiences conducting participant-observation and interviews with twenty-five HIV+ women in Ohio, as well as the ways in which the authors became—and remain—emotionally tied to them. Interspersed among transcriptions of interviews is a horizontally split text featuring the authors' reflections on their research—the former in larger font at the top of the page and the authors' reflections in smaller font underneath. The authors also include what they call "[angel] inter-texts" to serve as "breathers" between the women's experiences and emotions, a deliberate and calculated imposition of scientific interpretation, including "fact boxes" offering statistical and medical context. Finally, the text includes the women's writing in the form of poems, letters, speeches, and emails. The combined result is a purposefully discomforting text that delves deeply into the lives of the participants. By denying a straightforward, linear story, *Troubling the Angels* is destabilizing for the reader. In their epilogue, Lather and Smithies even note that participants found an earlier self-published version of the text disconcerting.

Parallel writing can have numerous effects—from successfully bringing varied voices or perspectives together to pairing different styles of writing, to being quite jarring for the reader (as Lather and Smithies's participants complained). Whatever the ultimate result, which can also be different for different audiences, this style forces us to consider the intent and purposes of what and how we write.

Autoethnography and Ethnographic Memoir

The final creative form of ethnographic writing highlighted in this section involves deep reflection on the ethnographer's role in the process of fieldwork and writing. The term **autoethnography** emerged as a blend of autobiographical and ethnographic writing and incorporates the perspective and experience of other interlocutors (such as participants in research, but also oftentimes family or colleagues). Although the terms autobiography and memoir are frequently used interchangeably in popular speech, memoir refers to an author's reflection on a particular period of their life. Ethnographic memoirs typically focus on an ethnographer's time conducting fieldwork.

A classic in the autoethnographic tradition in feminist ethnography is anthropologist Ruth Behar's widely read *Translated Woman: Crossing the Border with Esperanza's Story*. She traces her journey as a Cuban American feminist anthropologist with Esperanza Hernández, a Mexican street peddler with whom she became *comadres* during her fieldwork in Mexico. Reflecting on her approach to telling Esperanza's story and her own, Behar writes, "By using both a novelistic style and a dialogical style in this book, I've tried to keep Esperanza's voice at the center of the text, while also showing my efforts to hear and understand her, efforts that led me, ultimately, to my own voice."[20] In her preface to the tenth anniversary edition of *Translated Woman*, Behar notes that weaving her own biography with Esperanza's story, especially the intimate details of her own life that she reveals in the final chapter, received "mixed" responses. Indeed, critics of autoethnography often disparage it as "navel-gazing," merely a chance to write about oneself rather than one's ethnographic work. Feminist ethnographers have taken up this challenge in a variety of ways, including the value of reflecting on one's own position to give context and nuance to ethnographic work as a key feature of this genre.

Anthropologist Irma McClaurin emphasizes that autoethnography is a particular reflexive form that is "simultaneously autobiographical and communal, as the Self encounters the Collective."[21] For an ethnographer who is a "native" in the community they are studying, their "work resonates with a reflexivity grounded in a social reality of which [they are] both a product and a producer."[22] McClaurin argues that autoethnography holds particular importance for anthropologists of color, whose work is cited less often, yet whose stories are often appropriated. We should be mindful of the transformative possibilities for particular types of scholarship, as well as historical and disciplinary trends that have extended **ethnographic authority** to some authors and not others.

Indigenous scholars have also likened autoethnography to "Indigenous storywork," a term coined by Indigenous studies scholar Jo-Ann Archibald, also known as Q'um Q'um Xiiem, from the Sto:lo First Nation in British Columbia, Canada. The experiential is key to this type of storytelling:

> Neither ethnographic detail, no matter how "rich and thick," nor ethnographic interpretation, no matter how close to "truth," can replace living with the people

and being "initiated" into their cultural community. . . . If the reader wants to gain an understanding of the oral tradition, she/he cannot be a passive observer or armchair reader.[23]

The ability of a writer to make readers feel like they were "there" through vivid descriptions that engage senses beyond the visual is often cited as a key skill of the ethnographer. Allowing the reader to experience discomfort, sometimes even through the use of humor, can be a powerful way of connecting to audiences that may lack the experiences or heritage of the ethnographer themselves.

A striking example of this is anthropologist Gina Athena Ulysse's *Downtown Ladies: Informal Commercial Importers, a Haitian Anthropologist and Self-Making in Jamaica*, where she writes in what she calls a "third world subaltern female" voice to confront popular archetypes of Black women in the Caribbean.

🧠 ESSENTIAL

Excerpt from *Downtown Ladies*, "My Jelly Platform Shoes" by Gina Athena Ulysse

Gina Athena Ulysse *is trained as an anthropologist at the University of Michigan and is an accomplished performance artist, poet, and multimedia artist. She is a full professor of Feminist Studies at University of California, Santa Cruz, and the author of* Downtown Ladies: Informal Commercial Importers, a Haitian Anthropologist and Self-Making in Jamaica *(2007). In this book, Ulysse exposes the personal and professional challenges that reflexivity and autoethnography pose for the young, Black, female ethnographer. Yet she also eloquently demonstrates throughout the book how things that an ethnographer may initially perceive as trivial—in this excerpt a seemingly mundane fashion choice—can expose the nuanced understanding of intersecting racialized histories, forms of cultural capital, and local norms of consumption. The following is an autoethnographic excerpt from* Downtown Ladies *from a section called "My Jelly Platform Shoes."*

In October 1995, I went to conduct field research in Kingston. One of my prized possessions was a pair of platform jellies. I had worn them the entire summer in Ann Arbor as I had waited to go into "the field." The shoes were in. Throughout the U of M campus, students and even professors wore these jellies or some variation of them. In Jamaica, I wore them everywhere, because they were comfortable, especially during the rainy season. I wore them until the buckle broke. That day, a dark-skinned Jamaican friend, Miss Q. (who is first generation middle class), was visiting. She seemed relieved and expressed happiness that I would finally stop wearing my jellies. "Well, thank God! You won't have to wear those ghastly shoes ever again. They're going in the bin." Surprised, actually shocked, I asked her why. "Oh Gina! Get serious . . . These shoes are so common," she exclaimed. . . .

These moments did not occur in a vacuum but rather within cultural borders with specific definitions of consumption and presentation that affected all interactions. Before I begin an examination of this moment, let me note that historically, in Jamaica, shoes have been a marker of distinction, which at times separated a field hand from a house slave. The cleanliness of one's feet and the type and style of shoes that encase them are visible signs of position. Feet covered in dust differentiate someone who walks to and from a bus from one who rides in a car. Whether feet are sheathed in plastic, synthetic, or leather shoes, these coverings have various capital signs that both mark and reinforce difference. Contemporary anthropological research on shoes is limited. The role of shoes in making gender has been explored more in cultural and literary studies, which have raised a plethora of questions concerning such things as desire, identity, feminism, and globalization. Thicker description[1] of my platform shoes necessitates a broader field of examination that can ultimately provide knowledge that crosses various disciplines. This is particularly relevant to Caribbean anthropology, where issues of gender and feminism, until recently, were disparate and thus hardly focused on this intersection. Yet, this theoretical crossroads is central to understanding color-, gender-, and class-based inequalities, as these do not rest solely on material differences, but are fully entrenched in the symbolic.

[After further discussing the reception of her jellies, in the context of other fieldwork experiences and interdisciplinary scholarship on race and class, Ulysse concludes:] Indeed, for dark-skinned, lower-class individuals, money buys character and, in the process, lightens one's color only when it is accompanied with other cultural capital that are determinants of class identities such as education, taste, and presentation.

Source: Ulysse, Gina A. *Downtown Ladies: Informal Commercial Importers, a Haitian Anthropologist, and Self-Making in Jamaica. Women in Culture and Society.* Chicago: University of Chicago Press, 2007, 232.

[1] Here Ulysse draws on anthropologist Clifford Geertz, who describes the term "thick description" as the object of ethnography. Not only should an ethnographer describe human behavior, but they should also offer readers the cultural context to better understand the meaning of such a behavior. Geertz uses the example of a blink or wink of an eye to clarify: Is it merely a twitch, someone rapidly contracting an eyelid, or is the person "practicing a burlesque of a friend faking a wink to deceive an innocent into thinking a conspiracy is in motion"? Clifford Geertz, "Thick Description: Toward an Interpretive Theory of Culture," 1973, 7.

The methodological textbook authored by communications scholar Carolyn Ellis, *The Ethnographic I: A Methodological Novel about Autoethnography*, combines autoethnography and fiction. She writes, for instance, about a fictional graduate course to teach the craft of autoethnographic writing. She favors the terms memoir and autoethnography over what some have called a "confessional," reminiscent of Bronislaw Malinowski's controversial diary,[24] published posthumously, recounting his fieldwork experiences in early twentieth-century New Guinea and the Trobriand Islands in ways that critics have called narcissistic and ethnocentric. Departing from Malinowski's scientific, ostensibly objective presentation of the Trobrianders in his famous 1922 ethnographic monograph, *Argonauts of the Western Pacific*,[25] among other academic publications, when his diaries were published in 1989, his personal writing revealed **ethnocentrism** and insensitivity about his research subjects.

In contrast to autoethnography, which is usually written for an academic audience, ethnographic memoir, which chronicles personal ethnographic experience, is a genre typically intended for a broader readership. An ethnographic memoir that has drawn both praise and criticism is Karla Poewe's *Reflections of a Woman Anthropologist: No Hiding Place*, which she wrote under the pseudonym Manda Cesara in 1982.[26] It was one of the first memoirs of ethnography to offer an "extremely revealing account" of an author's experience, which some reviewers have described as "painful," "uncomfortable," and even "tortuous to read."[27] "Cesara" details her early life experiences growing up in Germany, including strained relationships with her Canadian and German family. These experiences serve as background for excerpts from her diary and letters during her fieldwork in Zambia (which she refers to as "Lenda" in the anonymized account) and extensive conversations about existential philosophy. Her deeply personal reflections include descriptions of her attenuated relationship with her husband and love affairs with a local magistrate and other African men who also served as her informants. "Cesara" positions herself as a feminist in the account, arguing for what she describes as a new feminism, one where "men and women, but especially women . . . realize that another man, even another human being, cannot become their whole existence."[28]

Following the publication of *Reflection of a Woman Anthropologist*, queer feminist anthropologist Esther Newton (see Essential in chapter 2), whose work is cited heavily by "Cesara," wrote her an open letter in 1984, which was later published in Newton's intellectual autobiography *Margaret Mead*.[29] Newton priased "Cesara's" (aka Poewe's) "spirit of self-examination and revelation" that she espoused and "courageously practiced." However, Newton fervently contested the use of her own work in "a homophobic diatribe worthy of the Moral Majority in the conclusion, citing my work in support of . . . abuse."[30] "Cesara"/Poewe had written, for instance:

> I tolerated homosexuality before I went to the field. While I tolerate it now, I agree with Newton's observation that gays "will always be traitors in the battle of the sexes" (1979:xii). I admired the ongoing "battle of the sexes" in Lenda. By contrast, I deplore the cultural principles which nourish American homosexuality, such as: (1) domination in sex; (2) obsession with youth; (3) obsession with extreme forms of masculinity and femininity; (4) commercialization of physical beauty; (5) egotism; (6) excessive status consciousness; (7) a flippant emotional freedom; (8) manipulation of sex-roles; (9) tendency to produce ersatz cowboys, imitation Hell's Angels, phony oppositions between make-believe men and make-believe woman, and so on. American homosexuality is inauthentic.[31]

Newton's response speaks to what she felt was the blatant misuse of her work:

> I put my career on the line to write [*Mother Camp: Female Impersonators in America*, the first ethnography to substantively address a gay and transgender community, which was published in 1972] (without a pseudonym, I might add). To see you misuse my book to denounce the group I was attempting to dignify . . . is a bitter, bitter irony. As a final insult, you omit my book from your bibliography; readers won't be able to check for themselves.[32]

It is important to interrogate texts in light of feminist sensibilities writ large. This is an instructive example: Poewe/"Cesara" represents a scholar who pushed boundaries within the field—in terms of self-revelation and personal reflection—yet also utilized the anonymity of a pseudonym to make discriminatory claims and mischaracterize another feminist ethnographer's work.

THINKING THROUGH . . .

Citational Politics, Revisited in the Age of #MeToo

Esther Newton's experience having elements of her work cherry-picked (and ultimately left off the bibliography) to uphold homophobic beliefs antithetical to her own raises important questions (again) about citational politics. All writers open themselves to critique when they make their work public—through publishing books or articles, but also via blogs and social media. For comparative example, consider the role of citation in the context of the #MeToo Movement, especially #MeToo_Academia and #MeTooPhD, established to allow those who have experienced sexual harassment or abuse by professors, advisors, and other mentors to report their experience with the goal of prompting more frank conversations about the breadth and depth of this problem in academic settings.[1] (How) Should a writer, especially a student writer, concern themselves with contemporary public controversies or whether an author expresses (or has expressed) views that contradict contemporary values (like Poewe/"Cesara")? And what should be considered when deciding whether (or how) to cite a well-known author's works if they have been charged publicly of abuse or harassment?[2] To address the complexities of these issues, break into two debate groups (or more in a larger class). Prepare arguments in response to the following questions and stage a class debate on how a feminist ethnographer could productively respond to these issues in different ways (*hint:* there isn't one "right" answer).

1. What are some of the strategies you can use to develop a robust and capacious, but also discerning, citational politics?
2. What are the politics of *avoiding* the citation of particular authors?
3. How much should we acknowledge controversies in our work?
4. And perhaps most important, why do we often have to dig to find out a person's divisive politics or harmful actions?

[1] See, for instance, Karen Kelskey, "#MeTooPhD—Sexual Harassment in the Academy Survey," *The Professor Is In*, 2017.

[2] Dan Souleles, "What to Do with the Predator in Your Bibliography?" *Allegra Lab: Anthropology for Radical Optimism* (blog), September 15, 2020.

How Can We Make Feminist Ethnography Publicly Accessible?

Many of the creative examples in the previous section aim to make ethnographic work accessible to audiences beyond academia, but that is not—nor should it always be—the intent of all creative work. In fact, creative approaches to collaborative writing or autoethnography (often published by academic presses) can deeply enrich the field of (feminist) ethnography but may not necessarily reach audiences outside of academia. In this section, we address efforts that explicitly engage with nonacademic audiences. Social scientists have become increasingly "public" in recent years, aiming to extend their work to audiences beyond their scholarly peers. Many ethnographers have become active contributors of op-eds for newspapers and YouTube videos (one of our favorites is "The Anthropology Song: A Little Bit Anthropologist" by Dai Cooper, when she was a Master's Student in Anthropology at the University of Toronto), as well as blogs devoted to ethnography. *Anthro{dendum}* is a popular group blog about sociocultural anthropology and specifically about "doing anthropology in public," which has featured posts by feminist ethnographers, such as Elizabeth Chin, Dána-Ain, and Gina Ulysse, and a series "Trauma and Resilience" curated by anthropologists Beatriz Reyes-Foster and Rebecca Lester in collaboration with the Anthropology of Mental Health Interest Group.[33] *The Feminist Wire* is another blog operated by an editorial collective of scholars, activists, and writers that provides a sociopolitical and cultural critique of antifeminist, racist, and imperialist politics. It regularly publishes work by feminist ethnographers, such as Dána-Ain and Christa's 2013 op-ed "Equity at the Peril of Normativity: A Feminist Anthropological Take on Race, Marriage and Justice,"[34] and work by other feminist ethnographers such as Monica Casper, Aimee Meredith Cox, and Michelle Téllez.

In this vein, feminist ethnographers have made wide use of social media and blogs in recent years to bring their analyses to broader audiences. For instance, many have been featured prominently on *The Huffington Post* and the *King's Review* in the United Kingdom, writing about race and feminism, same-sex marriage, "cyberbullying," and revitalization efforts in Haiti following the 2010 earthquake. To appeal to nonacademic audiences, ethnographers must think about both the accessibility of their language and the placement of research to reach desired audiences. What sorts of journals, magazines, online sites, digital, and nondigital formats should we favor for circulating our work? This answer will vary based on the ethnographer's goals. It is worthwhile for feminist ethnographers committed to analyzing inequalities to ask themselves questions like: What about my study would be interesting, relevant, or meaningful to those beyond academia? Earlier we discussed being attentive to the desires of those we study, and as we prepare to make our work more public, what would engage readers who may not know very much about the subject or geographical location? While not every ethnographic study lends itself to broad audiences, we would argue that for feminist ethnographers, part of contributing to social justice work is considering how our research might cross these boundaries.

One example is ethnographic filmmaking. Since the 1980s, ethnographers have moved beyond presenting visual images as merely supplementary to ethnographic insights, using visual images as an alternative. These attempts have broken from a conventionally discursive or didactic mode of knowledge production. Filmmaker and women's studies scholar Trinh T. Minh-ha (Trinh Thi Minh-Há) has produced numerous films that have brought into question notions of memory, sensation, and perception in the ethnographic encounter. She is widely known for her award-winning film *Reassemblage* (1982), in which she aims "not to speak about/just speak nearby," the lives of rural women in Senegal, and takes a similar approach in *Surname Viet Given Name Nam* (1989) about five Vietnamese women in the United States. In her important 1989 book, *Woman, Native, Other: Writing Postcoloniality and Feminism*,[35] she positions her work as (un/non)ethnography, in contrast to more conventional ethnographic documentary films, that has often purported to translate the experiences of groups deemed "other."

Harjant Gill on Film as a Powerful Feminist Medium

Harjant Gill *is an associate professor of Anthropology at Towson University, Maryland. His research examines the intersections of masculinity, modernity, transnational migration, and popular culture in India. Gill is also an award-winning filmmaker and has made five ethnographic films that have screened at international film festivals and on television channels worldwide, including* BBC, Doordarshan (Indian National TV), *and* PBS. *Gill is also a recipient of the Point Foundation Scholarship, Fulbright-Nehru Research Fellowship, American Institute of Indian Studies Performing Arts Fellowship, the Institute for Citizens & Scholars' Career Enhancement Fellowship, and the Whiting Foundation Public Engagement Fellowship. Gill is currently developing a nine-part immersive virtual reality web series exploring Indian masculinities titled "Tales from Macholand." His website is HarjantGill.com.*

My films [use] queer, feminist, and transnational studies' theoretical frameworks to explore how masculinities are defined and reinforced within traditionally patriarchal societies like Punjab. While these films are not auto-ethnographic, they are equally informed by personal interests and experiences having grown up as a man with a Punjabi Sikh family in North India. Having been introduced to feminist and queer studies during my undergraduate training in anthropology at San Francisco State University, the two have [also] profoundly shaped my own approach to ethnographic film, in terms of how I think about the content, the form, the style, and treatment of my films. In making *Milind Soman Made Me Gay*, I drew directly on the works of feminist and queer ethnographers and filmmakers like Trinh T. Minh-Ha, Cherríe Moraga, Gloria E. Anzaldúa, Marlon Riggs, Pratibha Parmar, Richard Fund, Safina Uberoi. The title *Milind Soman Made Me Gay* is a direct reference to Esther Newton's seminal text, *Margaret Mead Made Me Gay*, which was my introduction to queer anthropology. Unlike the conventional approaches to ethnographic film and documentary which seems to perennially concern itself with boundary policing (trying to determine what is and what is not an ethnographic film), I found feminist and queer approaches very liberating, permitting me to disregard conventions by placing individual narratives before the form, permitting me to experiment with different conceptual styles and approaches, and thereby defining my own perimeters for ethnographic/documentary film. Similarly, treatment of my more recent films on Indian masculinities including *Roots of Love* and *Mardistan* has been influenced more so by feminist and queer approaches to ethnography in thinking about the experiences of men in India, and in critiquing the role the state and the legal system plays in keeping patriarchal privilege intact. Feminist studies, particularly the scholarship of bell hooks, has also taught me the importance of treating my participants (the subjects of my documentaries) with love and compassion, stressing the importance of depicting them as individuals with agency rather than mere victims of their circumstances.

While I produce work in both filmic and textual forms, I find film to be a much more accessible form of disseminating my research and scholarship, and engaging with audiences both within and outside of the academy. As an anthropologist deeply invested in the idea of doing public anthropology, I find film as an effective tool for dialogue, engagement, and advocacy. I also find that film can offer a kind of an immediate sensorial experience of a given topic or community, through the use of image and sound, which make up the medium, in ways that text alone cannot accomplish. Audiences (including my students) are able to visualize and experience what a young Sikh boy experiences the first time a turban is tied around his head, or what a young Sikh man experiences when he has his first haircut. The affective quality and experience of film as a medium are incredibly powerful for audiences being introduced to narratives or communities they have not encountered before. More so than text, film as a medium allows our participants/our interlocutors to speak and share their experiences in their own voice, which is incredibly important within a discipline with a history marred with issues and concerns around representation. Film can and has been used as a powerful collaborative tool for anthropologists to work with the community members, empowering them to share their own stories in their own voice rather than speaking on their behalf.

While film is a powerful medium, I also recognize its limitations—in not being able to provide the kinds of contextual and analytic insights text or a monograph can offer. I don't think film and text should be mutually exclusive. In fact, in my personal experience, the two mediums are most effective when they complement each other. I have written extensively about my film work, and I've used film as windows of insight into my larger, more expansive project on Punjabi masculinities, which I am in the process of developing into a monograph. Currently I am most excited about the possibility of using new media technologies to incorporate my films into my writing in the form of interactive and dynamic e-books, areas with tremendous opportunities for experimentation and growth.

Anthropologist Harjant Gill's elegant documentary films interrogate topics related to gender, sexuality, and religion in India and among Indians in the diaspora. His academic writing examines notions of belonging and citizenship among gay South Asian men. His film *Mardistan (Macholand)* demonstrates new possibilities for documenting a range of Indian masculinities.

Mardistan (Macholand) is an exploration of Indian manhood articulated through the voices of four men from different generations and backgrounds. A middle-aged writer trying to make sense of the physical and sexual abuse he witnessed studying in an elite military academy, a Sikh father of twin daughters resisting the pressure to produce a son, a young 20-year-old college student looking for a girlfriend with whom he can lose his virginity, and a working-class gay activist coming out to his wife after twenty years of marriage. Together, their stories make up different dimensions of what it means to be a man in India today. Mardistan (Macholand) starts a conversation on critical issues including patriarchy, son preference, sexual violence and homophobia in a nation increasingly defined by social inequalities.[36]

Gill's work has been screened at academic institutions and conferences—which we had the pleasure of viewing at the 2015 American Anthropological Association conference—as well as public film festivals, and it has been shown on *BBC World News*, *PBS*, and *Doordarshan* (Indian National TV). The films' wide distribution has reached audiences far beyond academia.

Digital formats that can blend multiple sensory experiences and offer content in a free, **open-access** format have also become popular among ethnographers in recent years—for public accessibility as well as creative possibilities. For instance, Elisia Ixchelle Campos, who graduated from the College of Wooster in 2016, sought to make her research more accessible by partnering with artists Vero Majano, DJ Brown Amy (Amy Martinez), and Kari Orvik, whose gallery opening at Galería de la Raza in the Mission District of San Francisco for their photography series *The Q-Sides* inspired Campos's ethnographic study of queer Latinx community lowrider culture.

> My choice to have music and photos accompany my thesis was intentional to force the reader to see and hear the struggle of queer Latinx people in the lowrider culture. Ultimately, my goal is that you can empathize with the emotion felt through the stories being told in two sensory experiences.

Campos organized her analysis around songs from the doo-wop and soul oldies albums that were used in *The Q-Sides* exhibit from *East Side Story, Volumes 1–12* and created an iBook, featuring the artists' recreation of iconic photos of lowriders to reimagine queer inclusion within the traditionally heterosexual public image of lowrider culture. Campos' iBook—which you can view at https://openworks.wooster.edu/independentstudy/7203/—won a prize in digital scholarship. Campos also archived her interviews with the artists for their use in future exhibits and for other scholars. Since completing her undergraduate thesis, Campos has spoken with academic audiences and community groups about her work, as well as her experience as a first generation College student.

In the project that led to Christa's publication of *Reproductive Losses: Challenges to LGBTQ Family-Making*, her witnessed the acute need for resources among LGBTQ+ people who had experienced miscarriage, adoption loss, infertility, and/or sterility. She knew that a book from an academic press would be outside the price range of many people she spoke with, most talked about searching (often unsuccessfully) for online support resources that included families like their own. While Christa's physical book centered on the stories of LGBTQ people, she also worked with Digital Curation Librarian Catie Heil and student research assistants Hannah Lane-Davies and Ella Lang to launch a free, open-access website https://www.lgbtqreproductiveloss.org/. The website includes interactive elements, such as digital collages of advice from participants and a contribution plug-in that allows visitors to contribute new content, such as photographs of memorials and commemorative tattoos. These are also presented in text reader-friendly formats to support accessibility for those with a range of abilities and inclusion of those without high-speed Internet access.[37]

A final note on accessibility—not just availability—is important. Much ink has been spilled (and blog posts typed) about controversies over trigger warnings in academia, publishing, social media, and beyond. While it is beyond the scope of this book to delve deeply into this debate, many students, as well as seasoned feminist ethnographers, question whether warnings about the content (neither of us is fond of the gun metaphor) are necessary or desirable in ethnographic accounts that often chronicle tragic and sometimes violent experiences. A scholar who writes elegantly about this is genderqueer disability activist Eli Clare, who co-organized the first Queer Disability Conference in 2002 that drew academics, activists, and artists. In his 2017 book, *Brilliant Imperfection: Grappling with Cure*, Clare offers the following in the prefatory note:

> Some of the fragments in this book are razor sharp. The histories, ideas, realities I'm grappling with are full of pain and violence, grief and rage—involuntary sterilization, ritual abuse, suicide, centuries of colonialism, and bison massacre to name a few. These fragments might slice old wounds open, might remind us of scars long

forgotten, might catapult us into past trauma. They might *trigger* us. I use that word intentionally to reflect the abrupt, visceral tailspin some of us experience when encountering or being caught off guard by particular images or stories, smells or sounds, memories or emotions.

In the late 1980s and 1990s, feminists developed the practice of trigger warnings to give people a heads-up before details of violence were spoken out loud. We weren't engaging in censorship or avoiding contentious issues, as some academics and activists claim today. Rather we knew that without trigger warnings many of us would lose access to conversations, communities, and learning spaces.

In his own work, Clare found these lessons difficult to apply, since he frequently felt unsure about what to tag, when to mark particular passages, and how often to provide written warnings as he wrote when almost every essay could have merited a trigger warning. Ultimately, he created what he describes as a mosaic: some stories have warnings, whereas others on difficult subjects are marked as stories that do not have gratuitous details or extended descriptions of violence. His goal was one of accessibility, but he also acknowledges that naming particular content has the potential to create incomplete access for some readers as well. Although Clare's work is not ethnographic, we find this advice instructive for any of us who want to grapple thoughtfully with questions about accessibility in different ethnographic contexts.

How Do Feminist Ethnographers Engage in Creative and Artistic Projects?

As evidenced above, the creative processes of conducting fieldwork and crafting ethnography can also lend themselves to producing creative formats for circulation. In this section, we focus on feminist ethnographers who have distributed their work through performance, dance, song, plays, and graphic novels. In the late 1980s, for instance, Faye V. Harrison wrote and performed "Three Women, One Struggle," a one-woman show organized around the voices of three Black women from Washington, DC, Jamaica, and South Africa. Performed in Louisville, Kentucky, on International Women's Day, Harrison writes:

> Anthro-performances . . . even when published are much more than what can be read from a printed page. Although performances can be recorded through video or film, and hence, viewed by bigger audiences, the dynamics of the wider social event(s) of which a performance is a part may be hard to capture.[38]

Gina Athena Ulysse's TEDx Talk "Untapped Fierceness/My Giant Leaps" is a beautiful example of her use of song, dance, performance, and personal revelation—and well worth watching. She opens the talk by singing and follows with a performance of her poetry about containment. "You either do that [contain yourself] or you disappear," she says, before asking rhetorically, "Why do they think that so many Black women in anthropology keep turning to the arts?" The piece she performed is one she wrote after defending her dissertation as a first-generation student. Her "giant leaps" through academia as a Haitian American woman are told through monologue, poetry, and song. She concludes by explaining that her own "untapped potential" is in the merging of her childhood goals of being a rock star and her academic journey to theorize oppression and serve as a change agent in her birth country, Haiti. Through performance, she dramatizes her ethnographic work, and her scholarly work informs her performance. As she says, "Little bits of theory started to spill into my songs. And then I started to reference everybody . . . to such a point that when you hear me [sing], you need a bibliography."

Her CD *I Am Storm: Songs and Poems for Haiti* has received critical acclaim, and her one-woman performance piece "Because God Is Too Busy: Haiti, Me and the World" is a dramatic monologue that weaves spoken word poetry and Vodou chants into a fierce critique of the post-earthquake dehumanization of Haitians in the global media.

Another example is an Argentine political theorist and anthropologist Marta Elena Savigliano, who pairs textual analysis with multiart presentation in *Angora Matta: Actos Fatales De Traduccion Norte-Sur/Fatal Acts of North-South Translation*, a bilingual, interdisciplinary text that incorporates what Savigliano calls "writerly experimentation [that] challenges the conventions of fiction and scholarly writing."[39] *Angora Matta* was originally conceived as a libretto for a thriller opera of tangos, developed with composer Ramon Pelinski, choreographer Susan Rose, and animation director Miguel Angel Nanni. The main portion of the text features the original Spanish on the left-hand column and translation/*traducción* of English "subtitles" on the right, interspersed with photos, scene description, and other performative elements. Savigliano builds upon her training in dance, political science, and anthropology to challenge the racialized, exoticized, and eroticized representations of "other" in "traditional" dance forms fetishizing and isolating the communities that perform them from the global flow of international politics. In addition, she coproduced an experimental presentation of this work in 2002, involving thirty US and Argentine artists in the Teatro Presidente Alvear of Buenos Aires. Savilgiano draws upon feminist scholarship to critique the representational politics of ethnography, and offers novel alternatives.

For the sake of comparison, it is instructive to look at Savigliano's work in relation to anthropologist Julie Taylor's *Paper Tangos*, which also takes up the art and politics of tango in Argentina in the context of military dictatorships and violence.[40] Taylor is a classically trained ballet dancer born in the United States, who chronicles her life crossing borders between the United States and Latin America. A notable element of the book is the experimental design, which includes photographs on the lower corner of every right-hand page so that when a reader thumbs through it, a flip-book sequence of a tango appears. Taylor describes this as an effort to convey body knowledge by introducing movement onto each page of her written words. Yet, unlike Savigliano, Taylor does not explicitly position her account as emerging from feminist theory or ethnographic practice.

THINKING THROUGH . . .

Experimental Design

Read Marta Elena Savigliano's *Angora Matta* and Julie Taylor's *Paper Tangos*. Write a brief comparison of the ways that each author characterizes the experimental design of her work. What differences do you see in an explicitly feminist approach versus one that does not identify as such?

Performance can also be designed to engage other scholars and students of ethnography in conversation. For instance, Dána-Ain and Aimee Meredith Cox created an experimental performance designed to engage and enliven discussion at the American Anthropological Association (AAA) conference in 2009. The piece was developed as part of a performative session organized by Elizabeth Chin and was eventually included in written form in *Katherine Dunham: Recovering an Anthropological Legacy, Choreographing Ethnographic Futures*.[41] The AAA session celebrated the work of Katherine Dunham (1909–2006), a dancer, choreographer, social activist, and anthropologist who was a pioneer in ethnochoreography and African American modern dance and an expert on religion and culture in Haiti. Dána-Ain has also embarked on a new collaboration with birth worker and graphic artist Cheyenne Varner, which they envision as "an effort in disobedience against the 'typical' academic form."[42] Together, they created an illustrated story featuring the birth stories of Black women in a way that moves their voices and experiences—particularly with obstetric racism—from margin to center. Their first graphic rendition was published in a 2021 special issue of *Anthropology News* "Graphic Ethnography," based on a story Dána-Ain collected. Working with public health scholar and poet LeConté J. Dill, the three collaborated to recount Dill's story about her birth and postpartum experience. Reflecting on their process, they write:

> Illustrating racism and adverse birth outcomes is complicated by, among other things, the ethnographic research mandate of anonymity and the use of pseudonyms, citations, footnotes, and theoretical references. But something about illustration breathes a different kind of life and knowingness into that mandate. . . . Sharing a birth story of obstetric racism, any story really, accompanied by illustrations and poetry is one way in which people who live in the world uninvited, are able to enter a world with witnesses, with others, with other senses—the heart, the eyes, and the ears.[43]

Another evocative illustration of the collaboration process involved in graphic ethnography (pun intended) is anthropologist Alisse Waterston and illustrator Charlotte Corden's work on *Light in Dark Times: The Human Search for Meaning*. Waterston is no stranger to creative approaches—recall her intimate ethnography, *My Father's Wars*, introduced in chapter 3. That book, which spanned the genres of biography, memoir, autoethnography, and cultural history, featured links to photographs, audio-recordings, and videos, and other artifacts on the book's companion website, offering readers a variety of sensory ways to experience the material. "Making Light in Dark Times"—also featured in *Anthropology News*' "Graphic Ethnography" series—records their serendipitous partnership and creative journey after Corden sent Waterston an illustration she made following Waterston's 2017 presidential address to the American Anthropological Association that ultimately inspired them to co-create *Light in Dark Times* as a graphic ethnography.[44]

Conclusion

As this chapter demonstrates, there are many ways to produce interesting, engaging, and impactful feminist ethnography. One thing gained from ethnographic performance and creative nontraditional forms of ethnography is the ability to reach various audiences. We also gain the chance to be emotive as scholars—feeling (not just theorizing in isolation) our way through crises, challenging situations, the traumas we may witness, or the joys we may encounter. These creative mechanisms are a useful way to share the stories of participants and to translate theory. Through creative production, we open up the possibility of moving our viewers, listeners, and readers to think, act, and respond critically. It is certainly a productive alternative to generating data in more positivist terms. Creativity then may be viewed as an interpretive domain, which expands critical **pedagogy**, the philosophy of teaching and learning, as well as scholarship.

> ## THINKING THROUGH . . .
>
> ## Developing Creative Ethnography
>
> If you have been working on an ethnographic project this term, take this opportunity to write, create, or perform about it in a way that is new to you. Presumably, you have turned in a paper about the project aimed at your professor (an academic audience). What would it look like to write a fictional account about an event you observed? Or create a dance performance inspired by your fieldwork? Think about your options and choose one aimed at distributing your ethnographic knowledge in a different way. Write a brief reflection on the differences you observe in the two styles to a different audience.

Suggested Resources

Ruth Behar, and Deborah A. Gordon (1996) *Women Writing Culture*.

Toni Morrison (2007) *Playing in the Dark*.

Kirin Narayan (2012) *Alive in the Writing: Crafting Ethnography in the Company of Chekhov*.

Gina Athena Ulysse (2013, May 4) "Untapped Fierceness/My Giant Leaps." TEDxUofM Talk, https://www.youtube.com/watch?v=xHhngXU8Zw4.

Go to museums, dance performances, and other performative events.

Read well-written work—fiction, poetry, ethnography, whatever inspires you.

Notes

[1] Octavia Butler, "Furor Scribendi," in *Bloodchild and Other Stories*, 1996, 141–142.

[2] Anne Lamott, "Shitty First Drafts," in *Bird by Bird*, 1995.

[3] Ibid., 25–26.

[4] Soyini D. Madison, *Critical Ethnography: Methods, Ethics, Performance*, 2005, 211.

[5] Margery Wolf, *A Thrice Told Tale: Feminism, Postmodernism and Ethnographic Responsibility*, 1992.

[6] Margery Wolf, *The House of Lim: A Study of a Chinese Farm Family*, 1968.

[7] Savannah Shange argues that "ovaric"—sometimes used as an insulting term to refer to ovaries and menstruation as attributes that make women "stupid" about masculine-identified pursuits like cars and power tools—also reinstantiates assumptions about binary gender and the centrality of biological reproduction in governing the pursuit of knowledge (*Progressive Dystopia*, 2019, 95).

[8] It is also important to note that the use of language changes over time and reflects different cultural and linguistic trends. An informal study by law professors on the blog *BlackProf*, for instance, showed that the use of "seminal" nearly quintupled in law journals and reviews between the 1980s and early 2000s and far outpaces the use of "germinal" (though it also shows a slight increase). Al Brophy, "Seminal and Germinal: A Study in Progression and Retrogression," *BlackProf* blog, November 2016 (no longer available), reposted on March 30, 2010, at *The Faculty Lounge: Conversations about Law, Culture and Academia* (blog), https://www.thefacultylounge.org/2010/03/seminal-and-germinal-a-study-in-progression-and-retrogression.html.

[9] Megan Sinnott, *Toms and Dees*, 2004; Gayatri Reddy, *With Respect to Sex*, 2005; Rudolf Gaudio, *Allah Made Us*, 2009; Elisabeth Engebretsen, *Queer Women in Urban China*, 2013; Elisabeth Engebretsen, Will Schroeder, and Hongwei Bao, eds. *Queer/Tongzhi China*, 2015; Marlon Bailey, *Butch Queens Up in Pumps*, 2013; Gloria Wekker, *The Politics of Passion*, 2006.

[10] Tom Boellstorff, *The Gay Archipelago: Sexuality and Nation in Indonesia*, 2005, 82.

[11] Kale Fajardo, *Filipino Crosscurrents: Oceanographies of Seafaring, Masculinities, and Globalization*, 2011, 154–155. Fajardo follows Kanaka Maoli Studies scholar and historian Noenoe Silva in

her choice not to highlight Hawaiian words when she wrote a comprehensive history of Hawai'i that drew from Hawaiian-language sources, *Aloha Betrayed: Native Hawaiian Resistance to American Colonialism*, 2004.

12 The Latina Feminist Group, *Telling to Live: Latina Feminist Testimonios*, 2001.

13 Jenny Sundén, and Malin Sveningsson, *Gender and Sexuality in Online Game Cultures*, 2012, 17, 19.

14 Ella Cara Deloria, *Waterlily*, 1988.

15 Susan Gardner, "Introduction" to *Waterlily*, 2009, xxxiii.

16 Elenore Smith Bowen (Laura Bohannon), *Return to Laughter: An Anthropological Novel*, 1964.

17 The fully revised second edition features the imagined childcare guides for new societies, including contemporary China and the West Bank, migrant mothers in Israel, Guinean Muslim families in Portugal, Andean families in Peru, and displaced Somali refugees in Minneapolis. Both editions demonstrate, without a doubt, the myriad "right" ways to raise a child, as well as an inventive and accessible approach to ethnographic writing.

18 Annemarie Mol, *The Body Multiple: Ontology in Medical Practice*, 2003.

19 Patricia Lather and Chris Smithies, *Troubling the Angels*, 1997.

20 Ruth Behar, *Translated Woman*, 2003, 13–14.

21 Irma McClaurin, *Black Feminist Anthropology*, 2001, 69.

22 Ibid., 67.

23 Jo-Anne Archibald (Q'um Q'um Xiiem), *Indigenous Storywork: Educating the Heart, Mind, Body, and Spirit*, 2008, 31. See also Jo-Ann Archibald, Jenny Bol Jun Lee-Morgan, and Jason De Santolo, eds., *Decolonizing Research: Indigenous Storywork as Methodology*, 2019.

24 Carolyn Ellis, *The Ethnographic I*, 2004; Bronislaw Malinowski, *A Diary in the Strictest Sense of the Term*, 1989.

25 Bronislaw Malinowski, *Argonauts of the Western Pacific*, 1922.

26 Manda Cesara, *Reflections of a Woman Anthropologist*, 1982. Poewe's pseudonym is acknowledged on her website.

27 John L. Wengle, *Ethnographers in the Field*, 1988; Martha Ward, "Reflections of a Woman Anthropologist: No Hiding Place. Manda Cesara (Book Review)," *American Anthropologist*, 1985; Carolyn Sargent, "Manda Cesara, 'Reflections of a Woman Anthropologist. No Hiding Place' (Book Review)," *Canadian Journal of African Studies/Revue Canadienne Des Études Africaines*, 1983.

28 Manda Cesara, *Reflections of a Woman Anthropologist*, 1982, 188.

29 Esther Newton, *Margaret Mead Made Me Gay*, 2000.

30 Ibid., 227.

31 Manda Cesara, *Reflections of a Woman Anthropologist*, 1982, 211.

32 Esther Newton, *Margaret Mead Made Me Gay*, 2000, 227.

33 *Anthro{dendum}*, https://anthrodendum.org/; formerly known as *Savage Minds* (2005–2017).

34 Dána-Ain Davis, and Christa Craven, "Equity at the Peril of Normativity: A Feminist Anthropological Take on Race, Marriage and Justice," *The Feminist Wire*, 2013. http://thefeministwire.com/2013/06/equity-at-the-peril-of-normativity-a-feminist-anthropological-take-on-race-marriage-justice/.

35 Trinh T. Minh-Ha, *Woman, Native, Other*, 2009.

36 Harjant Gill, "Mardistan (Macholand) Reflections on Indian Manhood," 28 Mins. In Punjabi & English w/subtitles. Directed by Harjant Gill Produced by PSBT (Public Service Broadcasting Trust), 2014.

37 Christa Craven, *Reproductive Losses: Challenges to LGBTQ Family-Making*, 2019; Christa Craven, "LGBTQ+ Reproductive Loss," 2019, https://www.lgbtqreproductiveloss.org/.

38 Faye V. Harrison, *Outsider Within*, 2008, 291.

39 Marta Savigliano, *Angora Matta*, 2003, xi.

40 Julie M. Taylor, *Paper Tangos*, 1998.

41 Elizabeth Chin, ed., *Katherine Dunham*, 2014; Dána-Ain Davis, "Katherine Dunham Made Me . . .," in *Katherine Dunham, Elizabeth Chin, ed.*, 2014, 118.

42 Dána-Ain Davis, Cheyenne Varner, and LeConté J. Dill, "A Birth Story," *Anthropology News* website, August 27, 2021.

43 Davis, Varner, and J. Dill, "A Birth Story"; Davis, *Reproductive Injustice*, 2019.

44 Alisse Waterston and Charlotte Corden, "Making Light in Dark Times," *Anthropology News* website, August 12, 2021; Waterson, *My Father's Wars*, 2013; Waterston and Corden, *Light in Dark Times*, 2020.

CHAPTER 7

Feminist Activist Ethnography

In order to identify and evaluate the role activism can play in feminist ethnography, this chapter will guide you through the following questions:

- What does it mean to be a feminist activist ethnographer?
- What should feminist activist ethnography seek to accomplish?
- Is feminist ethnography inherently activist?
- What forms can feminist activist ethnography take?
- How can feminist activist ethnographers reflect upon our practice?

Spotlights in this chapter:

- Tom Boellstorff on New Technologies and Activism
- Michelle Téllez on Activism Through Storytelling in Visual Media
- Leith Mullings on Keeping Feminist Ethnography Meaningful

Essentials in this chapter:

- Susan Brin Hyatt, "'Water Is Life—Meters Out!'"
- Jennifer Goett, Black Autonomy: Race, Gender, and Afro-Nicaraguan Activism
- Fed Up Honeys, "Makes Me Mad! Stereotypes of Young Urban Womyn of Color"
- Dorothy Hodgson, "Introduction: Comparative Perspectives on the Indigenous Rights Movement in Africa and the Americas"

You will also be **Thinking Through** . . .

- Engaging in Public Scholarship
- Working with Activists

In 2003, then American Anthropological Association president Louise Lamphere argued that an engaged anthropology was vital, given the host of critical issues that anthropologists were researching.[1] Similarly, in his Presidential Address to the American Sociological Association (ASA) in 2004, Michael Burawoy spoke about the critical turn toward public scholarship within sociology:

> As mirror and conscience of society, sociology must define, promote and inform public debate about deepening class and racial inequalities, new gender regimes, environmental degradation, market fundamentalism, state and non-state violence. I believe that the world needs public sociology—a sociology that transcends the academy—more than ever. Our potential publics are multiple, ranging from media audiences to policy makers, from silenced minorities to social movements. They are

local, global, and national. As public sociology stimulates debate in all these contexts, it inspires and revitalizes our discipline. In return, theory and research give legitimacy, direction, and substance to public sociology.[2]

Over the past decade, many disciplines have increased their commitment to more public and engaged scholarship. In fact, a decade after these conversations began at ASA and AAA conferences, AAA president Leith Mullings noted in her 2013 address to members that calls for engaged, public, and activist scholarship have ignited the discipline of anthropology and making such interventions have become not only accepted but often expected.

This chapter examines the role of activism within feminist ethnography and a variety of ways that feminist ethnographers engage in activist work. Many would argue that being a feminist activist ethnographer is practicing a form of scholarship committed to human liberation. It requires that you have commitments beyond the academy—that you are committed to a struggle.

To explore the subject of activist ethnography as it intersects with feminist ethnography, there are several things that should be considered. First, ethnographers collect data that can be used to illuminate social problems and can often have an impact on policy or serve as a mechanism to activate community groups. Second, feminist social inquiry owes a debt to politically engaged action, particularly the civil rights and feminist movements of the 1960s and 1970s. Feminist ethnography is unquestionably indebted to the visions, risks, and sacrifices that have enabled gender-conscious struggles for the rights of full citizenship and for human rights and dignity into the twenty-first century.[3] Third, social critique by feminist scholars has played an important role in contemporary understandings of social justice.

Feminist ethnographic research and activism have contributed to the development of the activist-scholar model. For instance, writing about the perils and possibilities for feminist scholar-activists and activist-scholars, sociologist Manisha Desai reflects on her experiences with activist ethnography in the early 1980s, when she came to the United States for graduate school following her training in social work in India:

> I assumed the identity of a scholar-activist from the beginning of my graduate school career. This identity was facilitated by changes in the U.S. academy at the time, in particular the institutionalization of feminist scholarship, which highlighted the intrinsic relationships between the intellectual and activist projects of feminism. It was understood that feminist scholars would have an activist commitment, which often was the focus of their research, and that this commitment would be reflected in their analysis and writing.[4]

Feminism is a prescriptive project, with a social justice vision that attempts to explain, in analytical terms, power differentials of a number of processes including colonialism, capitalism, militarism, ableism, homophobia, among others. We recognize that the term "scholar-activist" is the term most commonly used by activist researchers and that some, like Desai, utilize both terms to describe their work. However, we choose the term "activist-scholar" strategically to underscore how feminist activism and principles so often guide the research of those we discuss in this chapter.

Critics of activist scholarship have claimed that researchers may lose objectivity if they work with a particular group or community for extended periods of time and view themselves as part of that groups' goals—in other words, we run the risk of "going native." In our view, it is often the passion for issues—be it reproductive justice, LGBTQI+ rights, antiracist initiatives, access to public safety nets, or prison reform—that leads many of those who become feminist ethnographers to pursue an academic career in the first place. In turn, formal training in feminist ethnography, epistemology, and theory provides the tools to engage critically with inequity and contribute to social justice.

What Does It Mean to Be a Feminist Activist Ethnographer?

Given that feminist politics both respond to and draw from a social justice perspective, an element of that sensibility is to think about the ethnographer's role in how information is gathered and for whom or in whose interest the research being done. Ida Susser, an anthropologist whose research is on HIV/AIDS, among other topics, argues that it is almost impossible to engage in ethnography and not intervene or advocate when you do research with people who have preventable illnesses or face challenges that can be addressed, such as homelessness. In these instances, she posits activism as an integral part of the research.[5] The political contexts in which research and activism occur vary over time. For instance, in the neoliberal moment, market- and consumption-based strategies are advanced as the solution for addressing social problems and feminist activist research helps to demystify and highlight other ways of knowing. Commitments beyond the academy play an important part in being an activist-scholar. Yet only making one's work available to various publics does not constitute engaging in activism; it requires a particular intent on the part of the feminist ethnographer.

Many researchers come to feminist ethnography with preexisting involvements in activist struggles, such as human rights advocacy, racial and economic justice, disability rights, anti-domestic violence, and/or LGBTQI+ equity. A history of engagement in activist efforts undoubtedly shapes and may become part of the ways we approach our research. For some, this may guide them toward particular research projects. For others, these commitments may influence the way they approach a topic that may have no direct relation to their previous work.

Being an activist-scholar has a long history in disciplines like anthropology and sociology, some dating that relationship to early-twentieth-century figures, such as Ruth Benedict, Katherine Dunham, and Margaret Mead. What did it mean to be a public ethnographer advocating what would now be characterized as feminist goals in the 1920s? In many ways, it was a personal decision to be a **public intellectual**. Using Mead as our example, she had a public persona and wrote for popular journals, using the knowledge she had gathered through ethnographic fieldwork. She entered into public conversation about contemporary societal concerns. Mead wrote a column in the 1960s for *Redbook*, a popular magazine targeted at young married women, and engaged in public dialogue about subjects from adolescence to women's sexuality to environmentalism on radio and television. She was a public scholar in that she engaged in public debates. For example, Mead gave Congressional testimony toward the legalization of marijuana. And at the time of her death, she was working on the Congressional passage of childhood nutrition legislation. Her notoriety, indicated by the political and media responses to her efforts, is a strong indication of her role as a public intellectual. In 1969, the then-governor of Florida Claude Kirk referred to Mead as a "dirty old lady," and various cartoons during the 1960s and 1970s mocked Mead's position on the legalization of marijuana and presented her being searched by customs at the US-Mexico border, presumably for drugs.[6]

How does Mead's public engagement and activism differ from more contemporary feminist ethnographers' activist roles? One might say that being a public intellectual today centers around a commitment to ensuring that one's scholarship is accessible to the general public in the form of performance, graphic novels, or films, writing for popular newspapers or blogs, or participating on talk shows or in events that are live-streamed for public consumption. In that regard, being a public ethnographer during Margaret Mead's time is not so different from the contemporary moment—apart from the technologies that are used to do it.

The contributions feminist ethnographers have made to activism and activist scholarship are evident by engaging in critical analysis of social situations aimed at changing social structures. For instance, consider the legions of feminist ethnographers whose work has contributed boldly to reproductive health struggles. In illuminating and challenging the intentions of some conservatives to undermine women's reproductive rights, research by feminist scholars has informed those debates. Exploring the politics of reproduction and reproductive access within the context of shifting economic strategies, anthropologist Emily Martin's *The Woman in the Body: A Cultural Analysis of Reproduction* was one of the first to illuminate how medical language exploited industrial metaphors to describe and pathologize women's bodies.[7] Other scholars confronted the logic of positioning fetuses as more important than women, such as sociologist Monica J. Casper's *The Making of the Unborn Patient: A Social Anatomy of Fetal Surgery*.[8] Still others examined the implications of new reproductive technologies, such as sociologist Barbara Katz Rothman in her text on how prenatal testing changed the landscape for women's experience of pregnancy, *The Tentative Pregnancy: How Amniocentesis Changes the Experience of Motherhood*, and anthropologist Sarah Franklin's scholarship on the cultural dimensions of assisted reproduction and the debates surrounding them, documented in *Embodied Progress: A Cultural Account of Assisted Conception* and *Biological Relatives: IVF, Stem Cells and the Future of Kinship*.[9] Interventions may also be found in the work of scholars who use a critical race perspective within both activist efforts and scholarship on reproduction. For instance, legal scholar Dorothy Roberts's *Killing The Black Body: Race, Reproduction, and the Meaning of Liberty* argues that one can never understand reproduction without considering race.[10] Anthropologist Khiara Bridges explores how processes of racialization are evident in prenatal care in *Reproducing Race: An Ethnography of Pregnancy as a Site of Racialization*.[11] Social critique can be valuable for activist-scholars, because it works to transform our thinking in ways that can influence organizing strategies and approaches, as well as open up new avenues of inquiry and intervention for other scholars to pursue.

What are the other ways feminist ethnographic work is utilized in the sphere of reproduction? One example comes from the use of the term "obstetric racism" from Dána-Ain Davis's article "Obstetric Racism: The Racial Politics of Pregnancy and Birthing."[12] Obstetric racism sits at the intersection of medical racism and obstetric violence and is used to explain forms of abuse that medical personnel and institutions perpetrate against women during conception, pregnancies, childbirth, and postpartum. Obstetric racism is enacted on racialized bodies that have experienced historically constituted forms of subjugation.

The phrase has migrated from the social sciences to the clinical domain: a research team in California used the framework as the foundation to create a measure a measure to capture and provide data about various domains of obstetric racism that Black women experience in hospital settings. This represents an elaboration of the sites of social justice and how ethnographic research can be used not only in activist work but also in policy and public health toward activist ends.

Other scholars are involved in activist work more directly, engaging with and in movements for social change. One example that builds on the social critique of reproductive politics highlighted above is the Advocacy Committee established by the Council on Anthropology and Reproduction (CAR), a special interest group of the Society for Medical Anthropology. CAR has been active for the past decade, working with groups like National Advocates for Pregnant Women and contributing to policy brief drafts used to influence policy. For instance, CAR published a statement vehemently opposing legislation that creates barriers to safe abortion care, encouraging readers to contact lawmakers opposing such legislation and work with organizations like Planned Parenthood that provide reproductive healthcare to low-income women and are being targeted by these laws.[13]

THINKING THROUGH . . .

Engaging in Public Scholarship

One way to engage in public scholarship is to edit a public resource like Wikipedia. This is particularly important for feminists because Wikipedia's articles on women, people of color, LGBTQI+ figures, and feminist/queer organizations are often incomplete, "stubs," of low quality, or simply nonexistent. Wikipedia is the seventh "most read" website on the Internet (falling behind only search engines, YouTube, and social media sites).

Look up WikiProjects on Feminism, Gender Studies, LGBT Studies, or WikiProjects relevant to countering systematic bias. From those pages, you can choose a "stub" (an incomplete article), conduct your own research, and add your content. See also Wikipedia links to "How to" Guides (and a video tutorial), as well as suggestions for writing about women, transgender, nonbinary, and intersex people linked to the WikiProjects mentioned above. Write a brief reflection about the experience (why did you choose a particular topic? what state was it in prior to your intervention? why did you make the changes that you did? what interactions, if any, did you have with Wikipedia administrators and/or other users?).

What Should Feminist Activist Ethnography Seek to Accomplish?

Feminist ethnographers contribute to many types of activism, including those that lean toward conservatism (see discussion of Poewe/"Cesara's" ethnographic memoir in chapter 6). This textbook is primarily oriented toward engagement or activism that is politically *progressive*, concerned with both feminism and social justice. By social justice, we mean understanding how power works and seeking to ensure equitable treatment.

In the twenty-first century, being an activist-scholar often means developing formal relationships with organizations or community-based programs in which research priorities are determined by the organizations for their benefit. Whether engaged, activist, or public, any one of these terms (often used interchangeably by scholars) means that feminist ethnographers consciously put themselves in public dialogue about issues of injustice. That public may be a general listening public, a government-related public, or a community-based public, such as an activist organization. The point is that the feminist ethnographer who seeks to be public, engaged, or activist aims to accomplish research that is meaningful for those who participate in it.

In "'Water Is Life—Meters Out!' Women's Grassroots Activism and the Privatization of Public Amenities,"[14] anthropologist Susan Brin Hyatt discusses her ethnographic project on the privatization of water in a deindustrialized town in the United Kingdom. Essentially, Hyatt attempts to see the way that women, through the lens of activism, understood their structural disadvantage. One of the things that Hyatt found in researching and documenting activist work was that people could envision the possibility of making common causes with other groups whom they previously had seen as the root of the problem.

Women organized campaigns against companies that were selling water, which they thought should be provided by the state. Privatizing water increased the likelihood that poor and working-class families would be unable to pay their bills at some point. In order to have a "seat" at the table to air their concerns, the women bought shares in the water company so they could attend the annual shareholders meeting. Hyatt also bought one share, and she, too, attended (see *Essential*). This offers a glimpse into the role that a feminist activist ethnographer can play in both conducting research and contributing to the issue under study.

A second example illustrating feminist activist ethnography is evident in Bianca Williams's work. Williams embodies being an academic and an activist. She was a coleader of Black Lives Matter 5280, the Denver chapter of the national Black Lives Matter (BLM) organization. Williams's research includes focusing on the emotional well-being of Black women as it contributes to the group's five Community Commitments, including striving for justice; affirming Black women leadership; inclusivity; serving Black communities; and cultivating Black love. Her activism informs her scholarship such that in the past year and a half, as Black women across the globe have risen as founders, organizers, and leaders in the BLM movement, Williams is undertaking a research project that documents and analyzes how they participate in radical self- and communal care. As part of their initiative, BLM encourages organizers and leaders to prioritize self-care in the struggle for racial justice, going as far as to have a "Healing Justice" committee dedicated to creating strategies "to assist communities who are rising up and fighting back against anti-Black state and state-sanctioned violence to care for themselves, move through grief, heal from trauma, and attend to their emotional and physical safety in protest spaces."[15]

🌼 **ESSENTIAL**

Excerpt from "Water Is Life— Meters Out!" by Susan Brin Hyatt

Susan B. Hyatt is Professor of Anthropology at Indiana University—Purdue University Indianapolis (IUPUI) and former Chair of the Anthropology Department. She received her BA in Anthropology from Grinnell College and her MA from the University of Michigan before working for eight years as a community organizer in southwest Chicago, working to fight racially discriminatory real estate and lending practices. She then resumed her studies at the University of Massachusetts where she completed her PhD in 1996. In her dissertation fieldwork, she documented and analyzed activism among working-class women living in peripheral public housing in northern England, who were contesting the impact of neoliberal policies on their beleaguered communities. She joined the faculty at IUPUI in 2005, after teaching for eight years at Temple University in Philadelphia. She has involved her students in a number of collaborative research projects with Indianapolis communities and has received several awards for civic engagement and service learning. She has been an active member of the Association for Feminist Anthropology and currently serves as a member of the editorial board for the journal Feminist Anthropology. *She also edited several issues of* Voices, *the former newsletter of the Association for Feminist Anthropology.*

One of the most active campaigns I observed and participated in was a campaign organized and participated in primarily by low-income women against the effects of water privatization. . . .

The annual meeting was scheduled for a day in late September 1994. We decided that we would have a little demonstration outside of the building where the meeting was to be held before it began. I suggested that we collect some bottled waters (which I bought in the supermarket) and set up a little "stand" where we would display the bottled waters alongside other bottles labeled, "Water from the Meters of Lower Grange." Everyone agreed to this plan and we spent an afternoon making placards with the message, "Water for Sale! Is Social Justice Also for Sale?" and fliers that read: First there was the craze for Perrier, then it was other bottled waters like Highland Spring or Buxton. Will the next fashion for expensive, over-priced water be Water from the Meters of Lower Grange? SHOULD WATER FEEL MORE LIKE A LUXURY THAN A NECESSITY?

We arrived at the shareholders' meeting early the next morning in festive spirits. Needless to say, the majority of shareholders were not sympathetic to the cause, but the media and various and sundry other groups who were also there to protest came by the table we had set up and chatted with us.

Source: Brin Hyatt, Susan. "'Water Is Life—Meters Out!' Women's Grassroots Activism and the Privatization of Public Amenities." *Occasional Papers on Globalization*. University of South Florida. Vol. 1(7), (2004), 8.

It is also important to note that it is not always feasible for scholars (feminist or otherwise) to identify themselves during fieldwork as activists or engage in direct activism. Sometimes this is the case due to geopolitical constraints, which may be a barrier to assuming the role of activist or advocate. Geopolitics is a complex and complicated issue that can be unpredictable in the ways it motivates and/or encumbers an ethnographer. Nonetheless, feminist activist researchers often find alternative ways to engage in change. For example, serving in an intermediary capacity allows one to take part in a dialogue or conversation, while at the same time maintaining a kind of distance from the issue under discussion, in ways that may prove to be more useful to a long-term project.

Is Feminist Ethnography Inherently Activist?

As Indigenous rights activist and education scholar Linda Tuhiwai Smith has written, "There is no easy or natural relationship between activism and research. Although some activists are also researchers, and have to undertake their own research, and researchers may also be activists, the roles are very different."[16] However, we believe it is accurate to say that most feminist ethnographers have shaped their work in relation to broader political concerns, despite the fact that professional ethnographers are sometimes treated with skepticism by the academy when they engage in activism. When you consider yourself a feminist activist ethnographer, it is a priority to have feminist principles as a researcher that merge both research and activism. In so doing, there is a shift in the responsibility that a feminist ethnographer has to those they study.

Performance studies scholar D. Soyini Madison has written on the use of what she terms critical ethnography, which we view as similar to activist ethnography:

> Critical ethnography . . . begins with an ethical responsibility to address processes of unfairness or injustice within a particular lived domain. By "ethical responsibility" I mean a compelling sense of duty and commitment based on moral principles of human freedom and well-being and hence a compassion for the suffering of living beings. The conditions for existence within a particular context are not as they could be for specific subjects; as a result, the researcher feels a moral obligation to make a contribution toward changing those conditions toward greater freedom and equity. The critical ethnographer also takes us beneath surface appearances, disrupts the status quo, and unsettles both neutrality and taken-for-granted assumptions by bringing to light underlying and obscure operations of power and control. Therefore, the critical ethnographer resists domestication and moves from "what is" to "what could be."[17]

One thing is certain: proponents of feminist activist ethnography are opposed to the idea that any research can be "objective" or neutral. In fact, they highlight that discussing inequities is, in effect, a political position by itself. Feminist activist ethnographers are conscious of—and must be reflective about—their desire for their research to be politically relevant.

One of the mid-twentieth century's most vocal activist feminist scholars in the discipline of anthropology was Eleanor "Happy" Leacock. She believed that feminist anthropology was part of a broader radical critique of the origins of inequality in which detailed attention needed to be paid to historical processes. Her scholarship covered many subjects, such as Indigenous issues, poverty, education, and racism in schools, and one of the most important contributions to feminist scholarship was Leacock's introduction to the reissue of Friedrich Engels's *Origins of the Family, Private Property and the State*,[18] which locates the origins of women's oppression in economic systems. Although she struggled to find academic employment during the 1950s because of her political work—for example, as an activist with the group Harlem Fight Back—Leacock modeled what it means to be a feminist and activist. Leacock was a founder of the New York Women's Anthropology Caucus, which, among other things, challenged sexism in the academy. Her research among the Montagnais-Naskapi in the northern Labrador region of Canada shed light on how industrial capitalism impacted Indigenous people's lives, essentially destroying egalitarian relationships. It was Leacock's political commitments to equality that often drove her research. Yet during the McCarthy era, when many Americans were accused of being Communists or Communist sympathizers, Leacock was careful about calling herself an "activist."

The simplest answer to the question in this section is that not every feminist ethnographic project is activist in intent, and not every ethnographic project on feminist activism produces feminist ethnography. One would be hard pressed to pose ethnography as intrinsically activist. Yet we believe that learning about activist possibilities enhances all work that aims to be attentive to issues of power, privilege, and inequality.

What Forms Can Feminist Activist Ethnography Take?

Many feminist activist ethnographers engaged with social issues come to be viewed as experts. In fact, feminist ethnographers' expertise may be used in many ways: from teaching to public education, from publishing to collaboration, and from conducting research to working on campaigns. They use their skills and **cultural capital** to raise awareness, inform policy, engage with media, and serve as expert witnesses in human rights and legal cases.

In many instances, feminist scholars have sought to develop projects that bridged the gaps between the researcher and the researched, between subjectivity and objectivity, between theory and practice. Here we might reconsider the import of expertise. Ethnographic knowledge can serve as a form of witnessing and exploring the processes through which activist practice can emerge. In the field of theology, we see the use of ethnography as a form of witnessing. According to Christian theologians Christian Scharen and Aana Marie Vigen in *Ethnography as Christian Theology and Ethics*, when scholars divest themselves from being an expert, they can become "witnesses to truth on a more profound level."[19] Likewise, women's studies scholar Deborah Gordon in the article "Border Work: Feminist Ethnography and the Dissemination of Literacy"[20] discusses witnessing and the role it plays in reinventing stories of suffering that can be used in support of social justice. Accordingly, witnessing can be a fundamentally important component of feminist activist ethnography.

While there are many forms that feminist activist ethnography can take, the scales of that activism—that is, how much a researcher interacts with organizers, the intention of their ethnographic work, et cetera—differ across projects. Zethu Matebeni is an interdisciplinary feminist scholar and activist whose research is linked to queer issues, sexuality, gender, race, HIV and AIDS, film, cinema, and photography. Along with three other scholars—psychologist Vasu Reddy, clinical psychiatry research scientist Theo Sandfort, and LGBTI program coordinator for the Open Society Initiative for Southern Africa Ian Southey-Swartz—Matebeni wrote about a community study based on in-depth interviews with twenty-four self-identifying African lesbians living with HIV in South Africa, Zimbabwe, and Namibia. The study focused on the women's personal experiences and circumstances, making the point that women's experiences shed light on and challenge popular notions of lesbian risk. Matebeni also curates exhibits and book projects, including "Jo'burg TRACKS: Sexuality in the City" and the book project *Reclaiming Afrikan: Queer Perspectives on Sexual and Gender Identities*.[21]

Feminist activist ethnographers often document and analyze local or community-based movements. Consider, for example, anthropologist Michelle Marzullo's analysis of a local instantiation of same-sex marriage. In her article, "Seeking Marriage Material: Rethinking the U.S. Marriage Debates Under Neoliberalism,"[22] Marzullo examines the circumstances and outcomes of Mayor Jason Wests's decision to perform same-sex marriages in the Hudson Valley city of New Paltz, New York, in 2004. Wests's decision was prompted by his interest in his city doing its part to contribute to the larger goal of legalizing same-sex marriage. Marzullo's focus on this particular local effort may be viewed in contrast to a researcher who might document and analyze same-sex marriage conceptually in terms of family making or national efforts to legalize same-sex marriage.

Other feminist activist ethnographers prioritize translating their work so that it can be of use to the communities with which they work. For example, anthropologist Jennifer Goett has parlayed her scholarly work on Afro-descendant Creole communities in Nicaragua to develop evidence that has been marshaled by community members in their struggles against state and private interests in order to attain territorial autonomy.

ESSENTIAL

Excerpt from *Black Autonomy: Race, Gender, and Afro-Nicaraguan Activism* by Jennifer Goett

Jennifer Goett *trained in anthropology at the University of Texas at Austin and is an associate professor of Comparative Cultures and Politics at Michigan State University. She has published activist scholarship on Afro-descendant social movements in Nicaragua and on state violence, land dispossession, infrastructure megaprojects, and youth activism. Her current research focuses on the political activism and migration experiences of Nicaraguan asylum seekers in Costa Rica and the United States. In addition, she works as a pro bono expert witness for asylum cases in US immigration court. In this excerpt, she talks about her path from beginning her research as a graduate student and becoming a feminist activist ethnographer.*

Photo Credit: Waseem El-Rayes

I entered into the work as a graduate student with a certain degree of youthful idealism and a sense of optimism that I could help create a more just and egalitarian world through activist research. Although my political commitments remain the same fifteen years later, my estimation of the impact of my activist scholarship is more circumspect. . . . At the end of the day, I am infinitely more indebted to my community allies in Nicaragua than they are to me. . . . Many of my research goals have emerged from dialogue and collaboration with local activists, but I have pursued other goals because I found them to be urgent and relevant to the broader themes of autonomous rights and activism. For instance, as a feminist scholar, much of my research on gender and sexuality is of minimal interest to male leaders who are primarily concerned with cultural and race-based rights to territory and self-determination. Doing feminist activist research with groups that may not have woman-centered politics does not always lend itself to a seamless alignment of research goals. . . . The broader political goals that drive my activist scholarship are shared goals born of long-term engagement and collaboration with Indigenous and Afrodescendent communities.

Source: Goett, Jennifer. *Black Autonomy: Race, Gender, and Afro-Nicaraguan Activism*. Stanford, CA: Stanford University Press, 2016.

Collaboration and Participatory Action Research

The line between collaborative research and participatory action research (PAR) is often a thin one. Here we highlight the ways that PAR (introduced briefly in chapter 4) involves methods and political strategies that are developed for a research project *with* the people being studied. Anthropologist Luke Eric Lassiter discusses feminist approaches to collaborative research in *The Chicago Guide to Collaborative Ethnography*, such as cowriting the outcome of the research with the participants.[23] Ideally, this process will benefit both the researcher and the subjects of inquiry, enabling participants to serve as partners in the production of knowledge. Participants are also explicitly consulted in almost all steps in the research process.

Education scholars T.J. Jourian and Z. Nicolazzo note that "many of the frameworks for collaborative research methodologies have been informed by highly marginalized communities themselves."[24] Jourian and Nicolazzo's approach to their respective ethnographic projects with trans* students and educators in higher education emerged from their long-held commitments to social activism among queer and trans* people of color. Experience with coalitional work in the grassroots organizations like the Sylvia Rivera Law Project and the Audre Lorde Project, among others, gave them tangible examples of what they hoped to achieve by working "with" and alongside participants rather than conceptualizing their research as "on," "about," or "for" trans* communities. This allowed them to foreground an ethic of care and compassion as they worked to generate new knowledge and create social change alongside participants.

An early example of collaborative research was the four-year literacy project that was directed by urban affairs and public policy scholar Rosa Torruellas, along with oral historians Ana Jurabe and Rina Benmayor. Between 1985 and 1989, the Center for Puerto Rican Studies at Hunter College in New York City initiated and ran a Spanish-language adult literacy program in East Harlem.[25] The researchers created the project to study educational patterns in a community with high dropout rates and promoted women's empowerment through Spanish-language literacy. The most profound outcome of collaborative and public scholarship is that it shifts the role of more passive research informants to consultants or participants who may take on a number of roles such as cointerpreters, coresearchers, or collaborators.

A more contemporary example of collaborative research is environmental psychologist Caitlin Cahill's community-based PAR project with young people investigating the everyday experiences of global urban restructuring. The project "Makes Me Mad: Stereotypes of Young Urban Womyn of Color" involved Cahill and six young women researchers living on the Lower East Side of Manhattan.[26] Together they investigated the relationship between the gentrification of their community, public (mis)representations, and their self-understanding. Because the project was developed for and by young urban womyn of color, it reflects their concerns.

🧠 **ESSENTIAL**

Excerpt from "Makes Me Mad! Stereotypes of Young Urban Womyn of Color" by the Fed Up Honeys

The Fed Up Honeys *collective developed as part of a critical participatory action research (PAR) project addressing the concerns of women of color living in the Lower East Side in New York City. One of the researchers is feminist ethnographer Caitlin Cahill, an environmental psychologist from New York City. Committed to interdisciplinary, engaged scholarship, Cahill works in intergenerational collaboratives to explore and take action upon the everyday intimate experiences of racial capitalism, specifically as it concerns gentrification, immigration, education, and state violence. She has published extensively on critical PAR research. Together, Indra Rios-Moore, Erica Arenas, Jennifer*

Young Urban Womyn of Color are...

Likely to Become Teen Moms

Stereotype #1
www.fed-up-honeys.org

Young Urban Womyn of Color are...

In Abusive Relationships

Stereotype #3
www.fed-up-honeys.org

Young Urban Womyn of Color are...

Promiscuous

Stereotype #5
www.fed-up-honeys.org

Young Urban Womyn of Color are...

Lazy and on Welfare

Stereotype #2
www.fed-up-honeys.org

Young Urban Womyn of Color are a ...

Burden To Society

Stereotype #4
www.fed-up-honeys.org

Young Urban Womyn of Color are...

Uneducated

Stereotype #6
www.fed-up-honeys.org

Contreras, Na Jiang, Tiffany Threatts, Shamara Allen, and Caitlin Cahill published a research report "Makes Me Mad: Stereotypes of Young Urban Womyn of Color" and launched the website www.fed-up-honeys.org. The following excerpt from one coauthored publication by Cahill, Rios-Moore, and Threatts discusses the genesis of their collaborative research and activist outcomes of the Fed Up Honeys' work.

Our study considered the relationship between the lack of resources in our community, the Lower East Side neighborhood of New York City, and mischaracterizations of young women. When we first began our project, we did not know what we were going to research. The area of investigation was open as the study was broadly defined as "the everyday lives of young women in the city." We collectively determined the focus of the project after working together for several weeks, and after doing preliminary research on our neighborhood and our own everyday experiences. . . . The project is for and by young urban women of color and is reflective of our own concerns and the issues that personally affected us. We represent a diverse collection of personalities and backgrounds; the fact that we all felt so passionately about this topic is a testament to its likely importance to all young women affected by stereotypes that are pervasive in popular culture and the self-image issues that stem from them. . . .

As is evident in the title for our project "Makes Me Mad," we wanted to express our anger in order to engage others, depending on who they are, to either feel their own pain or experience the pain and guilt of acknowledging racism. With our "stereotype stickers" we wanted to "prick the 'psychic amnesia' that has infected America" (Torre and Fine 2006). Each sticker features a stereotype about young urban women of color including: "Likely to become teen moms," "In abusive relationships," "Promiscuous," "Uneducated," "Lazy and on Welfare," and "Burden to society." In the sticker campaign we hoped to upset and motivate "to go against the grain, to prove everyone wrong" and "to realize what it is we have against us." We created the stickers especially for other young women of color, but we posted them all over our neighborhood as we hoped to provoke the public in general into rethinking these stereotypes and how they related to the gentrification of our community. We also used the stereotype stickers to "advertise" our website.

Our website www.fed-up-honeys.org, "created by young womyn of color for young womyn of color," is a kind of one-stop-shop experience where visitors can find out about the "Makes Me Mad" research project. On our website you can download our study and learn more about our research. We have a page devoted to the Lower East Side that includes links to community organizations and businesses that connect to young people's interests. We have a page of resources especially for young women (links to other websites with information about health, sexuality, financial resources). We also have a "rant" page because venting was key to our own process so we wanted to create a virtual space for self-expression, where people can post their frustration. Another page includes poetry of relevance to other young people of color and features a beautiful poem about taking cold showers in the projects. . . .

Through the fed-up-honeys website and our sticker campaign, we want to stress the importance of self-directed and community-supported action for change. Using the vehicles of action research, research products such as our stickers, and the website, we want to help in the process of motivating and taking part in a revitalization of active community participation. We believe that by simply living your truth and encouraging others to do the same, you can participate in your community's growth. In the process of being true to yourself and the network of people that make up your community, you can help to knock down the myths that hold down our communities.

Source: Cahill, Caitlin, Indra Rios-Moore, and Tiffany Threatts. "Different Eyes/Open Eyes." *Revolutionizing Education*, 2008, 94, 117–119.

Dána-Ain worked on a PAR project with students from Queens College with the Office of Community Studies (OCS) and the Griot Circle, an organization founded to meet the needs of elder LGBT people of color. Wanting to address the problem of Access-a-Ride, a paratransit service for people with limited mobility, operated by New York's Mass Transit Authority (MTA), Griot sought a research partner to help understand the problems its members had with Access-a-Ride. Due to time and budgetary constraints, they agreed to use survey methodology. They wanted the OCS student researchers and Dána-Ain to conduct the research, analyze the data, and develop an agenda to advocate for better services. Members of Griot and the executive director collaborated in developing the first draft of the survey. Then Dána-Ain, working with three master's-level students, refined the survey after consultation with OCS staff. A second draft went back to Griot Circle for members to review. In return, they received a third draft, which OCS staff finalized. At the moment that Dána-Ain thought they had finished with the back and forth, the executive director sent an email stating that since the survey would be aimed at members of other elder-focused programs beyond Griot, they, too, wanted some input in the survey instrument. Although this project is not explicitly feminist, the analysis of the data includes attention to gender and gender variance in relationship to accessing these services. The back and forth that Dána-Ain experienced with Griot is not unusual in the PAR process. In order to maintain the integrity of a participatory research project grounded in feminist principles, a researcher must be willing to accept the full participation of community members in the process. This can be daunting, and quite a bit of time is necessary to ensure that all parties experience full investment and ownership in the project.

Social Media and Film

Social media, according to some, has changed activism because it facilitates an almost lightening-speed circulation of information. It generates an urgency in ways that are almost unprecedented. For example, in 2014, a full-fledged campaign "Bring Back Our Girls" took off on social media, in response to the kidnapping of 276 schoolgirls in Nigeria. The ensuing campaign received widespread coverage on Facebook, Twitter, and other social media.

In an article in the *New Yorker Magazine* in 2010, however, columnist Malcolm Gladwell wrote an editorial critical of such "new" forms of activism, in which he describes the 1960 scene in Greensboro, North Carolina, where "Negro" students staged a sit-in at Woolworth's protesting the fact that Blacks were not served.[27] They risked their lives and limbs during the protest, and Gladwell distinguishes between this form of activism versus cyberactivism, whereby one can push a button to sign a petition or post their outrage over a particular injustice on Facebook or Twitter. Gladwell holds that these forms of digital protest are weak.

But social media has clearly changed activism, and there are possibilities for cyber-engagement that can draw activist-scholars into struggles beyond clicking a button or buying a coffee to support a particular cause. The possibilities are ones that we hope will engage a new generation of feminist ethnographers. In our interview with anthropologist Tom Boellstorff, who has conducted extensive ethnographic research in virtual communities, he offers a more optimistic perspective than Gladwell, which we appreciate (see *Spotlight* below).

A powerful use of visual media as a form of feminist activist ethnography is the use of film. In 2010, an earthquake hit Haiti and the viewing public witnessed the devastation, largely via social media. The popular media portrayed Haiti as a miserable country with little ability to deal with the catastrophe. The groundbreaking 2009 film *Poto Mitan: Haitain Women, Pillars of the Global Economy* has served as an important counternarrative. With anthropologist Mark Schuller as codirector and coproducer, anthropologist Gina Athena Ulysse and international education scholar Claudine Michel as associate producers, and filmmaker Renée Bergan, the documentary sought to make Haitian women's voices more accessible to US audiences. *Poto Mitan* is based on Schuller's ethnographic work and features the perspectives of five women and how they have survived neoliberal globalization by using their collective activism to make change.

ꕥ SPOTLIGHT ꕥ

Tom Boellstorff on New Technologies and Activism

Tom Boellstorff *received his PhD in anthropology at Stanford University and teaches anthropology at the University of California, Irvine. His publications include* The Gay Archipelago: Sexuality and Nation in Indonesia *(2005),* A Coincidence of Desires: Anthropology, Queer Studies, Indonesia *(2007),* Coming of Age in Second Life: An Anthropologist Explores the Virtually Human *(2008, with a new second edition in 2015), and the coauthored* Ethnography and Virtual Worlds: A Handbook of Method *(2012). He has served as editor-in-chief of* American Anthropologist, *the flagship journal*

of the American Anthropological Association, is a Fellow of the American Association for the Advancement of Science, and has been engaged in HIV/AIDS and LGBT activism in the United States, Indonesia, Malaysia, and Russia, with groups such as OutRight Action International. In our interview, Boellstorff addressed the virtual possibilities for activism and feminist ethnography.

Thinking about the multiple meanings of activism as they are changed by technology is really important. I do agree that there's a critique of this kind of "Click a link activism" where people are like "Oh I'm so activist, I clicked on this link that audoubon.org had." But at the same time, if a million people pick up one piece of trash. . . . I don't want to throw out the baby with the bathwater and just say that's meaningless. I think these new emerging technologies do give us ways to do half-hearted activism, busy activism, multi-tasking activism, that could be meaningful and actually part of the equation for making social change. Not that it's better or necessarily more effective, but I get worried about [calling it] inauthentic or bad. That, to me, is a little too hasty and prevents us from thinking about what might be some cool things that are happening in this space that we could be using for activist work and that could play a role in building coalitions and informing people and doing other kinds of stuff. For newer generations, as these technologies continue to transform the world in so many ways, thinking about technology and activism is something that I'm interested in. And what really interests me are things that we can do that make these new intersections of technology and activism not a way to be self-satisfied and not do the real thing, but a way of doing the real thing. Because technology nowadays *is* part of the real thing.

Poto Mitan's unique quality rests upon the women's acute understanding of the power of film. Citing the Haitian proverb, "hearing and seeing are two different things," the women implored Dr. Schuller to share their stories with people in the U.S., people who have the power to make change.[28]

Schuller returned to Haiti as a member of one of the first teams to respond following the devastating 7.0 earthquake in 2010 through a grassroots medical mission in his neighborhood. His objective in producing this film was to raise Haiti's profile and standards for media about Haiti, increase awareness of revitalization efforts within Haiti, identify funds to support that work, and promote people's voices to demand change.

Importantly, as Schuller has emphasized in his scholarly presentations, he realizes that his role is to document and observe social and political conditions, but not necessarily spearhead public activism. Distinguishing himself from local activists allowed him to connect with people in power with whom he might not otherwise have been able to access. Schuller's ability to bring issues pertaining to Haiti to the forefront of people's attention is not necessarily embedded in activism but rather with him serving as an interlocutor.

> ## THINKING THROUGH . . .
>
> ### Working with Activists
>
> Identify an organization online, based anywhere in the world, that addresses an activist issue (an antiviolence campaign, LGBTQ rights, disability rights, anti-racism, et cetera). Write a brief summary, explaining their mission and organizational goals, and reflect on how a feminist activist ethnographer could collaborate with organizers to assist their work, virtually or in person.

The power of social justice film, documentaries, and social media is that they have the ability to make you think, make you mad, or make you act. Visual media also has the power to motivate people, because when it documents or narrates inequality, abuse, and devastation, they are often produced out of passion and anger. Indeed, the intent is to stimulate discussion among the viewers. Consider, for instance, two popular films, *An Inconvenient Truth* and *Born into Brothels*, both of which had wide releases and deeply influenced the public's perception about global warming and the children of prostitutes living in Calcutta, India, respectively. Media, whatever the form, can help shape and circulate ideas about subjects that may not be well understood. We expect to be told real things about life and situations and to have our awareness raised. That is why some feminist activist ethnographers may decide to make films or use social media to stimulate the public's interest in issues of inequity or discrimination, and sometimes to rally the public to respond.

A final example of a feminist ethnographic film that has been used widely by worker's rights activists, as well as in the academy, is Michelle Téllez's "Workers on the Rise." Téllez collaborated with a Phoenix-based editor Justine García and members of the Arizona Worker Rights Center, which tracks labor rights violations, challenges abusive employers, promotes worker-friendly legislation, and develops worker leadership and community in Phoenix. The film was originally sold in hard copy to fundraise for the nonprofit organization it is centered around and is now available for free viewing on Vimeo.[29]

> ### ➳ SPOTLIGHT ➳
>
> ### Michelle Téllez on Activism Through Storytelling in Visual Media
>
> *Michelle Téllez is an Associate Professor in the Department of Mexican American Studies at the University of Arizona. She writes about transnational community formations, Chicana feminism, and gendered migration through her research, public scholarship, and digital humanities work. A founding member of the Chicana M(other)work collective, the Arizona Son Jarocho Collective, and the Binational Arts Residency project, Téllez has a long history in grassroots organizing projects and community-based arts and performance. She coedited* The Chicana M(other)work Anthology:

Porque Sin Madres No Hay Revolución *(2019)*. *Her newest book is* Border Women and the Community of Maclovio Rojas: Autonomy in the Spaces of Neoliberal Neglect *(2021)*.

There is a quote I live by: "No hay que luchar para destruir hay que luchar para crear (We mustn't struggle to destroy, we must struggle to create)." Feminist praxis requires reflexivity and a desire to produce research that can transform—transform our minds, our ideologies, our perceptions of truth—and without an intersectional lens that centers the voices that are often ignored in positivist research paradigms then we are not pursuing that transformation. When I learned about ethnography, it gave me the tools to tell the stories that I so deeply wanted to tell. . . . I came across visual media through the women's multimedia center of Claremont, California and it opened brand new possibilities of storytelling to me. I've played with different methods behind the camera and mostly I've found that coediting and filming—that is, collaborating on a project—shapes what stories are told, what voices are centered and the final product becomes a radical way of shifting how documentaries are made and by whom.

Gender is something that is ignored oftentimes when we're trying to tell stories, right? So what lens is being used to tell a story? I'm a feminist, I'm a feminist ethnographer, and so this kind of goes with me everywhere I go. It's almost like second nature, so I'm always thinking about what story hasn't been told, what visual hasn't been shared, what experience is often ignored. That is what feminism is about, right? It's not just about what is found in the theoretical field; it's about transformation. For me, it's bringing to life [the stories]. Writing is one way of getting out the stories that must be heard. But when you actually get to see the experience, the visual experience, it tells something different, especially for those that are unfamiliar with the topic. This is true for migration, this is true for activism, this is true for community members trying to revive and share their cultural center. Visuals create relationality and viewers can find their mutual humanity in that. That is an essential part of feminist ethnography, right? That's storytelling. You're trying to transform, and I think that storytelling through visual media is absolutely important because it's accessible.

Serving as an Interlocutor

Like Mark Schuller, some feminist ethnographers do not assume the identity of being an activist—at least not in one's field sites. Rather, they prefer to serve as interlocutors, whereby they can offer social critique and simultaneously disentangle the webs of power in which people live. This is the case for anthropologist Dorothy Hodgson, who does ethnography in Tanzania, where she positions herself as an interlocutor. In her documentation of the continuing land grabs of Maasai land, her position as researcher/interlocutor (rather than being directly identified as an activist) enabled her Maasai participants to use her documentation work in court cases toward their own political project.

While value is often derived from scholars' data collection used toward social movements or social justice, it is possible that participants may be placed at risk for being associated with a scholar who identifies as an activist, making the very term problematic since sometimes activists are viewed as agitators. Engaging in activist research must account for the ways in which researchers often have resources upon which they can call if their participation instigates or involves some form of danger or harm. It is important to be sensitive to the fact that research participants associated with scholars who identify as activists can experience danger but may not have the same access to resources. This is particularly significant since it is the researcher's responsibility to do no harm, but if one is an activist-scholar, we also have a responsibility to attempt to do good.

🧠 ESSENTIAL

Excerpt from "Introduction: Comparative Perspectives on the Indigenous Rights Movement in Africa and the Americas" by Dorothy Hodgson

Dorothy Hodgson *earned her PhD in anthropology at the University of Michigan and is Dean of the School of Arts and Sciences and Professor of Anthropology at Brandeis University director at Rutgers University. She has published numerous books on gender and social inequality among Maasai, including her most recent* Being Maasai, Becoming Indigenous: Postcolonial Politics in a Neoliberal World *(2011).*

[Feminist ethnographers have] a range of overlapping positions, from advocacy and collaboration, to dialogue and discussion, to scholarly detachment. Some anthropologists like David Maybury-Lewis have been relentless advocates for indigenous rights, working through nonprofit organizations such as Cultural Survival, IWGIA, and Survival International to facilitate and finance indigenous networking and advocacy. Others, like Les Field, argue for a position that combines scholarship and collaboration. Field describes himself as

> an academic who works within the metropolitan academy as a theorist critical of conventional and particularly colonial-derived categories and also collaborates with an indigenous community and its intellectuals in their various projects, attempting to negotiate and reconcile these very different kinds of work. [Field 1999:195]

Some anthropologists, like myself, might characterize our position as "interlocutors" rather than "collaborators," that is, as scholars who share our ideas and work with indigenous groups in ongoing, constructive, and, perhaps, even occasionally contentious dialogues and debates in an effort to inform and shape their policies and practices, without directly aligning ourselves with one group or faction of the movement (cf. Jackson 1999). As I have written elsewhere, drawing on Gupta and Ferguson (1997:30), I see our "political task not as 'sharing' knowledge with those who lack it but as forging links between different knowledges that are possible from different locations and tracing lines of possible alliance and common purpose between them" (Hodgson 1999:214). As such, our "interlocutors" may be many and varied, including not just indigenous activists but the constituencies, institutions, organizations, and people with which we, and they, engage and interact.

Source: Hodgson, Dorothy L. "Introduction: Comparative Perspectives on the Indigenous Rights Movement in Africa and the Americas." *American Anthropologist* 104, no. 4 (2002):1037–1049, 1044–1045.

How Can Feminist Activist Ethnographers Reflect upon Our Practice?

When we look back on the practice of feminist activist ethnography, we must not obscure its conflictual history. Many scholars view activism as an important goal of feminist and progressive research. However, others critique the idea of being politically engaged when one is an intellectual. Anthropologists Setha Low and Sally Engle Merry's article, "Engaged Anthropology: Diversity and Dilemmas,"[30] lays out some of the issues that have been raised. One point is that anthropologists from the United States in particular have been engaged since the discipline's beginning. We saw evidence of this in the work of Margaret Mead, a public academic. Low and Engle chronicle the inclusion of scholars in projects supported by the Works Progress Administration during the 1930s and 1940s, the largest project to promote the development of public infrastructure, such as roads and buildings, in the United States. In some instances, this engagement was not representative of the kind of progressive politics we have highlighted in this text. A different form of engagement arose after World War II when scholars based in the United States were asked to provide their knowledge and expertise to projects financed by the military, such as **Project Camelot**, creating ethical controversy about the appropriate role of the ethnographer as both a researcher and a citizen.

Low and Engle identify three difficulties scholars may face when being activists. The first is whether one should be involved in the research or serve as a non-biased observer. On the one hand, the argument is that the dynamics of the research changes when you become involved. On the other hand, what about the ethics of not responding when an intervention is necessary? The second dilemma concerns criticizing those who have power over the people or situation you are researching, particularly if you are conducting research in someplace other than your home country. The final concern is the long-standing debate over providing anthropological insights to governments, militaries, and development agencies. One challenge is the possibility that those entities could appropriate an ethnographer's data and potentially use it to harm research participants or their communities.

Further, anthropologist Charles Hale notes that activist scholarship may be called into question when it is posed in terms that are too celebratory or sanguine, as opposed to being in relation to confrontation and contradiction.[31] Some would argue that there are consequences for pointing out contentious social issues and then being directly in the line of fire when people disagree with the researcher's perspective. Alongside the dilemmas laid out by Low and Engles, and Hale—and there are certainly others—we would add the possibility that the researchers' agenda may differ from those of the participants. For example, Dána-Ain points out in *Battered Black Women and Welfare Reform: Between a Rock and a Hard Place*[32] that one major goal of her research was to reshape welfare policy and the negative perspectives many policymakers held about working class and poor women on welfare. However, women's priorities were much more individually oriented because they needed housing and employment and implored Dána-Ain to assist them in securing those resources, which she tried to do, as an advocate. Dána-Ain came to see more clearly after reflecting back on her research that her advocacy had very limited outcomes.

Morgensen (see *Spotlight* in chapter 1) points out that neither activism nor advocacy guarantees justice, empowerment, or resources: "If anti-oppressive commitments are crucial to feminist activist ethnography, all who wish to pursue such work must take care not to imagine that their activist sites provide a counter or a solution to the power relations in their research."[33] What feminist activist ethnography does, however, is reveal the various ways in which power can be negotiated in the research context and that critical reflection may generate, as Morgensen notes, potentially productive tactics. A potent example of this is anthropologist and visual artist Beth Uzwiak's research on an international women's human rights agency in New York City.[34] Her research reveals a dramatic disconnection between the NGO's feminist mission and the façade it creates to maintain legitimacy with transnational human rights structures. Uzwiak calls into question the inequitable internal labor practices of feminist NGOs, which often go unnoticed—even by worker/activists themselves—in the context of the laudable broader goals of feminist organizations to achieve social justice for women around the world. Ultimately, the NGO creates an environment where workers are ideologically committed to women's human rights but, because of this commitment, do not openly refute their own mistreatment within the agency. Uzwiak questions: How much (or *how*) should we, as feminist activist ethnographers, reveal in our critical work, especially when such revelations can potentially complicate unwavering support of feminist organizations? We side with Uzwiak in this debate. Ultimately, we believe that it is incumbent upon feminist activist ethnographers to remain reflective and critical both about our own work and about the work of organizations with feminist goals.

Another factor in reflecting upon our practice of feminist activist ethnographers is that in some cases, our desire to collect data and narratives may be refused. As Savannah Shange's reflection on her interactions with Tarika demonstrates, the people we seek out to interview or build relationships with may refuse to participate in our research (see *Essential* in chapter 6). Feminist ethnographers frequently valorize ethnographic engagements that include assuming all of our interlocutors will want to share their lives with us. But in some instances, feminist ethnographers must also accept refusal, particularly if the project is about documenting painful experiences or substantiating various forms of oppression.

Urban education researcher and Indigenous (Unangax̂) scholar Eve Tuck describes the complicated relationship she has with social science research: "As fraught as research is in its complicity with power, it is one of the last places for legitimated inquiry. It is at least still a space that proclaims to care about curiosity."[35] Yet it is also a space of settler-colonial knowledge that has long denied the agency of those that are researched and the legitimacy of their own interpretations. One of the most important things contemporary researchers can do to challenge these histories is to determine limits on what they will ask and what they will write. This might take the form of turning off a recording, listening to a story but not retelling it, and choosing not to "traffic theories that cast communities as in need of salvation."[36]

While it is essential for feminist ethnographers to respect refusal among participants—and continue to probe the shortcomings of ethnographic research—we do a disservice to those whose voices are often silenced or ignored if we turn away entirely from its potential. Feminist activist ethnography offers vital opportunities to create meaningful research and relationships, contribute to social and political change, and move toward a broader vision of social justice.

◄◄ SPOTLIGHT ►►

Leith Mullings on Keeping Feminist Ethnography Meaningful

Leith Mullings *graduated from the University of Chicago and became a distinguished professor of anthropology at the Graduate Center of the City University of New York. Mullings served as president of the American Anthropological Association from 2011 to 2013. She is the author of influential articles, such as "Households Headed by Women," and the book* On Our Own Terms *(1996). Mullings's scholarship is consistently linked to her work with activist organizations for racial, economic, and social justice. In her interview for this book, conducted by Talisa Feliciano as part of her final project for Dána-Ain's course in Feminist Ethnographies at the Graduate Center CUNY in 2014, Mullings described her work as socialist feminist ethnography to signal an emphasis on the analysis of inequality, the ways in which it is produced and reproduced, and how it can be addressed. She explained that at this point in time, feminist anthropology is generally accepted in the academy, particularly the stream that emphasizes cultural critique. Yet an enduring challenge that Mullings emphasized for feminist ethnographers is how we must work to keep our scholarship meaningful.*

It is one thing to do analytic, scholarly work that your colleagues read. It's quite another thing to do work that can affect people's lives for the better. That is a challenge that I would hope feminist ethnography would address. As scholars, we have to think about how that can be done from the very outset of our work. But not all scholars are necessarily concerned about that. . . .

The challenge of making your work meaningful to the problems of ordinary people is first to make it accessible with respect to language and availability and second to the extent that you can, to work in the context of and with social movements that can use your work to help bring about change. In an era when social movements are not as intense as they were in the 1960s and 1970s, this may be more difficult. Collaborative research helps to address that. If you work with communities, not only does it make your research better, but you are also more likely to produce work that is relevant, that can help people and can be used to empower subaltern populations.

Conclusion

We have discussed activism and its connection to feminist ethnography and want to conclude by considering how activism has changed during the time that feminist ethnography has emerged as a field. Consider, for instance, how aspects of activism have transformed as social change has become increasingly linked to consumption. The (RED) Campaign, for instance, founded by U2 singer Bono and Bobby Shriver in 2006, involved business and individual consumers in the fight against AIDS by shopping. In order to create sustained flows of capital to fight AIDS, through the sales of products like Starbucks and Gap, they advocated a consumer-based approach to social change. These consumerist shifts have not necessarily changed what feminist ethnographers feel committed to in developing activist scholarship, but they are problematic for reducing activism to a financial engagement that is more available to some than to others. Indeed, consumer-based activism has not diluted the need for research, nor our willingness to participate in social movements. It is knowing of people's burdens that motivates many feminist ethnographers to do what we do and engage with activist movements and organizations.

Suggested Resources

Mary K. Anglin (2006) "Whose Health? Whose Justice? Examining Quality of Care and Breast Cancer Activism through the Intersections of Gender, Race, Ethnicity, and Class." In Health at the Intersections of Gender, Race, and Class.

Caitlin Cahill (2004) "Defying Gravity? Raising Consciousness through Collective Research." *Children's Geographies.*

Jeffrey S. Juris, and Alex Khasnabish, eds. (2013) *Insurgent Encounters: Transnational, Activism, Ethnography, and the Political.*

New Day Films https://www.newday.com/films.

Lynne Phillips and Sally Cole (2013) *Contesting Publics: Feminism, Activism, Ethnography.*

Julia Sudbury and Margo Okazawa-Rey (2009) *Activist Scholarship: Antiracism, Feminist and Social Change.*

Jennifer R. Wies and Hillary J. Haldane, eds. (2015) *Applying Anthropology to Gender-Based Violence: Global Responses, Local Practices.*

Notes

[1] Louise Lamphere, "The Perils and Prospects for an Engaged Anthropology: A View from the United States," *Social Anthropology*, 2003.

[2] Michael Burawoy, "2004 American Sociological Association Presidential Address: For Public Sociology," *American Sociological Review*, 2005.

[3] Faye V. Harrison, "Navigating Feminist Activist Ethnography," in *Feminist Activist Ethnography*, eds. Christa Craven and Dána-Ain Davis, 2013.

[4] Manisha Desai, "The Possibilities and Perils for Scholar-Activists and Activist-Scholars," in *Insurgent Encounters*, eds. Jeffrey S. Juris and Alex Khasnabish, 2013, 90.

[5] Ida Susser, "The Anthropologist as Social Critic: Working Towards a More Engaged Anthropology." *Current Anthropology*, 2010.

[6] Library of Congress, "Margaret Mead as a Cultural Commentator," 2001.

[7] Emily Martin, *The Woman in the Body: A Cultural Analysis of Reproduction*, 2001.

[8] Monica J. Casper, *The Making of the Unborn Patient: A Social Anatomy of Fetal Surgery*, 1998.

[9] Barbara Katz Rothman, *The Tentative Pregnancy: How Amniocentesis Changes the Experience of Motherhood*, 1993; Sarah Franklin, *Embodied Progress: A Cultural Account of Assisted* Conception, 2002 and Biological *Relatives: IVF, Stem Cells and the Future of Kinship*, 2013.

[10] Dorothy Roberts, *Killing The Black Body: Race, Reproduction, and the Meaning of Liberty*, 1998.

[11] Khiara Bridges, *Reproducing Race: An Ethnography of Pregnancy as a Site of Racialization*, 2011.

[12] Dána-Ain Davis, "Obstetric Racism: The Racial Politics of Pregnancy and Birthing," *Medical Anthropology*, 2018.

13 Council on Anthropology and Reproduction Advocacy Committee, "CAR Opposes Legislation that Creates Barriers to Safe Abortion Care," *Medical Anthropology Quarterly*, 2015.

14 Susan Brin Hyatt, "'Water Is Life—Meters Out!' Women's Grassroots Activism And the Privatization of Public Amenities," 2004.

15 "Black Lives Matter," accessed October 4, 2015, http://blacklivesmatter.com/.

16 Linda Tuhiwai Smith, *Decolonizing Methodologies*, 2012, 217.

17 Soyini D. Madison, *Critical Ethnography*, 2005, 5.

18 Eleanor B. Leacock, "Introduction to the Origin of the Family, Private Property, and the State, by Frederick Engels," 1972.

19 Christian Scharen and Aana Marie Vigen, *Ethnography as Christian Theology and Ethics*, 2011, 22.

20 Deborah A. Gordon, "Border Work: Feminist Ethnography and the Dissemination Literacy," in *Women Writing Culture*, eds. Ruth Behar and Deborah A. Gordon, 1995, 383.

21 Zethu Matabeni, ed., *Reclaiming Afrikan*, 2014.

22 Michelle Marzullo, "Seeking 'Marriage Material': Rethinking the U.S. Marriage Debatees Under Neoliberalism," in *Feminist Activist Ethnography*, eds. Christa Craven and Dána-Ain Davis, 2013.

23 Luke Eric Lassiter, *The Chicago Guide to Collaborative Ethnography*, 2005.

24 T.J. Jourian and Z Nicolazzo, "Bringing our Communities to the Research Table: The Liberatory Potential of Collaborative Methodological Practices Alongside LGBTQ Participants," 2017, 599.

25 Rina Benmayor, Rosa M. Torruellas, and Ana L. Juarbe, *Responses to Poverty among Puerto Rican Women*, 1992.

26 Indra Rios-Moore et al., *Makes Me Mad: Stereotypes of Young Urban Womyn of Color*, 2004.

27 Malcolm Gladwell, "Small Change, Why the Revolution Will Not Be Tweeted," *New Yorker*, 2010.

28 "Poto Mitan: Haitian Women Pillars of the Global Economy," accessed October 4, 2015. http://potomitan.net/.

29 Michelle Téllez, "Workers on the Rise," 2012, https://vimeo.com/85164509.

30 Setha M. Low and Sally Engle Merry, "Engaged Anthropology: Diversity and Dilemmas," *Current Anthropology*, 2010.

31 Charles R. Hale, *Theory, Politics and Methods of Activist Scholarship*, 2008.

32 Dána-Ain Davis, *Battered Black Women and Welfare Reform*, 2006.

33 Scott L. Morgensen, "Reflection: Fearlessly Engaging Complicity," in *Feminist Activist Ethnography*, eds. Christa Craven and Dána-Ain Davis, 2013, 72.

34 Beth Uzwiak, "Fracturing Feminism: Activist Research and Ethics in a Women's Human Rights NGO," in *Feminist Activist Ethnography*, eds. Christa Craven and Dána-Ain Davis, 2013.

35 See, for example, Eve Tuck and K. Wayne Wang, "R-Words: Refusing Research" in *Humanizing Research: Decolonizing Qualitative Inquiry with Youth and Communities*, 2014, 223, 244–245.

36 Ibid., 245.

CHAPTER 8

Thinking Through the Futures of Feminist Ethnography

> Feminist methodologies have a task.
> We conclude by asking:
> What will be yours?

In the Introduction to this textbook, we discussed the multiple ways of thinking through feminist ethnography—as project, process, product, and outcomes that can be linked to the aims of social justice. A central part of this engagement has been constructing a history of the field. Clearly, we have placed quite a bit of emphasis on the past, which is suggestive of our thinking about its importance. In our opinion, charting the past also helps to understand the present, as well as future possibilities. We invoke the past, as it relates to feminist ethnography by thinking through histories. Knowing the histories of feminist ethnography, from the early contributions of female ethnographers to the diverse and critical strands that have emerged in recent years, facilitates achieving some degree of intellectual integrity. But it also facilitates the understanding that feminist ethnography is an entanglement and its lineage is often linked to the discipline of the feminist practitioner.

What you can learn from examining histories is about not only the scope of the research and ethnography that came before but also how its practice and definition have changed over time. Definitions are particularly sticky issues, and attempts to define feminist ethnography reveal there is no one single definition. What is also clear is that in defining feminist ethnography, one inevitably ends up discussing the "doing" of feminist ethnography. Feminist ethnography does not have a single scholarly trajectory, historical course or topical focus and has circulated as a methodological tool to study culture. While the exploration of culture has most often been viewed as the purview of anthropologists, in fact feminist ethnography has rarely been only a cultural project. Its political inclinations, in both theory and practice, have been aimed at interrogating power. The flexibility of feminist ethnography is evidenced by the ways it has been shaped and produced in the hands of feminist ethnographers. As a genre, it has a long history of drawing on innovative production that seeks to expand the circulation of ideas by reaching a variety of publics. Feminist ethnography is much more than a practice, more than theory, more than principles and producing texts, performances, and engaging in social media. Feminist ethnography is praxis—an actively engaging process that is embodied, taught, learned, and relearned. Beyond that, most feminist ethnographers believe that feminist ethnography has great value because of its potential to move us toward a just and equitable world.

Feminist ethnography—as a process, practice, and product—motivates us to think politically about our work. Feminist ethnography is an approach that opens up possibilities for understanding the world in new ways and ushering in social change. As Leith Mullings explained in a 2014 interview:

> [Feminist ethnography is] the ability to step out of the traditional canon to understand and engage in analyses that can lead you to a different place, a different conclusion, a different way of seeing the world, and perhaps a different way of participating in changing the world. I do not believe that all feminist ethnography necessarily leads us to this place. It is about a philosophical worldview and political commitments. There are many different ways of doing feminist ethnography and many different types of commitment. Feminist ethnography that focuses on the conditions of women and takes a collaborative methodological approach is exciting, but for me what is much more exciting is a feminist ethnography that seeks to understand the foundations of inequality and to change them.

We do so through various lenses, including our political commitments and our ability to engage in reflexivity. While reflexivity is sometimes dismissed as a form of self-absorption, it is a strategy to think through complex power relations between the feminist ethnographer and research participants. It also centers on the relationality between the voice of research participants and the voice of the researcher. These concerns are profoundly evident in the work of feminist ethnographers of color and Indigenous scholars who have interrogated the roles of colonialism, imperialism, settler colonialism, and enslavement in the construction of knowledge and experience, recognizing that "ethnography is a gift of reciprocity, not an imperial entitlement."[1]

We believe that feminist research holds the possibility of building coalitional knowledge. That knowledge is developed through relational practices, including collaborations, supporting movements or communities, and incorporating participants into the development of the research project and the possibility of engaging in analysis. Jennifer Goett, in her research for *Black Autonomy: Race, Gender and Afro-Nicaraguan Activism* (see *Essential* excerpt in chapter 7), illustrates important coalitional possibilities for politically engaged research. Goett is committed to the activist struggle of Afro-descendant Nicaraguans and is attentive to her own racial class and national privilege as a white woman raised in the United States. She writes about how she built relationships with community members centered on political solidarity and worked collaboratively with community members who are attentive to local and global systems of oppression.

One of the most urgent interventions of feminist praxis is the consideration of citational politics. There is ample evidence across a broad range of disciplines that publications by women and nonbinary authors are cited less frequently than male authors.[2] Black women are significantly undercited by other scholars, including those who identify themselves as feminists.[3] It is incumbent upon all of us to attend to the reality that feminist scholars often reproduce exclusionary practices. Developing a citational practice cannot be done in isolation, nor in a hollow effort to position oneself as "more woke than thou." Rather, it must involve connecting with others who share these commitments who will both encourage *and* hold one another accountable. For white women in particular—and really all who benefit from privilege in the academy and beyond—this requires self-reflection about one's own positionality in relation to power and privilege. It also necessitates a collective vigilance as we engage with each other as peer reviewers, teachers, and both formal and informal reviewers. This collaborative work is, in itself, a form of transformational politics within and among communities of feminist ethnographers.

The pulse of change, a phrase used by Faye Harrison in her book *Outsider Within: Reworking Anthropology in the Global Age*,[4] aptly characterizes how feminist ethnography can intersect with activism. Many of the people we interviewed realize the force activism carries, even when it comes in different forms. Some have made choices about how to best position themselves so that they can do activist work—whether that be movement building, teaching, political lobbying, and so on. However, the possibilities for linking scholarship to activism were not always available to academics, as Louise Lamphere recalls:

> I don't think the kind of activism that [some younger people] on the panel are talking about was as possible in the 70s and 80s. . . . And when you get up to the 2000s, first of all—there are a lot of social movements that people have been studying that focus on different issues like climate, sustainability, food insecurity, LGBT marriage issues. And folks are studying those movements and are working in activist movements themselves, so the line between "I do my activism on Sundays or Saturdays and in the evenings and I do my teaching over here" has collapsed. I think [a lot of activism] has been going on among feminist anthropologists and other anthropologists for a long time. But there are other, more collaborative things [now] and the actual work on policy and/or on working for political change because you're part of a movement that's doing demonstrations or whatever, that's the new piece. . . . It doesn't mean we weren't doing some activist stuff, but we didn't engage, it wasn't possible at that point to do it in our writing and in our research in quite the same direct way that it's possible now.

The possibilities envisioned by feminist ethnographers over the past few decades have often centered around its production. Some people wanted to see more results of ethnographic research publicized beyond academic circles and feminist ethnographers produce ethnography in many ways—both on the page and off, through performance, film, and other creative projects—and there are still many opportunities for innovative work. We need not see theoretical inquiry as separate from creative work.

The choices we make about how we conduct research, who we cite, and how we produce and circulate our work must also extend to our commitments to foster the work of feminist ethnography both within and outside academia. As we point out throughout the book, ultimately the onus remains on each of us—scholars and students of feminist ethnography—to assure that we actively seek out and hold up the innovative work by women and nonbinary researchers, scholars of color, authors outside of the Global North, disabled scholars, and other groups that have been frequently overlooked in previous scholarship. In this way, we are each in a position not only to enhance our own scholarship but also to create a future for feminist ethnography that continues to push against boundaries and invigorate the field.

Notes

[1] Renée Alexander Craft, Meida Mcneal, Mshaï S. Mwangola, and Queen Meccasia E. Zabriskie, "The Quilt: Towards a Twenty-First-Century Black Feminist Ethnography," *Performance Research*, 2007, 67.

2 In addition to those reviewed in chapter 4, see recent blog posts that have emerged in response, such as Stephanie Halmhofer's "Celebrating the Women of Archaeology – 2017 Edition," *Bones, Stones, and Books* blog, 2018; and Andrea Eidinger and Krista McCraken's "Celebrating Women and Non-Binary Historians," *Unwritten Histories* blog, 2019.

3 Lynn Bolles, "Telling the Story Straight: Black Feminist Intellectual Thought in Anthropology." *Transforming Anthropology*, 2013; Christen Smith's Special Issue on the Cite Black Women Movement in *Feminist Anthropology* 1(2), 2021.

4 Faye V. Harrison, *Outsider Within*, 2008.

abolitionist movement A movement to end slavery; in the United States, the movement sought to end the African and Indian slave trade and free enslaved Africans.

adjudication board Organizational bodies that assess the merits of a claim (i.e., against ethical standards) and assess a legal punishment.

Afrofuturism A philosophy that imagines alternative visions of the future and aesthetically synthesizes astral jazz, African American sci-fi, hip-hop, historical fiction, fantasy, Afrocentricity, magic realism, and technology. It is a critique of the dilemmas that people of color experience and offers a reexamination of possibilities.

agency The capacity for an individual to act.

androcentric A focus on men, often concerning research focused primarily on men.

autoethnography A form of writing that uses self-reflection and the researcher's experience in relation to broad cultural meanings.

big data A field that uses computational analysis to reveal patterns and trends, especially relating to human behavior and interactions, with data sets that are too large or complex to be dealt with by traditional statistical tools.

binary Having two parts in contrast to each other—for example, black/white or public/private.

BIPOC Black, Indigenous, (and) people of color, frequently abbreviated to BIPOC, is a term popularized in 2020. It centers Black and Indigenous people's oppressions, though includes all people of color to acknowledge shared oppressions in white-dominated cultures. The acronyms POC and WoC (women of color) are also used by many feminist writers.

canon A body of work influential in shaping a topic or discipline.

cisgender Someone whose assigned sex and gender identity are in alignment

Chican@/Xicanx/Latin@/Latinx Gender-expansive alternatives to Chicano (also Chicano/a), Latino (also Latino/a). Xicanx is also used to identify with Indigenous heritage.

code A process of looking at data and identifying or labeling themes.

confidentiality A primary responsibility a researcher has to keep a person's information private.

consanguinity Relation by blood.

cultural asset mapping A method of collecting information about cultural resources, networks, and patterns of usage within a site or community to engage in a place-based planning process that recognizes, tracks, and promotes them.

cultural capital The nonfinancial assets, such as family status or political influence, one has to promote mobility and access to resources.

cultural relativism The notion that a culture must only be judged within its own cultural context.

cyberfeminism A term used to describe feminists involved in the use of new media technology.

demographic information/data Information about characteristics, such as gender identity, race, ancestry, nationality, religious background, or age; often used to provide background for ethnographic narratives or interviews and/or to compile statistical data for a community.

descriptive statistics Summary information, often presented in percentages, about a population.

digital humanities (digital social sciences) The application of computational and digital analysis tools and methods to humanities disciplines such as literature, history, and philosophy. Increasingly, these forms of analysis are becoming common among a wide array of social science fields.

donor agency An entity that provides financial resources for projects.

economic liberalism An economic perspective centered on the belief that individuals should make the greatest number of economic decisions.

emic The perspective of a person within a community.

empirical Verifiable research, based on observation or experience.

epistemology The nature and scope of knowledge.

essentialize/essentialism To reduce to an essence; to attribute a "natural" set of characteristics to a specific group, such as, "women are emotional."

ethnocentrism The belief that one's own culture is the appropriate standard against which to measure all others.

ethnographic authority The notion that an ethnographer holds authority by virtue of having "been there" in the field.

etic The analytical perspective of a researcher.

etiology The cause of a condition.

eugenics Controversial beliefs, laws, practices with the goal of improving genetic quality of human populations.

feminist standpoint theory An argument that when women recognize and confront the systems that keep them oppressed, they can understand that oppression from the perspective of who they are.

genocide The intentional killing of a group, usually an ethnic, racial, or religious group.

geopolitics Issues relating to nation, geography, and economics, such as diplomacy, security, financial markets, and sometimes civil disruption.

heteronormativity A perspective that heterosexuality is the "normal" sexual orientation.

hierarchize To arrange in a ranked order.

hybridity A cross between two things.

intellectual genealogy Refers to the authors one has read and who have influenced their thinking.

interdisciplinary Crossing academic or disciplinary boundaries.

intersectionality An analysis of intersecting identities—such as race, class, gender, sexuality, ability, and nation—in relation to systems of oppression.

informed consent The permission granted to the researcher by the research participant to conduct research.

informed refusal When a potential research participant chooses not to grant access to the researcher.

interlocutor A person who participates in a dialogue.

IRB (Institutional Review Board) A committee designated to review and approve research projects involving human subjects.

longitudinal Something that occurs over a long period of time, often used to describe a long-term research project and/or one where a researcher returns to the field after a period of time to obtain additional data.

means of production The nonhuman items needed to produce things, such as machines, buildings, and tools.

mestizo (masculine, or mestiza, feminine) A term used to describe a person who is of combined descent.

mixed-methods Utilizing qualitative and quantitative methods or using different methodological strategies in concert to collect data.

moral relativism A philosophical argument that all standards of right and wrong are products of time and culture; thus, we should tolerate all cultural behaviors, even when we disagree about the morality of them.

NAFTA (North Atlantic Free Trade Agreement) The 1994 agreement between Canada, the United States, and Mexico that created a trilateral rules-based trade block.

netnography Originally coined in the context of consumer research, the term refers to applying ethnographic data analysis techniques to data collected from public conversations on digital communication networks. Ethnography in the digital landscape within the social sciences is more frequently referred to as virtual ethnography or digital ethnography.

neoliberalism An economic approach that shifts away from government spending to privatization.

NGO (non-governmental organization) An organization that is typically set up by citizens as a nonprofit and is not run by any government agency.

obstetrical racism The experience of racism, particularly for Black women, during medical encounters during pregnancy labor and delivery.

open-access Free access to research; materials are often available online, free of cost or other access readers.

open-source A type of computer software that people can modify and share because its design is publicly accessible; because such applications are often developed collaboratively, they often contain fewer errors and last longer than proprietary ones.

participatory action research (PAR) A research approach involving participation and action by members of a community or group under study.

participant-observation A method or process in which the researcher participates in activities with and observes a group.

patriarchy A societal form where men hold power and women are largely excluded from it.

pedagogy A method of teaching.

periodization To divide into portions of time.

polyvocality Use of multiple voices as a way to narrate.

positionality Describes how one is situated in relation to others.

positivist Knowledge based on observable facts.

postmodernism A late-twentieth-century movement away from modernism. In the social sciences it resulted in skepticism about cultural interpretation. It is often associated with new forms of writing.

poststructuralism A mid- to late-twentieth-century intellectual movement that developed in Europe away from structuralism. As a strategy, it interrogates linguistic and other structures to demonstrate how knowledge is produced by understanding objects—such as texts.

praxis The application of knowledge and skills.

Project Camelot The code name for a counterinsurgency project launched by the US Army in 1964, which recruited anthropologists, psychologists, sociologists, economists, and other intellectuals to provide information about the cultures of countries targeted by the US military, especially in Latin America.

public intellectual A person whose scholarship and ideas go beyond the academy and circulate in nonacademic spheres.

reflexive/reflexivity To be self-referential, looking back on one's actions.

reproductive justice The complete physical, mental, spiritual, political, social, and economic well-being of women and girls based on the full achievement and protection of women's human rights.

reproductive labor Refers to the work that is done in the domestic sphere, which sustains the household and society.

reproductive loss The experience of miscarriage, stillbirth, failed adoption, infertility, and/or sterility.

settler colonialism An ongoing system of power that is characterized by the elimination of Indigenous culture and normalization continuous occupation by a dominant culture—often disguised as paternalistic benevolence.

taxonomy Classification of things.

temperance movement A nineteenth-century social movement against consuming alcohol.

Title VII Part of the Civil Rights Act of 1964 prohibiting discrimination against employees based on sex, race, color, national origin, and religion.

transcripts Typed copies of a recorded interview.

Abramovitz, Mimi, and Sandra Morgen, eds. *Taxes Are a Woman's Issue: Reframing the Debate*. New York: Feminist Press, 2006.

Abu-Lughod, Lila. "Can There Be a Feminist Ethnography?" *Women & Performance: A Journal of Feminist Theory* 5, no. 1 (1990): 7–27.

———. *Veiled Sentiments: Honor and Poetry in a Bedouin Society*. Updated ed. with a new preface. Berkeley: University of California Press, 1999 (orig. 1986).

———. *Do Muslim Women Need Saving?* Cambridge, MA: Harvard University Press, 2013.

Aenerud, Rebecca. "Thinking Again: This Bridge Called My Back and the Challenge to Whiteness." In *This Bridge We Call Home: Radical Visions for Transformation*, edited by Gloria Anzaldúa and AnaLouise Keating. New York: Routledge, 2002.

Agathangelou, Anna M., and Lily H. M. Ling. "An Unten (ur) Able Position: The Politics of Teaching for Women of Color in the US." *International Feminist Journal of Politics* 4, no. 3 (2002): 368–98.

Ahmed, Sara. *The Cultural Politics of Emotion*. New York: Routledge, 2004.

———. *Queer Phenomenology: Orientations, Objects, Others*. Durham, NC: Duke University Press, 2006.

———. *The Promise of Happiness*. Durham, NC: Duke University Press, 2010.

Alexander, M. Jacqui, and Chandra Talpade Mohanty. *Feminist Genealogies, Colonial Legacies, Democratic Futures*. New York: Routledge, 1997.

Allen, Jafari. *¡Venceremos?: The Erotics of Black Self-making in Cuba*. Durham, NC: Duke University Press, 2011.

American Anthropological Association. "Code of Ethics of the American Anthropological Association." *AAA Ethics Blog: A Forum Sponsored by the AAA Committee on Ethics*, 2012. http://ethics.aaanet.org/category/statement/.

American Sociological Association. "American Sociological Association Code of Ethics." The American Sociological Association, 2008. http://www.asanet.org/images/asa/docs/pdf/CodeofEthics.pdf.

Andaya, Elise. *Conceiving Cuba: Reproduction, Women, and the State in the Post-Soviet Era*. New Brunswick, NJ: Rutgers University Press, 2014.

Angel-Ajani, Asale. *Strange Trade: The Story of Two Women Who Risked Everything in the International Drug Trade*. Berkeley, CA: Seal Press, 2010.

Anglin, Mary.0 "Whose Health? Whose Justice? Examining Quality of Care and Breast Cancer Activism through the Intersections of Gender, Race, Ethnicity, and Class." In *Health at the Intersections of Gender, Race, and Class*, edited by Amy Schulz and Leith Mullings, 313–41. New York: Jossey-Bass/Pfeiffer, 2006.

Anzaldúa, Gloria. *Borderlands/La Frontera: The New Mestiza*. San Francisco, CA: Aunt Lute, 1987.

Archibald, Jo-Ann (Q'um Q'um Xiiem). *Indigenous Storywork: Educating the Heart, Mind, Body, and Spirit*. Vancouver: University of British Columbia Press, 2008.

Archibald, Jo-Ann, Jenny Bol Jun Lee-Morgan, and Jason De Santolo, eds. *Decolonizing Research: Indigenous Storywork as Methodology*. London: Zed Books, 2019.

Aretxaga, Begoña. *Shattering Silence: Women, Nationalism, and Political Subjectivity in Northern Ireland*. Princeton: Princeton University Press, 1997.

Asch, Adrienne, and Michelle Fine. "Shared Dreams: A Left Perspective on Disability Rights and Reproductive Rights." *Radical America* 18, no. 4 (1984): 51–58.

Association for Queer Anthropology. "Awards." *Association for Queer Anthropology*, n.d. http://queeranthro.org/awards/.

Atay, Ahmet. *Globalization's Impact on Cultural Identity Formation: Queer Diasporic Males in Cyberspace*. Lanham, MD: Lexington Books, 2015.

Aizura, Aren Z. *Mobile Subjects: Transnational Imaginaries of Gender Reassignment*. Durham, NC: Duke University Press,: Duke University Press, 2018.

Babb, Florence. *Between Field and Cooking Pot: The Political Economy of Marketwomen in Peru*. Austin: University of Texas Press, 1989.

———. *After Revolution: Mapping Gender and Cultural Politics in Neoliberal Nicaragua*. Austin: University of Texas Press, 2001.

———. *The Tourism Encounter: Fashioning Latin American Nations and Histories*. Stanford: Stanford University Press, 2011.

Baca Zinn, Maxine, and Bonnie Thornton Dill, eds. *Women of Color in U.S. Society*. Philadelphia, PA: Temple University Press, 1993.

Bailey, Marlon M. *Butch Queens Up in Pumps: Gender, Performance, and Ballroom Culture in Detroit*. Ann Arbor: University of Michigan Press, 2013.

Bailey, Moya. "#transform(ing)DH Writing and Research: An Autoethnography of Digital Humanities and Feminist Ethics." *Digital Humanities Quarterly* 9, no 2 (2015).

———. *Misogynoir Transformed: Black Women's Digital Resistance*. New York: New York University Press, 2021.

Baker, Lee D. *From Savage to Negro: Anthropology and the Construction of Race, 1896–1954*. Berkeley: University of California Press, 1998.

———. *Anthropology and the Racial Politics of Culture*. Durham, NC: Duke University Press, 2010.

Baker, Lee, ed. *Life in America: Identity and Everyday Experience*. Malden, MA: Wiley-Blackwell, 2003.

Basu, Srimati. "Hiding in Plain Sight: Disclosure, Identity, and the Indian Men's Rights Movement," *QED: A Journal in GLBTQ Worldmaking* 5, no. 3 (2018): 117–29.

Bates, Daisy. *My Natives and I*. Edited by Peter J Bridge. Carlisle, Western Australia: Hesperian Press, 2004.

Battle-Baptiste, Whitney. *Black Feminist Archaeology*. Walnut Creek, CA: Left Coast Press, 2011.

Baumgardner, Jennifer, and Amy Richards. *Manifesta: Young Women, Feminism and the Future*. New York: Farrar, Straus and Giroux, 2000.

Behar, Ruth. *The Vulnerable Observer: Anthropology That Breaks Your Heart*. Boston, MA: Beacon Press, 1996.

———. *Translated Woman: Crossing the Border with Esperanza's Story*. 2nd ed. Boston, MA: Beacon Press, 2003.

Behar, Ruth, and Deborah A. Gordon. *Women Writing Culture*. Berkeley: University of California Press, 1996.

Bell, Diane, Pat Caplan, and Wazir Jahan Karim. *Gendered Fields: Women, Men and Ethnography*. New York: Routledge, 2013.

Benmayor, Rina, Rosa M. Torruellas, and Ana L. Juarbe. *Responses to Poverty among Puerto Rican Women: Identity, Community, and Cultural Citizenship*. Centro de Estudios Puertorriqueños, Hunter College of the City University of New York, 1992.

Berry, Maya J., Claudia Chávez Argüelles, Shanya Cordis, Sarah Ihmoud, and Elizabeth Velásquez Estrada. "Toward a Fugitive Anthropology: Gender, Race, and Violence in the Field." *Cultural Anthropology* 32, no. 4 (November 20, 2017): 537–65.

Blake, Samantha. "Why Some People Still Think 'Feminist' Is a Dirty Word." *Medium*. September 1, 2020. https://medium.com/equality-includes-you/why-some-people-still-think-feminist-is-a-dirty-word-4583e8a1dd94, 2020.

"Black Lives Matter." Accessed October 4, 2015. http://blacklivesmatter.com/.

Blackwood, Evelyn. *The Many Faces of Homosexuality: Anthropological Approaches To Homosexuality*. New York: Routledge, 1986.

———. "Tombois in West Sumatra: Constructing Masculinity and Erotic Desire." *Cultural Anthropology* 13, no. 4 (1998): 491–521.

———. *Falling into the Lesbi World: Desire and Difference in Indonesia*. Honolulu: University of Hawaii Press, 2010.

Blackwood, Evelyn, and Saskia Wieringa, eds. *Same-Sex Relations and Female Desires: Transgender Practices Across Cultures*. New York: Columbia University Press, 1999.

Blee, Kathleen. *Women of the Klan: Racism and Gender in the 1920s*. Berkeley: University of California Press, 2008 (orig. 1991).

Boddy, Janice Patricia. *Civilizing Women: British Crusades in Colonial Sudan*. Princeton: Princeton University Press, 2007.

Boellstorff, Tom. *The Gay Archipelago: Sexuality and Nation in Indonesia*. Princeton: Princeton University Press, 2005.

———. "Queer Studies in the House of Anthropology." *Annual Review of Anthropology* 36 (2007): 17–35.

———. *Coming of Age in Second Life: An Anthropologist Explores the Virtually Human*. Princeton: Princeton University Press, 2008.

Boellstorff, Tom, Bonnie Nardi, Celia Pearce, and T. L. Taylor, eds. *Ethnography and Virtual Worlds: A Handbook of Method*. Princeton: Princeton University Press, 2012.

Bolles, A. Lynn. *Sister Jamaica: A Study of Women Work and Households in Kingston*. Lanham, MD: University Press of America, 1996.

———. *We Paid our Dues: Women Trade Union Leaders of the Caribbean*. Washington, DC: Howard University Press, 1996.

———. "Telling the Story Straight: Black Feminist Intellectual Thought in Anthropology." *Transforming Anthropology* 21, no. 1 (2013): 57–71.

Bookman, Ann, and Sandra Morgen, eds. *Women and the Politics of Empowerment*. Philadelpha: Temple University Press, 1988.

Bourque, Susan, and Kay Warren. *Women of the Andes: Patriarchy and Social Change in Two Peruvian Towns*. Ann Arbor: University of Michigan Press, 1981.

Bowen, Elenore Smith. *Return to Laughter: An Anthropological Novel*. New York: Anchor, 1964.

Bradley, Candice. "Doing Fieldwork with Diabetes." *Cultural Anthropology Methods* 9, no. 2 (1997): 1–8.

Bridges, Khiara M. *Reproducing Race: An Ethnography of Pregnancy as a Site of Racialization*. Berkeley: University of California Press, 2011.

Bridgman, Rae, Sally Cole, and Heather Howard-Bobiwash, eds. *Feminist Fields: Ethnographic Insights*. Ontario: Broadview Press, 1999.

Brodkin Sacks, Karen. *Caring by the Hour: Women, Work, and Organizing at Duke Medical Center*. Champaign: University of Illinois Press, 1988.

Brophy, Al. "Seminal and Germinal: A Study in Progression and Retrogression," *BlackProf* blog, November 2016 (no longer available), reposted on at *The Faculty Lounge: Conversations about Law, Culture and Academia* (blog), March 30, 2010, https://www.thefacultylounge.org /2010/03/seminal-and-germinal-a-study -in-progression-and-retrogression.html.

Brown, Lindsey, and Felicity K. Boardman. "Accessing the Field: Disability and the Research Process." *Social Science & Medicine* 72, no. 1 (2011): 23–30.

Browne, Kath, and Catherine J. Nash, eds. *Queer Methods and Methodologies: Intersecting Queer Theories and Social Science Research*. Farnham, Surrey, UK; Burlington, VT: Ashgate, 2010.

Brown University, Pembroke Center for Teaching and Research on Women. "Exhibit—The Lamphere Case: The Sex Discrimination Lawsuit That Changed Brown," 2015. http://www.brown.edu /research/pembroke-center/archives/ christine-dunlap-farnham-archives/lou ise-lamphere-v-brown-university/exhibit -lamphere-case-.

Burawoy, Michael. "2004 American Sociological Association Presidential Address." *American Sociological Review* 70 (2005): 4–28.

Butler, Octavia. "Furor Scribendi." In *Bloodchild and Other Stories*, 139–42. New York: Seven Stories Press, 1996.

Cahill, Caitlin. "Defying Gravity? Raising Consciousness through Collective Research." *Children's Geographies* 2, no. 2 (2004): 273–86.

Cahill, Caitlin, Indra Rios-Moore, and Tiffany Threatts. "Different Eyes/Open Eyes." *Revolutionizing Education: Youth Participatory Action in Motion*, edited by Julio Cammarota and Michelle Fine, 89–124. New York: Routledge, 2008.

Caldwell, Kia Lilly, Kathleen Coll, Tracy Fisher, Renya K. Ramirez, and Lok Siu, eds. *Gendered Citizenships: Transnational Perspectives on Knowledge Production, Political Activism, and Culture*. New York: Palgrave Macmillan, 2009.

Campos, Elisia Ixchelle. "Cruising the Borderlands: Queer Latinx Creating Space in Lowrider Culture," *Senior Independent Study Theses*. Paper 7203, 2016. https:/ /openworks.wooster.edu/independentstud y/7203.

Casper, Monica J. *The Making of the Unborn Patient: A Social Anatomy of Fetal Surgery*. New Brunswick, NJ: Rutgers University Press, 1998.

Castillo, Ana. *Massacre of the Dreamers: Essays on Xicanisma*. Albuquerque: University of New Mexico Press, 1994.

Cesara, Manda. *Reflections of a Woman Anthropologist: No Hiding Place*. Studies in Anthropology. London; New York: Academic Press, 1982.

Chari, Sharad, and Henrike Donner. "Ethnographies of Activism." Special Double Issue, *Cultural Dynamics* 22(2) (2010): 75–85.

Cheater, Christine. "Kaberry, Phyllis Mary (1910–1977)." In *Australian Dictionary of Biography*. Canberra: National Centre of Biography, Australian National University. Accessed October 4, 2015. http://adb.anu.edu.au/biography/kaberry-phyllis-mary-10654.

Chin, Elizabeth. *Purchasing Power: Black Kids, America and Consumer Culture*. Minneapolis: University of Minnesota Press, 2001.

———. "The Neoliberal Institutional Review Board, or Why Just Fixing the Rules Won't Help Feminist (Activist) Ethnographers." In *Feminist Activist Ethnography: Counterpoints to Neoliberalism in North America*, edited by Christa Craven and Dána-Ain Davis, 201–116. Lanham, MD: Lexington Books, 2013.

———. *My Life with Things: The Consumer Diaries*. Durham, NC: Duke University Press, 2016.

Chin, Elizabeth, ed. *Katherine Dunham: Recovering an Anthropological Legacy, Choreographing Ethnographic Futures*. Advanced Seminar Series. Santa Fe: School for Advanced Research Press, 2014.

Chodorow, Nancy. Family Structure and Feminine Personality. In *Woman, Culture, and Society*, edited by Michelle Rosaldo and Louise Lamphere, 43–66. Stanford: Stanford University Press, 1974.

Christian, Barbara. "The Race for Theory." *Cultural Critique* 6 (1987): 51–63.

Christian, Tanya A. "Trending Topics," *Essence*. 48, no. 11 (April 2018): 61–62.

Cite Black Women website, accessed January 8, 2020, https://www.citeblackwomencollective.org/.

City University of New York Graduate Center, PhD Program in Anthropology. "The Impact of Welfare Reform on Two Communities in New York City." W. K. Kellogg Foundation. Accessed January 15, 2016. http://www.wkkf.org/resource-directory/resource/2003/01/the-impact-of-welfare-reform-on-two-communities-in-new-york-city.

Clair, Robin Paric. "The Changing Story of Ethnography." In *Expressions of Ethnography: Novel Approaches to Qualitative Methods*, edited by Robin Paric Clair, 3–28. Albany: State University of New York Press, 1992.

Cohen, Cathy J. *Democracy Remixed: Black Youth and the Future of American Politics*. Oxford; New York: Oxford University Press, 2010.

———. "Black Youth Project." *Black Youth Project*. Accessed October 4, 2015. http://www.blackyouthproject.com/.

Cole, Sally Cooper, Rae Bridgman, and Heather Howard-Bobiwash. *Feminist Fields: Ethnographic Insights*. Ontario: Broadview Press, 1999.

Collins, Patricia Hill. *Black Feminist Thought: Knowledge, Consciousness, and the Politics of Empowerment*, 2nd ed. New York: Routledge, 2009 [orig. 1990].

Collins, Patricia Hill and Sirma Bilge. *Intersectionality*. Malden, MA: Polity Press, 2016.

Combahee River Collective. *The Combahee River Collective Statement: Black Feminist Organizing in the Seventies and Eighties*. New York: Kitchen Table, Women of Color Press, 1986.

Compton, D'Lane R., Tey Meadow, and Kristen Schilt, eds. *Other, Please Specify: Queer Methods in Sociology*. Oakland, CA: University of California Press, 2018.

Conquergood, Dwight. "Performing as a Moral Act: Ethical Dimensions of the Ethnography of Performance," *Literature in Performance 5*, no. 2 (1985): 1–13.

Council on Anthropology and Reproduction. "The Council on Anthropology and Reproduction (CAR) Opposes Legislation That Creates Barriers to Safe Abortion Care." *Medical Anthropology Quarterly* 30: Na–Na (2015).

Cox, Aimee Meredith. *Shapeshifters: Black Girls and the Choreography of Citizenship*. Durham, NC: Duke University Press, 2015.

Craft, Renée Alexander, Meida Mcneal, Mshaï S. Mwangola, and Queen Meccasia E. Zabriskie. "The Quilt: Towards a Twenty-First-Century Black Feminist Ethnography." *Performance Research* 12, no. 3 (2007): 55–73.

Craven, Christa. *Pushing for Midwives: Homebirth Mothers and the Reproductive Rights Movement*. Philadelphia, PA: Temple University Press, 2010.

———. "Reproductive Rights in a Consumer Rights Era: Toward the Value of 'Constructive' Critique." In *Feminist Activist Ethnography: Counterpoints to Neoliberalism in North America*, edited by Christa Craven and Dána-Ain Davis, 100–116. Lanham, MD: Lexington Books, 2013.

———. *Reproductive Losses: Challenges to LGBTQ Family-Making*, in "Gender and Sexualities in Psychology" Book Series (Elizabeth Peel and Elizabeth Stokoe, eds.) with Routledge Press, 2019.

———. "LGBTQ+ Reproductive Loss." LGBTQ+ Reproductive Loss companion website, 2019. https://www.lgbtqreproductiveloss.org/.

Craven, Christa, and Dána-Ain Davis, eds. *Feminist Activist Ethnography: Counterpoints to Neoliberalism in North America*. Lanham, MD: Lexington Books, 2013.

Crenshaw, Kimberlé. "Mapping the Margins: Intersectionality, Identity Politics and Violence Against Women of Color." *Stanford Law Review* 43, no. 6 (1991): 1241–99.

Dahl, Ulrika. "Femme on Femme: Reflections on Collaborative Methods and Queer Femme-inist Ethnography." In *Queer Methods and Methodologies*, edited by Kath Browne and Catherine J. Nash, 143–66. Farnham, Surrey, UK; Burlington, VT: Ashgate, 2010.

Dahl, Ulrika, and Jenny Payne Gunnarson, eds. "Special Issue: Kinship & Reproduction." *Lambda Nordica*, no. 3/4 (2014). http://www.lambdanordica.se/en/2015/06/03/nytt-nummer-3-42014-kinship-reproduction/.

Dahl, Ulrika, and Del LaGrace Volcano. *Femmes of Power: Exploding Queer Femininities*. London: Serpent's Tail, 2009.

Dave, Naisargi. *Queer Activism in India: A Story in the Anthropology of Ethics*. Durham, NC: Duke University Press, 2012.

Davids, Tine. "Trying to Be a Vulnerable Observer: Matters of Agency, Solidarity and Hospitality in Feminist Ethnography." *Women's Studies International Forum* 43, March–April (2014): 50–58.

Davis, Angela Y. *Women, Race, & Class*. New York: Vintage, 2011 (Orig. 1981).

Davis, Dána-Ain. *Battered Black Women and Welfare Reform: Between a Rock and a Hard Place*. Albany: State University of New York Press, 2006.

———. "Border Crossings: Intimacy and Feminist Activist Ethnography in the Age of Neoliberalism." In *Feminist Activist Ethnography: Counterpoints to Neoliberalism in North America*, edited by Christa Craven and Dána-Ain Davis, 29–38. Lanham, MD: Lexington Books, 2013.

———. "Katherine Dunham Made Me . . ." In *Katherine Dunham: Recovering an Anthropological Legacy, Choreographing Ethnographic Futures*, edited by Elizabeth Chin, 101–26. Advanced Seminar Series. Santa Fe: School for Advanced Research Press, 2014.

———. "Obstetric Racism: The Racial Politics of pregnancy and Birthing." *Medical Anthropology*, 38, no. 3 (2018): 1–14.

———. *Reproductive Injustice: Racism, Pregnancy, and Premature Birth*. New York: New York University Press, 2019.

Davis, Dána-Ain, Ana Aparicio, Audrey Jacobs, Akemi Kochiyama, Leith Mullings, Andrea Queeley, and Beverly Thompson. "Working It Off: Welfare Reform, Workfare and Work Experience Programs in New York City." *Souls: A Critical Journal of Black Politics, Culture and Society* 5, no. 2 (2003): 22–41.

Davis, Dána-Ain, and Christa Craven. "Revisiting Feminist Ethnography: Methods and Activism at the Intersection of Neoliberal Policy." *Feminist Formations* 23, no. 2 (2011): 190–208.

———. "Equity at the Peril of Normativity: A Feminist Anthropological Take on Race, Marriage and Justice." *The Feminist Wire*, 2013. http://thefeministwire.com/2013/06/equity-at-the-peril-of-normativity-a-feminist-anthropological-take-on-race-marriage-justice/.

Davis, Dána-Ain, and Shaka McGlotten, eds. *Black Genders and Sexualities*. New York: Palgrave Macmillan, 2012.

Davis, Dána-Ain, Cheyenne Varner, and LeConté J. Dill. "A Birth Story," *Anthropology News* website, August 27, 2021.

Deacon, Desley. *Elsie Clews Parsons: Inventing Modern Life*. Women in Culture and Society Series. Chicago, IL: University of Chicago Press, 1997.

DeLoache, Judy S., and Alma Gottlieb, eds. *A World of Babies: Imagined Childcare Guides for Seven Societies*. Cambridge; New York: Cambridge University Press, 2000.

Deloria, Ella Cara. *Waterlily*. Lincoln: University of Nebraska Books, 1988.

Deomampo, Daisy. *Deomampo, Daisy. Transnational Reproduction: Race, Kinship, and Commercial Surrogacy in India*. New York: New York University Press, 2016.

Desai, Manisha. "The Possibilities and Perils for Scholar-Activists and Activist-Scholars: Reflections on the Feminist Dialogues." In *Insurgent Encounters: Transnational Activism, Ethnography, and the Political*, edited by Jeffrey S. Juris and Alex Khasnabish, 89–107. Durham, NC: Duke University Press, 2013.

di Leonardo, Micaela, ed. *Gender at the Crossroads of Knowledge*. Berkeley: University of California Press, 1991.

———. "Introduction: Gender, Culture and Political Economy: Feminist Anthropology in Historical Perspective." In *Gender at the Crossroads of Knowledge*, edited by Micaela di Leonardo, 1–49. Berkeley: University of California Press, 1991.

di Leonardo, Micaela, and Roger Lancaster. "Gender, Sexuality, Political Economy." *New Politics* 6, no. 1 (1996).

Dill, Bonnie Thornton, and Ruth Enid Zambrana, eds. *Emerging Intersections: Race, Class, and Gender in Theory, Policy, and Practice*. New Brunswick, NJ: Rutgers University Press, 2009.

Dominguez, Virginia, Matthew Guttman, and Catherine Lutz. "Problem of Gender and Citations Raised Again in New Research Study." *Anthropology News* (2014): 19.

Durban, Erin L. 2021. "Anthropology and Ableism." *American Anthropologist* 124 (4): 1–14.

Eidinger, Andrea, and Krista McCraken. 2019. "Celebrating Women and Non-Binary Historians," *Unwritten Histories* (blog), January 8, 2019. https://www.unwrittenhistories.com/celebrating-women-and-non-binary-historians/.

Ellingson, Laura L. 2006. "Embodied Knowledge: Writing Researchers' Bodies into Qualitative Health Research." *Qualitative Health Research* 16 (2): 298–310.

Ellis, Carolyn. *The Ethnographic I: A Methodological Novel about Autoethnography*. Lanham, MD: Rowman Altamira, 2004.

Engebretsen, Elisabeth L. *Queer Women in Urban China: An Ethnography*. New York: Routledge, 2015.

Engebretsen, Elisabeth L., William F. Schroeder, and Hongwei Bao, eds. *Queer/Tongzhi China: New Perspectives on Research, Activism, and Media*. Copenhagen, Denmark: Nordic Institute of Asian Studies Press, 2015.

Engels, Frederich. *The Conditions of the Working Class in England*. Leipzig, Germany: Otto Wigand, 1845.

———. *Origin of the Family, Private Property and the State*, Hottingen-Zürich, Germany: Verlag der Schweizerischen, Volkbuchhandlung, 1884.

Enloe, Cynthia. *Seriously! Investigating Crashes and Crises as If Women Mattered*. Berkeley and Los Angeles: University of California Press, 2013.

Enloe, Cynthia H. *Globalization and Militarism: Feminists Make the Link*. Lanham, MD: Rowman & Littlefield, 2007.

Erzen, Tanya. *Straight to Jesus: Sexual and Christian Conversions in the Ex-Gay Movement*. Berkeley: University of California Press, 2006.

———. *Fanpire: The Twilight Saga and the Women Who Love It*. Boston, MA: Beacon Press, 2012.

Espiritu, Yen Le. *Asian American Panethnicity: Bridging Institutions and Identities*. Philadelphia: Temple University Press, 1993.

Fajardo, Kale. *Filipino Crosscurrents: Oceanographies of Seafaring, Masculinities, and Globalization*. Minneapolis: Minnesota University Press, 2011

Families of Choice in Poland, Institute of Psychology, Polish Academy of Sciences. "Conference: Queer Kinship and Relationships," June 2015. https://www.ncfr.org/events/calendar/queer-kinship-and-relationships-2015-conference.

"The Feminist Ethnographer's Dilemma." Accessed October 5, 2015. http://bcrw.barnard.edu/videos/the-feminist-ethnographers-dilemma/.

Feministing. "Katherine Cross Archive." Accessed October 4, 2015. http://feministing.com/author/katherinecross/.

feministkilljoys. "Making Feminist Points." *Feministkilljoys*, September 11, 2013. http://feministkilljoys.com/2013/09/11/making-feminist-points/.

Fernández-Kelley, Maria Patricia. *For We Are Sold, I and My People: Women and Industry in Mexico's Frontier*. Albany: State University of New York Press, 1984.

Fernea, Elizabeth Warncock. *Guests of the Sheik: An Ethnography of an Iraqi Village*. New York: Doubleday Anchor, 1969.

Field, Les W. "Complicities and Collaborations: Anthropologists and the 'Unacknowledged Tribes' of California."

Current Anthropology 40, no. 2 (1999): 193–210.

Fine, Michelle, Maria Elena Torre, Iris Boudin, Judith Clark, Donna Hylton, Migdalia Martinez, "Missy" Melissa Rviera, Rosemarie Roberts, Pamela Smart, and Debora Upegui. *Changing Minds: The Impact of College In a Maximum-Security Prison*. A Collaborative Research Project by the Graduate Center of the City University of New York and the Women in Prison at the Bedford Hills Correctional Facility, 2001.

Fisher, Melissa. *Wall Street Women*. Durham, NC: Duke University Press, 2012.

Fisher, Tracy. *What's Left of Blackness: Feminisms, Transracial Solidarities, and the Politics of Belonging in Britain*. Comparative Feminist Studies. New York: Palgrave Macmillan, 2012.

Fletcher, Alice Cunningham, and Francis A. LaFlesche. *The Omaha Tribe*, Vol 2. Bison Book Edition reproduced form the 27th Annual Report of the Bureau of American Ethnology to the Secretary of the Smithsonian Institution, 1905–1906. Washington: Government Printing Office, 1911.

Franklin, Sarah. *Embodied Progress: A Cultural Account of Assisted Conception*. New York: Routledge, 2002.

———. *Biological Relatives: IVF, Stem Cells, and the Future of Kinship*. Durham, NC: Duke University Press, 2013.

Frederickson, Mary E., and Delores M. Walters, eds. *Gendered Resistance: Women, Slavery, and the Legacy of Margaret Garner*. New Black Studies. Urbana: University of Illinois Press, 2013.

Freeman, Carla. *High Tech and High Heels in the Global Economy: Women, Work, and Pink-Collar Identities in the Caribbean*. Durham, NC: Duke University Press, 2000.

Freidan, Betty. *The Feminine Mystique*. New York: W. W. Norton, 1963.

Freire, Paulo. *Pedagogy of the Oppressed*. 30th anniversary ed. New York: Continuum, 2000.

Garcia, Sandra E. 2020. "Where Did BIPOC Come From?" New York Times (Online). New York, United States: New York Times Company. June 15, 2020. http://www.proquest.com/docview/2413212043/citation/C0B82141984A42D2PQ/1.

Gardner, Susan. "Introduction." In *Waterlily*, xxxiii. University of Nebraska, 2009.

Gaudio, Rudolf Pell. *Allah Made Us: Sexual Outlaws in an Islamic Society*. Malden, MA: Wiley-Blackwell, 2009.

Ghaziani, Amin and Matt Brim, eds. *Imagining Queer Methods*. New York: New York University Press, 2019.

Geertz, Clifford. "Thick Description; Toward an Interpretive Theory of Culture." In *The Interpretation of Cultures*, 3–30. New York: Basic Books, 1973.

Gill, Harjant, dir. *Milind Soman Made Me Gay*. 27 mins. In Punjabi & English w/subtitles. Produced by Tilotama Productions, 2007.

———. *Roots of Love*. 26 mins. In Punjabi & English w/subtitles. Produced by PSBT (Public Service Broadcasting Trust), 2011.

———. *Mardistan (Macholand) Reflections on Indian Manhood*. 28 mins. In Punjabi & English w/subtitles. Produced by PSBT (Public Service Broadcasting Trust), Tilotama Productions, 2014.

Ginsburg, Faye. "Procreation Stories: Reproduction, Nurturance, and Procreation in Life Narratives of Abortion Activists." *American Ethnologist* 14, no. 4 (1987): 623–36.

———. *Contested Lives: The Abortion Debate in an American Community*. Berkeley: University of California Press, 1998.

Gladwell, Malcolm. "Small Change, Why the Revolution Will Not Be Tweeted." *New Yorker*, October 4, 2010.

Gordon, Deborah A. "Border Work: Feminist Ethnography and the Dissemination of Literacy." In *Women Writing Culture*, edited by Ruth Behar and Deborah A. Gordon, 373–89. Berkeley: University of California Press, 1995.

Gottlieb, Alma and Judy DeLoache, Eds. *A World of Babies: Imagined Childcare Guides for Eight Societies* Updated Edition, 2016. Cambridge: Cambridge University Press.

Gray, Mary L. *Out in the Country: Youth, Media, and Queer Visibility in Rural America*. New York: New York University Press, 2009.

———. "Stop Blaming Dharun Ravi: Why We Need to Share Responsibility for the Loss of Tyler Clementi." *The Huffington Post*, 2012. Accessed October 5, 2015. http://www.huffingtonpost.com/mary

-l-gray-phd/tyler-clementi_b_1317688
.html.

———. "Why LGBT Communities and Our
Allies Should Care about Net Neutrality." *The Huffington Post*, 2014. http://
www.huffingtonpost.com/mary-l-gray
-phd/why-lgbt-communities-and-_b
_6147802.html.

Gupta, Akhil, and James Ferguson. "Discipline and Practice: 'The Field' as Site,
Method, and Location in Anthropology."
*Anthropological Locations: Boundaries
and Grounds of a Field Science* 100
(1997): 1–47.

Gutmann, Matthew C. *The Meanings of
Macho: Being a Man in Mexico City*.
Men and Masculinity 3. Berkeley: Uni-
versity of California Press, 1996.

Hale, Charles R. *Engaging Contradictions:
Theory, Politics, and Methods of Activist
Scholarship*. Berkeley: University of Cali-
fornia Press, 2008.

Halmhofer, Stephanie. 2018. "Celebrating the Women of Archaeology—2017
Edition." *Bones, Stones, and Books*
(blog). January 4, 2018. https://bon-
esstonesandbooks.com/2018/01/04/cele-
brating-the-women-of-archaeology-2017
-edition/.

Hancock, Ange-Marie. *Intersectionality: An
Intellectual History*. New York: Oxford
University Press, 2016.

Harding, Sandra G. *Feminism and Methodology: Social Science Issues*. Bloomington: Indiana University Press, 1987.

Harrison, Faye V. "'Three Women, One
Struggle': Anthropology, Performance,
and Pedagogy." *Transforming Anthropology* 1, no. 1 (1990): 1–9.

———. "Feminist Methodology as a Tool for
Ethnographic Inquiry on Globalization."
In *The Gender of Globalization: Women
Navigating Cultural and Economic Mar-
ginalities*, edited by Nandini Gunewar-
dena and Ann Kingsolver, 23–31. Santa
Fe, NM: School for Advanced Research
Press, 2007.

———. *Outsider Within: Reworking
Anthropology in the Global Age*. Chicago: University of Illinois Press, 2008.

———. "Navigating Feminist Activist Ethnography." In *Feminist Activist Ethnography: Counterpoints to Neoliberalism in
North America*, edited by Dána-Ain Davis
and Christa Craven, ix–xv. Lanham, MD:
Lexington, 2013.

Harrison, Faye V., ed. *Decolonizing
Anthropology: Moving Further Toward
an Anthropology for Liberation*. Washington, DC: Association of Black
Anthropologists, American Anthropological Association, 1991.

Heath, James. 2021. "Opinion: The Term
'BIPOC' Is a Bad Fit for the Canadian Discourse on Race." *The Globe and Mail*, May
28, 2021. https://www.theglobeandmail
.com/opinion/article-the-term-bipoc-is-a
-bad-fit-for-the-canadian-discourse-on-race/.

Herdt, Gilbert. *Guardians of the Flutes:
Idioms of Masculinity: A Study of Rit-
ualized Homosexual Behavior*. New
York: McGraw-Hill Book Co, with
Company, 1981.

Hernández, Graciela. "Multiple Mediations
in Zora Neale Hurston's *Mules and
Men*." *Critique of Anthropology* 13, no.
4 (1993): 351–62.

Hesse-Biber, Sharlene Nagy. *Feminist
Research Practice: A Primer*. 2nd ed.
Thousand Oaks, CA: SAGE Publi-
cations, 2014.

Ho, Karen. *Liquidated: An Ethnography
of Wall Street*. Durham: Duke University
Press, 2009.

Hodgson, Dorothy L. "Critical Inter-
ventions: Dilemmas of Accountability in
Contemporary Ethnographic Research."
Identities 6, no. 2–3 (1999): 201–24.

———. "Introduction: Comparative
Perspectives on the Indigenous Rights
Movement in Africa and the Americas." *American Anthropologist* 104, no.
4 (2002): 1037–49.

———. *Being Maasai, Becoming Indigenous: Postcolonial Politics in a Neoliberal World*. South Bend, IN: Indiana
University Press, 2011.

hooks, bell. *Feminist Theory: From Margin
to Center*. Cambridge, MA: South End
Press, 2000.

Huggins, Martha K., and Marie-Louise
Glebbeek, eds. *Women Fielding Danger:
Negotiating Ethnographic Identities in
Field Research*. Lanham, MD: Rowman
& Littlefield Publishers, 2009.

Hunter, Nan D. "Contextualizing the
Sexuality Debates: A Chronology
1966–2005." In *Sex Wars: Sexual
Dissent and Political Culture*, edited by
Lisa Duggan and Nan D. Hunter, 10th
Anniversary Edition, 15–28. New York:
Taylor & Francis, 2006.

Hurston, Zora Neale. *Mules and Men.* Urbana and Chicago: University of Chicago Press, 1978 (orig. 1935).

———. *Their Eyes Were Watching God.* New York: Harper Perennial Modern Classics, 2013 (orig. 1937).

———. *Tell My Horse: Voodoo and Life in Haiti and Jamaica.* New York: Harper Collins, 1990 (orig. 1938).

Hurtado, Aída. *The Color of Privilege: Three Blasphemies on Race and Feminism.* Ann Arbor: University of Michigan Press, 1997.

Hyatt, Susan Brin. "Water Is Life—Meters Out! Women's Grassroots Activism And the Privatization of Public Amenities." *Globalization Research Center. Occasional Papers on Globalization,* University of South Florida, Vol. 1 (7) (June 2004).

Hyatt, Susan Brin, Boone W. Shear, and Susan Wright, eds. *Learning under Neoliberalism: Ethnographies of Governance in Higher Education.* New York: Berghahn Books, 2015.

Inhorn, Marcia C. *Quest for Conception: Gender, Infertility and Egyptian Medical Traditions.* Philadelphia: University of Pennsylvania Press, 1994.

———. *The New Arab Man: Emergent Masculinities, Technologies, and Islam in the Middle East.* Princeton: Princeton University Press, 2012.

Jackson, Antoinette T. "Daisy M. Bates: Ethnographic Work among the Australian Aborigines." Unpublished paper, 1998.

Jackson, Jean. "The Politics of Ethnographic Practice in the Colombian Vaupés." *Identities: Global Studies in Culture and Power* 6, no. 2–3 (1999): 281–317.

Johnson, E. Patrick. *Black. Queer. Southern. Women: An Oral History.* Greensboro: University of North Carolina Press, 2018.

Johnson, Jessica Marie. "Thinking About the 'X.'" *African American Intellectual Society* (blog), December 12, 2015, http://aaihs.org/thinking-about-an-x/.

———. "Markup Bodies: Black [Life] Studies and Slavery [Death] Studies at the Digital Crossroads." *Social Text* 36, no. 4 (137) (2018): 57–79.

Jourian, T.J., and Z. Nicolazzo. "Bringing our Communities to the Research Table: The Liberatory Potential of Collaborative Methodological Practices Alongside LGBTQ Participants," *Educational Action Research* 25, no. 4 (2017): 594–609.

Juris, Jeffrey S., and Alex Khasnabish, eds. *Insurgent Encounters: Transnational Activism, Ethnography, and the Political.* Durham, NC: Duke University Press, 2013.

Kaberry, Phyllis Mary. *Aboriginal Woman: Sacred and Profane.* London; New York: Routledge, 2004.

Kanaaneh, Rhoda Ann. *Birthing the Nation: Strategies of Palestinian Women in Israel.* Berkeley: University of California Press, 2002.

Kelskey, Karen. "#MeTooPhD-Sexual Harrassment in the Academy Survey," *The Professor Is In,* 2017.

Kingston, Maxine Hong. *The Woman Warrior: Memoirs of a Girlhood among Ghosts.* Vintage, 2010 (orig. 1976).

Koyama, Emi. "The Transfeminist Manifesto." In *Catching a Wave: Reclaiming Feminism for the Twenty-First Century,* edited by Rory Decker and Alison Piepmeier, 244–59. Chicago: Northwestern University Press, 2003 (orig. 2001).

Kozinets, Robert. *Netnography: Doing Ethnographic Research Online.* Thousand Oaks, CA: Sage Publications, 2009.

Lamott, Anne. "Shitty First Drafts." In *Bird by Bird: Some Instructions on Writing and Life,* 20–27. New York: Anchor Books, 1995.

Lamphere, Louise. "The Perils and Prospects for an Engaged Anthropology. A View from the United States," *Social Anthropology* 11, no. 2 (2003): 153–68.

———. "Feminist Anthropology Engages Social Movements: Theory, Ethnography and Activism." In *Mapping Feminist Anthropology in the Twenty-First Century,* edited by Ellen Lewin and Leni M. Silverstein. New Brunswick, NJ: Rutgers University Press, 2016.

Lamphere, Louise, Eva Price, Carole Cadman, and Valerie Darwin. *Weaving Women's Lives: Three Generations in a Navajo Family.* Albuquerque: University of New Mexico Press, 2007.

Lamphere, Louise, Helena Ragoné, and Patricia Zavella, eds. *Situated Lives: Gender and Culture in Everyday Life.* New York: Routledge, 1997.

Lamphere, Louise, Rayna Rapp, and Gayle Rubin. "Anthropologists Are Talking about Feminist Anthropology." *Ethnos* 72, no. 3 (2007): 408–26.

Lamphere, Louise, Patricia Zavella, and Felipe Gonzales. *Sunbelt Working Mothers: Reconciling Family and Factory.* Ithaca, NY: Cornell University Press, 1993.

Landes, Ruth *City of Women*. New York: Macmillan, 1947.

Lareau, Annette. *Home Advantage: Social Class and Parental Intervention in Elementary Education*. Lanham, MD: Rowman & Littlefield Publishers, 1989.

———. "Common Problems in Fieldwork." In *Journeys Through Ethnography: Realistic Accounts of Fieldwork*, edited by Annette Lareau and Jeffrey Shultz, 195–236. Boulder, CO: Westview Press, 1996.

———. "Reflections on Longitudinal Ethnography and the Families' Reactions to Unequal Childhoods." In *Unequal Childhoods: Class, Race, and Family Life*, 2nd ed., 312–32. Berkeley: University of California Press, 2011.

———. *Unequal Childhoods: Class, Race, and Family Life*. 2nd ed. Berkeley: University of California Press, 2011.

Lassiter, Luke Eric. *The Chicago Guide to Collaborative Ethnography*. Chicago: University of Chicago Press, 2005.

Lather, Patti. "Postbook: Working the Ruins of Feminist Ethnography." *Signs: Journal of Women and Society* 27, no. 1 (2001): 199–227.

Lather, Patti, and Chris Smithies. *Troubling the Angels: Women Living with HIV/AIDS*. Boulder, CO: Westview Press, 1997.

Latina Feminist Group. *Telling to Live: Latina Feminist Testimonios*. Durham, NC: Duke University Press, 2001.

Leacock, Eleanor B. "Introduction to *The Origin of the Family, Private Property, and the State*, by Frederick Engels," 7–67. New York: International, 1972.

———. "Theory and Ethics in Applied Urban Anthropology." In *Cities of the United States*, edited by Leith Mullings, 317–36. New York: Columbia University Press, 1987.

Leacock, Eleanor, and Richard Lee. *Politics and History of Band Societies*. Politics and History of Band Societies. New York: Cambridge University Press, 1982.

Lee, Latoya A. "Black Twitter: A Response to Bias in Mainstream Media" *Social Sciences* 6 (2017): 26

Lewin, Ellen, *Lesbian Mothers: Accounts of Gender in American Culture*. Ithaca, NY: Cornell University Press, 1993.

———. *Recognizing Ourselves*. New York: Columbia University Press, 1999.

———. *Gay Fatherhood: Narratives of Family and Citizenship in America*. Chicago: University of Chicago Press, 2009.

Lewin, Ellen, ed. *Inventing Lesbian Cultures*. Boston, MA: Beacon Press, 1996.

———. *Feminist Anthropology: A Reader*. Malden, MA: Wiley-Blackwell, 2006.

Lewin, Ellen, and William L. Leap, eds. *Out in Public: Reinventing Lesbian/Gay Anthropology in a Globalizing World*. Chichester, UK; Malden, MA: Wiley-Blackwell, 2009.

———. *Out in the Field: Reflections of Lesbian and Gay Anthropologists*. Urbana: University of Illinois Press, 1996.

———. *Out in Theory: The Emergence of Lesbian and Gay Anthropology*. Urbana: University of Illinois Press, 2002.

Library of Congress. "Margaret Mead As a Cultural Commentator - Margaret Mead: Human Nature and the Power of Culture | Exhibitions - Library of Congress." Web page, November 30, 2001. http://www.loc.gov/exhibits/mead/oneworld-comment.html.

Longman, Chia, and Tamsin Bradley. *Interrogating Harmful Cultural Practices: Gender, Culture and Coercion*. Farnham, Surrey, UK; Burlington, VT: Ashgate, 2015.

López, Iris. *Matters of Choice: Puerto Rican Women's Struggle for Reproductive Freedom*. New Brunswick, NJ: Rutgers University Press, 2008.

———. "Negotiating Different Worlds: An Integral Ethnography of Reproductive Freedom and Social Justice." In *Feminist Activist Ethnography: Counterpoints to Neoliberalism in North America*, edited by Christa Craven and Dána-Ain Davis, 145–80. Lanham, MD: Lexington Books, 2013.

Lorber, Judith. *Gender Inequality: Feminist Theories and Politics*. New York: Oxford University Press, 2010.

Love, Barbara J., ed. *Feminists Who Changed America, 1963–1975*. Urbana: University of Illinois, 2006.

Low, Setha, and Sally Engle Merry. "Engaged Anthropology: Diversity and Dilemmas." *Current Anthropology* 51, no. S2 (2010): S203–S226.

Lurie, Nancy O. "Women in Early American Anthropology." In *Pioneers of American Anthropology: The Uses of Biography*, edited by June Helm, 29–82. Seattle: University of Washington Press, 1966.

Lutz, Catherine, and Jane Collins. *Reading National Geographic*. Chicago: University of Chicago Press, 1993.

Madison, Soyini D. *Critical Ethnography: Methods, Ethics, Performance*. Los Angeles, CA: Sage, 2005.

Maguire, Patricia. *Doing Participatory Research: A Feminist Approach*. Amherst, MA: Center for International Education, School of Education, University of Massachusetts, 1987.

Makana, Selina. "Contested Encounters: Toward a Twenty-First-Century African Feminist Ethnography." *Meridians: Feminism, Race, Transnationalism* 17, no. 2 (November 2018): 361–75.

Malinowski, Bronislaw. *Argonauts of the Western Pacific: An Account of Native Enterprise and Adventure in the Archipelagoes of Melanesian New Guinea*. London: George Routledge & Sons, Ltd., 1922.

———. *A Diary in the Strictest Sense of the Term*. Vol. 235. Stanford University Press, 1989.

Manalansan, Martin F., IV. *Global Divas: Filipino Gay Men in the Diaspora*. Durham, NC: Duke University Press, 2003.

Marcus, Eric. "Stonewall Revisited." *Independent Gay Forum*, Vol. 30 (1999).

Marcus, George E. *Ethnography through Thick and Thin*. Princeton: Princeton University Press, 1998.

Martin, Emily. *The Woman in the Body: A Cultural Analysis of Reproduction*. Boston, MA: Beacon Press, 2001.

Marzullo, Michelle. "Seeking 'Marriage Material': Rethinking the U.S. Marriage Debates Under Neoliberalism." In *Feminist Activist Ethnography: Counterpoints to Neoliberalism*, edited by Dána-Ain Davis and Christa Craven, 77–100. Lanham, MD: Lexington Books, 2013.

Matabeni, Zethu, ed. *Reclaiming Afrikan: Queer Perspectives on Sexual and Gender Indentities*. Cape Town, South Africa: Modjaji Books, 2014.

Matebeni, Zethu, Vasu Reddy, Theo Sandfort, and Ian Southey-Swartz. "'I Thought We Are Safe': Southern African Lesbians' Experiences of Living with HIV." *Culture, Health & Sexuality* 15, no. 1 (2013): 34–47.

Matto de Turner, Clorinda *Aves Sin Nido*. Lima: Imprenta del Universo de Carlos Prince, 1889.

Maynard, Mary. *Researching Women's Lives from a Feminist Perspective*. New York: Routledge, 2013 (Orig. 1994).

McClaurin, Irma. *Black Feminist Anthropology: Theory, Politics, Praxis, and Poetics*. New Brunswick, NJ: Rutgers University Press, 2001.

McGlotten, Shaka and Dána-Ain Davis, eds. *Black Genders and Sexualities*. Critical Black Studies. New York: Palgrave Macmillan, 2012.

Medicine, Beatrice. "Native American (Indian) Women: A Call for Research." *Anthropology and Education* 19, no. 2 (1988): 86–92.

Mendez, Jennifer Bickham. *From the Revolution to the Maquiladoras: Gender, Labor and Globalization in Nicaragua*. Durham, NC: Duke University Press, 2005.

———. "Globalizing Scholar Activism: Opportunities and Dilemmas Through a Feminist Lens." In *Engaging Contradictions: Theory, Politics, and Methods of Activist Scholarship*, edited by Charles R. Hale, 136–63. Berkeley: University of California Press, 2008.

Meyer, Doug. *Violence against Queer People: Race, Class, Gender, and the Persistence of Anti-LGBT Discrimination*. New Brunswick, NJ: Rutgers University Press, 2015.

———. "Researching Violence and Asking People to Describe Traumatic Experiences." Accessed September 30, 2015. https://gendersociety.wordpress.com/2015/01/30/researching-violence/.

Minh-ha, Trinh T., *producer and director*. *Reassemblage*. New York: Women Make Movies, Inc., 1982.

———. *Surname Viet Given Name Nam*. New York: Women Make Movies, 1989.

———. *Woman, Native, Other: Writing Postcoloniality and Feminism*. Bloomington: Indiana University Press, 2009.

Mohanty, Chandra Talpade. "Cartographies of Struggle: Third World Women and the Politics of Feminism." In *Third World Women and the Politics of Feminism*, edited by Chandra Talpade Mohanty, Ann Russo, and Lourdes Torres, 1–47. Bloomington: Indiana University Press, 1991.

———. "Under Western Eyes." In *Third World Women and the Politics of Feminism*. Bloomington: Indiana University Press, 1991.

———. *Feminism Without Borders: Decolonizing Theory, Practicing Solidarity*. Durham, NC: Duke University Press, 2003.

———. "'Under Western Eyes' Revisited: Feminist Solidarity through Anticapitalist Struggles." *Signs: Journal of Women and Society* 28, no. 2 (2003): 499–535.

Mohanty, Chandra Talpade, Ann Russo, and Lourdes Torres, eds. *Third World Women and the Politics of Feminism*. Bloomington: Indiana University Press, 1991.

Mol, Annemarie. *The Body Multiple: Ontology in Medical Practice*. Durham, NC: Duke University Press, 2003.

Monáe, Janelle. The Electric Lady. © 2013 by Bad Boy, Atlantic, Wondaland Arts Society. Digital Recording.

Moore, Henrietta L. *Feminism and Anthropology*. Feminist Perspectives. Cambridge, UK: Polity Press in association with B. Blackwell, Oxford, UK, 1988.

Moore, Mignon R. "Challenges, Triumphs, and Praxis: Collecting Qualitative Data on Less Visible and Marginalized Populations." In *Other, Please Specify: Queer Methods in Sociology*, edited by D'Lane R. Compton, Tey Meadow, and Kristen Schilt, 169–84. Oakland: University of California Press, 2018.

———. *Invisible Families: Gay Identities, Relationships, and Motherhood among Black Women*. Berkeley: University of California Press, 2011.

Moraga, Cherríe, and Gloria Anzaldúa. *This Bridge Called My Back: Writings of Radical Women of Color*. New York: Kitchen Table, Women of Color Press, 1983.

Morgan, Robin. *Sisterhood Is Global: The International Women's Movement Anthology*. New York: The Feminist Press at City University of New York, 1996.

Morgen, Sandra. *Into Our Own Hands: The Women's Health Movement in the United States, 1969–1990*. New Brunswick, NJ: Rutgers University Press, 2002.

———, ed. *Gender and Anthropology: Critical Reviews for Research and Teaching*. Washington, DC: American Anthropological Association, 1989.

Morgensen, Scott L. *Spaces Between Us: Queer Settler Colonialism and Indigenous Decolonization*. Minneapolis: University of Minnesota Press, 2011.

———. "Reflection: Fearlessly Engaging Complicity." In *Feminist Activist Ethnography: Counterpoints to Neoliberalism in North America*, edited by Christa Craven and Dána-Ain Davis, 69–74. Lanham, MD: Lexington Books, 2013.

Morrison, Toni. *The Bluest Eye*. New York: Random House, 1999 (orig. 1970).

———. *Song of Solomon*. New York: Random House, 2014 (orig. 1977).

———. *Playing in the Dark*. New York: Vintage, 2007.

Mullings, Leith. "Households Headed by Women: The Politics of Race, Class and Gender." In *Conceiving the New World Order: The Global Politics of Reproduction*, edited by Faye Ginsburg and Rayna Rapp, 122–39. Oakland: University of California Press, 1995.

———. *On Our Own Terms: Race, Class, and Gender in the Lives of African-American Women*. New York: Routledge, 1997.

———. "African American Women Making Themselves: Notes on the Role of Black Feminist Research." *Souls: A Critical Journal of Black Politics, Culture and Society* 2, no. 4 (2000): 18–29.

Mullings, Leith, and Amy J. Schulz. "Intersectionality and Health: An Introduction." In *Gender, Race, Class, and Health: Intersectional Approaches*, edited by Amy J. Schulz and Leith Mullings, 3–19. San Francisco: Jossey Bass, 2006.

Mullings, Leith, and Alaka Wali. *Stress and Resilience: The Social Context of Reproduction in Central Harlem*. New York: Kluwer Academic/Plenum Publishers, 2001.

Muñoz, Lorena. "Brown, Queer and Gendered: Queering the Latina/o 'StreetScapes' in Los Angeles." In *Queer Methods and Methodologies*, edited by Kath Browne and Catherine J. Nash, 55–67. Farnham, Surrey, UK; Burlington, VT: Ashgate, 2010.

Murphy, Robert Francis. *The Body Silent*. New York: Henry Holt and Company, Inc., 1987.

Mwaria, Cheryl. "Biomedical Ethics, Gender, and Ethnicity: Implications for Black Feminist Anthropology." In *Black Feminist Anthropology: Theory, Politics, Praxis, and Poetics*, edited by Irma McClaurin, 187–210. New Brunswick, NJ: Rutgers University Press, 2001.

———. "Questioning the Role of Race and Culture Versus Racism and Poverty in Medical Decision-Making." In *Health at the Intersections of Gender, Race, and*

Class, edited by Amy Schulz and Leith Mullings, 289–312. New York: Jossey-Bass/Pfeiffer, 2006.

Naaeke, Anthony, Anastacia Kurylo, David Linton, Michael Grabowski, and Marie L Radford. "Insider and Outsider Perspective in Ethnographic Research." Report No. 9. *Proceedings of the New York State Communication Association*, 2011. http://docs.rwu.edu/cgi/viewcontent.cgi?article=1017&context=nyscaproceedings.

Nader, Laura. "Up the Anthropologist: Perspectives Gained from Studying Up." In *Reinventing Anthropology*, 284–311. New York: Vintage Books, 1972.

Nagar, Richa. *Muddying the Waters: Coauthoring Feminisms across Scholarship and Activism*. Chicago: University of Illinois Press, 2014.

Nagar, Richa, and Susan Geiger. "Reflexivity, Positionality, and Languages of Collaboration in Feminist Fieldwork." In *Muddying the Waters: Coauthoring Feminisms across Scholarship and Activism*, 81–104. Urbana, Chicago, and Springfield: University of Illinois Press, 2014.

Naples, Nancy A. *Grassroots Warriors: Activist Mothering, Community Work, and the War on Poverty*. New York: Routledge, 1998.

———. *Feminism and Method: Ethnography, Discourse Analysis, and Activist Research*. New York: Routledge, 2003.

Naples, Nancy A., ed., *Companion to Feminist Studies*. Hoboken, NJ: Wiley-Blackwell, 2020.

Naples, Nancy A., and Karen Bojar, eds. *Teaching Feminist Activism: Strategies from the Field*. New York: Routledge, 2002.

Naples, Nancy A., and Manisha Desai, eds. *Women's Activism and Globalization: Linking Local Struggles to Global Politics*. New York: Routledge, 2002.

Naples, Nancy A., and Jennifer Bickham Mendez, eds. *Border Politics: Social Movements, Collective Identities, and Globalization*. New York: New York University Press, 2014.

Narayan, Kirin. *Storytellers, Saints, and Scoundrels: Folk Narrative in Hindu Religious Teaching*. Philadelphia: University of Pennsylvania Press, 1989.

———. "How Native Is a 'Native' Anthropologist?" *American Anthropologist* 95, no. 3 (1993): 671–86.

———. *Alive in the Writing: Crafting Ethnography in the Company of Chekhov*. Chicago: University of Chicago Press, 2012.

Nash, Jennifer C. *Black Feminism Reimagined: After Intersectionality*. Durham, NC: Duke University Press, 2019.

Nash, June. *We Eat The Mines and the Mines Eat Us: Dependency and Exploitation in Bolivian Tin Mines*. New York: Columbia University Press, 1979.

Navarro, Tami, Bianca Williams, and Attiya Ahmad. "Sitting at the Kitchen Table: Fieldnotes from Women of Color in Anthropology." *Cultural Anthropology* 28, no. 3 (2013): 443–63.

Nelson, Jennifer. *Women of Color and the Reproductive Rights Movement*. New York: New York University Press, 2003.

Newton, Esther. *Mother Camp: Female Impersonators in America*. Englewood Cliffs, NJ: Prentice-Hall, 1972.

———. *Cherry Grove, Fire Island: Sixty Years in America's First Gay and Lesbian Town*. Durham, NC: Duke University Press, 1993.

———. *Margaret Mead Made Me Gay: Personal Essays, Public Ideas*. Durham, NC: Duke University Press, 2000.

———. "Too Queer for College: Notes on Homophobia 1987." In *Margaret Mead Made Me Gay: Personal Essays, Public Ideas*, 219–24. Durham, NC: Duke University Press, 2000.

Noble, Safiya Umoja. *Algorithms of Oppression: How Search Engines Reinforce Racism*. New York: New York University Press, 2018.

Oakley, Ann. "Gender Methodology and People's Ways of Knowing: Some Problems with Feminism and the Paradigm Debate in Social Science." *Sociology* 32, no. 4 (1998): 707–31.

Ong, Aihwa. *Spirits of Resistance and Capitalist Discipline: Factory Women in Malaysia*. Albany: State University of New York Press, 1987.

Parezo, Nancy J. "Matilda Coxe Stevenson: Pioneer Ethnologist." In *Hidden Scholars: Women Anthropologists and the Native American Southwest*, edited by Nancy J. Parezo, 38–62 Albuquerque: University of New Mexico Press, 1999.

Parsons, Elsie Worthington Clews. *The Journal of a Feminist*. Bristol, UK: Thoemmes Continuum, 1994.

Pascoe, C. J. *Dude, You're a Fag: Masculinity and Sexuality in High School*. 2nd ed., with a New Preface. Berkeley: University of California Press, 2011.

Paxson, Heather. *Making Modern Mothers: Ethics and Family Planning in Urban Greece*. Berkeley: University of California Press, 2004.

Pérez, Gina M. *The Near Northwest Side Story: Migration, Displacement, and Puerto Rican Families*. Berkeley: University of California Press, 2004.

———. "Methodological Gifts in Latina/o Studies and Feminist Anthropology." *Anthropology News* 48, no. 7 (October 1, 2007): 6–7.

Personal Narratives Group. *Interpreting Women's Lives: Feminist Theory and Personal Narratives*. Bloomington: Indiana University Press, 1989.

Phillips, Lynne, and Sally Cole. *Contesting Publics: Feminism, Activism, Ethnography*. London: Pluto Press, 2013.

Piepzna-Samarasinha, Leah Lakshmi. *Care Work: Dreaming Disability Justice*. Vancouver: Arsenal Pulp Press, 2018.

Pinho, Osmundo. "Ethnographies of the Brau: Body, Masculinity and Race in the Reafricanization in Salvador." *Estudos Feministas* 13, no. 1 (2006): 127–45.

Popham, James and Latasha VanEvery. "Representing Indigenous Protest on Twitter: Examining the Social Media Dialogue that Accompanied a Single Image of the DAPL Protests at Standing Rock," *The Annual Review of Interdisciplinary Justice Research,* Volume 7, edited by Steven Kohm, Kevin Walby, Kelly Gorkoff, Michelle Bertrand and Bronwyn Dobchuk-Land, 149–80. The University of Winnipeg Centre for Interdisciplinary Justice Studies, 2018.

"Poto Mitan: Haitian Women Pillars of the Global Economy." Webpage, accessed October 4, 2015. http://potomitan.net/.

Powdermaker, Hortense *After Freedom: A Cultural Study In the Deep South*. New York: Viking, 1939.

Queeley, Andrea. "*Somos Negros Finos*: Anglophone Caribbean Cultural Citizenship in Revolutionary Cuba." In *Global Circuits of Blackness: Interrogating the African Diaspora*, edited by Jean Muteba Rahier, Percy C. Hintzen, and Felipe Smith, 201–22. Champaign: University of Illinois Press, 2010.

Radcliffe-Brown, A. R. "The Social Organization of Australian Tribes." *Oceania* 1, no. 1 (1930): 206–46.

Ransby, Barbara. *Eslanda: The Large and Unconventional Life of Mrs. Paul Robeson*. New Haven and London: Yale University Press, 2013.

Rapp, Rayna. *Testing Women, Testing the Fetus: The Social Impact of Amniocentesis in America*. New York: Routledge, 1999.

Raymond, Janice G. *The Transsexual Empire: The Making of the She-Male*. Boston, MA: Beacon Press, 1979.

Reedy, Gayatri. *With Respect to Sex: Negotiating Hijra Identity in South India*. Chicago: University of Chicago Press, 2005.

Reinharz, Shulamit. *Feminist Methods in Social Research*. New York: Oxford University Press, 1992.

Reiter (now Rapp), Rayna. *Toward an Anthropology of Women*. New York: Monthly Review Press, 1975.

Rios-Moore, Indra, Erica Arenas, Jennifer Contreras, Na Jiang, Tiffany Threatts, Shamara Allen, and Caitlin Cahill. "Makes Me Mad: Stereotypes of Young Urban Womyn of Color." New York: Center for Human Environments, The Graduate Center, City University of New York, 2004.

Roberts, Dorothy. *Killing the Black Body: Race, Reproduction, and the Meaning of Liberty*. New York: Vintage, 1998.

Rodriguez, Cheryl. "Black Feminist Anthropology for the 21st Century." *Anthropology News* 48, no. 7 (2007): 7.

Rodriguez, Cheryl R., and Dzodzi Tsikata, and Akosua Adomako Ampofo, eds. *Transatlantic Feminisms: Women and Gender Studies in Africa and the Diaspora*. Lanham, MD: Lexington Books, 2015.

Rooke, Alison. "Queer in the Field: On Emotions, Temporality and Performativity in Ethnography." In *Queer Methods and Methodologies*, edited by Kath Browne and Catherine J. Nash, 1:25–41. Farnham, Surrey, UK; Burlington, VT: Ashgate, 2010.

Rosaldo, Michelle, and Louise Lamphere, eds. *Woman, Culture, and Society*. Stanford: Stanford University Press, 1974.

Ross, Loretta *The Origin of the Phrase "Women of Color."* 2011. https://www.youtube.com/watch?v=82vl34mi4Iw.

Rothman, Barbara Katz. *The Tentative Pregnancy: How Amniocentesis Changes the Experience of Motherhood*. New York: W. W. Norton & Company, 1993.

Rubin, Gayle. "The Traffic in Women: Notes on the 'Political Economy' of Sex." In *Toward an Anthropology of Women*, edited by Rayna Reiter, 157–209. New York: Monthly Review Press, 1975.

———. "Thinking Sex: Notes for a Radical Theory of the Politics of Sexuality, in Pleasure and Danger: *Exploring Female Sexuality,* edited by Carole Vance, 143–78. New York: Routledge, 1984.

Sandoval, Chela. *Methodology of the Oppressed.* Theory out of Bounds, v. 18. Minneapolis: University of Minnesota Press, 2000.

Sanford, Victoria, and Asale Angel-Ajani, eds. *Engaged Observer: Anthropology, Advocacy, and Activism.* New Brunswick, NJ: Rutgers University Press, 2006.

Sangtin Writers Collective, and Richa Nagar. *Playing with Fire: Feminist Thought and Activism through Seven Lives in India.* Minneapolis: University of Minnesota Press, 2006.

Sargent, Carolyn. "Manda Cesara, 'Reflections of a Woman Anthropologist. No Hiding Place' (Book Review)." *Canadian Journal of African Studies/Revue Canadienne Des Études Africaines* 17, no. 3 (1983): 564.

Savigliano, Marta. *Angora Matta: Actos Fatales De Traduccion Norte-Sur/Fatal Acts of North-South Translation.* Lebanon, NH: University Press of New England, 2003.

Scharen, Christian, and Aana Marie Vigen. *Ethnography as Christian Theology and Ethics.* London: Continuum International Publishing Group, 2011.

Schrock, Richelle D. "The Methodological Imperatives of Feminist Ethnography." *Journal of Feminist Scholarship* 5, no. 1 (2013): 48–60.

Schuller, Mark, and Renée Bergan, dirs. *Poto Mitan: Haitian Women Pillars of the Global Economy.* Produced by Tèt Ansanm Productions, 2009. http://www.potomitan.net/.

Shabazz, Rashad. *Spatializing Blackness: Architectures of Confinement and Black Masculinity in Chicago.* Chicago: University of Illinois Press, 2015.

Shange, Savannah. *Progressive Dystopia: Abolition, Antiblackness and Schooling in San Francisco.* Durham, NC: Duke University Press, 2019.

Shostak, Marjorie. *Nisa: The Life and Words of a !Kung Woman.* Ann Arbor: University of Michigan Press, 1981.

———. *Return to Nisa.* Cambridge, MA: Harvard University Press, 2000.

Silliman, Jael Miriam, Marlene Gerber Fried, Loretta Ross, and Elena Gutiérrez. *Undivided Rights: Women of Color Organize for Reproductive Justice.* Cambridge, MA: South End Press, 2004.

Silva, Noenoe. *Aloha Betrayed: Native Hawaiian Resistance to American Colonialism.* Durham, NC: Duke University Press, 2004.

Simpson, Audra. "On Ethnographic Refusal: Indigeneity, 'Voice,' and Colonial Citizenship." *Junctures* 9 (2007): 67–80.

Sinnott, Megan. *Toms and Dees: Transgender Identity and Female Same-Sex Relationships in Thailand.* Honolulu: University of Hawai'i Press, 2004.

Sins Invalid. *Skin, Tooth, and Bone: The Basis of Movement Is Our People: A Disability Justice Primer*, 2nd Edition. Berkeley: Sins Invalid, 2019.

Skeggs, Beverly. "Feminist Ethnography." In *Handbook of Ethnography*, edited by Paul Atkinson, Amanda Coffey, Sara Delamont, John Lofland, and Lyn Lofland. London: Sage Publications, 2001.

Smith, Barbara. *The Truth That Never Hurts: Writings on Race, Gender, and Freedom.* New Brunswick, NJ: Rutgers University Press, 1998.

Smith, Christen A. "An Introduction to Cite Black Women." *Feminist Anthropology* 2, no. 1 (2021): 6–9.

———, ed. "Special Issue: Cite Black Women." *Feminist Anthropology* 2, no. 1 (2021): 1–191.

Smith, Dorothy E. *Writing the Social: Critique, Theory, and Investigations.* Ontario: University of Toronto Press, 1999.

———. *Institutional Ethnography: A Sociology for People.* The Gender Lens Series. Walnut Creek, CA: AltaMira Press, 2005.

Smith, Linda Tuhiwai. *Decolonizing Methodologies: Research and Indigenous Peoples.* 2nd ed. London: Zed Books, 2012 (orig. 1999).

Smiths, Mary. *Baba of Karo, a Woman of the Muslim Hausa.* New Haven, CT: Yale University Press, 1954.

Souleles, Dan. "What to Do with the Predator in Your Bibliography?" *Allegra*

Lab: Anthropology for Radical Optimism (blog). September 15, 2020. https://allegralaboratory.net/what-to-do-with-the-predator-in-your-bibliography/.

South African History Online. "Charlotte (née Manye) Maxeke." Text, February 17, 2011. http://www.sahistory.org.za/people/charlotte-n%C3%A9e-manye-maxeke.

Spector, Janet. *What This Awl Means: Feminist Archaeology at a Wahpeton Dakota Village*. St. Paul: Minnesota Historical Society Press, 1993.

Speed, Shannon. *Rights in Rebellion: Indigenous Struggle and Human Rights in Chiapas*. Stanford: Stanford University Press, 2008.

Speed, Shannon, R. Aída Hernández Castillo, and Lynn M. Stephen, eds. *Dissident Women: Gender and Cultural Politics in Chiapas*. Austin, TX: University of Texas Press, 2006.

Sprague, Joey. *Feminist Methodologies for Critical Researchers: Bridging Difference*. Walnut Creek, CA: Alta Mira, 2005.

Spry, Tami. "Bodies of/as Evidence in Autoethnography." *International Review of Qualitative Research* 1, no. 4 (2009): 583–90.

Stacey, Judith. "Can There Be A Feminist Ethnography?" *Women's Studies International Forum* 11, no. 1 (1988): 21–27.

———. *Brave New Families: Stories of Domestic Upheaval in Late-Twentieth-Century America*. Berkeley: University of California Press, 1990.

———. *Unhitched: Love, Marriage, and Family Values from West Hollywood to Western China*. New York: New York University Press, 2011.

Steinmetz, Katy. "Which Word Should Be Banned in 2015?" *Time Magazine*, November 12, 2014. http://time.com/3576870/worst-words-poll-2014/.

Sterk, Claire E. *Tricking and Tripping: Prostitution in the Era of AIDS*. Putnam, NY: Social Change Press, 2000.

Strathern, Marilyn. "An Awkward Relationship: The Case of Feminism and Anthropology." *Signs: Journal of Women and Society* 12, no. 2 (1987): 276–92.

Stryker, Susan. *Transgender History: The Roots of Today's Revolution*. Second edition, New York: Seal Press, 2017 (orig. 2008).

Stryker, Susan, and Aren Aizura, eds. *The Transgender Studies Reader 2*. New York: Routledge, 2013.

Sudbury, Julia, and Margo Okazawa-Rey, eds. *Activist Scholarship: Antiracism, Feminism, and Social Change*. Boulder, CO: Paradigm Publishers, 2009.

Su, Karen. "Translating Mother Tongues: Amy Tan and Maxine Hong Kingston on Ethnographic Authority." *Feminist Fields: Ethnographic Insights*, edited by Rae Bridgman, Sally Cole, and Heather Howard-Bobiwash, 33–53. Ontario: Broadview Press, 1999.

Sundén, Jenny, and Malin Sveningsson. *Gender and Sexuality in Online Game Cultures: Passionate Play*. Routledge Advances in Feminist Studies and Intersectionality 8. New York: Routledge, 2012.

Susser, Ida. "The Anthropologist as Social Critic: Working Towards a More Engaged Anthropology." *Current Anthropology* 51, no. 2 (2010): S227–33.

Swarr, Amanda Lock. *Sex in Transition: Remaking Gender & Race in South Africa*. Albany, NY: State University of New York Press, 2012.

Taylor, Julie M. *Paper Tangos*. Public Planet Books. Durham, NC: Duke University Press, 1998.

Te Awekotuku, Ngahuia, and Manatu Maori. *He Tikanga Whakaaro: Research Ethics in the Maori Community*. Wellington, New Zealand: Manatu Maori, 1991.

Téllez, Michelle. "Doing Research at the Borderlands: Notes from a Chicana Feminist Ethnographer." *Chicana/Latina Studies* 4, no. 2 (2005): 46–70.

Téllez, Michelle, dir. Workers on the Rise, 2012. https://vimeo.com/85164509.

Torre, Maria E., and Michelle Fine. "Participatory Action Research (PAR) by Youth." *Youth Activism: An International Encyclopedia* 2 (2006): 456–62.

#transformDH. 2015. "About #transformDH." *#TransformDH* (blog). June 2, 2015. http://transformdh.org/about-transformdh/. Accessed June 13, 2021.

Tristan, Flora. *Promenades dans Londre*. Paris: H.-L. Delloye; Londres: W. Jeffs, Libraire, 1840.

Tsing, Anna Lowenhaupt. *In the Realm of the Diamond Queen: Marginality in an Out-of-the-Way Place*. Princeton: Princeton University Press, 1993.

Tuck, Eve and K. Wayne Yang. "R-Words: Refusing Research." In *Humanizing Research: Decolonizing Qualitative Inquiry with Youth and Communities*, edited by Django Paris and Maisha T.

Winn, 223–48. Thousand Oaks, CA: Sage Publications, 2014.

Ulysse, Gina Athena. *Downtown Ladies: Informal Commercial Importers, a Haitian Anthropologist, and Self-Making in Jamaica*. Women in Culture and Society. Chicago: University of Chicago Press, 2007.

———. *I Am Storm: Songs and Poems for Haiti*, © 2010. Compact disc.

———. "Faye V. Harrison and Why Anthropology Still Matters." The Huffington Post, December 20, 2013, http://www.huffingtonpost.com/gina-athena-ulysse/anthropology-still-matters-faye-v-harrison_b_4259423.html.

———. *Untapped Fierceness/My Giant Leaps*. TEDxUofM, 2013. https://www.youtube.com/watch?v=xHhngXU8Zw4.

Underhill, Ruth Murray. *Papago Woman: An Intimate Portrait of American Indian Culture*. Case Studies. Prospect Heights, IL: Waveland Press, 1985 (orig. 1936).

Uzwiak, Beth. "Fracturing Feminism: Activist Research and Ethics in a Women's Human Rights NGO." In *Feminist Activist Ethnography: Counterpoints to Neoliberalism in North America*, edited by Christa Craven and Dána-Ain Davis, 119–36. Lanham, MD: Lexington Books, 2013.

Valentine, David. *Imagining Transgender: An Ethnography of a Category*. Durham, NC: Duke University Press, 2007.

Venugopal, Arun. "Museums as White Spaces," 2015. accessed May 21, 2021, https://www.wnyc.org/story/museums-white-spaces/.

Visweswaran, Kamala. *Fictions of Feminist Ethnography*. Minneapolis: University of Minnesota Press, 1994.

———. "Histories of Feminist Ethnography." *Annual Review of Anthropology* 26 (1997): 591–621.

Viteri, María Amelia. *Desbordes: Translating Racial, Ethnic, Sexual, and Gender Identities Across the Americas*. Albany: State University of New York Press, 2014.

Walker, Alice. *Meridian*. Open Road Media, 2011 (orig. 1976).

———. *The Color Purple*. New York: Harcourt Brace Jovanovich, 1982.

Walker, Rebecca "Becoming the Third Wave." *Ms.* Magazine, 11, no. 2 (1992): 39–41.

Walters, Delores. "Cast Among Outcastes: Interpreting Sexual Orientation, Racial, and Gender Identity in the Yemen Arab Republic." In *Out in the Field: Reflections of Lesbian and Gay Anthropologists*, edited by Ellen Lewin and William L. Leap, 58–69. Urbana and Chicago: University of Illinois Press. 1996.

Wang, Carolyn, and Mary Ann Burris. "Photovoice: Concept, Methodology, and Use for Participatory Needs Assessment." *Health, Education & Behavior* 24, no. 3 (1997): 369–87.

Ward, Martha. "Reflections of a Woman Anthropologist: No Hiding Place. Manda Cesara (Book Review)." *American Anthropologist* 87, no. 2 (1985): 476–78.

Waterston, Alisse. *My Father's Wars: Migration, Memory, and the Violence of a Century*. New York: Routledge, 2013.

Waterson, Alisse, and Maria D. Vesperi, eds. *Anthropology Off the Shelf: Anthropologists on Writing*. New York: Blackwell, 2009.

Waterston, Alise and Charlotte Corden. *Light in Dark Times: The Human Search for Meaning*. Toronto: University of Toronto Press, 2020.

———. "Making Light in Dark Times." *Anthropology News* website, August 12, 2021.

Weiner, Annette. *The Trobrianders of Papua New Guinea*. Ann Arbor: University of Michigan Press, 1988.

Weiss, Margot. *Techniques of Pleasure: BDSM and the Circuits of Sexuality*. Durham, NC: Duke University Press, 2011.

Wekker, Gloria. *The Politics of Passion: Women's Sexual Culture in the Afro-Surinamese Diaspora*. New York: Columbia University Press, 2006.

Wengle, John L. *Ethnographers in the Field: The Psychology of Research*. Tuscaloosa: University of Alabama Press, 1988.

Weston, Kath. *Families We Choose: Lesbians, Gays, Kinship*. New York: Columbia University Press, 1991.

Wies, Jennifer R., and Hillary J. Haldane, eds. *Applying Anthropology to Gender-Based Violence: Global Responses, Local Practices*. Lanham, MD: Lexington Books, 2015.

Wilchins, Riki Anne. *Read My Lips: Sexual Subversion and the End of Gender*. Ithaca, NY: Firebrand Books, 1997.

Williams, Erica Lorraine. *Sex Tourism in Bahia: Ambiguous Entanglements*. Chicago: University of Illinois Press, 2013.

Wolf, Deborah Goleman. *Lesbian Community*. Berkeley: University of California Press, 1979.

Wolf, Diane L. *Beyond Anne Frank: Hidden Children and Postwar Families in Holland*. Berkeley: University of California Press, 2007.

Wolf, Diane L., ed. *Feminist Dilemmas in Fieldwork*. Boulder, CO: Westview, 1996.

Wolf, Margery. *The House of Lim: A Study of a Chinese Family*. Princeton: Pearson, 1968.

———. *A Thrice-Told Tale: Feminism, Postmodernism, and Ethnographic Responsibility*. Stanford, CA: Stanford University Press, 1992.

Wollstonecraft, Mary. *A Vindication of the Rights of Woman*. London: Joseph Johnson, 1792.

Yale University Lesbian, Gay, Bisexual, and Transgender Studies. "Conference: Queering Anthropology." *Yale University Lesbian, Gay, Bisexual, and Transgender Studies*, February 2015. http://lgbts.yale.edu/event/conference-queering-anthropology.

Zavella, Patricia. *Women's Work and Chicano Families: Cannery Workers of the Santa Clara Valley*. Ithaca: Cornell University Press, 1987.

———. "Feminist Insider Dilemmas: Constructing Ethnic Identity with Chicana Informants." In *Feminist Dilemmas in Fieldwork*, edited by Diane L. Wolf, 138–59. Boulder, CO: Westview, 1996.

Zinn, Maxine Baca, and Bonnie Thornton Dill, eds. *Women of Color in U.S. Society*. Women in the Political Economy. Philadelphia, PA: Temple University Press, 1994.

Index

abolitionist movement, 17, 18
Aboriginal issues and communities. *See* Indigenous issues and communities
abortion and reproductive rights, 18–19, 22, 85, 109, 184
Abramovitz, Mimi, 133, 146, 147
Abu-Lughod, Lila, 64, 67, 81–82
active and passive writing voice, 154–55
activist ethnography: activating, 207; Burawoy on, 181–82; definition of, 185; difficulties, 199; Downs on, 145; Fed Up Honeys, 191–93; forms of, 189–99; geopolitics and, 187; goals of, 185–87; Gray on, 86–87; Morgen on, 146–47; Mullings on, 201; nature of, 87–88, 183–85, 187–88; reflections on, 199–201; self-care and, 186; social media and film, 194–97
activist-scholars, 4, 182–85, 190–93, 194, 198
adjudication boards, 124
African American issues and communities: activist-scholars and, 184–85, 191–93; Afrofuturism, 67; alienation, 20; battered women, 67, 98, 118–19, 128, 130, 199–200; birth control, 19; Black folklore, 41; Black Lives Matter, 103, 186; Black Twitter, 112; Black Youth Project, 2; citational politics and, 76–79, 206; Davis and, 118–19; Harlem Birth Right project, 97–98; Harlem Fight Back, 188; Hurston and, 41; medical racism, 119, 184; Mullings and, 51, 97–98; performance projects about, 175–76; queer experiences, 55; stereotypes, 192–93; Strawberry Mansion neighborhood, North Philadelphia, 117. *See also* Black feminism
African issues and communities: Bantu Women's League, 16; "Bring Back Our Girls" campaign, 194; digital repositories, 111; female genital cutting, 113, 136; !Kung San women, 106; LGBTQ+, 189; Maasai, 197, 198; Pan-Africanist scholars, 87; SANNC, 16; smallpox epidemic, 163–64
Afrofuturism, 67
agency, 42

Ahmad, Attiya, 47, 49–50
Ahmed, Sara, 79, 80
AIDS (Acquired Immune Deficiency Syndrome), 101, 165, 202
Aizura, Aren Z., 128–29
Alive in the Writing: Crafting Ethnography in the Company of Chekhov (Narayan), 154, 156–57
Allen, Jafari, 76
American Anthropological Association (AAA), 37, 64, 78, 126, 176–77, 182
American Birth Control League (ABCL), 19
Andaya, Elise, 83
androcentric research, 36
Angel-Ajani, Asale, 162–63
Anthony, Susan B., 18
anthropology, 11, 27, 52–53, 62; and trans studies, 55–56; Tylor on, 36
Anzaldúa, Gloria, 2
archaeology and literary fiction, 113–15
Archibald, Jo-Ann (Q'um Q'um Xiiem), 166–67
Argüelles, Claudia Chávez, 134–35
argumentation, 14
Arizona Worker Rights Center, 196
artistic and creative projects, 174, 175–77
Asch, Adrienne, 22
Asian American Panethnicity: Bridging Institutions and Identities (Espiritu), 51
Asian issues and communities: intersectional analysis, 51–52; masculinity, 56, 172–73; Men's Rights Movement, 140–41; Meratus Dayaks, 52; Sangtin Writers Collective, 159, 160–61
Association of Feminist Anthropology (AFA), 62
Atay, Ahmet, 83–84
audience, nonacademic, 170–71
Audre Lorde Project, 191
autoethnography and ethnographic memoir, 84, 166–69

Babb, Florence, 44–45, 54, 97
Bailey, Marlon M., 55
Bailey, Moya, 124
Baker, Lee, 57–58, 113
Bantu Women's League, 16
Barbin, Herculine, 59n2

Basu, Srimati, 140–41

Bates, Daisy, 39

Battered Black Women and Welfare Reform: Between a Rock and a Hard Place (Davis), 67, 98, 118–19, 128, 130, 199–200

Battle-Baptiste, Whitney, 113–15

Baumgardner, Jennifer, 22

BDSM. *See* bondage, dominance and submission, sadomasochism

Behar, Ruth, 137, 152, 166

Bell, Diane, 132

Benedict, Ruth, 40

Benmayor, Rina, 191

Bergan, Renée, 194

Berry, Maya J., 134–35

bias, 111, 112, 137, 145

big data, 111

binarisms, 31

BIPOC (Black, Indigenous, [and] people of color), 5n3

birth control, 18–19

"A Birth Story" (Davis, Varner, and Dill), 177

Black Autonomy: Race, Gender, and Afro-Nicaraguan Activism (Goett), 190

Black feminism: in archaeology, 113–15; citational politics and, 76–79; Combahee River Collective, 9, 28–29, 76; historical aspects of, 27–28; intersectional analysis, 51, 76; masculinity research and, 56. *See also* African American issues and communities

Black folklore, 41

Black Lives Matter, 103, 186

Black queer studies, 55, 109

Black Twitter, 112

Blackwood, Evelyn, 54

Black Youth Project, 2

Blee, Kathleen, 138

blog(s), 1, 2, 127; *Anthro(dendum)*, 171; *BlackProf*, 178n8; *feministkilljoys*, 79, 80; *The Feminist Wire*, 171; Meyer's, 141

Boardman, Felicity, 127

Boas, Franz, 32n2

Boddy, Janice, 113

The Body Multiple: Ontology in Medical Practice (Mol), 165

Boellstorff, Tom, 100, 156, 194–95

Bohannon, Laura (Elenore Smith Bowen), 163–64

Bolles, Lynn, 52, 76, 77

bondage, dominance and submission, sadomasochism (BDSM), 56

Bono (U2 singer), 202

"Border Crossing: Intimacy and Feminist Activist Ethnography in the Age of Neoliberalism" (Davis), 67

Bourque, Susan, 46

Bowen, Elenore Smith. *See* Bohannon, Laura

Bradley, Candice, 127

Bread and Roses (consciousness raising group), 44

Bridges, Khiara, 184

Brilliant Imperfection: Grappling with Cure (Clare), 174–75

British anthropology, 36

Brodkin Sacks, Karen, 43, 96

Brown, Lindsay, 127–28

Brown University, 47, 48–49

Burawoy, Michael, 181–82

Burris, Mary Ann, 116–17

Butler, Octavia, 152

Cahill, Caitlin, 191–93

Campos, Elisia Ixchelle, 174

"Can There Be a Feminist Ethnography" (Stacey), 65–66

capitalism, 25, 52–53, 188

Caplan, Pat, 132

Casper, Monica J., 171, 184

"Cast among Outcastes: Interpreting Sexual Orientation, Racial and Gender Identity on the Yemen Arab Republic" (Walters), 131–32

Center for Democratic Renewal (CDR), 139

Cesara, Manda. *See* Poewe, Karla

challenges of feminist ethnographers: Code of Ethics, 124; difficult experiences, 136–38, 154; ethical concerns, 136–44; funders' interests, 62; geopolitics, 126, 130, 187; logistical constraints, 126–35; politics, 138

Chase, Cheryl, 21

Chavez, Leo, 52–53

Chekhov, Anton, 154

Chiapas, Mexico, 74

Chicano/a/@/x: Chicana movement, 46, 70; etymology, 6n11. *See also* Latino/a/@/x issues and communities

childcare practices, 164–65

Chin, Elizabeth, 79, 124, 125, 143, 176

Chodorow, Nancy, 25

un choque (cultural collisions), 2, 22

citational politics, 75–80, 166, 169, 170, 206–7

Citing Black Women campaign, 76–79

Clare, Eli, 174–75

coalition building, 20

Cochran, Floyd, 139, 140

Code of Ethics, 64, 124

coding, of photographs, 110

Cohen, Cathy, 2

Cole, Johnetta, 42

collaborative research, 96–97, 104–5, 118, 201; PAR and, 190–93
collaborative writing, 158–61
Collins, Jane, 109–10
Collins, Patricia Hill, 74–75, 81
colonialism and research, 63–64
Combahee River Collective, 9, 28–29, 76
Comision Femenil Mexicana Nacional, 46
Committee on the Mothers of the Disappeared, 62
community activism, 191–93
Comparative Perspectives on the Indigenous Rights Movement in Africa and the Americas (Hodgson), 198–99
confidentiality, 124
Conquergood, Dwight, 66
consanguinity, 55
consciousness raising (CR) groups, 44
consumer-based activism, 202
Contested Lives: The Abortion Debate in an American Community (Ginsburg), 136–37
Cooper, Dai, 171
Corden, Charlotte, 177
Cordis, Shanya, 134–35
Council on Anthropology and Reproduction (CAR), 184–85
COVID-19, 100, 101–5, 130
Cox, Aimee Meredith, 99, 171, 176–77
Craven, Christa: citational politics and, 76; collaborative writing of, 159; consumer rights language and, 147; LGBTQ+ reproductive loss website, 174; logical constraints of, 128; op-ed of, 171; politics and, 140; as primary advisor, 102; *Pushing for Midwives*, 10; *Reproductive Losses*, 98, 108, 174; research of, 10, 108, 140
creative and artistic projects, 174, 175–77
creative writing, 161–63
Crenshaw, Kimberlé, 60n34
crip, terminology, 33n21
critical ethnography, 188. *See also* activist ethnography
Cross, Katherine, 2
cultural asset mapping, 117–18
cultural capital, 167–68, 189
cultural feminism, 25, 42
cultural materials, analysis of, 109–10
cultural relativism, 138
curiosity, feminist, 145
cyberactivism, 194, 195
cyberethnography. *See* virtual ethnography
cyberfeminism, 67

Dahl, Ulrika, 96–97
Daly, Mary, 20

dance projects, 176
Dave, Naisargi, 99–100
Davids, Tine, 137
Davis, Dána-Ain: activism and, 199–200; activist ethnography of, 193; *Battered Black Women and Welfare Reform*, 67, 98, 118–19, 128, 130, 199–200; *Black Genders & Sexualities*, 55; "Border Crossing," 67; collaborative writing of, 159; donations by, 143; experimental project of, 176–77; logistical constraints of, 128; "Obstetric Racism," 184; op-ed of, 171; *Reproductive Injustice*, 119; use of an interpretive community, 118–19
Davis, Katherine Bement, 40
Davuluri, Nina, 51
deaf culture, 82
debates and interventions: "Can There Be a Feminist Ethnography," 65–66; citational politics, 75–80; insider/outsider dilemma, 69–75, 81–82; "post-" discussions, 68–69
Declaration of Sentiments (Seneca Falls), 17–18
Decolonizing Anthropology: Moving Further Toward an Anthropology for Liberation (Harrison), 88
Decolonizing Methodologies: Research and Indigenous Peoples (Smith), 63–64
de la Cruz, Sor Juana Inés, 16
DeLoache, Judy, 164–65
Deloria, Ella Cara, 42, 152, 163
demographic information, 107–8
Deomampo, Daisy, 2
Desai, Manisha, 182
descriptive statistics, 108
Diamond, Norma, 43–44
diasporic masculinity, 83–84
di Leonardo, Micaela, 62, 68–69
Dill, LeConté J., 177
disability, of researchers, 127–28
disability justice, 86
disability rights, 22
discourse analysis, 31
discrimination, employment, 47–50
donor agencies, 62
Douglass, Frederick, 17, 18
Downs, Kiersten, 144–46
Downtown Ladies, "My Jelly Platform Shoes" (Ulysse), 167–68
drug smuggling, 162–63
Du Bois, W. E. B., 151–52
Dunham, Katherine, 177

Ebron, Paulla A., 152
economic liberalism, 53–54
Ellingson, Laura, 128

Ellis, Carolyn, 168
emic *versus* etic perspectives, 11, 69, 73
employment discrimination, 47–50
Engebretsen, Elisabeth Lund, 95–96
Enloe, Cynthia, 133, 145
Erzen, Tanya, 141–42
Espiritu, Yen Le, 51
essentialize/essentialism, 20
ethical concerns, 64, 84, 104, 111, 124,
    128, 136–44, 188, 199
ethnocentrism, 168
ethnographic authority, 166
ethnographic content analysis (ECA), 112
*The Ethnographic I: A Methodological
    Novel about Autoethnography* (Ellis),
    168
ethnographic memoir, 166–69
ethnography, definition of, 9–14; etymology
    of, 151; "thick description," 168
ethnohistory, 113–15
etic point of view, 11, 69, 73
etiology, 24
eugenics, 19
experimental ethnographic projects, 163,
    175–77

Fajardo, Kale, 156, 178n11
fashion, 167–68
Fed Up Honeys, 191–93
female genital cutting (FGC), 113, 136
The Feminine Mystique (Friedan), 14
feminism: challenges, 2; definition of, 8, 10
feminism, historical aspects: attitudes
    toward, 1–2, 62–63; "First Wave," 8,
    16–19; phases of, 7–8, 15; "Second
    Wave," 15, 19–22, 25, 42–50, 62, 188;
    "Third Wave," 22–23
feminism, types of: Black, 27–28; cultural,
    25, 42; lesbian, 20–21, 47; liberal,
    8, 24, 133; Marxist, 25–26, 27, 43;
    postcolonial and transnational, 29–31,
    51–52; postmodern, 31; radical, 19–22,
    25, 67, 188; socialist, 26. *See also*
    activist ethnography; Black feminism;
    transnational feminism
*Feminism and Method: Ethnography,
    Discourse Analysis, and Activist
    Research* (Naples), 67, 68
Feminist Dilemmas in Fieldwork (Wolf),
    132
feminist epistemology, 10
feminist ethnographic production:
    1920s–1960s, 40–42; 1960s–1980s,
    42–50; 1990s to present, 50–57, 62;
    early contributors, 36–39; forms of,
    152; publicly accessible, 170–75; twin
    ethnography, 159. *See also* creative and

artistic projects; methods, ethnographic;
    writing, ethnographic
feminist ethnography: contemporary
    applications, 2–3; defining, 9–13, 205–6;
    emergence of, 11–12, 14, 36; etymology
    of ethnography, 151; histories of, 61–62,
    205; outcomes of, 144–48; purpose of,
    123, 201; queer ethnography, 54–55.
    See also activist ethnography; challenges
    of feminist ethnographers; debates and
    interventions; feminist ethnographic
    production
feminist histories, 57–58
"Feminist Insider Dilemmas: Constructing
    Ethnic Identity with 'Chicana'
    Informants" (Zavella), 70–71
feministkilljoys blog, 79, 80
feminist knowledge, 14
feminist sensibility, 4, 54
feminist standpoint theories, 74–75
*Femmes of Power: Exploding Queer
    Femininities* (Volcano and Dahl), 96
Fernández-Kelly, M. Patricia, 46
fiction and fiction writers: archaeology and,
    113–15; Bohannon and, 163–64; Deloria
    and, 42, 163; Hurston and, 41, 115,
    152, 163; Wolf and, 153–54; women of
    color writers, 45. *See also* creative and
    artistic projects; creative writing
films, 171–73, 194–97
Fine, Michelle, 22
"First Wave" feminism, 8, 16–19
Fisher, Melissa, 133
Fisher, Tracy, 106–7
Fletcher, Alice, 37–38
Frank, Geyla, 152
Franklin, Sarah, 184
Freeman, Carla, 53
Friedan, Betty, 14, 21
Fried, Marlene Gerber, 19

García, Justine, 196
Geertz, Clifford, 168
Geiger, Susan, 75
gender analysis, 10, 51; dependency theory
    and, 46
*Gender and Sexuality in Online Game
    Cultures: Passionate Play* (Sundén and
    Sveningsson), 159
*Gender at the Crossroads of Knowledge:
    Feminist Anthropology in the
    Postmodern Era* (di Leonardo), 68–69
GenderPAC, 21
geopolitics, 126, 130, 187
Gidding, Franklin H., 38
Gill, Harjant, 172–73
Ginsburg, Faye, 136–37

Gladwell, Malcolm, 194
Glebbeek, Marie-Louise, 136
globalization, gendered effects of, 51–52, 53
Goett, Jennifer, 189–90, 206
Golde, Peggy, 43
Gordon, Deborah, 152, 189
Gottlieb, Alma, 164–65
Gray, Mary L., 86–87
Green, Vera, 42
Griot Circle, 193
Gruenbaum, Ellen, 136
Gutiérrez, Elena, 19
Guttmann, Matthew, 56, 95

Haitian American women, 175–76
Haitian women, 194–95
Hale, Charles R., 199
Haraway, Donna, 42
Harding, Sandra, 42, 92
Harlem Fight Back, 188
Harrison, Faye V., 87–88, 92–93, 175, 207
hashtags, 2, 112, 113, 124
hate groups, 138, 139–40
health, of researchers, 127–28
Heil, Catie, 174
Herdt, Gilbert, 54
Hermaphrodites With Attitude, 21
Hernández, Graciela, 41
heteronormativity, 20
hierarchizing difference, 24
histories, feminist, 57–58
HIV/AIDS, 101, 165, 202
Ho, Karen, 133
Hodgson, Dorothy, 197, 198–99
home births, 10
Huggins, Martha, 136
Hurston, Zora Neale: Battle-Baptiste on, 115; fiction of, 152; impact of, 162; *Mules and Men*, 41; significance of, 41; *Their Eyes Were Watching God*, 41
Hurtado, Aída, 51
husain, saeed, 102, 104, 105
Hyatt, Susan Brin, 186–87
hybridity, 71–72

identity: citational practice and, 79; fieldwork and, 69–75; research and, 85; researcher's, 128
Ihmoud, Sarah, 134–35
INCITE: Women of Color Against Violence, 16
inclusion: of Indigenous women, 21; of nonbinary people, 6n11; of queer, 174; of transgender, 23
Indigenous issues and communities: Archibald (Xiiem) and, 166; Bates and, 39; Fletcher and, 37; Hodgson on, 198–

99; insider/outsider dilemma in relation to, 72–74; Māori people, 64; Medicine and, 21; Narayan and, 71; researchers of, 40; Sioux culture, 42, 163; Smith and, 63–64; Speed, 72–74; Standing Rock protests, 112; study of, 40, 188; Zuni women, 37
Indigenous storywork, 166–67
Indigenous terminology, 155–56
Industrial Workers of the World, 16
informed consent, 104, 111, 124
informed refusal, 125–26
Inhorn, Marcia, 56
Inside-Out Program, 3
insider/outsider dilemma, 69–75, 81–82
Institutional Review Boards (IRBs), 124–25, 126
interlocutors, 197–99
Interpreting Women's Lives: Feminist Theory and Personal Narratives (Personal Narratives Group), 119
interpretive communities, 118–19
intersectional analysis, 50–51, 60n34, 76
Intersex Society of North America, 21
Inter-university Research Group Exploring the Intersection of Race and Gender, 51
interviewing, 98, 100–105
Invisible Families: Gay Identities, Relationships, and Motherhood among Black Women (Moore), 109
Isoke, Zenzele, 8–9

Johnson, E. Patrick, 66–67
Johnson, Jessica Marie, 111
Jones, Claudia, 16
Jones, Mary Harris (Mother Jones), 16
Jourian, T. J., 191
Journal of a Feminist (Parsons), 38
Jurabe, Ana, 191

Karim, Wazir Jahan, 132
Kayberry, Phyllis, 40
Kingston, Maxine Hong, 45
knowledge production, 14, 64, 69; citational politics, 75–80; coalitional, 206; reflexivity and, 75. *See also* methods, ethnographic
Kochiyama, Yuri, 20
Kondo, Dorinne, 152
Koyama, Emi, 23
Kozinets, Robert, 110
Ku Klax Klan, 138
Kurylo, Anastacia, 72

labor: of feminist ethnography, 86–87; of women, 46, 51
labor rights, 196

LaFlesche, Francis, 37–38

LaFlesche, Susan, 37

Lamott, Anne, 153

Lamphere, Louise, 43, 44, 45, 47, 48–49, 62, 152, 207

Lamphere v. Brown, 47, 48–49

Landes, Ruth, 42, 43

Lane-Davies, Hannah, 102, 104, 105, 174

Lang, Ella, 102, 104–5, 174

language, accessible, 13, 171

language use, 154–56, 178nn7–8

Lareau, Annette, 132

Lassiter, Luke Eric, 190–91

Lather, Patti, 165–66

Latino/a/@/x issues and communities: Afro-Latina Creole communities, 189–90; Chiapas, Mexico, 74; *Comision Femenil Mexicana Nacional*, 46; Committee of the Mothers of the Disappeared, 62; Cuban women, 76; education, 191; elite Mexican women, 137; JROTC program, 53; Latina Feminist Group, 159; LGBT, 174; "Methodological Gifts in Latina/o Studies and Feminist Anthropology," 52–53; Puerto Rican women, 109; *¡Venceremos?*, 76; *Women's Work and Chicano Families*, 51; Zavella and, 51, 70–71. *See also* Chicano/a/@/x

lavender menace, 21

Leacock, Eleanor "Happy," 44, 188

Leap, William, 54

Lee, Jarena, 16

Lee, Latoya, 112

lesbian feminism, 20–21, 47

Lesbian Mothers (Lewin), 54

Lewin, Ellen, 54

Lewis, Diane K., 42

LGBTQI+ issues and communities: activist ethnography and, 189, 193; Black, 55; "Cast among Outcastes," 131–32; Chinese, 95–96; ethnographic studies, 54–55; ex-gay movement, 141–42; *Femmes of Power*, 96; film and, 172, 173; Gray on, 87; Hermaphrodites With Attitude, 21; intersex, 59n2; Latino, 174; lesbian feminism, 20–21; mobility, 193; Newton on, 54, 169; *Queer Activism in India*, 99–100; queer studies, 22–23, 55, 56, 83–84, 103, 108, 109, 174–75, 189; *Reproductive Losses*, 174; South African, 189; "Too Queer for College," 46–47; transgender inclusion, 23; trans mobilities, 128, 129; trans studies, 55–56. *See also* sexuality

liberal feminism, 8, 24, 133

life history/oral history, 106–8, 144

Light in Dark Times: The Human Search for Meaning (Waterston and Corden), 177

literature. *See* fiction and fiction writers

logistical constraints, 126–35

longitudinal study, 132

López, César Oswaldo, 102, 103

López, Iris, 108–9

Lorde, Audre, 20, 28

Love, Barbara J., 46

Low, Setha, 199

lowrider culture, 174

Lutz, Catherine, 109–10

Madison, D. Soyini, 153, 188

Maguire, Patricia, 115

Maher, Lee, 131–32

Makana, Selina, 71

"Makes Me Mad: Stereotypes of Urban Womyn of Color," 191–93

Malinowski, Bronislaw, 11, 168

Māori people, 64

Mardistan (film: Gill), 173

Marshall, Gloria (Niara Sudarkasa), 42

Martin, Emily, 184

Marxist feminism, 25–26, 27, 43

Marzullo, Michelle, 189

masculinities, 56, 83–84, 95, 172–73

Massacre of the Dreamers: Essays on Xicanisma (Castillo), 6n11

Matebeni, Zethu, 189

Matters of Choice: Puerto Rican Women's Struggle for Reproductive Freedom (López), 108–9

Matto de Turner, Clorinda, 16

Mauldin, Laura, 82–83

Maxeke, Charlotte Manye, 16

McCaffrey, Brenna, 84–85

McClaurin, Irma, 166

McGlotten, Shaka, 55

Mead, Margaret, 40, 57, 183, 199

medical racism, 119, 184

memoir, 166–69

Mendez, Jennifer Bickham, 94

Men's Rights Movement (MRM), Indian, 140–41

Merry, Sally Engle, 199

"Method and Methodology" (Harrison), 92–93

"Methodological Gifts in Latina/o Studies and Feminist Anthropology" (Pérez), 52–53

methodologies, research: definition of, 92–93; ethnohistory, 113–15; literary fiction in, 113–15; personal experience in, 81–84; personal impulses in,

162–63; Rodriguez on, 93; Rooke on, 91. *See also* Black feminism; feminist ethnographic production; queer studies

methods, ethnographic: choosing, 94–97; creative and artistic projects, 175–77; cultural materials, 109–10; definition of, 92; digital, 110–13; interpretive communities, 118–19; interviewing, 98, 100–105; mixed-methods, 86, 97–98, 118; netnography, 110, 111; oral history/life history, 106–8, 144; participant-observation, 11, 72, 73, 98–100; participatory action research, 115–16, 190–93; participatory research, 115–18; photovoice, 116–18; survey, 108–9

Mexican masculinity, 56, 95

Meyer, Doug, 141

Meyerhoff, Barbara, 152

Michel, Claudine, 194

midwifery, 10, 136, 140, 147

Minh-Ha, Trinh T. (Trinh Thi Minh-Hà), 171

"mini-ethnographies," 99

mixed-methods research, 86, 97–98, 118

Mobile Subjects: Transnational Imaginaries of Gender Reassignment (Aizura), 129

Mock, Janet, 124

Mohanty, Chandra Talpade, 30, 33n25

Mol, Annemarie, 165

Monae, Janelle, 67

monographs, ethnographic, 151

Moore, Mignon, 109

moral relativism, 138

Morgan, Robin, 29, 67

Morgen, Sandra, 133, 146–47

Morgensen, Scott L., 15, 200

Ms. magazine, 22

Mules and Men (Hurston), 41

Mulla, Sameena, 78–79

Mullings, Leith, 3, 12, 51, 97–98, 117, 182, 201, 206

Muñoz, Lorena, 72

Nader, Laura, 132–33

Nagar, Richa, 75, 159, 160–61

Naples, Nancy A., 67, 68

Narayan, Kirin, 71, 154, 156–57

Nash, June, 44, 46

National Organization for Women (NOW), 21, 23

National Women's Studies Association (NWSA), 13, 29

Native issues and communities. *See* Indigenous issues and communities

Navarro, Tami, 47, 49–50

neoliberalism, 67, 183

netnography, 110, 111

Newton, Esther, 46–47, 54, 169, 170

New Yorker Magazine, 194

New York State Scholar Practitioner team, 117

New York Women's Anthropology Caucus, 188

New Zealand Association of Social Anthropologists, 64

NGOs (non-governmental organizations), 159, 200

Nicolazzo, Z., 191

Nisa: The Life and Words of a !Kung Woman (Shostak), 106

Nolan, Hayden Ruairí, 102, 103

nonbinary, 4, 6n11, 103, 206, 207

Norris, Denise, 21

Oakley, Ann, 86

objectivity *versus* subjectivity, 69–70, 85, 182, 188

obstetric racism, 119, 184

Office of Community Studies (OCS), 193

O'Leary, Ana Ochoa, 53

The Omaha Tribe (Fletcher and LaFlesche), 37–38

Ong, Aihwa, 52

On Our Own Terms (Mulling), 51

op-ed writing, 171

open-access content, 174

open-ended interviews, 101

open-ended methodology, 81

oral history/life history, 106–8, 118, 144

Osaze, Dyese, 12

Pan-Africanist scholars, 87

parallel writing, 165–66

Parsons, Elsie Clews, 38, 152

participant-observation, 11, 72, 73, 98–100

participants, research: as coresearchers and coproducers of research, 95–97, 191; "give back" to, 143–44; protection of, 163–64; refusal by, 200; researcher relationship and, 65–67, 69–75, 81, 84; terminology referring to, 93–94

participatory action research (PAR), 115–16, 190–93

Pascoe, C. J., 56

passive and active writing voice, 154–55

patriarchy, 20, 42, 67, 115

Payne, Hakima Tafunzi, 125–26

Pérez, Gina, 52–53

performance projects, 175–77

persistence, determinant of a good writer, 152

personal experiences of ethnographers, 81–84

Personal Narratives Group, 119
Personal Responsibility and Work Opportunity and Reconciliation Act (PRWORA), 117, 146
photography projects, 174, 176
photovoice, 116–18
Piepzna-Samarasinha, Leah Lakshmi, 86, 104
Pinho, Osmunco, 56
Planned Parenthood, 19, 23, 185
Plascencia, Luis, 53
Playing with Fire: Feminist Thought and Activism Through Seven Lives in India (Sangtin Writers and Nagar), 159, 160–61
Poewe, Karla (Manda Cesara), 169
politics: Black women participation in, 28; Mexican women participation in, 137; political perspectives, 14, 15, 205, 206; writing feminist ethnography and, 154
politics of reciprocity and mediation, 141–42
polyvocality, 67, 153, 158
Popham, James, 112
positionality, 72, 73, 74, 81–82, 84
positivism, 42, 84, 86
postcolonial feminism, 29–31, 51–52
postmodern feminism, 31
postmodernism and poststructuralism, 67, 69
Poto Mitan: Haitian Women, Pillars of the Global Economy, a Documentary, 194–95
Powdermaker, Hortense, 42
power differentials, 67, 69: challenging aspects, 65, 132–33; method in relation to, 98, 113
privatization, of public amenities, 186, 187
problem-based learning, 1, 4
Progressive Dystopia: Abolition, Antiblackness, and Schooling in San Francisco (Shange), 157–58
Project Camelot, 199
Promenande dans Londre (Tristan), 11
public archaeology, 114–15
public ethnographers. *See* activist ethnography
public intellectuals, 183–84. *See also* activist ethnography
Pushing for Midwives: Homebirth Mothers and the Reproductive Rights Movement (Craven), 10

qualitative research, 10
Queeley, Andrea, 130
Queens College, 193
Queer Activism in India: A Story in Anthropology of Ethics (Dave), 99–100

queer studies, 23, 54–56, 103, 108, 109, 174–75, 189; diasporic, 83–84
Q'um Q'um Xiiem (Jo-Ann Archibald), 166–67

racism: within feminist movement, 20, 76–79; obstetric racism, 119, 184; research and, 41
Radcliffe-Brown, Alfred, 39
radical feminism, 19–22, 25, 67, 188
Ramos Zayas, Ana Yolanda, 53
Ransby, Barbara, 39
Rapp, Rayna. *See* Reiter (Rapp), Rayna
Raymond, Janice, 21
Reassemblage (film: Minh-Ha), 171
reciprocity and mediation, 141–42
The (RED) Campaign, 202
Reddy, Vasu, 189
Reflection of a Woman Anthropologist (Poewe), 169
reflexivity, 69, 75, 83–84, 137, 161, 206
Reichard, Gladys, 40
Reinhartz, Shulamith, 115
Reiter (Rapp), Rayna, 43–44, 45, 52, 62, 81
reproductive health, 174, 184–85
Reproductive Injustice: Pregnancy, Racism, and Premature Birth (Davis), 119
reproductive justice, 22, 85, 119, 138
Reproductive Losses: Challenges to LGBTQ Family-Making (Craven), 98, 108, 174
research participants. *See* participants, research
Return to Laughter: An Anthropological Novel (Bohannon), 163–64
Richards, Amy, 22
Roberts, Dorothy, 184
Roberts, Rosemarie A., 13–14
Robeson, Eslanda Goode, 39, 59n12
Robeson, Paul, 39, 59n12
Rodriguez, Cheryl, 93
Roe v. Wade, 22
Rohrlich-Leavitt, Ruby, 44
Rooke, Alison, 91
Rosaldo, Michelle, 43, 44, 45, 62
Ross, Loretta, 5n3, 19, 138–40
Rothman, Barbara Katz, 184
Rubin, Gayle, 26–27, 44
Ruth Benedict Collective (RBC), 44

Safa, Helen, 52
safety, 127, 140–41
same-sex marriage, 23, 24, 189
Sandfort, Theo, 189
Sanger, Margaret, 19
Sangtin Writers collective, 159, 160–61

Sappho, 16

Savigliano, Marta Elena, 176

Scharen, Christian, 189

scholar-activist. *See* activist ethnography; activist-scholars

Schoolcraft, Henry R., 32n2

Schuller, Mark, 194–95

"Second Wave" feminism, 15, 19–22; impact of, 42–50; lesbian feminism during, 20–21; mainstream feminists, 20; nature of, 19; Newton on, 47; perspectives in relation to, 8; queer activism and, 23; reproductive rights issues, 22; texts of, 62; women oppression issues, 25, 35–36, 188

self-care, 186

self-naming, 5n3

self-promotion, 13, 14

Seneca Falls Convention, 17–18

settler colonialism, 42

sexism, 4, 27

sex-positive feminism, 22

sexuality: anthropologists and, 72; *Gender and Sexuality in Online Game Cultures*, 159; scholarship on, 54–55; study of, 40. *See also* LGBTQI+ issues and communities

"sex wars," 22–23

sex work, 54–55, 101

Shabazz, Rashad, 56

Shange, Savannah, 157–58, 178n7, 200

Shostak, Marjorie, 106

Shriver, Bobby, 202

Silliman, Jael, 19

Silva, Noenoe, 178n11

Silverstein, Leni, 44

Skeggs, Beverly, 11

skinheads, 139–40

Slutwalk protests, 23

Smith, Barbara, 76

Smith, Christen A., 76–79

Smith, Dorothy E., 74, 81

Smith, Linda Tuhiwai, 63–64, 187

Smithies, Chris, 165–66

Snorton, C. Riley, 55–56

socialist feminism, 26; Black feminism and, 27–28

social justice, defined, 185

social media, 104, 110–13, 124, 171, 194–96

social movements, 207; gendered dimensions of 53–54; movement building, 146–47

South African Native National Congress (SANNC), 16

Southey-Swartz, Ian, 189

Speed, Shannon, 72–74

Spock, Benjamin, 164

Spry, Tami, 84

Stacey, Judith, 64, 65–66, 67, 115

Standing Rock protests, 112

Stanton, Elizabeth Cady, 17, 18–19

stereotypes, 112, 192

Sterk, Claire, 101

Stevenson, Matilda Coxe and James, 36, 37

Stewart, Emery, 85

Stonewall riots (1969), 21

storytelling in visual media, 196–97

Strathern, Marilyn, 64

Stryker, Susan, 21

Su, Karen, 45

Sudanese women, 113, 136

Sudarkasa, Niara (Gloria Marshall), 42

suffrage, women's, 16, 17–19, 24, 62

Sundén, Jenny, 159

Surname Viet Given Name Nam (film: Minhha), 171

survey, 108–9, 193

Sveningsson, Malin, 159

Sylvia Rivera Law Project, 191

taxes, 133, 146–47

taxonomy, 79

Taylor, Julie, 176

Te Awekotuku, Ngahuia, 64

Téllez, Michelle, 171, 196–97

"Telling the Story Straight: Black Feminist Intellectual Thought in Anthropology" (Bolles), 77

Telling to Live: Latina Feminist Testimonios (Latina Feminist Group), 159

temperance movement, 18

terminology: dubbing culture, 156; research participants, 93–94; ways of using, 155–56

Their Eyes Were Watching God (Hurston), 41

theology, 189

"Third Wave" feminism, 1, 22–23

Third World feminism, 29. *See also* transnational feminism

This Bridge Called My Back: Writings by Radical Women of Color (Anzaldúa), 45

Thornton, Bonnie Dill, 3, 51

A Thrice Told Tale: Feminism, Postmodernism and Ethnographic Responsibility (Wolf), 153–54

Time, 1

tokenism, 58, 79

"Too Queer for College: Notes on Homophobia" (Newton), 46–47

topic selection, 94–97

Torruellas, Rosa, 191

"Toward a Fugitive Anthropology: Gender, Race, and Violence in the Field" (Berry et al.), 135

Toward an Anthropology of Women (Reiter, now Rapp), 43–44, 45, 62, 76

"The Traffic in Women: Notes on the 'Political Economy' of Sex" (Rubin), 26–27

transcripts, 96

Transexual Menace, 21

transfeminism, 23, 24

transgender activism, 21, 23

Transgender History (Stryker), 21

Translated Woman: Crossing the Border with Esperanza's Story (Behar), 166

transnational feminism, 29–31

trans studies, 55–56

travel constraints, 126–27, 130

Trinh Thi Minh-Hà, 171

Tristan, Flora, 11

Troubling the Angels: Women Living with HIV/AIDS (Lather and Smithies), 165–66

Truth, Sojourner, 18

Tsing, Anna Lowenhaupt, 52

Twitter, 112, 124

Tylor, Edward B., 36

Ulysse, Gina Athena, 87, 167–68, 175–76, 194

Underhill, Ruth, 40

"Under Western Eyes Revisited: Feminist Solidarity Through Anticapitalist Struggles" (Mohanty), 30–31

Undivided Rights: Women of Color Organize for Reproductive Justice (Silliman et al), 19

Uzazi Village, 125–26

Uzwiak, Beth, 117–18, 200

Valentine, David, 21

Varner, Cheyenne, 177

Veiled Sentiments: Honor and Poetry in a Bedouin Society (Abu-Lughod), 81

Velásquez Estrada, Elizabeth, 134–35

¡Venceremos? The Erotics of Black Self-making in Cuba (Allen), 76

veterans, women, 144–45

Vigen, Aana Marie, 189

violence: against LGBTQ, 141; against women, 23, 25, 130, 135

virtual ethnography, 83, 100, 110

Visweswaran, Kamala, 36, 40, 64

Volcano, Del LaGrace, 96

Wali, Alaka, 97

Walker, Alice, 45, 163

Walker, Rebecca, 22

Walters, Dolores M., 130–32

Wang, Caroline C., 116–17

Warren, Kay, 46

"Water Is Life—Meters Out! Women's Grassroots Activism and the Privatization of Public Amenities" (Hyatt), 186–87

Waterlily (Deloria), 42, 163

Waterston, Alisse, 84, 177

waves of feminism: critique of, 7, 15–17; Rubin on, 26–27; significance of, 8. *See also* "First Wave" feminism; "Second Wave" feminism; "Third Wave" feminism

Weiss, Margot, 56

Wekker, Gloria, 55

welfare reform, 117, 146–47

West, Jason, 189

Weston, Kath, 54

white supremacists, 138, 139–40

Wilchins, Riki Ann, 21

Williams, Bianca, 47, 49–50, 186

Williams, Erica Lorraine, 54–55

witnessing, 189

Wolf, Arthur, 153

Wolf, Deborah Goleman, 54

Wolf, Diane, 132

Wolf, Margery, 94, 153–54

Wollstonecraft, Mary, 16, 24

Woman, Culture, and Society (Rosaldo and Lamphere), 25, 43–44, 45, 62, 76

Woman Writing Culture (Behar and Gordon), 152

Women in the Field: Anthropological Experiences (Golde), 43

women of color: activist ethnography and, 191–93; "Common Differences: Third World Women and Feminist Perspectives" conference, 45–46; etymology of, 5n3; exclusion in research, 51; scholarship of, 45, 50–55; "Third Wave" feminism and, 22

women of color faculty, 47, 49–50

Women of Color in U.S. Society (Thornton and Zinn), 51

women's movement. *See* feminism, historical aspects; feminism, types of; waves of feminism

Women's National Indian Association, 37

Women's Work and Chicano Families: Cannery Workers of the Santa Clara Valley (Zavella), 51

A World of Babies (DeLoache and Gottlieb), 164–65
Worthey, Perry, 102, 103
writing, ethnographic: autoethnography, 84, 166–69; creative forms, 161–63; fiction, 163–65; forms of, 40–41; how to write, 152–61; monographs, 151; parallel, 165–66; participant's perspectives in, 143; publicly accessible, 170–75

Xicanisma, 6n11

Zavella, Patricia, 51, 70–71
Zinn, Maxine Baca, 3, 51
Zuni women, 37

www.ingramcontent.com/pod-product-compliance
Ingram Content Group UK Ltd.
Pitfield, Milton Keynes, MK11 3LW, UK
UKHW031827160925
462988UK00007B/88

9 781538 129791